RAGGED DICK; OR, STREET LIFE IN NEW YORK WITH THE BOOT-BLACKS

and

RISEN FROM THE RANKS; OR, HARRY WALTON'S SUCCESS

W0010526

broadview editions
series editor: Martin R. Boyne

RAGGED DICK; OR, STREET LIFE IN NEW YORK WITH THE BOOT-BLACKS

and

RISEN FROM THE RANKS; OR, HARRY WALTON'S SUCCESS

Horatio Alger Jr.

edited by
Gary Scharnhorst

broadview editions

BROADVIEW PRESS – www.broadviewpress.com
Peterborough, Ontario, Canada

Founded in 1985, Broadview Press remains a wholly independent publishing house. Broadview's focus is on academic publishing; our titles are accessible to university and college students as well as scholars and general readers. With over 600 titles in print, Broadview has become a leading international publisher in the humanities, with world-wide distribution. Broadview is committed to environmentally responsible publishing and fair business practices.

The interior of this book is printed
on 30% recycled paper.

© 2017 Gary Scharnhorst

Library and Archives Canada Cataloguing in Publication

Alger, Horatio, Jr., 1832–1899
[Novels. Selections]
   Ragged Dick; or, Street life in New York with the boot-blacks and Risen from the ranks; or, Harry Walton's success / Horatio Alger Jr. ; edited by Gary Scharnhorst.

Includes bibliographical references.
ISBN 978-1-55481-236-3 (softcover)

   I. Scharnhorst, Gary, editor II. Alger, Horatio, Jr., 1832–1899. Ragged Dick. III. Alger, Horatio, Jr., 1832–1899. Risen from the ranks. IV. Title. V. Title: Ragged Dick. VI. Title: Street life in New York with the boot-blacks. VII. Title: Risen from the ranks. VIII. Title: Harry Walton's success. IX. Title: Novels. Selections.

PS1029.A3A6 2017   813'.4   C2016-907628-8

Broadview Editions
The Broadview Editions series is an effort to represent the ever-evolving canon of texts in the disciplines of literary studies, history, philosophy, and political theory. A distinguishing feature of the series is the inclusion of primary source documents contemporaneous with the work.

Advisory editor for this volume: Michel Pharand

Broadview Press handles its own distribution in North America
PO Box 1243, Peterborough, Ontario K9J 7H5, Canada
555 Riverwalk Parkway, Tonawanda, NY 14150, USA
Tel: (705) 743-8990; Fax: (705) 743-8353
email: customerservice@broadviewpress.com

Distribution is handled by Eurospan Group in the UK, Europe, Central Asia, Middle East, Africa, India, Southeast Asia, Central America, South America, and the Caribbean. Distribution is handled by Footprint Books in Australia and New Zealand.

Broadview Press acknowledges the financial support of the Government of Canada through the Canada Book Fund for our publishing activities.

Canada

Typesetting and assembly: True to Type Inc., Claremont, Canada
Cover Design: Aldo Fierro

PRINTED IN CANADA

For Rebecca, Jeremy, Jasiah, and Cole

Contents

Acknowledgements

I am indebted to Bradford Chase, Lynne Thomas, and Brian Conant for their help in obtaining a copy of the cover of *Joe's Luck* (1910) suitable for reproduction. I also wish to thank the interlibrary loan staff at the University of New Mexico, especially Joe Lane and Frances Lopez-Smith, for their patience and assistance over the years; and my friend and collaborator Jack Bales of the University of Mary Washington, who long ago proved his mettle as a writer and researcher.

Introduction

Horatio Alger Jr. (1832–99) was born in Chelsea, Massachusetts, to an obscure Unitarian minister and failed farmer. After graduating with Phi Beta Kappa honors from Harvard College in 1852, Alger worked for several years as a teacher and journalist while contributing to such New England literary weeklies as *True Flag*, *Olive Branch*, *American Union*, and *Yankee Blade*. His first book, *Bertha's Christmas Vision: An Autumn Sheaf*, a sampler of eleven sentimental tales and eight poems, appeared to favorable reviews in 1855. The *Monthly Religious Magazine*, for example, commended the "collection of stories and verses, written in an uncommonly pure spirit and graceful style," by "a literary gentleman of high promise."[1]

Ill-suited for a teaching career yet unable to earn a comfortable living by his pen, Alger entered the Harvard Divinity School in 1857 to train for the ministry. Meanwhile, he wrote sensation novels on moral themes, with such titles as "Manson, the Miser" and "The Mad Heiress." After graduating from the Divinity School in 1860, he enjoyed a *Wanderjahr* in Europe, loitering at length in England, France, and Italy, while defraying part of his expenses by sending a battery of travel letters to the *Sun* and other papers. Exempted from the Civil War draft because he was short and nearsighted, Alger supported the Union cause by writing unsigned patriotic fiction and verse for *Harper's Weekly*. After he was paid only a dollar per page for an article published in the *North American Review* in 1863, however, he turned to juvenile fiction. He later explained that "the *res angusta domi* [limited wealth at home] of which Horace speaks compelled me years since to forsake the higher walks of literature and devote myself to an humbler department which would pay me better."[2] Alger's first juvenile novel, *Frank's Campaign* (1864), was designed "to show how boys can be of most effectual service in assisting to put down the Rebellion." The abolition journalist Thomas Wentworth Higginson considered it "a good story of home life" during the war.[3] In December 1864, Alger was or-

1 *Monthly Religious Magazine* 15 (January 1856): 57.
2 Gary Scharnhorst with Jack Bales, *The Lost Life of Horatio Alger, Jr.* (Bloomington: Indiana UP, 1985), 61.
3 Thomas Wentworth Higginson, "Children's Books of the Year," *North American Review* 102 (January 1866): 242–43.

dained the minister of the Unitarian Society in Brewster, Massachusetts, though he was accused fifteen months later of sexually molesting boys in his congregation—a charge he did not deny—and forced to resign.[1]

He moved to New York in April 1866 to earn his living as a writer, and there he began to frequent such charitable institutions as the Five Points mission, the YMCA, and the Newsboys' Lodging House of the Children's Aid Society. Within days of his arrival in the city, moreover, he composed a ballad that both betrayed his remorse for the events in Brewster and foreshadowed a major structural change he soon introduced in his juvenile fiction: the figure of the adult benefactor of the street urchins. In "Friar Anselmo," a clergyman committed "one sad day a deadly sin" and "drew back, self-abhorred, / From the rebuking presence of the Lord." He is roused from his guilt when,

> looking down from the convent window high,
> He saw a wounded traveler gasping lie
> Just underneath, who, bruised and stricken sore,
> Had crawled for aid unto the convent door.

Anselmo (= Horatio) launches a "blessed ministry of noble deeds" by bathing the wounds of the stranger who, suddenly transformed into an angel, admonishes him:

> "Courage, Anselmo, though thy sin be great,
> Grants thee life that thou may'st expiate.
> Thy guilty stains shall be washed white again,
> By noble service done thy fellow-man."[2]

In brief, Alger's life and career pivoted abruptly in April 1866 as a result of the Brewster scandal. "I have a natural liking for boys, which has made it easy for me to win their confidence and become intimately acquainted with them," he reflected late in life.[3] "What gratifies me most," he allowed privately in 1897, "is that boys, though strangers, seem to regard me as a personal friend."[4] For the record, there is no evidence Alger ever repeated his earlier crimes.

---

1   Scharnhorst with Bales, *Lost Life* 1–3.
2   Alger, *Grand'ther Baldwin's Thanksgiving* (Boston: Loring, 1875), 51–54.
3   "Advice from Horatio Alger, Jr.," *Writer* 6 (January 1892): 16.
4   Qtd. in Scharnhorst with Bales, *Lost Life* 136.

In *Ragged Dick; or, Street Life in New York with the Boot-blacks* (1868), his most successful book and the first juvenile tale he wrote after settling in the city, Alger codified the basic formula he would follow, with only minor variations, in nearly a hundred subsequent novels for boys: a young hero, inexperienced in the temptations of the city but morally armed to resist them, is forced to earn a livelihood. His exemplary struggle—to retain his virtue, to clear his name of false accusations, to gain economic independence from the evil squires or stepmothers who seek to oppress him—was the stuff of the standard Alger plot. Even in his lowly position, Dick seems destined to rise to the middle class. Though poor, he is energetic and alert for business. He frustrates a clerk's attempt to cheat him, thwarts a confidence game, and exposes the tricks of a dishonest clothier. With the money he earns for escorting a young gentleman around the city—the novel through chapter XII may easily be read as a tour guide to lower Manhattan—Dick abandons his alley, hires a room, begins to attend church, and, after rescuing the son of a rich banker, is awarded an entry-level job in a counting house that will pay him ten dollars a week. It enables him to quit bootblacking, and on the last page of the novel he changes his name to Richard Hunter, Esq.—a rite of passage that epitomizes his initiation into adulthood.

In *Ragged Dick*, moreover, Alger introduced to his cast of stock characters the figure of the adult benefactor, modeled on Friar Anselmo, who materially aids the struggling young hero. No figure resembling this patron had appeared in his earlier three-volume "Campaign series" of juvenile novels (1864–66). In fact, he depicted no fewer than three patrons in *Ragged Dick*: Mr. Whitney urges Dick to aspire to middle-class respectability and replaces Dick's ragged George Washington coat and Louis-Napoléon pants, emblems of his affinity with the Father of His Country and the first and only president of the French Second Republic, with a neat cast-off suit, signaling the beginning of his maturation. Mr. Greyson, Dick's future father-in-law, instructs him in his religious duties; and James Rockwell eventually employs him.

Not only is *Ragged Dick* in part a guidebook to the city but it also resembles a conduct book for young adult readers. Throughout his career, in fact, Alger negotiated a middle course between the domestic banalities of so-called Sunday school fiction and the lurid blood-and-thunder sensationalism of cheap juvenile novels. Unlike the immaculate hero of the Rollo novels by Jacob Abbott (1803–79) and the insufferable protagonists of the books that

Mark Twain (1835–1910) burlesqued in such sketches as "The Story of the Bad Little Boy Who Did Not Come to Grief" (1875), Dick is a flawed character, a precursor of the type of rapscallion featured in Thomas Bailey Aldrich's *The Story of a Bad Boy* (1869), Twain's *The Adventures of Tom Sawyer* (1876) and *Huckleberry Finn* (1885), and George W. Peck's "Bad Boy" stories. "Our ragged hero wasn't a model boy in all respects," Alger concedes in the first chapter of his novel. "I am afraid he swore sometimes, and now and then he played tricks upon unsophisticated boys from the country, or gave a wrong direction to honest old gentlemen unused to the city" (p. 58). He sometimes squanders his hard-earned money in a notorious gambling hall, where "a vile mixture of liquor" is served for "two cents a glass" (p. 59). The father of Dick's friend Johnny Nolan is an incorrigible and violent drunk. Dick's housemate James Travis works, too, as "a bar-tender in a low groggery in Mulberry Street, and ... from his appearance, evidently patronized liberally the liquor he dealt out to others." One evening, after "reeling upstairs" to his room "in a state of intoxication" (p. 155), Travis steals Dick's bankbook, though he is immediately caught and justly punished. Similarly, the villains in *Risen from the Ranks* toast "each other in a fiery fluid which was not very likely to benefit either of them" (p. 201). In half of his juvenile books Alger also admonished his readers to avoid the tobacco habit. "No boy of fourteen can smoke without being affected injuriously," he declares in an authorial intrusion in *Ragged Dick*. "Men are frequently injured by smoking, and boys always" (p. 58). Other characters in the novel, especially Frank Whitney and his uncle, often echo this brand of heavy-handed moralizing in their own voices.

Under the ameliorating influences of his adult patrons, Dick resolves "to turn over a new leaf, and try to grow up 'spectable" (p. 110) by developing better habits. While still a bootblack, Dick forms "the habit of spending a portion of every evening in improving reading or study,"[1] because self-culture is a virtue in its own right. "If my feller-citizens should want me to go to Congress some time," he jokes, "I shouldn't want to disapp'int 'em; and then readin' and writin' might come handy" (p. 158). Through self-reform, Dick gains "something more valuable than money" (p. 149). With the help of his roommate Henry Fosdick, he is able by the close of the novel to "read well, write a fair hand, and had studied arithmetic as far as Interest. Besides this he had obtained

---

1 Alger, *Mark the Match Boy* (1869; rpt. Philadelphia: Winston, 1897), 15.

some knowledge of grammar and geography" (p. 149). In the sequel *Fame and Fortune* (1868), in fact, he gains a rudimentary knowledge of French[1] (a language Alger had begun to learn at the age of thirteen[2]), but not because it might lead to financial profit or economic advantage. Dick's linguistic skills will have little commercial value in the counting room where he works. Like Oscar Vincent in *Risen from the Ranks* (and like Alger), Frank Whitney also studies Latin and Greek at a prep school, not for their practical use but because they are required for admission to Harvard and other elite colleges that offered a classical curriculum. Dick also becomes more frugal with his money, opens a savings account, and adopts a higher standard of personal hygiene. His transformation from so-called "street Arab" to aspiring middle-manager may be attributed to his natural aristocracy of virtue and talent. As the novel ends, the well-dressed and well-groomed Richard Hunter, according to Fosdick, appears to be a "young gentleman on the way to fame and fortune" (p. 184).

In each of the two domestic melodramas in this Broadview edition, moreover, Alger decries the obsession with crass materialism and the rush to the California mining camps much as Henry David Thoreau (1817–62) regarded the Gold Rush as a turning point in American history. Thoreau lamented in his journal on 1 February 1852, for example, that "so many are ready to get their living by the lottery of gold-digging without contributing any value to society."[3] Predictably, the villain in *Ragged Dick* is "quite dazzled" by the prospects of easy money in the gold fields and "inflamed with the desire to go out to California" (p. 158), though he is ultimately disappointed; similarly, the ne'er-do-wells John Clapp and Luke Harrison in *Risen from the Ranks* discover that their western excursion was not "all that it was cracked up to be" (p. 326).

Alger's most succinct statement of his attitudes toward business appeared in a biographical sketch of the department-store magnate A.T. Stewart (1803–76) written for the juvenile magazine *Golden Argosy* in 1883: "1) Strict honesty in all dealings with customers. 2) One price for all. 3) Cash on delivery. 4) Business to be done as business, and without reference to any other consideration. 5) Courtesy to all, at whatever rank."[4] But Alger fore-

---

1 Alger, *Fame and Fortune* (Boston: Loring, 1868), 14.
2 Scharnhorst with Bales, *Lost Life* 14.
3 *The Writings of Henry David Thoreau*, ed. Bradford Torrey (Boston and New York: Houghton Mifflin, 1906), IX, 265.
4 Alger, "A.T. Stewart," *Golden Argosy* (10 March 1883).

shadowed his approval of this business code in *Ragged Dick*. As Frank Whitney explains to the hero, Stewart resolved from the first "that he would be strictly honorable in all his dealings, and never overreach any one for the sake of making money" (p. 92). Dick intuitively understands the point, if from a different perspective. He once lost money in the match business because he was exploited by well-to-do misers: An "old lady" who "lived in a big brick house ... beat me down so, that I didn't make no profit at all; but she wouldn't buy without, and I hadn't sold none that day; so I let her have them. I don't see why rich folks should be so hard upon a poor boy that wants to make a livin'" (p. 92). Implicit in Alger's defense of fair trade practices in all business dealings is his corollary belief that an employer, the purchaser of labor, is entitled to an honest day's work for an honest day's pay. Alger's protagonists invariably pledge their loyalty to their employers—"I'll try to serve you so faithfully, sir, that you won't repent having taken me into your service" (p. 182), as Ragged Dick assures Mr. Rockwell—hardly the resolution of a budding entrepreneur. As John G. Cawelti concludes, "Emphasis on fidelity to the employer's interests is perhaps the worst advice Alger could have given his young readers if financial success was of major interest to them."[1]

The conservative Republican bent of *Ragged Dick* is no less apparent in its implicit critique of the Democratic machine politics of Tammany Hall. With the support of Irish ward heelers and voters rewarded with jobs, "Boss" Tweed (William Magear Tweed, 1823–78) ran New York with a gloved fist from 1858 until 1877, when he was convicted of corruption. For his part, Alger supported anti-Tammany candidates in municipal elections and advocated civil-service reform. His portrayal of the gang leader Micky Maguire illustrates his distrust of the Irish voting bloc. If the young thug "had been fifteen years older, and had a trifle more education," Alger warns, "he would have interested himself in politics, and been prominent at ward meetings, and a terror to respectable voters on election day" (p. 118). Fortunately, like Dick, after his release from jail in *Fame and Fortune* Micky becomes a "useful employé of the establishment which he had entered" and is "saved from vicious habits and converted from a vagabond to a useful member of society."[2]

---

1   John G. Cawelti, *Apostles of the Self-Made Man* (Chicago: U of Chicago P, 1965), 119.

2   Alger, *Fame and Fortune*, 277.

Alger and the Country-Boy Myth

Ragged Dick also contains the germ of such later novels as *Bound to Rise* (1873) and its sequel *Risen from the Ranks* (1874), in which Alger apotheosized the character of the American country boy. Rooted in the agrarian idealism and American exceptionalism of Thomas Jefferson (1743–1826), who famously declared in *Notes on the State of Virginia* (1787) that "those who labor in the earth are the chosen people of God, if ever He had a chosen people," this tradition celebrates the yeoman farmers or rural folks who, in Jefferson's view, are morally, intellectually, and physically superior to city dwellers. Jefferson urged that "our work-shops remain in Europe" rather than fester in the cities of the New World.[1] According to R. Richard Wohl, moreover, Alger was "one of the architects of the country boy legend" in nineteenth-century American fiction.[2] To be sure, this strain of Alger's formula evolved over the years. In chapter X of *Ragged Dick*, a country rube is targeted by a city shark and bilked out of fifty dollars. Dick "contemptuously" dismisses the bumpkin as "a baby" unable to protect himself (p. 104). Later in the novel, however, Frank Whitney's uncle reminisces about his success. He had "entered a printing-office as an apprentice, and worked for some years." After he was obliged to quit the trade, "I went into the country, and worked on a farm," where he invented a machine that made him rich (p. 107). In *Risen from the Ranks*, moreover, the hero hails from the country and one of the students at the Prescott Academy has earned his school expenses by working "on a farm for two years" (p. 229). In short, in such novels as *Bound to Rise* and *Risen from the Ranks* and Alger's biography of Daniel Webster, *From Farm Boy to Senator* (1882), the rural hero succeeds despite the paucity of economic opportunities in the country. Harry Walton in fact prefers to remain a small-town editor at the close of *Risen from the Ranks* because, as he explains, "if I want to go into politics, there would be more chance in the country than in the city" (p. 314). The novel not only celebrates the village virtue of the American country boy; it also represents a variation on Alger's street-boy success formula and so may fairly be considered a worthy companion piece to *Ragged Dick*.

---

1   Thomas Jefferson, *Notes on the State of Virginia* (London: Stockdale, 1787), 274.
2   R. Richard Wohl, "The 'Country Boy Myth' and Its Place in American Urban Culture: The Nineteenth-Century Contribution," *Perspectives in American History* 3 (1969): 104.

Alger's didactic fiction formula may be said to have originated in parody, more specifically Benjamin Franklin's parody in his *Autobiography* of Christ's parable of the prodigal son. In the parable, of course, the errant son flees his inglorious life in a "far country" and returns home to a grateful father and a fatted calf. For his part, Franklin (1706–90) returns to Boston from Philadelphia sporting a new suit and a watch, the symbols of success Alger appropriated in his juvenile fiction. Alger's reverence for Franklin ran like a recurrent theme through his writings. The hero of *The Tin Box* (1882) reads Franklin's autobiography with the approval of his uncle: "You couldn't read anything better. Old Ben is a good model for American boys. He was a great man."[1] Alger quoted Poor Richard's maxims in both *The Young Explorer* (1880) and *Digging for Gold* (1891); and in *Bernard Brooks' Adventures* (1894) the hero is, according to family legend, descended from Franklin. In this context, "Ragged Dick" simply seems a rephrasing of "Poor Richard."

In all, Alger alluded to Franklin in seven of his books for boys, particularly in *Bound to Rise* and *Risen from the Ranks*, in which the hero patterns his life upon Franklin's autobiography. For example, W.D. Howells (1837–1920), former editor of the *Atlantic Monthly*, declared that "Franklin's is one of the greatest autobiographies in literature."[2] Woodrow Wilson (1856–1924), a professional historian, future president of Princeton University, governor of New Jersey, and twenty-eighth president of the United States, asserted in his introduction to the *Autobiography* in 1901 that Franklin, a "typical American," could hardly have been born or brought to the full light of fame anywhere but in America;[3] and Charles W. Eliot (1834–1926), president of Harvard University, published Franklin's memoirs in the first volume of his multi-volume Harvard Classics. Put another way, the *Autobiography* became an American culture-text and archetypal success story that resonated with readers of every social class—though Mark Twain famously punctured Franklin's inflated reputation in his comic article "The Late Benjamin Franklin" (1870), reprinted as Appendix B3 (pp. 358–60).

Alger acknowledged Franklin's exalted reputation in both *Bound to Rise* and *Risen from the Ranks*. In the former novel,

---

1   Alger, *The Tin Box* (1882; rpt. New York: Burt, n.d.), 216.

2   W.D. Howells, "Editor's Study," *Harper's Monthly* 119 (October 1905): 795–76.

3   Woodrow Wilson, "Introduction" to Franklin's *Autobiography* (New York: Century, 1901), vi, x, xi, xii.

Harry Walton, the son of a poor but proud New England farmer, wins a copy of "the life of the great American philosopher and statesman, Benjamin Franklin," in a declamation contest. As he reads it, he is "surprised to find that Franklin was a poor boy, and had to work for a living. He started out in life on his own account, and through industry, frugality, perseverance, and a fixed determination to rise in life, he became a distinguished man in the end, and a wise man also, though his early opportunities were very limited." Harry resolves to model his own life after Franklin's, whose memoirs became "the chart by which he meant to steer." He applies for work in a print shop and tells the owner that he "shouldn't expect to turn out a Franklin," but "I think one couldn't help being improved by the business."[1]

The sequel opens as Harry begins his newspaper apprenticeship, harboring an ambition to become an editor like Franklin. His employer introduces him to the other shop-workers as the "second Benjamin Franklin" (*Risen*, p. 199). Resolving "to get some books and study a little every day ... the way Franklin did" (p. 203), Harry meets a wealthy young Boston patrician, a student at a local academy, through whose agency he is elected to membership in the local Clionian Society, an association of young intellectuals akin to Franklin's Junto.[2] Encouraged to publish his ideas, Harry submits an essay entitled "Ambition," signed with the pseudonym "Franklin," to a Boston newspaper. Even in this endeavor, as Alger explains, Harry "was influenced by the example of Franklin, who, while yet a boy in his teens, contributed articles to his brother's paper" under the *nom de plume* "Silence Dogood" (p. 250). Under the pseudonym "Frank Lynn," Harry soon earns a literary reputation. He eventually becomes editor of the weekly *Centreville Gazette*, is elected to the New Hampshire legislature, and at the ripe age of 28 to Congress, where he devotes his life to public service. He "had never sought wealth," Alger assures his readers. "He was content with a comfortable support and a competence.... He was ambitious, but it was a creditable and honorable ambition. He sought to promote the public welfare, and advance the public interests" (p. 337). It was a comforting message only a year after the 1872

---

1 Alger, *Bound to Rise* (Boston: Loring, 1873), 53, 55, 68, 269.
2 The Junto was "a club of mutual improvement" that Franklin founded in Philadelphia in 1727. Alger's "Clionian" society is named for Clio, the Greek muse of history.

Crédit Mobilier scandal in Congress ruined the reputations of several prominent American politicians.[1]

Points of Similarity and Difference

Ragged Dick and *Risen from the Ranks* share several plot points. Like Dick, Harry embarks on a program of self-improvement. He forms "the habit of self-denial," which is even more valuable than the money he saves (p. 317). He develops strict study habits in the belief that "knowledge may be acquired in a printing office as well as within the walls of an academy or college" (p. 203), and his friend Ferguson cites an adage often attributed to Abraham Lincoln: "the printing office is the poor man's college" (p. 221). But Harry is not interested in acquiring only practical knowledge. Like Dick, he studies French, not that the language is liable to have any more utility in the print shop than in the counting room. Ferguson adds that in many cases "[e]ducation will make a man more competent to earn money," but "it isn't for the money alone that an education is worth having. There is a pleasure in being educated" (p. 241). Moreover, Harry is as wary as Dick of cultivating bad habits. Both of them shun tobacco. As Harry explains, "There is no danger of my smoking. I don't think it would do me any good. Besides, it is expensive" (p. 198). To their credit, both Dick and Harry accept skilled jobs at lower wages than they had earned by menial labor but with the expectation of advancement, and both of them pledge loyalty to their employers. Both heroes must ignore the sneers and insinuations of well-born snobs, Roswell Crawford in *Ragged Dick* and Fitzgerald Fletcher in *Risen from the Ranks*; and both are rewarded in the end with respectable careers and happy marriages to the daughters of their benefactors, Dick to Ida Greyson and Harry to Maud Vincent. The typical Alger hero, therefore, improves his station as much by a stroke of luck (e.g., saving the child of a rich banker from drowning, rescuing the child of a rich banker from a runaway horse) and/or by marrying well as by dint of hard work. He may deserve his good fortune, but he does not entirely earn it.

---

1 The officers of a dummy financial company, the Crédit Mobilier, bribed 15 political figures, including congressmen and the vice-president of the United States, with $9 million in stock in return for favors during the construction of the eastern route of the Union Pacific Railroad. The scandal came to light in 1872–73.

Risen from the Ranks also differs dramatically from *Ragged Dick*, however, in a couple of ways that subtly undermine the coherence of Alger's formula. In chapter XIX, in the midst of a subplot that seems a digression, Alger effectively satirizes the ending of his most popular novel. The confidence man Ferdinand B. Kensington purports to have saved a New York banker from drowning after falling overboard from the Brooklyn ferry, much as Alger's eponymous hero fortuitously rescues James Rockwell's son in chapter XXVI of *Ragged Dick*. "More than once I have swum all the way from New York to Brooklyn," Kensington brags to his would-be aunt (p. 271), much as Dick brags that he can "swim like a top" (p. 180). "I caught Mr. Clayton by the collar, as he was sinking for the third time, and shouted to a boatman near by to come to my help," the swindler claims, exactly as Dick saves Johnny Rockwell. Clayton ostensibly rewards him with a diamond ring and a new suit of clothes, much as James Rockwell buys new attire for Dick. But the episode raises a troubling question: Why would Alger parody the happy ending of *Ragged Dick* unless he realized that the plot twist was unbelievably contrived? It is as if the author understood the falsity of his own fabrication.

Moreover, according to the logic of Alger's formula, the distinguished editor of a Boston daily paper, John Vincent, should have been his primary benefactor. The elder Vincent is wealthy—his family resides in Beacon Street, the toniest address in America—and interested in boosting Harry. Instead, the hero is bankrolled, not by a former printer's devil cast in the Franklin mold, but by his former employer Professor Henderson, a professional illusionist, who suddenly reappears out of the blue in the final pages of the novel to float the loan that enables Harry and Ferguson to buy the *Centreville Gazette*. Why does Alger replace Mr. Vincent—who according to the logic of the plot should sponsor Harry—with a semi-comic figure? The answer is almost inescapable: the author again subverts his formula with an implicit admission that it is unrealistically fanciful.

Alger at the Close of the Nineteenth Century

Never a literary lion, Alger enjoyed the middle-class social station to which most of his characters aspired. He joined the Harvard Club of New York and the historical society in his parents' hometown in Massachusetts. To supplement his income from writing, he tutored the children of some prominent local Jewish families, including Edwin R.A. Seligman (1861–1939), later a professor of political economy at Columbia University; Benjamin Cardozo (1870–1938), later an associate justice of the US Supreme Court; and Lewis Einstein (1877–1967), later a career diplomat. During Alger's second grand tour of Europe in 1873, he completed *Bound to Rise* and traveled by train to the Pacific coast in 1877 and again in 1890 to gather local color for a series of juvenile novels set in the West.

Meanwhile, Alger's juvenile stories came under increasing fire from ministers and librarians, the so-called custodians of culture, for their alleged sensationalism. The *Boston Herald* editorialized that only children "raw at reading" would be attracted to the "fighting, killing, and thrilling adventures" found in Alger's novels.[1] At the dedication of a branch of the Boston Public Library in 1877, James Freeman Clarke (1810–88), a distinguished Unitarian minister and a member with Ralph Waldo Emerson (1803–82) and Thoreau of the famous Transcendental Club, denounced the "endless reams" of "drivel poured forth by Horatio Alger, Jr.";[2] and in 1879 the Fletcher Free Library in Burlington, Vermont, became the first public library in the country to remove Alger's books from its shelves.[3] Fifteen years later, in 1894, of the 145 libraries surveyed by the American Library Association, over a third banned Alger's books.[4]

Retiring to Natick, Massachusetts, in 1896, Alger died from congestive heart failure—in declining circumstances but by no means destitute—in July 1899. In order to conceal his homosexuality, he bequeathed his private papers to his sister, who destroyed them after his death.[5] Not a single letter written to him, nor a page of any personal diary, is extant. One of his obituarists reported that he had been "perhaps better known to boys of thirty years ago than to the present generation."[6] Available sales statistics tend to support this assertion. Alger's only best-sellers had been published between 1868 and 1871,[7] and his early modest popularity had so waned by 1881 that he had been surprised by

---

1 "Boys and Girls' Reading," *Boston Herald* (8 May 1881): 7.
2 "Literary Rubbish," *Boston Advertiser* (7 December 1877): 2; rpt. *Library Journal* 2 (January–February 1878): 299.
3 *Library Journal* 6 (May 1881): 161.
4 Lutie E. Stearns, "Report on Reading for the Young," *Library Journal* 19 (December 1894): 83.
5 Scharnhorst with Bales, *Lost Life* 145–46.
6 E.S. Martin, "This Busy World," *Harper's Weekly* (5 August 1899): 761.
7 Frank Luther Mott, *Golden Multitudes* (New York: Macmillan, 1947), 309, 321, 322.

the sale of 20,000 copies of his biography of James Garfield, the American president assassinated that year, which he wrote in only 14 days.[1] A prolific writer, Alger completed over a hundred juvenile books during his career, yet by his own estimate in 1897 his aggregate sales totaled only about 800,000 volumes.[2] Sales of the six volumes in the early "Ragged Dick series" (1868–70) account for about one-fifth of this total. After his death, however, Alger's popularity soared. By 1910, his juvenile novels were enjoying *annual* sales of over one million[3]—that is, more Alger novels were sold each year during the decade after his death than were sold in total during his life. His books, of which an estimated 17–20 million copies were sold in all,[4] remained popular until about 1920, when sales plummeted. By 1926, the circle of Alger's middle-class readers had so contracted[5] that the leading publisher of his books stopped issuing them. By 1932, less than 20 per cent of 7,000 surveyed New York boys recognized Alger's name and only about 14 per cent admitted to having read even one of his books.[6] He was described that year in the pages of one mass-circulation periodical as "forgotten," and two years later in the pages of another as "extinct."[7] In 1947, a poll of 20,000 New York children revealed that 92 per cent of them "had never heard of Alger. Less than 1 per cent had read any of his books."[8]

1   Scharnhorst with Bales, *Lost Life* 121. The heirs of James R. Gilmore filed suit in federal court in 1887, alleging that Alger plagiarized much of his *From Canal Boy to President* (1881) from Gilmore's *Life of James Garfield* (1880): "a large portion of his book had been taken bodily and inserted word for word in Mr. Alger's life of the President." After a judge ruled in the plaintiff's favor in the spring of 1889, the parties settled out of court. See "Accused of Plagiarism," *Brooklyn Eagle* (13 February 1887): 16; "The Suit as to Alger's 'From Canal Boy to President,'" *Publishers' Weekly* (2 February 1889): 101; and "Would Like to Have a Settlement," *Pittsburgh Dispatch* (16 May 1889): 4.

2   *Who's Who in America 1899–1900* (Chicago: Marquis, 1899), 10.

3   Everett T. Tomlinson, "The Perpetual 'Best-Sellers,'" *World's Work* 20 (June 1910): 13045.

4   Mott 159.

5   Arthur M. Jordan, *Children's Interests in Reading* (Chapel Hill: U of North Carolina P, 1926).

6   "The Cynical Youngest Generation," *Nation* (17 February 1932): 186.

7   "A Forgotten Boy's Classic," *Literary Digest* (30 January 1932): 20; Winifred King Rugg, "A Library Exile," *Christian Science Monitor* (19 November 1934): 7.

8   "Horatio Alger Is an Unknown to 92% of Boys and Girls in Seven Clubs in City," *New York Times* (13 January 1947): 23.

But if Alger's didactic tales were more popular in 1869 than in 1899, why did he enjoy such phenomenal posthumous popularity? And, more importantly, if Alger was virtually forgotten by the late 1920s, how did he acquire modern renown as a success mythmaker? As Malcolm Cowley has complained, "I cannot understand how [Alger] should come to be regarded as the prophet of business enterprise; nor why the family melodrama that he wrote and rewrote for boys should be confused with the American dream of success."[1] As long ago as 1945, Cowley noted this discrepancy between what Alger is believed to have written and what he actually wrote. He observed that the original Alger hero was not a poor boy who became a millionaire by dint of honest enterprise and patience, but a poor boy who rose to bourgeois respectability as a reward for his filial piety.[2] Despite the popular notion that his heroes rise "from rags to riches," moreover, only a few of his characters garner fabulous wealth. Alger's unearned reputation as a success mythmaker was institutionalized only two years later with the inauguration, in 1947, of the Horatio Alger Awards for meritorious service to the causes of political or religious conservatism and economic orthodoxy. By tracing apparent transformations in the image of success associated with Alger in the mass media, including literature, between the Civil War and World War II, one can silhouette the network of assumptions governing the American idea of success over several generations.

The Growth of Alger's Reputation

During the last third of the late nineteenth century, a period known in America as the Gilded Age (rather than a golden age),[3] Alger was viewed, much as he wished to be viewed,[4] simply as a writer of didactic juvenile stories. His tales were invariably evaluated according to the standard of moral influence—for good or ill—which they exerted on impressionable young minds. Particu-

---

1 Malcolm Cowley, "Horatio Alger: Failure," *Horizon* 12 (Summer 1970): 65.

2 Cowley, "Holy Horatio," *Time* (13 August 1945): 98.

3 Coined by Mark Twain and Charles Dudley Warner, the phrase "the gilded age" refers to the period between the end of the Civil War and the end of the nineteenth century, an era marked by explosive growth in the US economy but punctuated by labor strikes, a concentration of wealth in the upper class, and financial panics, particularly in 1873 and 1893, that precipitated long economic depressions.

4 Alger, "Writing Stories for Boys," *Writer* 9 (February 1896): 36.

larly during the late 1860s and 1870s, critical opinion of Alger's fiction, expressed in such prestigious periodicals as *Putnam's Monthly* and the *Nation*, was generally favorable.[1] From the earliest years of Alger's career, his defenders insisted that "a fine vein of high morality ... pervades everything from his pen."[2] However, these defenders gradually were overwhelmed by the superior forces of those who complained about the potentially nefarious effect of his unrealistic and sensational fiction. As early as 1869, parents were warned to beware of Alger's crippling influence on children by a reviewer in the *Nation*, one of the first American magazines to promote literary realism.[3] This complaint, echoed in a variety of forums, crescendoed through the 1870s and 1880s. For example, a reviewer for the children's magazine *St. Nicholas* charged that Alger's *Brave and Bold* (1872) contained characters "such as we do not meet in real life—and we are very glad that we don't meet them."[4] These criticisms tended to undermine Alger's modest initial popularity, and their appearance coincided with the first precipitous decline in the sales of his books. The earliest parodies of Alger's novels, such as Charles Battell Loomis's "Bernard the Bartender" (1894) and Stephen Crane's "A Self-Made Man" (1899), lampooned the formula at precisely these points: the mediocrity of the supposedly moral hero and the dreariness of Alger's prose. Still, whether defenders or detractors, all applied the same didactic standard to Alger's fiction: Does it improve and instruct its readers?

During the heyday of his popularity early in the twentieth century, Alger acquired a reputation as a champion of self-help whose formulaic fiction blended ethical heroism with economic success. As early as 1898, he was credited in a religious magazine for his "clever trick of turning incidents to account," a twist on the old complaint about his unrealistic plots; and his latest hero was commended as "an admirable boy with [a] wonderful ability to take care of himself."[5] Three years later, Carolyn Wells publicly celebrated Alger for teaching "bravery, courage, and pluck through the medium of such characters as newsboys, shoe-blacks, match-sellers and luggage boys, who almost invariably

1   E.g., "Literature," *Putnam's* ns 2 (July 1868): 120; and "Children's Holiday Books," *Nation* (3 December 1874): 368.
2   "Editor's Literary Record," *Harper's Monthly* 43 (August 1871): 459.
3   "The Last of the Children's Books," *Nation* (30 December 1869): 587.
4   "Books for Boys and Girls," *St. Nicholas* 2 (January 1875): 190.
5   *Independent* (20 October 1898): 1128.

rise to fame and fortune by their own persevering efforts."[1] Such comments indicate that Alger's original reputation as a writer of simple moral tales for boys had begun to morph. When he was criticized, he was less liable to be charged with writing unwholesome fiction than reprimanded for emphasizing the receipt of material rewards.[2] Whatever the personal taste of the reader, when read according to the standards that prevailed early in that century, his moral tracts seemed to praise entrepreneurs who earned and spent their wealth honestly. His books were popular during this Progressive era (1890s to the 1920s)—a period of intense nostalgia for an imaginary past of equal opportunity and equitable trade policies—because they satisfied the popular desire to reform the institutions of business and government through a "return to fundamental morality."[3] As Richard Weiss has noted, Alger became "a nostalgic spokesman of a dying order. Of middle-class rural origins, he was always an alien in the industrially dominated society of his adulthood.... Alger's work reflects an attempt to re-create the more harmonious society in which he was raised."[4] Because he idealized in his juvenile fiction the moral assurances of a pre-industrial economy, Alger ironically enhanced his appeal to a later generation of readers for whom he was reinvented as a kind of Progressive prophet. Significantly, some of his books were even packaged for sale as Progressive reform tracts. At least four editions of his novels issued during the first decade of the new century—the Street and Smith edition of *Tom Brace* (1901) and the New York Book Company editions of *Andy Gordon/Bob Burton, Mark Mason's Triumph/Joe's Luck*, and *Only an Irish Boy/Tom the Bootblack* (1910)—pictured President Theodore Roosevelt on the cover, though Alger died before Roosevelt assumed the presidency and had not referred to him in any of his stories. The evolution in Alger's reputation can even be inferred from a pair of frontispieces to the "Ragged Dick series." In the original illustration from 1868, four street boys attired in shabby clothes—among them a newsboy and a bootblack—stare blankly at the artist. In a revision of the image published in Alger editions over forty years later, however, the same four boys have aged, sport polished boots, and wear more fashionable outfits.

---

1   "Writers of Juvenile Fiction," *Bookman* 14 (January 1901): 352.

2   *Public Libraries* 16 (1911): 454.

3   Robert H. Wiebe, *The Search for Order, 1877–1920* (New York: Hill and Wang, 1967), 8.

4   Richard Weiss, *The Myth of American Success* (New York: Basic, 1969), 49, 59–60.

MEDAL LIBRARY No. 122

Tom Brace

WHO HE WAS
AND HOW HE FARED

By HORATIO ALGER JR.

STREET & SMITH, PUBLISHERS, NEW YORK

Figure 1. Cover of *Tom Brace* (1901). Editor's collection.

Figure 2. Cover of *Andy Gordon* / *Bob Burton* (New York Book Co., 1910). Editor's collection.

Figure 3. Frontispiece to "Ragged Dick series" (Loring, 1868). Editor's collection.

Figure 4. Frontispiece to "Ragged Dick series" (Winston, 1910). Editor's collection.

These two illustrations read Alger's moral fables through different lenses. Like a Rorschach test, his novels were open to a variety of interpretations.

Alger's new-found popularity as a champion of economic success also influenced so-called "serious" authors during this period. Theodore Dreiser (1871–1945), who avidly read Alger novels as a Hoosier farm boy,[1] probably modeled a chapter of *Sister Carrie* (1900) on an episode in Alger's *Helen Ford* (1866).[2] Moreover, Dreiser apparently meant the middle name of Frank Algernon Cowperwood, the protagonist of his novels *The Financier* (1912), *The Titan* (1914), and *The Stoic* (1947), to be read literally: as *not* an Alger hero. Except for the fact that both earn money, Cowperwood and Alger's earnestly moral hero have little in common. Similarly, Sherwood Anderson (1876–1941) satirized the Progressive view of Alger in *Windy McPherson's Son* (1916), in which he described the hollow success won by an Iowa newsboy who goes to Chicago, becomes rich, and marries his boss's daughter. As long ago as 1916, Waldo Frank (1889–1967) discerned "the faint footprints of Horatio Alger" in the novel,[3] and Wright Morris (1910–98) has also claimed that the "strain of experience" in it "is closer to Horatio Alger" than to Anderson's own.[4] Sinclair Lewis (1885–1951) also adapted "the tradition of Horatio Alger" to the expectations of Progressive-era readers by depicting "the mystiques of mechanics, rather than the formula of hard work and brave honesty, as the key to economic success" in his early novel *The Trail of the Hawk* (1915).[5] Whereas the Alger formula was frequently employed in the fiction of the period, Alger had not yet acquired symbolic status as the progenitor of an American success myth. Dreiser, Anderson, and Lewis did not explicitly admit their debt to him because, despite the increased sales of his books, his name had not yet acquired widespread cachet in the popular culture.

---

1   Theodore Dreiser, *Dawn* (New York: Liveright, 1931), 122, 125.

2   Scharnhorst, "A Possible Source for Sister Carrie," *Dreiser Newsletter* 9 (Spring 1978): 1–4.

3   Waldo Frank, "Emerging Greatness," *Seven Arts* (November 1916); rpt. in *Sherwood Anderson: A Collection of Critical Essays*, ed. Walter Rideout (Englewood Cliffs, NJ: Prentice-Hall, 1974), 14, 15.

4   Wright Morris, "Windy McPherson's Son: The Storyteller's Story," *Windy McPherson's Son* (Chicago: U of Chicago P, 1965), x, xiii.

5   Mark Schorer, *Sinclair Lewis* (New York: McGraw-Hill, 1961), 225.

Alger's Canonization

The most radical transformations in Alger's reputation, his enshrinement as an American success mythmaker, occurred largely after 1920, as his books declined in popularity and lapsed from print. Much as his novels seemed to endorse Progressive reform when read in the benign *zeitgeist* of the Progressive age, a generation later these same novels, no longer submitted to the critical opinion of readers, were recollected in the acquisitive spirit of the Roaring Twenties. That is, Alger's hero was reinvented during this decade as a business tycoon. According to a *Time* magazine article published in 1928, "Ragged Dick, Phil the Fiddler, and the heroes of every one of his 119 books survived adversity, invariably achieved fame and fortune at the end of the last chapter."[1] Simply stated, Alger's moral tracts acquired new meanings in each new cultural context. No longer considered merely a writer of didactic fiction, he became, in the words of the *New York Times*, a mythologizer who created "successful protagonists, ambitious boys who, through one variation or other of an ever-efficient formula, found their way up the ladder of achievement."[2] The phrase "Horatio Alger hero" also entered the language during the 1920s—its first appearance in print may have occurred as late as 1926[3]—even as more libraries were removing his books from their shelves. By 1928, only the common proclamation of Alger's name reminded people of his earlier popularity. As one pundit that year asked rhetorically, "Everyone knows Alger—and yet, do they? To most people Alger is just a name."[4]

The first biography of Alger, issued in 1928, also serviced this popular impression of Alger as a success ideologue. The author assigned the task of writing it for a trade press, Herbert R. Mayes (1900–87), later director of the *Saturday Review* and editor of *Good Housekeeping*, faced a formidable problem: how to document a life about which almost nothing was known. He filled the void in the record with factoids. "All I had to do was come up with a fairy tale," Mayes explained a half-century later. "No research required. Nothing required but a little imagination." In *Alger: A Biography without a Hero*, as the title may indicate, Mayes

---

1 "Alger," *Time* (7 May 1928): 47.

2 Halsey Raines, "Horatio Alger Created 119 Synthetic Heroes," *New York Times Book Review* (22 April 1928): 2.

3 "Frank A. Munsey as a Horatio Alger Hero," *Literary Digest* (9 January 1926): 48.

4 Milton Byron, "New Biography," *Outlook* (11 April 1928): 598.

portrayed his subject as "a pathetic, quite ridiculous character,"[1] the victim of a tyrannical father who forbade his marriage to a childhood sweetheart and bullied him into the Unitarian ministry. As a result of his tragic adolescence (in Mayes's version of events), Alger became neurotically obsessed with the trappings of success. That the work was not recognized as potboiling histrionics seems hardly possible today, yet not until 1972 did Mayes finally admit publicly that his biography had been a hoax. The best explanation for the uncritical acceptance of his fictionalized biography is that its depiction of Alger as a success-worshipper reinforced the popular view of Alger at the time. "Nobody bothered to do any digging," Mayes later observed,[2] because his work satisfied the need for a usable past about Alger.

Ironically, Mayes's biography is valuable as a source of information, not about Alger's life, but about Alger's utility as a symbol of success. The desperate achievements of his heroes, according to Mayes, was less a reward for faithful service and moral behavior than the unconscious compensation of a writer who suffered his entire life from an inferiority complex and sought emotional catharsis in his fiction. "All of Horatio Alger's heroes started poor and ended up well-to-do. All of them were in search of money," Mayes insisted.[3] Thirty years later, Alger scholars were still reading the stories through a psychoanalytical lens based on a woefully inaccurate biography. For example, Kenneth S. Lynn claimed that by "[s]ublimating a lifetime which Alger himself judged to be ignominiously unheroic, he created the 'Alger hero,' and thereby became one of the great mythmakers of the modern world."[4] According to the psychoanalytical critic Norman N. Holland, Alger "remained a child all his life, an emotional cripple whose growth was twisted by the steady application of moral pressures in childhood." Little wonder that in the Alger novels the hero's biological father is often dead, supposedly dispatched by the author in an Oedipal rage and replaced by an adult patron, a surrogate or substitute father. Not that such narratorial moves compensated for the author's repressions: he was a "guilty, impotent failure" to the end of his life.[5] Obviously, Mayes's revelation that he invented his Alger

1 Mayes, "After Half a Century," introduction to *Alger: A Biography without a Hero* (Des Plaines, IL: Westgard, 1978), v–vi.
2 "Holy Horatio!" *Time* (10 June 1974): 18.
3 Mayes, *Alger: A Biography without a Hero* (New York: Macy-Masius, 1928), 220.
4 Kenneth S. Lynn, *The Dream of Success* (Boston: Little, Brown, 1955), 6.
5 Norman N. Holland, "Hobbling with Horatio, or the Uses of Literature," *Hudson Review* 12 (Winter 1959–60): 550, 556, 557.

biography from whole cloth undermines this tidy interpretation. Still, it is significant that the seed that produced this hybrid Alger was planted during the boom years of the 1920s.

During this decade, Alger's name and supposed authority as a popular proponent of business success also began to be invoked by some *literati* whose adolescence had coincided with the heyday of Alger's vogue early in the century. In 1923, Thomas Wolfe (1900–38), still a struggling young playwright in New York, complained that "I feel like Horatio Alger's boy hero: alone in the cit-ee—which has no pit-ee.... Unfortunately I have not the money-making penchant which all of Horatio's boy-heroes seemed to have."[1] Wolfe's identification with the Alger hero of economic myth acquires even greater significance in light of his allusions to Alger as a success ideologue in *Look Homeward, Angel* (1929). In that autobiographical novel, he described his hero reading "through all the infinite monotony of the Algers—Pluck and Luck, Sink or Swim, Grit, Jack's Ward, Jed the Poor-House Boy—and dozens more. He gloated over the fat money-making of these books ... reckoning up the amount of income, if it were not given, or if it were, dividing the annual sum into monthly and weekly portions, and dreaming on its purchasing power. His desires were not modest—no fortune under $250,000 satisfied him."[2] Wolfe's reminiscence vividly illustrates how easily the moral message of the original Alger books could be misappropriated, for Alger's heroes rarely won so large a reward as this.

Alger's symbolic status among writers of the 1920s is most apparent in the works of F. Scott Fitzgerald (1896–1940), whose satires of the Alger stories popular in his boyhood became a vehicle for his condemnation of the crass materialism rampant in his adulthood.[3] For example, in his little-known play *The Vegetable; or, From President to Postman* (1922)—its title a burlesque of such Alger titles as *From Canal Boy to President*—Fitzgerald parodied popular success literature in general and Alger's works in particular. The protagonist is an ironic Alger hero whose father, a doddering old fool named Horatio, is a caricature of Alger himself. Fitzgerald's failure with this play was one of execution, not intention, for in it he discovered the rich parodic vein profitably mined earlier by Crane and later by James Thurber

---

1   *The Letters of Thomas Wolfe*, ed. Elizabeth Nowell (New York: Scribner's, 1956), 53.

2   Thomas Wolfe, *Look Homeward, Angel* (New York: Scribner's, 1929), 85.

3   Scharnhorst, "Scribbling Upward: Fitzgerald's Debt of Honor to Horatio Alger," *Fitzgerald/Hemingway Annual* (1978): 162–69.

(1894–1961) and Nathanael West (1903–40).[1] Notably in *The Great Gatsby* (1925), he again paid curled-lip service to the popular image of success by satirizing Alger. While it has become a critical commonplace to observe that this novel "is a contemporary variation of an old American success pattern, the rags-to-riches story exalted by American legend,"[2] the extent to which Fitzgerald spoofed Alger specifically has not been fully appreciated. Rather than "an inverted Alger novel,"[3] it may be more accurately described as a sequel to an ironic Alger fable. Indeed, Fitzgerald probably parodied Alger's *Jed the Poor-House Boy* in chapter VI, in which he treated Gatsby's apprenticeship to a patron named Dan Cody. Like Alger's Jeb Gilman, young Jimmy Gatz (who shares his initials) meets his patron aboard a luxurious yacht and is given a job and a new suit of clothes. Moreover, in both novels the hero changes his name "at the specific moment that witnessed the beginning of his career."[4] However, whereas Jeb's patron is a neat and mannerly young gentleman, Dan Cody is a "pioneer debauchee." Whereas at the end of Alger's story the hero moves into his ancestral mansion and lives happily ever after on an annual bequest of $25,000, Gatsby is cheated of his $25,000 legacy and must survive by his wits. Fitzgerald's story is, in effect, a sequel to that ironic version of Alger. In all, these satires of the economic myth associated with Alger are another indication that by the 1920s, Alger had become both a saint in the cult of success and the butt of jokes among the unconverted.

Alger's Iconic Status

Alger ultimately was transformed from an economic mythmaker, a reputation he acquired during the Roaring Twenties, into a patriotic defender of the social and political status quo and erstwhile proponent of *laissez-faire* capitalism. During the Great Depression of the 1930s and the world war that followed, Alger's

---

1 F. Scott Fitzgerald, *The Vegetable; or, From President to Postman* (New York: Scribner's, 1922); James Thurber, "Tom the Young Kidnapper, or Pay Up and Live," *New Yorker* (10 June 1933): 14ff., 7.

2 Edwin Fussell, "Fitzgerald's Brave New World," *ELH* 19 (December 1952): 296.

3 Richard Lehan, "The Nowhere Hero," *American Dreams, American Nightmares*, ed. David Madden (Carbondale: Southern Illinois UP, 1970), 110.

4 Fitzgerald, *The Great Gatsby* (1925; rpt. New York: Scribner's, 1953), 98.

name became a shibboleth used to identify Americans who affirmed traditional verities and values. The characteristics that had come to be associated with the Alger hero—the potential greatness of commoners, rugged individualism, economic triumph in a fabled land of opportunity—seemingly summarized the American way of life threatened by the Depression and preserved by the war. Significantly, whereas Samuel Eliot Morison (1887–1976) and Henry Steele Commager (1902–98) in the original edition of their standard history textbook *The Growth of the American Republic*, published in 1930, did not mention Alger at all, in the second and third editions, published in 1937 and 1942, they asserted that Alger probably had exerted greater influence on the American character than any other writer except perhaps Mark Twain.[1] Moreover, the *Reader's Guide to Periodical Literature*, an index of articles published in popular magazines since 1892, finally catalogued its first article about Alger in 1932, the centenary of his birth—a telling clue to his enshrinement as a culture hero after his sales popularity had waned. As one writer observed in the *New York Times* that year, "It is difficult for an adult to appraise the Alger books unless he has read them during his boyhood. If this is the case he is likely to be lost in a glamour of pleasant memories."[2]

Read or selectively remembered during the Depression and the war, the novels seemed to be neither moral tracts nor simple success stories, but political propaganda. As the national economy collapsed, Alger's presumed celebration of the merits of free enterprise won popular acclaim. In 1932, on the hundredth anniversary of his birth, the *New York Times* editorially praised Alger for propagating a philosophy of self-help.[3] In 1934, a writer for the *Christian Science Monitor* assured his readers that despite hard times, "the Alger pattern still persists."[4] A popular biography of Frank Munsey (1854–1925) published in 1935 lauded that publishing entrepreneur as "an Alger hero."[5] Over the next few years, Alger enjoyed a steady crescendo of praise in the public

---

1 Samuel Eliot Morison and Henry Steele Commager, *The Growth of the American Republic*, 2nd and 3rd eds. (New York: Oxford UP, 1937 and 1942), 287–88.
2 David Ferris Kirby, "The Author of the Alger Books for Boys," *New York Times Magazine* (10 January 1932): 5.
3 "The Newsboys' Hero," *New York Times* (13 January 1932), 22.
4 Rugg 7.
5 George Britt, *Forty Years—Forty Millions* (New York: Farrar & Rinehart, 1935), 56 and passim.

media. In 1938, Frederick Lewis Allen repeated the by-then common opinion that Alger had "had a far-reaching influence upon the economic and social thought of America" and had helped "to determine the trend and tradition of American business life."[1] In 1939, on the fortieth anniversary of his death, Alger was eulogized in the *New York Times Magazine*: "His imprint on American life is still clear after forty years; the papers almost every week report the success of some 'typical Alger hero' of the present."[2]

The following year, Street and Smith published a comic-book version of Alger's *Mark the Match Boy* and NBC radio broadcast a dramatization of his *From Farm Boy to Senator*. During this program, the governor of New York, Herbert Lehman, declared that as a boy he had been an avid reader of Alger's fiction and that "I was particularly interested because he showed in his books that the United States was a country of great opportunity for all and he was always a steadfast advocate of the democratic principles on which our nation was created and which have made it great." Rather than despair during the Depression, Lehman adjured his listeners to affirm that, as in Alger's time, "Broad and unrestricted opportunities for success exist for those who have the vision, the equipment, the industry and the courage to seize them."[3] A week later, the *New York Times* editorially commended Lehman for "rallying to the defense of Horatio Alger, and confessing without shame that he was 'an Alger fan when a boy.' It was Alger's comforting thesis that virtue and industry are always rewarded.... Hard times come and go, but America is not going to shut up shop. We expect the country to prosper."[4] Lehman prescribed Alger as a home remedy for the economic ills of the nation.

With the advent of world war, Alger's iconic importance was enhanced. Barely a month after the bombing of Pearl Harbor in December 1941, Alger's birthday (13 January) was celebrated by the Children's Aid Society of New York—an annual event by this time, after the date had been ignored for decades—and the ceremony was publicized in the *New York Times*.[5] In the popular

---

1 Frederick Lewis Allen, "Horatio Alger, Jr.," *Saturday Review of Literature* (17 September 1938): 3, 17.

2 L.H. Robbin, "Alger: No Alger Hero," *New York Times Magazine* (16 July 1939): 11.

3 "Lehman Speaks as Old Alger Fan in Acclaiming Our Opportunities," *New York Times* (30 March 1940), 9.

4 "An Alger Fan," *New York Times* 6 April 1940: 16.

5 "Alger's Birthday Marked," *New York Times* 14 January 1942: 12.

wartime motion picture *Yankee Doodle Dandy* (1942), a biopic of the patriotic playwright George M. Cohan (1878–1942), the hero describes his life to President Franklin Roosevelt as a Horatio Alger story. In 1943, the *Atlantic Monthly*, a magazine that had never reviewed an Alger novel during the author's life, featured an article about Alger's influence entitled "They Made Me What I Am Today." Its author suggested that because "the generation that grew up ... before the last war" had, as boys, been inspired by Alger, their "faith in laissez-faire, in the best of all possible worlds, in the inevitability of rags to riches," served the nation well in the prosecution of the new war.[1]

After the war, as the country demobilized, Alger retained his political office. In 1947, the *New York Times* again praised him in its editorial pages, contending that only disillusioned historians "who wrote, or may still be writing, in strong disapproval of America as a whole" dared to criticize Alger and his legendary success story,[2] and *Advertising Age* called for a new Alger to inspire contemporary American youth with the self-reliance of their fathers and to counteract "government interference" in the private sector.[3] Meanwhile, Stewart Holbrook suggested that Alger had "put free and untrammeled competition on the side of the angels" so persuasively that "the Red Dawn [communism] never came up over the horizon. Too many Americans held the vision of Upward and Onward."[4] The same year, the Grolier Club of New York named *Ragged Dick* one of the hundred most influential American books published before 1900.[5] No longer perceived as merely moral fables, Alger's novels seemed more like tools of social control wielded by an entrenched ruling class.

Basking in popular esteem like a decorated war hero, the author lent his name and reputation to the Horatio Alger Awards, a merchandising vehicle for political and economic orthodoxy founded in 1947 by Norman Vincent Peale (1898–1993), the author of *The Power of Positive Thinking* (1952). Sponsored by the non-profit American Schools and Colleges Association, Inc. (today the Horatio Alger Association of Distinguished Ameri-

---

1 Newman Levy, "They Made Me What I Am Today," *Atlantic Monthly* 172 (November 1943): 117.

2 "Topics of the Times," *New York Times* 16 January 1947: 24.

3 Qtd. in Cawelti 102.

4 Holbrook, *Lost Men of American History* (New York: Macmillan, 1946), 228, 238.

5 *One Hundred Influential American Books Printed Before 1900*, ed. Frederick B. Adams (New York: Grolier Club, 1947), 107.

cans), which had become "concerned about the trend among young people towards the mind-poisoning belief that equal opportunity was a thing of the past," the Alger Awards Committee select annually "living individuals who by their own efforts had pulled themselves up by their bootstraps in the American tradition."[1] Past recipients include H. Ross Perot, Billy Graham, W. Clement Stone, Clarence Thomas, Roger Ailes, corporate raider T. Boone Pickens, Republican presidents Herbert Hoover, Dwight Eisenhower, Ronald Reagan, and Gerald Ford,[2] and fast-food magnates Herman Cain, Dave Thomas, Carl Karcher, Harlan Sanders, and Ray Kroc. Clearly, Alger's books were no longer considered simple literary texts but were evaluated according to the social and political ends they seemed to serve. Alger was read through a lens that distorted his original moral intention.

Ironically, many American novelists on the Left shared this perspective. In 1945, soon after leaving the Communist Party of the USA, Richard Wright (1908–60), author of *Native Son* (1940), argued that Alger had been "perhaps American capitalism's greatest and most effective propagandist."[3] Still, the most notorious citation of Alger as an apologist for capitalism in the literature of this period appeared in Nathanael West's caustic parody *A Cool Million* (1934). Shortly before his death in 1940, West (b. 1903) would write in an unproduced screen treatment of *A Cool Million* that "[o]nly fools laugh at Horatio Alger, and his poor boys who make good. The wise man who thinks twice about that sterling author will realize that Alger is to America what Homer was to the Greeks."[4] In his novel, he turned this American Homer on his head and satirized the facile optimism of Americans in their collective epic-dream. His absurd hero, Lemuel Pitkin, who is exploited throughout by an ironic patron, ex-president Nathan "Shagpoke" Whipple, loses his money, teeth, right eye, left thumb, a leg, his scalp, and finally his life in a *tour de force* of misadventures. In the grotesque tableau that ends the novel, Whipple eulogizes the martyred all-American boy

---

1   *Opportunity Still Knocks*, Jubilee ed. (New York: Horatio Alger Awards Committee, 1971), 3.

2   James Cannon, *Gerald R. Ford: An Honorable Life* (Ann Arbor: U of Michigan P, 2013), 43: "They were my favorite reading."

3   "Alger Revisited, or My Stars! Did We Read That Stuff?" *PM* (16 September 1945): 13.

4   Qtd. in Jay Martin, *Nathanael West: The Art of His Life* (New York: Farrar, Straus and Giroux, 1970), 219.

and inaugurates the fascist millennium. Selecting a style designed to serve his thematic purpose, West constructed his work from altered and rearranged shards of at least six Alger books. In all, over one-fifth of the novel is vintage Alger only slightly revised.[1] This systematic plagiarism went unrecognized for over thirty years because, much as Mayes had appropriated the popular impression of Alger as a success-worshipper in his biography, West had appropriated the image of Alger as a political ideologue in his parody. Significantly, however, West invented all the polemical passages that appear in his book, for he found no political manifesto in the actual Alger stories. He had to reinvent Alger even as he plagiarized him in order to serve his literary purpose and to appeal to Depression-era readers.

More recent invocations of the Alger myth, as in the annual ceremonies hosted by the Alger Awards Committee, suggest that Alger's reputation crystallized with his institutionalization around 1947, and that his utility as a political icon has remained essentially unchanged since the Depression. Each generation between the Civil War and World War II discovered its own usable past in Alger by reinventing him according to the milieu of the moment. Forty years after the publication of West's *A Cool Million*, John Seelye (b. 1931) focused his Alger parody *Dirty Tricks; or, Nick Noxin's Natural Nobility* (1974) on a particular political target: Richard Nixon during the Watergate and impeachment hearings. (Not only does "Nick" rhyme with "Dick," the diminutive of "Richard," but "Noxin," an anagram of "Nixon," rhymes with "toxin.") The transformations in Alger's reputation—from didactic writer for juvenile readers to Progressive moralist, economic mythmaker, and political ideologue—seem to have been dictated less by the content of his books than by the cultural context in which they were read or remembered. Unlike other juvenile novelists, Alger's themes were peculiarly adaptable to popular contemporary issues long after his death. An economic and political icon more by accident than design, "it was not until 1947 that anyone got around to exploiting him into an organized symbol."[2]

---

1 For more detailed descriptions of West's plagiarisms, see Douglas Shepard, "Nathanael West Rewrites Horatio Alger, Jr.," *Satire Newsletter* 3 (Fall 1965): 13–28; and Scharnhorst, "From Rags to Patches, or *A Cool Million* as Alter-Alger," *Ball State University Forum* 21.iv (1980): 58–65.

2 Richard Huber, *The American Idea of Success* (New York: McGraw-Hill, 1971), 43.

More than ever, Alger had become, with the features of his make-over complete, a victim of mistaken identity.

In his juvenile novels, to be sure, Alger influenced a generation of young readers early in the twentieth century. As one familiar only with his modern reputation might expect, many of these readers, such as Benjamin Franklin Fairless (1890–1962) of US Steel and James A. Farley (1888–1976) of Coca-Cola,[1] became real-life counterparts of the mythic Alger heroes. But to consider Alger simply as an apologist for business success is to distort grossly his basic humanitarian impulse. As one familiar only with his modern reputation might *not* expect, many well-known American writers on the left, including not only Dreiser, Wright, and West, but Jack London (1876–1916), Upton Sinclair (1878–1968), and Maya Angelou (1928–2014),[2] read Alger's books as youths and were not converted to capitalism. As Cawelti has concluded, "Judging from the prominence of his themes, there is as much evidence that Alger was an important influence on future reformers as a popular model for incipient robber barons."[3] Alger himself hardly could have imagined that he would be so long remembered, much less celebrated as an American mythologizer of success a half-century after his death. As he opined to a friend in 1897, "If I could come back 50 years from now probably I should feel bewildered in reading the New York *Tribune* of 1947."[4] He wrote these words with a soothsayer's prescience, for one of the items in the news that year which undoubtedly would have perplexed him beyond his wildest flights of fancy announced the inauguration of the annual Horatio Alger Awards. After fifty years, he would not have recognized his offspring.

1   *Opportunity Still Knocks*, Jubilee edition (New York: Horatio Alger Awards Committee, 1971), *passim*.

2   London, *John Barleycorn* (New York: Century, 1913), 133; Sinclair, *Autobiography* (New York: Harcourt, Brace, 1962), 9; Angelou, *I Know Why the Caged Bird Sings* (1970; rpt. New York: Bantam, 1993), 75.

3   Cawelti 117.

4   Scharnhorst with Bales, *Lost Life* 156.

Horatio Alger Jr.: A Brief Chronology

1829	Horatio Alger, father of the writer, graduates from Cambridge Divinity School.
1832	13 January: Horatio Alger Jr. born in Chelsea, Massachusetts.
1844	The elder Horatio Alger defaults on debts.
1844–47	Alger Jr., attends Gates Academy, Marlborough, Massachusetts, to prepare for college.
1848–52	Attends Harvard College.
1849	First publications in a nationally distributed magazine, *Pictorial National Library*.
1852	Phi Beta Kappa graduate from Harvard College.
1852–57	Works as a teacher, editor, and part-time writer.
1856	Publishes *Bertha's Christmas Vision: An Autumn Sheaf*, his first book.
1857–60	Attends Harvard Divinity School.
1860–61	First European grand tour.
1861–64	Resides in Cambridge, Massachusetts, while teaching and writing.
1863	Publishes essay in the *North American Review* on the funeral of Eugène Scribe.
1864	Publishes *Frank's Campaign*, his first novel for juveniles and first of three novels in the "Campaign series."
1864–66	Minister of the Unitarian Society in Brewster, Massachusetts. Contributes to *Harper's Weekly*, *Harper's Monthly*, and *Frank Leslie's Illustrated Newspaper*.
1866	Resettles in New York City. Composes poem, "Friar Anselmo's Sin."
1867	Serialization of *Ragged Dick* in *Student and Schoolmate*.
1868	5 May: Book publication of revised *Ragged Dick*, the first of six juvenile novels in the "Ragged Dick series." Publishes "John Maynard: A Ballad of Lake Erie."
1869	Publishes *Fame and Fortune*, the sequel to *Ragged Dick*.
1869–81	Tutors the sons of the banker Joseph Seligman, including Edwin R.A. Seligman.
1871–75	Publishes "Luck and Pluck series" of eight volumes, including *Bound to Rise* (1873) and *Risen from the Ranks* (1874).

1871–79	Publishes "Tattered Tom series" of eight juvenile novels, including *Phil the Fiddler* (1872) and *Julius, or The Street Boy Out West* (1874).
1872–77	Publishes "Brave and Bold series" of four juvenile novels, including *Shifting for Himself* (1876).
1873	Second European grand tour.
1875	Publishes *Grand'ther Baldwin's Thanksgiving with Other Ballads and Poems*.
1877	Travels via Union Pacific Railroad to the Pacific coast. Publishes *Life of Edwin Forrest* in collaboration with his cousin, William Rounseville Alger, and *The New Schoolma'am*, his best-reviewed adult novel.
1878	Travels as far west as Denver.
1878–82	Publishes "Pacific series" of four juvenile novels, including *The Young Miner* (1879).
1879	Alger's juvenile novels are removed from public libraries for the first time.
1881	A.K. Loring, the Boston publisher of all Alger juveniles to date, declares bankruptcy.
1881–83	Publishes juvenile biographies of James Garfield, Abraham Lincoln, and Daniel Webster.
1883	Hired to tutor Benjamin Cardozo, future associate justice of the Supreme Court.
1883–86	Publishes "Atlantic series" of four juvenile novels, including *The Young Circus Rider* (1883).
1887	Sued for plagiarism. Travels to Chicago to gather material for *Luke Walton, the Chicago Newsboy* (1889).
1887–90	Publishes "Way to Success series" of four volumes, including *Struggling Upward* (1890).
1890	Travels to California via the Northern Pacific Railroad. Publishes "Are My Boys Real?" in *Ladies' Home Journal*.
1892	Publishes *Digging for Gold: A Story of California*.
1892–93	Publishes "New World series" of three juvenile novels, including *In a New World* (1893).
1895	Publishes *The Disagreeable Woman*, his final novel for adults.
1896	Publishes "The Novel—Its Scope and Place in Literature" in *New York Railroad Men* and "Writing Stories for Boys" in the *Writer*. Retires to South Natick, Massachusetts.

1898	Appoints Edward Stratemeyer as his literary executor.
1899	18 July: Alger dies in South Natick of congestive heart failure.
1928	Publication of Herbert R. Mayes's *Alger: A Biography without a Hero*.
1986	Posthumous publication of *Mabel Parker; or, The Hidden Treasure*.

A Note on the Texts

Horatio Alger Jr. originally contributed *Ragged Dick; or, Street Life in New York* as a twelve-part serial to the Boston juvenile magazine *Student and Schoolmate* in 1867. He revised and enlarged the text for publication as a single volume issued by the A.K. Loring Company of Boston in May 1868. The text reproduced in this Broadview Edition is the unedited first Loring edition.

The volume also contains the complete text of the first edition of *Risen from the Ranks* (Boston: A.K. Loring, 1874).

RAGGED DICK; OR, STREET LIFE IN NEW YORK WITH THE BOOT-BLACKS

Contents

PREFACE

"Ragged Dick" was contributed as a serial story to the pages of the *Schoolmate*,[1] a well-known juvenile magazine, during the year 1867. While in course of publication, it was received with so many evidences of favor that it has been rewritten and considerably enlarged, and is now presented to the public as the first volume of a series intended to illustrate the life and experiences of the friendless and vagrant children who are now numbered by thousands in New York and other cities.

Several characters in the story are sketched from life. The necessary information has been gathered mainly from personal observation and conversations with the boys themselves. The author is indebted also to the excellent Superintendent of the Newsboys' Lodging House, in Fulton Street,[2] for some facts of which he has been able to make use. Some anachronisms may be noted. Wherever they occur, they have been admitted, as aiding in the development of the story, and will probably be considered as of little importance in an unpretending volume, which does not aspire to strict historical accuracy.

The author hopes that, while the volumes in this series may prove interesting stories, they may also have the effect of enlisting the sympathies of his readers in behalf of the unfortunate children whose life is described, and of leading them to co-operate with the praiseworthy efforts now making by the Children's Aid Society[3] and other organizations to ameliorate their condition.

New York, April, 1868

---

1 Alger dedicated *Ragged Dick* to the editor of *Student and Schoolmate*, Joseph Henry Allen (1820–98), a Harvard-educated Unitarian minister. Allen had co-edited the monthly *Christian Examiner* between 1863 and 1865 with William Rounseville Alger (1822–1905), Horatio's cousin.

2 Charles O'Connor (1826–87) was the superintendent of the Newsboys' Lodging House, sponsored by the Children's Aid Society, from 1858 until his death. See also his obituaries "A Friend of the Newsboys Gone," New York *Sun* 13 March 1887: 13; and "Charles O'Connor Dead," *New York Times* 13 March 1887: 7.

3 Founded in 1853 by Charles Loring Brace (1826–90), the Children's Aid Society is a private, non-profit child welfare agency in New York.

CHAPTER I:
RAGGED DICK IS INTRODUCED TO THE READER

"Wake up there, youngster," said a rough voice.

Ragged Dick opened his eyes slowly, and stared stupidly in the face of the speaker, but did not offer to get up.

"Wake up, you young vagabond!" said the man a little impatiently; "I suppose you'd lay there all day, if I hadn't called you."

"What time is it?" asked Dick.

"Seven o'clock."

"Seven o'clock! I oughter've been up an hour ago. I know what 'twas made me so precious sleepy. I went to the Old Bowery[1] last night, and didn't turn in till past twelve."

"You went to the Old Bowery? Where'd you get your money?" asked the man, who was a porter in the employ of a firm doing business on Spruce Street.

"Made it by shines, in course. My guardian don't allow me no money for theatres, so I have to earn it."

"Some boys get it easier than that," said the porter significantly.

"You don't catch me stealin', if that's what you mean," said Dick.

"Don't you ever steal, then?"

"No, and I wouldn't. Lots of boys does it, but I wouldn't."

"Well, I'm glad to hear you say that. I believe there's some good in you, Dick, after all."

"Oh, I'm a rough customer!" said Dick. "But I wouldn't steal. It's mean."

"I'm glad you think so, Dick," and the rough voice sounded gentler than at first. "Have you got any money to buy your breakfast?"

"No, but I'll soon get some."

While this conversation had been going on, Dick had got up. His bedchamber had been a wooden box half full of straw, on which the young boot-black had reposed his weary limbs, and slept as soundly as if it had been a bed of down. He dumped down into the straw without taking the trouble of undressing.

Getting up too was an equally short process. He jumped out of the box, shook himself, picked out one or two straws that had found their way into rents in his clothes, and, drawing a well-

---

1 The Old Bowery Theatre was located at 46 Bowery on the lower East Side of Manhattan.

worn cap over his uncombed locks, he was all ready for the business of the day.

Dick's appearance as he stood beside the box was rather peculiar. His pants were torn in several places, and had apparently belonged in the first instance to a boy two sizes larger than himself. He wore a vest, all the buttons of which were gone except two, out of which peeped a shirt which looked as if it had been worn a month. To complete his costume he wore a coat too long for him, dating back, if one might judge from its general appearance, to a remote antiquity.

Washing the face and hands is usually considered proper in commencing the day, but Dick was above such refinement. He had no particular dislike to dirt, and did not think it necessary to remove several dark streaks on his face and hands. But in spite of his dirt and rags there was something about Dick that was attractive. It was easy to see that if he had been clean and well dressed he would have been decidedly good-looking. Some of his companions were sly, and their faces inspired distrust; but Dick had a frank, straight-forward manner that made him a favorite.

Dick's business hours had commenced. He had no office to open. His little blacking-box was ready for use, and he looked sharply in the faces of all who passed, addressing each with, "Shine yer boots, sir?"

"How much?" asked a gentleman on his way to his office.

"Ten cents," said Dick, dropping his box, and sinking upon his knees on the sidewalk, flourishing his brush with the air of one skilled in his profession.

"Ten cents! Isn't that a little steep?"

"Well, you know 'taint all clear profit," said Dick, who had already set to work. "There's the *blacking* costs something, and I have to get a new brush pretty often."

"And you have a large rent too," said the gentleman quizzically, with a glance at a large hole in Dick's coat.

"Yes, sir," said Dick, always ready to joke; "I have to pay such a big rent for my manshun up on Fifth Avenoo, that I can't afford to take less than ten cents a shine. I'll give you a bully shine, sir."

"Be quick about it, for I am in a hurry. So your house is on Fifth Avenue, is it?"

"It isn't anywhere else," said Dick, and Dick spoke the truth there.

"What tailor do you patronize?" asked the gentleman, surveying Dick's attire.

"Would you like to go to the same one?" asked Dick, shrewdly.

"Well, no; it strikes me that he didn't give you a very good fit."

"This coat once belonged to General Washington,"[1] said Dick, comically. "He wore it all through the Revolution, and it got torn some, 'cause he fit so hard. When he died he told his widder to give it to some smart young feller that hadn't got none of his own; so she gave it to me. But if you'd like it, sir, to remember General Washington by, I'll let you have it reasonable."

"Thank you, but I wouldn't want to deprive you of it. And did your pants come from General Washington too?"

"No, they was a gift from Lewis Napoleon.[2] Lewis had outgrown 'em and sent 'em to me,—he's bigger than me, and that's why they don't fit."

"It seems you have distinguished friends. Now, my lad, I suppose you would like your money."

"I shouldn't have any objection," said Dick.

"I believe," said the gentleman, examining his pocket-book, "I haven't got anything short of twenty-five cents. Have you got any change?"

"Not a cent," said Dick. "All my money's invested in the Erie Railroad."[3]

"That's unfortunate."

"Shall I get the money changed, sir?"

"I can't wait; I've got to meet an appointment immediately. I'll hand you twenty-five cents, and you can leave the change at my office any time during the day."

"All right, sir. Where is it?"

"No. 125 Fulton Street. Shall you remember?"

"Yes, sir. What name?"

"Greyson,—office on second floor."

"All right, sir; I'll bring it."

"I wonder whether the little scamp will prove honest," said Mr. Greyson to himself, as he walked away. "If he does, I'll give him my custom regularly. If he don't, as is most likely, I shan't mind the loss of fifteen cents."

---

1 George Washington (1732–99) was commander-in-chief of the Continental Army during the Revolutionary War and first president of the United States.

2 As Napoleon III, Louis-Napoléon Bonaparte (1808–73) was emperor of the Second Empire (1852–70) in France.

3 The Erie Railroad, constructed between and 1836 and 1851, linked New York and Lake Erie. Alger featured it in his juvenile novel *The Erie Train Boy* (1890).

Mr. Greyson didn't understand Dick. Our ragged hero wasn't a model boy in all respects. I am afraid he swore sometimes, and now and then he played tricks upon unsophisticated boys from the country, or gave a wrong direction to honest old gentlemen unused to the city. A clergyman in search of the Cooper Institute[1] he once directed to the Tombs Prison,[2] and, following him unobserved, was highly delighted when the unsuspicious stranger walked up the front steps of the great stone building on Centre Street, and tried to obtain admission.

"I guess he wouldn't want to stay long if he did get in," thought Ragged Dick, hitching up his pants. "Leastways I shouldn't. They're so precious glad to see you that they won't let you go, but board you gratooitous, and never send in no bills."

Another of Dick's faults was his extravagance. Being always wide-awake and ready for business, he earned enough to have supported him comfortably and respectably. There were not a few young clerks who employed Dick from time to time in his professional capacity, who scarcely earned as much as he, greatly as their style and dress exceeded his. But Dick was careless of his earnings. Where they went he could hardly have told himself. However much he managed to earn during the day, all was generally spent before morning. He was fond of going to the Old Bowery Theatre, and to Tony Pastor's,[3] and if he had any money left afterwards, he would invite some of his friends in somewhere to have an oyster-stew; so it seldom happened that he commenced the day with a penny.

Then I am sorry to add that Dick had formed the habit of smoking. This cost him considerable, for Dick was rather fastidious about his cigars, and wouldn't smoke the cheapest. Besides, having a liberal nature, he was generally ready to treat his companions. But of course the expense was the smallest objection. No boy of fourteen can smoke without being affected injuriously. Men are frequently injured by smoking, and boys always. But large numbers of the newsboys and boot-blacks form the habit. Exposed to the cold and wet they find that it warms them up, and

---

1 Founded by the philanthropist Peter Cooper (1791–1883) in 1859, the Cooper Institute or Cooper Union is a private college located at Cooper Square and Astor Place in New York.

2 The original New York City prison, opened in 1838 on the block surrounded by Centre, Franklin, Elm, and Leonard Streets, was nicknamed the Tombs for its alleged resemblance to an Egyptian tomb.

3 Tony Pastor's Opera House opened in 1865 at 201 Bowery.

the self-indulgence grows upon them. It is not uncommon to see a little boy, too young to be out of his mother's sight, smoking with all the apparent satisfaction of a veteran smoker.

There was another way in which Dick sometimes lost money. There was a noted gambling-house on Baxter Street, which in the evening was sometimes crowded with these juvenile gamesters, who staked their hard earnings, generally losing of course, and refreshing themselves from time to time with a vile mixture of liquor at two cents a glass. Sometimes Dick strayed in here, and played with the rest.

I have mentioned Dick's faults and defects, because I want it understood, to begin with, that I don't consider him a model boy. But there were some good points about him nevertheless. He was above doing anything mean or dishonorable. He would not steal, or cheat, or impose upon younger boys, but was frank and straight-forward, manly and self-reliant. His nature was a noble one, and had saved him from all mean faults. I hope my young readers will like him as I do, without being blind to his faults. Perhaps, although he was only a boot-black, they may find something in him to imitate.

And now, having fairly introduced Ragged Dick to my young readers, I must refer them to the next chapter for his further adventures.

CHAPTER II: JOHNNY NOLAN

After Dick had finished polishing Mr. Greyson's boots he was fortunate enough to secure three other customers, two of them reporters in the Tribune establishment, which occupies the corner of Spruce Street and Printing House Square.[1]

When Dick had got through with his last customer the City Hall[2] clock indicated eight o'clock. He had been up an hour, and hard at work, and naturally began to think of breakfast. He went up to the head of Spruce Street, and turned into Nassau. Two blocks further, and he reached Ann Street. On this street was a

---

1 Printing House Square, on Park Row near City Hall, was the hub of the New York publishing industry, the locale of offices of many New York newspapers, including the *Sun*, *Tribune*, *World*, *Times*, and *Day Book*.

2 The New York City Hall, built between 1810 and 1812, is located in City Hall Park between Broadway and Chambers Street in lower Manhattan.

small, cheap restaurant, where for five cents Dick could get a cup of coffee, and for ten cents more, a plate of beefsteak with a plate of bread thrown in. These Dick ordered, and sat down at a table.

It was a small apartment with a few plain tables unprovided with cloths, for the class of customers who patronized it were not very particular. Our hero's breakfast was soon before him. Neither the coffee nor the steak were as good as can be bought at Delmonico's;[1] but then it is very doubtful whether, in the present state of his wardrobe, Dick would have been received at that aristocratic restaurant, even if his means had admitted of paying the high prices there charged.

Dick had scarcely been served when he espied a boy about his own size standing at the door, looking wistfully into the restaurant. This was Johnny Nolan, a boy of fourteen, who was engaged in the same profession as Ragged Dick. His wardrobe was in very much the same condition as Dick's.

"Had your breakfast, Johnny?" inquired Dick, cutting off a piece of steak.

"No."

"Come in, then. Here's room for you."

"I aint got no money," said Johnny, looking a little enviously at his more fortunate friend.

"Haven't you had any shines?"

"Yes, I had one, but I shan't get any pay till to-morrow."

"Are you hungry?"

"Try me, and see."

"Come in. I'll stand treat this morning."

Johnny Nolan was nowise slow to accept this invitation, and was soon seated beside Dick.

"What'll you have, Johnny?"

"Same as you."

"Cup o' coffee and beefsteak," ordered Dick.

These were promptly brought, and Johnny attacked them vigorously.

Now, in the boot-blacking business, as well as in higher avocations, the same rule prevails, that energy and industry are rewarded, and indolence suffers. Dick was energetic and on the alert for business, but Johnny the reverse. The consequence was that Dick earned probably three times as much as the other.

---

1 The flagship Delmonico's, featuring French cuisine, was located at 2 South William Street in lower Manhattan for most of the nineteenth century.

"How do you like it?" asked Dick, surveying Johnny's attacks upon the steak with evident complacency.

"It's hunky."

I don't believe "hunky" is to be found in either Webster's or Worcester's big dictionary;[1] but boys will readily understand what it means.

"Do you come here often?" asked Johnny.

"Most every day. You'd better come too."

"I can't afford it."

"Well, you'd ought to, then," said Dick. "What do you do I'd like to know?"

"I don't get near as much as you, Dick."

"Well you might if you tried. I keep my eyes open,—that's the way I get jobs. You're lazy, that's what's the matter."

Johnny did not see fit to reply to this charge. Probably he felt the justice of it, and preferred to proceed with the breakfast, which he enjoyed the more as it cost him nothing.

Breakfast over, Dick walked up to the desk, and settled the bill. Then, followed by Johnny, he went out into the street.

"Where are you going, Johnny?"

"Up to Mr. Taylor's, on Spruce Street, to see if he don't want a shine."

"Do you work for him reg'lar?"

"Yes. Him and his partner wants a shine most every day. Where are you goin'?"

"Down front of the Astor House.[2] I guess I'll find some customers there."

At this moment Johnny started, and, dodging into an entry way, hid behind the door, considerably to Dick's surprise.

"What's the matter now?" asked our hero.

"Has he gone?" asked Johnny, his voice betraying anxiety.

"Who gone, I'd like to know?"

"That man in the brown coat."

"What of him. You aint scared of him, are you?"

"Yes, he got me a place once."

"Where?"

---

1 Noah Webster's and Joseph Emerson Worcester's English dictionaries were rival reference tools in the so-called "dictionary wars" of the mid-nineteenth century.

2 The most famous hotel in America, the Astor House was built at the corner of Broadway and Vesey Street in lower Manhattan by John Jacob Astor (1763–1848) and opened in 1836.

"Ever so far off."

"What if he did?"

"I ran away."

"Didn't you like it?"

"No, I had to get up too early. It was on a farm, and I had to get up at five to take care of the cows. I like New York best."

"Didn't they give you enough to eat?"

"Oh, yes, plenty."

"And you had a good bed?"

"Yes."

"Then you'd better have stayed. You don't get either of them here. Where'd you sleep last night?"

"Up an alley in an old wagon."

"You had a better bed than that in the country, didn't you?"

"Yes, it was as soft as—as cotton."

Johnny had once slept on a bale of cotton, the recollection supplying him with a comparison.

"Why didn't you stay?"

"I felt lonely," said Johnny.

Johnny could not exactly explain his feelings, but it is often the case that the young vagabond of the streets, though his food is uncertain, and his bed may be any old wagon or barrel that he is lucky enough to find unoccupied when night sets in, gets so attached to his precarious but independent mode of life, that he feels discontented in any other. He is accustomed to the noise and bustle and ever-varied life of the streets, and in the quiet scenes of the country misses the excitement in the midst of which he has always dwelt.

Johnny had but one tie to bind him to the city. He had a father living, but he might as well have been without one. Mr. Nolan was a confirmed drunkard, and spent the greater part of his wares for liquor. His potations made him ugly, and inflamed a temper never very sweet, working him up sometimes to such a pitch of rage that Johnny's life was in danger. Some months before, he had thrown a flat-iron at his son's head with such terrific force that unless Johnny had dodged he would not have lived long enough to obtain a place in our story. He fled the house, and from that time had not dared to re-enter it. Somebody had given him a brush and box of blacking, and he had set up in business on his own account. But he had not energy enough to succeed, as has already been stated, and I am afraid the poor boy had met with many hardships, and suffered more than once from cold and hunger. Dick had befriended him more than once, and often given him a breakfast or dinner, as the case might be.

"How'd you get away?" asked Dick, with some curiosity. "Did you walk?"

"No, I rode on the cars."

"Where'd you get your money? I hope you didn't steal it."

"I didn't have none."

"What did you do, then?"

"I got up about three o'clock, and walked to Albany."

"Where's that?" asked Dick, whose ideas on the subject of geography were rather vague.

"Up the river."

"How far?"

"About a thousand miles," said Johnny, whose conceptions of distance were equally vague.

"Go ahead. What did you do then?"

"I hid on top of a freight car, and came all the way without their seeing me.[1] That man in the brown coat was the man that got me the place, and I'm afraid he'd want to send me back."

"Well," said Dick, reflectively, "I dunno as I'd like to live in the country. I couldn't go to Tony Pastor's or the Old Bowery. There wouldn't be no place to spend my evenings. But I say, it's tough in winter, Johnny, 'specially when your overcoat's at the tailor's, an' likely to stay there."

"That's so, Dick. But I must be goin', or Mr. Taylor'll get somebody else to shine his boots."

Johnny walked back to Nassau Street, while Dick kept on his way to Broadway.

"That boy," soliloquized Dick, as Johnny took his departure, "aint got no ambition. I'll bet he won't get five shines to-day. I'm glad I aint like him. I couldn't go to the theatre, nor buy no cigars, nor get half as much as I wanted to eat.—Shine yer boots, sir?"

Dick always had an eye to business, and this remark was addressed to a young man, dressed in a stylish manner, who was swinging a jaunty cane.

"I've had my boots blacked once already this morning, but this confounded mud has spoiled the shine."

"I'll make 'em all right, sir, in a minute."

"Go ahead, then."

---

1 [Alger's note:] A fact.

The boots were soon polished in Dick's best style, which proved very satisfactory, our hero being a proficient in the art.

"I haven't got any change," said the young man, fumbling in his pocket, "but here's a bill you may run somewhere and get changed. I'll pay you five cents extra for your trouble."

He handed Dick a two-dollar bill, which our hero took into a store close by.

"Will you please change that, sir?" said Dick, walking up to the counter.

The salesman to whom he proffered it took the bill, and, slightly glancing at it, exclaimed angrily, "Be off, you young vagabond, or I'll have you arrested."

"What's the row?"

"You've offered me a counterfeit bill."

"I didn't know it," said Dick.

"Don't tell me. Be off, or I'll have you arrested."

CHAPTER III: DICK MAKES A PROPOSITION

Though Dick was somewhat startled at discovering that the bill he had offered was counterfeit, he stood his ground bravely.

"Clear out of this shop, you young vagabond," repeated the clerk.

"Then give me back my bill."

"That you may pass it again? No, sir, I shall do no such thing."

"It doesn't belong to me," said Dick. "A gentleman that owes me for a shine gave it to me to change."

"A likely story," said the clerk; but he seemed a little uneasy.

"I'll go and call him," said Dick.

He went out, and found his late customer standing on the Astor House steps.

"Well, youngster, have you brought back my change? You were a precious long time about it. I began to think you had cleared out with the money."

"That aint my style," said Dick, proudly.

"Then where's the change?"

"I haven't got it."

"Where's the bill then?"

"I haven't got that either."

"You young rascal!"

"Hold on a minute, mister," said Dick, "and I'll tell you all about it. The man what took the bill said it wasn't good, and kept it."

"The bill was perfectly good. So he kept it, did he? I'll go with you to the store, and see whether he won't give it back to me."

Dick led the way, and the gentleman followed him into the store. At the reappearance of Dick in such company, the clerk flushed a little, and looked nervous. He fancied that he could browbeat a ragged boot-black, but with a gentleman he saw that it would be a different matter. He did not seem to notice the newcomers, but began to replace some goods on the shelves.

"Now," said the young man, "point out the clerk that has my money."

"That's him," said Dick, pointing out the clerk.

The gentleman walked up to the counter.

"I will trouble you," he said a little haughtily, "for a bill which that boy offered you, and which you still hold in your possession."

"It was a bad bill," said the clerk, his cheek flushing, and his manner nervous.

"It was no such thing. I require you to produce it, and let the matter be decided."

The clerk fumbled in his vest-pocket, and drew out a bad-looking bill.

"This is a bad bill, but it is not the one I gave the boy."

"It is the one he gave me."

The young man looked doubtful.

"Boy," he said to Dick, "is this the bill you gave to be changed?"

"No, it isn't."

"You lie, you young rascal!" exclaimed the clerk, who began to find himself in a tight place, and could not see the way out.

This scene naturally attracted the attention of all in the store, and the proprietor walked up from the lower end, where he had been busy.

"What's all this, Mr. Hatch?" he demanded.

"That boy," said the clerk, "came in and asked change for a bad bill. I kept the bill, and told him to clear out. Now he wants it again to pass on somebody else."

"Show the bill."

The merchant looked at it. "Yes, that's a bad bill," he said. "There is no doubt about that."

"But it is not the one the boy offered," said Dick's patron. "It is one of the same denomination, but on a different bank."

"Do you remember what bank it was on?"

"It was on the Merchants' Bank of Boston."[1]

"Are you sure of it?"

"I am."

"Perhaps the boy kept it and offered the other."

"You may search me if you want to," said Dick, indignantly.

"He doesn't look as if he was likely to have any extra bills. I suspect that your clerk pocketed the good bill, and has substituted the counterfeit note. It is a nice little scheme of his for making money."

"I haven't seen any bill on the Merchants' Bank," said the clerk, doggedly.

"You had better feel in your pockets."

"This matter must be investigated," said the merchant, firmly. "If you have the bill, produce it."

"I haven't got it," said the clerk; but he looked guilty notwithstanding.

"I demand that he be searched," said Dick's patron.

"I tell you I haven't got it."

"Shall I send for a police officer, Mr. Hatch, or will you allow yourself to be searched quietly?" said the merchant.

Alarmed at the threat implied in these words, the clerk put his hand into his vest-pocket, and drew out a two-dollar bill on the Merchants' Bank.

"Is this your note?" asked the shopkeeper, showing it to the young man.

"It is."

"I must have made a mistake," faltered the clerk.

"I shall not give you a chance to make such another mistake in my employ," said the merchant sternly. "You may go up to the desk and ask for what wages are due you. I shall have no further occasion for your services."

"Now, youngster," said Dick's patron, as they went out of the store, after he had finally got the bill changed. "I must pay you something extra for your trouble. Here's fifty cents."

"Thank you, sir," said Dick. "You're very kind. Don't you want some more bills changed?"

"Not to-day," said he with a smile. "It's too expensive."

"I'm in luck," thought our hero complacently. "I guess I'll go to Barnum's to-night, and see the bearded lady, the eight-foot

---

1   The Merchants' Bank of Boston had been founded in 1831.

giant, the two-foot dwarf, and the other curiosities, too numerous to mention."[1]

Dick shouldered his box and walked up as far as the Astor House. He took his station on the sidewalk, and began to look about him.

Just behind him were two persons,—one, a gentleman of fifty; the other, a boy of thirteen or fourteen. They were speaking together, and Dick had no difficulty in hearing what was said.

"I am sorry, Frank, that I can't go about, and show you some of the sights of New York, but I shall be full of business to-day. It is your first visit to the city, too."

"Yes, sir."

"There's a good deal worth seeing here. But I'm afraid you'll have to wait to next time. You can go out and walk by yourself, but don't venture too far, or you will get lost."

Frank looked disappointed.

"I wish Tom Miles knew I was here," he said. "He would go around with me."

"Where does he live?"

"Somewhere up town, I believe."

"Then, unfortunately, he is not available. If you would rather go with me than stay here, you can, but as I shall be most of the time in merchants'-counting-rooms, I am afraid it would not be very interesting."

"I think," said Frank, after a little hesitation, "that I will go off by myself. I won't go very far, and if I lose my way, I will inquire for the Astor House."

"Yes, anybody will direct you here. Very well, Frank, I am sorry I can't do better for you."

"Oh, never mind, uncle, I shall be amused in walking around, and looking at the shop-windows. There will be a great deal to see."

Now Dick had listened to all this conversation. Being an enterprising young man, he thought he saw a chance for a speculation, and determined to avail himself of it.

---

1 Alger added perhaps the most awkward phrase in the novel ("and see the bearded lady, the eight-foot giant, the two-foot dwarf, and the other curiosities, too numerous to mention") in revision. Barnum's American Museum, at the corner of Broadway and Ann Street from 1841 to 1865 and at 539–41 Broadway from 1865 to 1868, featured a "bearded lady," probably Delina Rose or Rossa; the wax effigy of a giant named Daniel Lambert (1770–1809); the 25-inch tall General Tom Thumb, aka Charles Sherwood Stratton (1838–85); and a theater or "lecture room."

Accordingly he stepped up to the two just as Frank's uncle was about leaving, and said, "I know all about the city, sir; I'll show him around, if you want me to."

The gentleman looked a little curiously at the ragged figure before him.

"So you are a city boy, are you?"

"Yes, sir," said Dick, "I've lived here ever since I was a baby."

"And you know all about the public buildings, I suppose?"

"Yes, sir."

"And the Central Park?"[1]

"Yes, sir. I know my way all round."

The gentleman looked thoughtful.

"I don't know what to say, Frank," he remarked after a while. "It is rather a novel proposal. He isn't exactly the sort of guide I would have picked out for you. Still he looks honest. He has an open face, and I think can be depended upon."

"I wish he wasn't so ragged and dirty," said Frank, who felt a little shy about being seen with such a companion.

"I'm afraid you haven't washed your face this morning," said Mr. Whitney, for that was the gentleman's name.

"They didn't have no wash-bowls at the hotel where I stopped," said Dick.

"What hotel did you stop at?"

"The Box Hotel."

"The Box Hotel?"

"Yes, sir, I slept in a box on Spruce Street."

Frank surveyed Dick curiously.

"How did you like it?" he asked.

"I slept bully."

"Suppose it had rained."

"Then I'd have wet my best clothes," said Dick.

"Are these all the clothes you have?"

"Yes, sir."

Mr. Whitney spoke a few words to Frank, who seemed pleased with the suggestion.

"Follow me, my lad," he said.

Dick in some surprise obeyed orders, following Mr. Whitney and Frank into the hotel, past the office, to the foot of the stair-

---

1 Central Park was established on 778 acres of city land in 1857 and was developed according to the design of landscape architects Frederick Law Olmsted (1822–1903) and Calvert Vaux (1824–95). Construction of the Park lasted over a decade.

case. Here a servant of the hotel stopped Dick, but Mr. Whitney explained that he had something for him to do, and he was allowed to proceed.

They entered a long entry, and finally paused before a door. This being opened a pleasant chamber was disclosed.

"Come in, my lad," said Mr. Whitney.

Dick and Frank entered.

CHAPTER IV: DICK'S NEW SUIT

"Now," said Mr. Whitney to Dick, "my nephew here is on his way to a boarding-school. He has a suit of clothes in his trunk about half worn. He is willing to give them to you. I think they will look better than those you have on."

Dick was so astonished that he hardly knew what to say. Presents were something that he knew very little about, never having received any to his knowledge. That so large a gift should be made to him by a stranger seemed very wonderful.

The clothes were brought out, and turned out to be a neat gray suit.

"Before you put them on, my lad, you must wash yourself. Clean clothes and a dirty skin don't go very well together. Frank, you may attend to him. I am obliged to go at once. Have you got as much money as you require?"

"Yes, uncle."

"One more word, my lad," said Mr. Whitney, addressing Dick; "I may be rash in trusting a boy of whom I know nothing, but I like your looks, and I think you will prove a proper guide for my nephew."

"Yes, I will, sir," said Dick, earnestly. "Honor bright!"

"Very well. A pleasant time to you."

The process of cleansing commenced. To tell the truth Dick needed it, and the sensation of cleanliness he found both new and pleasant. Frank added to his gift a shirt, stockings, and an old pair of shoes. "I am sorry I haven't any cap," said he.

"I've got one," said Dick.

"It isn't so new as it might be," said Frank, surveying an old felt hat, which had once been black, but was now dingy, with a large hole in the top and a portion of the rim torn off.

"No," said Dick; "my grandfather used to wear it when he was a boy, and I've kep' it ever since out of respect for his memory. But I'll get a new one now. I can buy one cheap on Chatham Street."

"Is that near here?"

"Only five minutes' walk."

"Then we can get one on the way."

When Dick was dressed in his new attire, with his face and hands clean, and his hair brushed, it was difficult to imagine that he was the same boy.

He now looked quite handsome, and might readily have been taken for a young gentleman, except that his hands were red and grimy.

"Look at yourself," said Frank, leading him before the mirror.

"By gracious!" said Dick, starting back in astonishment, "that isn't me, is it?"

"Don't you know yourself?" asked Frank, smiling.

"It reminds me of Cinderella,"[1] said Dick, "when she was changed into a fairy princess. I see [*sic*] it one night at Barnum's. What'll Johnny Nolan say when he sees me? He won't dare to speak to such a young swell as I be now. Aint it rich?" and Dick burst into a loud laugh. His fancy was tickled by the anticipation of his friend's surprise. Then the thought of the valuable gifts he had received occurred to him, and he looked gratefully at Frank.

"You're a brick," he said.

"A what?"

"A brick! You're a jolly good fellow to give me such a present."

"You're quite welcome, Dick," said Frank, kindly. "I'm better off than you are, and I can spare the clothes just as well as not. You must have a new hat though. But that we can get when we go out. The old clothes you can make into a bundle."

"Wait a minute till I get my handkerchief," and Dick pulled from the pocket of the pants a dirty rag, which might have been white once, though it did not look like it, and had apparently once formed a part of a sheet or shirt.

"You mustn't carry that," said Frank.

"But I've got a cold," said Dick.

"Oh, I don't mean you to go without a handkerchief. I'll give you one."

Frank opened his trunk and pulled out two, which he gave to Dick.

"I wonder if I aint dreamin'," said Dick, once more surveying himself doubtfully in the glass. "I'm afraid I'm dreamin', and shall wake up in a barrel, as I did night afore last."

---

1   The folk tale about Cinderella was popularized by Jacob (1785–1863) and Wilhelm (1786–1859) Grimm in the early nineteenth century.

"Shall I pinch you so you can wake here?" asked Frank, playfully.

"Yes," said Dick, seriously, "I wish you would."

He pulled up the sleeve of his jacket, and Frank pinched him pretty hard, so that Dick winced.

"Yes, I guess I'm awake," said Dick; "you've got a pair of nippers, you have. But what shall I do with my brush and blacking?" he asked.

"You can leave them here till we come back," said Frank. "They will be safe."

"Hold on a minute," said Dick, surveying Frank's boots with a professional eye, "you aint got a good shine on them boots. I'll make 'em shine so you can see your face in 'em."

And he was as good as his word.

"Thank you," said Frank; "now you had better brush your own shoes."

This had not occurred to Dick, for in general the professional boot-black considers his blacking too valuable to expend on his own shoes or boots, if he is fortunate enough to possess a pair.

The two boys now went downstairs together. They met the same servant who had spoken to Dick a few minutes before, but there was no recognition.

"He don't know me," said Dick. "He thinks I'm a young swell like you."

"What's a swell?"

"Oh, a feller that wears nobby clothes like you."

"And you, too, Dick."

"Yes," said Dick, "who'd ever have thought as I should have turned into a swell?"

They had now got out on Broadway, and were slowly walking along the west side by the Park, when who should Dick see in front of him, but Johnny Nolan?

Instantly Dick was seized with a fancy for witnessing Johnny's amazement at his change in appearance. He stole up behind him, and struck him on the back.

"Hallo, Johnny, how many shines have you had?"

Johnny turned round expecting to see Dick, whose voice he recognized, but his astonished eyes rested on a nicely dressed boy (the hat alone excepted) who looked indeed like Dick, but so transformed in dress that it was difficult to be sure of his identity.

"What luck, Johnny?" repeated Dick.

Johnny surveyed him from head to foot in great bewilderment.

"Who be you?" he said.

"Well, that's a good one," laughed Dick; "so you don't know Dick?"

"Where'd you get all them clothes?" asked Johnny. "Have you been stealin'?"

"Say that again, and I'll lick you. No, I've lent my clothes to a young feller as was goin' to a party, and didn't have none fit to wear, and so I put on my second-best for a change."

Without deigning any further explanation, Dick went off, followed by the astonished gaze of Johnny Nolan, who could not quite make up his mind whether the neat-looking boy he had been talking with was really Ragged Dick or not.

In order to reach Chatham Street it was necessary to cross Broadway. This was easier proposed than done. There is always such a throng of omnibuses, drays, carriages, and vehicles of all kinds in the neighborhood of the Astor House, that the crossing is formidable to one who is not used to it. Dick made nothing of it, dodging in and out among the horses and wagons with perfect self-possession. Reaching the opposite sidewalk, he looked back, and found that Frank had retreated in dismay, and that the width of the street was between them.

"Come across!" called out Dick.

"I don't see any chance," said Frank, looking anxiously at the prospect before him. "I'm afraid of being run over."

"If you are, you can sue 'em for damages," said Dick.

Finally Frank got safely over after several narrow escapes, as he considered them.

"Is it always so crowded?" he asked.

"A good deal worse sometimes," said Dick. "I knowed a young man once who waited six hours for a chance to cross, and at last got run over by an omnibus, leaving a widder and a large family of orphan children. His widder, a beautiful young woman, was obliged to start a peanut and apple stand. There she is now."

"Where?"

Dick pointed to a hideous old woman, of large proportions, wearing a bonnet of immense size, who presided over an apple-stand close by.

Frank laughed.

"If that is the case," he said, "I think I will patronize her."

"Leave it to me," said Dick, winking.

He advanced gravely to the apple-stand, and said, "Old lady, have you paid your taxes?"

The astonished woman opened her eyes.

"I'm a gov'ment officer," said Dick, "sent by the mayor to

collect your taxes. I'll take it in apples just to oblige. That big red one will about pay what you're owin' to the gov'ment."

"I don't know nothing about no taxes," said the old woman, in bewilderment.

"Then," said Dick, "I'll let you off this time. Give us two of your best apples, and my friend here, the President of the Common Council, will pay you."

Frank smiling, paid three cents apiece for the apples, and they sauntered on, Dick remarking, "If these apples aint good, old lady, we'll return 'em, and get our money back." This would have been rather difficult in his case, as the apple was already half consumed.

Chatham Street, where they wished to go, being on the East side, the two boys crossed the Park. This is an enclosure of about ten acres, which years ago was covered with a green sward, but is now a great thoroughfare for pedestrians and contains several important public buildings. Dick pointed out the City Hall, the Hall of Records, and the Rotunda.[1] The former is a white building of large size, and surmounted by a cupola.

"That's where the mayor's office is," said Dick. "Him and me are very good friends. I once blacked his boots by partic'lar appointment. That's the way I pay my city taxes."

CHAPTER V: CHATHAM STREET AND BROADWAY

They were soon in Chatham Street, walking between rows of ready-made clothing shops, many of which had half their stock in trade exposed on the sidewalk. The proprietors of these establishments stood at the doors, watching attentively the passersby, extending urgent invitations to any who even glanced at the goods to enter.

"Walk in, young gentlemen," said a stout man, at the entrance of one shop.

"No, I thank you," replied Dick, "as the fly said to the spider."

"We're selling off at less than cost."

"Of course you be. That's where you makes your money," said Dick. "There aint nobody of any enterprise that pretends to make any profit on his goods."

---

1   The Hall of Records, formerly the debtors' prison Old Gaol, and the Rotunda, home of the first civic art museum, were both located in City Hall Park.

The Chatham Street trader looked after our hero as if he didn't quite comprehend him; but Dick, without waiting for a reply, passed on with his companion.

In some of the shops auctions seemed to be going on.

"I am only offered two dollars, gentlemen, for this elegant pair of doeskin pants, made of the very best of cloth. It's a frightful sacrifice. Who'll give an eighth? Thank you, sir. Only seventeen shillings! Why the cloth cost more by the yard!"

This speaker was standing on a little platform haranguing to three men, holding in his hand meanwhile a pair of pants very loose in the legs, and presenting a cheap Bowery look.

Frank and Dick paused before the shop door, and finally saw them knocked down to rather a verdant-looking individual at three dollars.

"Clothes seem to be pretty cheap here," said Frank.

"Yes, but Baxter Street is the cheapest place."

"Is it?"

"Yes. Johnny Nolan got a whole rig-out there last week, for a dollar,—coat, cap, vest, pants, and shoes. They was very good measure, too, like my best clothes that I took off to oblige you."

"I shall know where to come for clothes next time," said Frank, laughing. "I had no idea the city was so much cheaper than the country. I suppose the Baxter Street tailors are fashionable?"

"In course they are. Me and Horace Greeley[1] always go there for clothes. When Horace gets a new suit, I always have one made just like it; but I can't go the white hat. It aint becomin' to my style of beauty."

A little farther on a man was standing out on the sidewalk, distributing small printed handbills. One was handed to Frank, which he read as follows,—

"GRAND CLOSING-OUT SALE!—A variety of Beautiful and Costly Articles for Sale, at a Dollar apiece. Unparalleled Inducements! Walk in, Gentlemen!"

"Whereabouts is this sale?" asked Frank.

"In here, young gentlemen," said a black-whiskered individual, who appeared suddenly on the scene. "Walk in."

"Shall we go in, Dick?"

"It's a swindlin' shop," said Dick, in a low voice. "I've been

---

1   Horace Greeley (1811–72) founded the *New York Tribune*, the most prestigious newspaper in America, in 1841.

there. That man's a reg'lar cheat. He's seen me before, but he don't know me coz of my clothes."

"Step in and see the articles," said the man, persuasively. "You needn't buy, you know."

"Are all the articles worth more'n a dollar?" asked Dick.

"Yes," said the other, "and some worth a great deal more."

"Such as what?"

"Well, there's a silver pitcher worth twenty dollars."

"And you sell it for a dollar. That's very kind of you," said Dick, innocently.

"Walk in, and you'll understand it."

"No, I guess not," said Dick. "My servants is so dishonest that I wouldn't like to trust 'em with a silver pitcher. Come along, Frank. I hope you'll succeed in your charitable enterprise of supplyin' the public with silver pitchers at nineteen dollars less than they are worth."

"How does he manage, Dick?" asked Frank, as they went on.

"All his articles are numbered, and he makes you pay a dollar, and then shakes some dice, and whatever the figgers come to, is the number of the article you draw. Most of 'em aint worth sixpence."

A hat and cap store being close at hand, Dick and Frank went in. For seventy-five cents, which Frank insisted on paying, Dick succeeded in getting quite a neat-looking cap, which corresponded much better with his appearance than the one he had on. The last, not being considered worth keeping, Dick dropped on the sidewalk, from which, on looking back, he saw it picked up by a brother boot-black who appeared to consider it better than his own.

They retraced their steps and went up Chambers Street to Broadway. At the corner of Broadway and Chambers Street is a large white marble warehouse, which attracted Frank's attention.

"What building is that?" he asked, with interest.

"That belongs to my friend A. T. Stewart," said Dick. "It's the biggest store on Broadway.[1] If I ever retire from boot-blackin', and go into mercantile pursuits, I may buy him out, or build another store that'll take the shine off this one."

"Were you ever in the store?" asked Frank.

---

1 [Alger's note:] Mr. Stewart's Tenth Street store was not open at the time. [In 1848, Alexander T. Stewart (1803–76) opened the first department store in New York on Broadway between Chambers and Reade Streets.]

"No," said Dick; "but I'm intimate with one of Stewart's partners. He is a cash boy, and does nothing but take money all day."

"A very agreeable employment," said Frank, laughing.

"Yes," said Dick, "I'd like to be in it."

The boys crossed to the West side of Broadway, and walked slowly up the street. To Frank it was a very interesting spectacle. Accustomed to the quiet of the country, there was something fascinating in the crowds of people thronging the sidewalks, and the great variety of vehicles constantly passing and repassing in the street. Then again the shop-windows with their multifarious contents interested and amused him, and he was constantly checking Dick to look in at some well-stocked window.

"I don't see how so many shopkeepers can find people enough to buy of them," he said. "We haven't got but two stores in our village, and Broadway seems to be full of them."

"Yes," said Dick; "and its [sic] pretty much the same in the avenoos, 'specially the Third, Sixth, and Eighth avenoos. The Bowery, too, is a great place for shoppin'. There everybody sells cheaper'n anybody else, and nobody pretends to make no profit on their goods."

"Where's Barnum's Museum?" asked Frank.

"Oh, that's down nearly opposite the Astor House," said Dick. "Didn't you see a great building with lots of flags?"

"Yes."

"Well, that's Barnum's.[1] That's where the Happy Family live,[2] and the lions, and bears, and curiosities generally. It's a tip-top place. Haven't you ever been there? It's most as good as the Old Bowery, only the plays isn't quite so excitin'."

"I'll go if I get time," said Frank. "There is a boy at home who came to New York a month ago, and went to Barnum's, and has been talking about it ever since, so I suppose it must be worth seeing."

"They've got a great play at the Old Bowery now," pursued Dick. "'Tis called the 'Demon of the Danube.'[3] The Demon falls

---

1 [Alger's note:] Since destroyed by fire, and rebuilt farther up Broadway, and again burned down in February.

2 The Happy Family Display at Barnum's featured natural predators and their prey co-existing in the same cage.

3 A fictional title, though Alger alluded to it again in both his novel *The Young Outlaw* (1875) and his short story "Gustavus Higgins; or, The Ill-Starred Genius" (1879).

in love with a young woman, and drags her by the hair up to the top of a steep rock where his castle stands."

"That's a queer way of showing his love," said Frank, laughing.

"She didn't want to go with him, you know, but was in love with another chap. When he heard about his girl bein' carried off, he felt awful, and swore an oath not to rest till he had got her free. Well, at last he got into the castle by some underground passage, and he and the Demon had a fight. Oh, it was bully seein' 'em roll round on the stage, cuttin' and slashin' at each other."

"And which got the best of it?"

"At first the Demon seemed to be ahead, but at last the young Baron got him down, and struck a dagger into his heart, sayin', 'Die, false and perjured villain! The dogs shall feast upon thy carcass!' and then the Demon give an awful howl and died. Then the Baron seized his body, and threw it over the precipice."

"It seems to me the actor who plays the Demon ought to get extra pay, if he has to be treated that way."

"That's so," said Dick; "but I guess he's used to it. It seems to agree with his constitution."

"What building is that?" asked Frank, pointing to a structure several rods back from the street, with a large yard in front. It was an unusual sight for Broadway, all the other buildings in that neighborhood being even with the street.

"That is the New York Hospital,"[1] said Dick. "They're a rich institution, and take care of sick people on very reasonable terms."

"Did you ever go in there?"

"Yes," said Dick; "there was a friend of mine, Johnny Mullen, he was a newsboy, got run over by a omnibus as he was crossin' Broadway down near Park Place.[2] He was carried to the Hospital, and me and some of his friends paid his board while he was there. It was only three dollars a week, which was very cheap, considerin' all the care they took of him. I got leave to come and see him while he was here. Everything looked so nice and comfortable, that I thought a little of coaxin' a omnibus driver to run over me, so I might go there too."

---

1   Founded in 1771, New York Hospital was located on Broadway between Anthony (or Duane) and Catherine (or Worth) Streets, a few blocks from City Hall.

2   Park Place runs from Broadway and Greenwich Street in lower Manhattan.

"Did your friend have to have his leg cut off?" asked Frank, interested.

"No," said Dick; "though there was a young student there that was very anxious to have it cut off; but it wasn't done, and Johnny is around the streets as well as ever."

While this conversation was going on they reached No. 365, at the corner of Franklin Street.[1]

"That's Taylor's Saloon,"[2] said Dick. "When I come into a fortun' I shall take my meals there reg'lar."

"I have heard of it very often," said Frank. "It is said to be very elegant. Suppose we go in and take an ice-cream. It will give us a chance to see it to better advantage."

"Thank you," said Dick; "I think that's the most agreeable way of seein' the place myself."

The boys entered, and found themselves in a spacious and elegant saloon, resplendent with gilding, and adorned on all sides by costly mirrors. They sat down to a small table with a marble top, and Frank gave the order.

"It reminds me of Aladdin's palace,"[3] said Frank, looking about him.

"Does it?" said Dick; "he must have had plenty of money."

"He had an old lamp, which he had only to rub, when the Slave of the Lamp would appear, and do whatever he wanted."

"That must have been a valooable lamp. I'd be willin' to give all my Erie shares for it."

There was a tall, gaunt individual at the next table, who apparently heard this last remark of Dick's. Turning towards our hero, he said, "May I inquire, young man, whether you are largely interested in this Erie Railroad?"

"I haven't got no property except what's invested in Erie," said Dick, with a comical side-glance at Frank.

"Indeed! I suppose the investment was made by your guardian."

"No," said Dick; "I manage my property myself."

---

1 [Alger's note:] Now the office of the Merchants' Union Express Company.

2 Established in 1851 by John Taylor at the corner of Broadway and Franklin Street, Taylor's Saloon was one of the most luxurious restaurants in New York at mid-century.

3 Alger alludes to "Aladdin's Lamp," one of the folk tales that originally appeared in the French translation of the *Arabian Nights' Entertainments* in the early eighteenth century.

"And I presume your dividends have not been large?"

"Why, no," said Dick; "you're about right there. They haven't."

"As I supposed. It's poor stock. Now, my young friend, I can recommend a much better investment, which will yield you a large annual income. I am agent of the Excelsior Copper Mining Company, which possesses one of the most productive mines in the world. It's sure to yield fifty per cent. on the investment. Now, all you have to do is to sell out your Erie shares, and invest in our stock, and I'll insure you a fortune in three years. How many shares did you say you had?"

"I didn't say, that I remember," said Dick. "Your offer is very kind and obligin', and as soon as I get time I'll see about it."

"I hope you will," said the stranger. "Permit me to give you my card. 'Samuel Snap, No. — Wall Street.' I shall be most happy to receive a call from you, and exhibit the maps of our mine. I should be glad to have you mention the matter also to your friends. I am confident you could do no greater service than to induce them to embark in our enterprise."

"Very good," said Dick.

Here the stranger left the table, and walked up to the desk to settle his bill.

"You see what it is to be a man of fortun', Frank," said Dick, "and wear good clothes. I wonder what that chap'll say when he sees me blackin' boots to-morrow in the street?"

"Perhaps you earn your money more honorably than he does, after all," said Frank. "Some of these mining companies are nothing but swindles, got up to cheat people out of their money."

"He's welcome to all he gets out of me," said Dick.

CHAPTER VI: UP BROADWAY TO MADISON SQUARE

As the boys pursued their way up Broadway, Dick pointed out the prominent hotels and places of amusement. Frank was particularly struck with the imposing fronts of the St. Nicholas and Metropolitan Hotels,[1] the former of white marble, the latter of a subdued brown hue, but not less elegant in its internal appointments. He was not surprised to be informed that each of these splendid structures cost with the furnishing not far from a million dollars.

---

1 The St. Nicholas Hotel opened in 1853 and was located on Broadway between Broome and Spring Streets. The Metropolitan Hotel opened in 1852 on the northeast corner of Broadway and Prince Street.

At Eighth Street Dick turned to the right, and pointed out the Clinton Hall Building now occupied by the Mercantile Library, comprising at that time over fifty thousand volumes.[1]

A little farther on they came to a large building standing by itself just at the opening of Third and Fourth Avenues, and with one side on each.

"What is that building?" asked Frank.

"That's the Cooper Institute," said Dick; "built by Mr. Cooper, a particular friend of mine. Me and Peter Cooper used to go to school together."

"What is there inside?" asked Frank.

"There's a hall for public meetin's and lectures in the basement, and a readin' room and a picture gallery up above," said Dick.

Directly opposite Cooper Institute, Frank saw a very large building of brick, covering about an acre of ground.

"Is that a hotel?" he asked.

"No," said Dick; "that's the Bible House.[2] It's the place where they make Bibles. I was in there once,—saw a big pile of 'em."

"Did you ever read the Bible?" asked Frank, who had some idea of the neglected state of Dick's education.

"No," said Dick; "I've heard it's a good book, but I never read one. I aint much on readin'. It makes my head ache."

"I suppose you can't read very fast."

"I can read the little words pretty well, but the big ones is what stick me."

"If I lived in the city, you might come every evening to me, and I would teach you."

"Would you take so much trouble about me?" asked Dick, earnestly.

"Certainly; I should like to see you getting on. There isn't much chance of that if you don't know how to read and write."

"You're a good feller," said Dick, gratefully. "I wish you did live in New York. I'd like to know somethin'. Whereabouts do you live?"

"About fifty miles off, in a town on the left bank of the Hudson.

---

1 [Alger's note:] Now not far from one hundred thousand. [The Mercantile Library of New York was located in Clinton Hall at 21 Astor Place from 1855 until 1932.]

2 The headquarters of the American Bible Society, the Bible House, on Astor Place at Third and Fourth Avenues and Ninth Street in New York, was built in 1852.

I wish you'd come up and see me sometime. I would like to have you come and stop two or three days."

"Honor bright?"

"I don't understand."

"Do you mean it?" asked Dick, incredulously.

"Of course I do. Why shouldn't I?"

"What would your folks say if they knowed you asked a boot-black to visit you?"

"You are none the worse for being a boot-black, Dick."

"I aint used to genteel society," said Dick. "I shouldn't know how to behave."

"Then I could show you. You won't be a boot-black all your life, you know."

"No," said Dick; "I'm goin' to knock off when I get to be ninety."

"Before that, I hope," said Frank, smiling.

"I really wish I could get somethin' else to do," said Dick, soberly. "I'd like to be a office boy, and learn business, and grow up 'spectable."

"Why don't you try, and see if you can't get a place, Dick?"

"Who'd take Ragged Dick?"

"But you aint ragged now, Dick."

"No," said Dick; "I look a little better than I did in my Washington coat and Louis Napoleon pants. But if I got in a office, they wouldn't give me more'n three dollars a week, and I couldn't live 'spectable on that."

"No, I suppose not," said Frank, thoughtfully. "But you would get more at the end of the first year."

"Yes," said Dick; "but by that time I'd be nothin' but skin and bones."

Frank laughed. "That reminds me," he said, "of the story of an Irishman, who, out of economy, thought he would teach his horse to feed on shavings. So he provided the horse with a pair of green spectacles which made the shavings look eatable. But unfortunately, just as the horse got learned, he up and died."

"The hoss must have been a fine specimen of architectur' by the time he got through," remarked Dick.

"Whereabouts are we now?" asked Frank, as they emerged from Fourth Avenue into Union Square.[1]

"That is Union Park," said Dick, pointing to a beautiful en-

---

1 Union Square Park is located between East 14th and East 17th Streets and Union Square East and West in New York.

closure, in the centre of which was a pond, with a fountain playing.

"Is that the statue of General Washington?"[1] asked Frank, pointing to a bronze equestrian statue, on a granite pedestal.

"Yes," said Dick; "he's growed some since he was President. If he'd been as tall as that when he fit in the Revolution, he'd have walloped the Britishers some, I reckon." Frank looked up at the statue, which is fourteen and a half feet high, and acknowledged the justice of Dick's remark.

"How about the coat, Dick?" he asked. "Would it fit you?"

"Well, it might be rather loose," said Dick, "I aint much more'n ten feet high with my boots off."

"No, I should think not," said Frank, smiling. "You're a queer boy, Dick."

"Well, I've been brought up queer. Some boys is born with a silver spoon in their mouth. Victoria's boys[2] is born with a gold spoon, set with di'monds; but gold and silver was scarce when I was born, and mine was pewter."

"Perhaps the gold and silver will come by and by, Dick. Did you ever hear of Dick Whittington?"[3]

"Never did. Was he a Ragged Dick?"

"I shouldn't wonder if he was. At any rate he was very poor when he was a boy, but he didn't stay so. Before he died, he became Lord Mayor of London."

"Did he?" asked Dick, looking interested. "How did he do it?"

"Why, you see, a rich merchant took pity on him, and gave him a home in his own house, where he used to stay with the servants, being employed in little errands. One day the merchant noticed Dick picking up pins and needles that had been dropped, and asked him why he did it. Dick told him he was going to sell them when he got enough. The merchant was pleased with his saving disposition, and when soon after, he was going to send a vessel to foreign parts, he told Dick he might send anything he

---

1 The oldest sculpture in the New York City Parks collection, this equestrian statue was executed by Henry Kirke Brown (1814–86) and dedicated in 1865.

2 Queen Victoria's four sons were Albert Edward (the future Edward VII, 1841–1910), Alfred Ernest Albert (1844–1900), Arthur William Patrick (1850–1942), and Leopold George Duncan (1853–84).

3 While Dick Whittington (c. 1354–1423) was indeed a long-time Lord Mayor of London, the folklore surrounding his acquisition of a fortune is entirely mythological.

pleased in it, and it should be sold to his advantage. Now Dick had nothing in the world but a kitten which had been given him a short time before."

"How much taxes did he have to pay on it?" asked Dick.

"Not very high, probably. But having only the kitten, he concluded to send it along. After sailing a good many months, during which the kitten grew up to be a strong cat, the ship touched at an island never before known, which happened to be infested with rats and mice to such an extent that they worried everybody's life out, and even ransacked the king's palace. To make a long story short, the captain, seeing how matters stood, brought Dick's cat ashore, and she soon made the rats and mice scatter. The king was highly delighted when he saw what havoc she made among the rats and mice, and resolved to have her at any price. So he offered a great quantity of gold for her, which, of course, the captain was glad to accept. It was faithfully carried back to Dick, and laid the foundation of his fortune. He prospered as he grew up, and in time became a very rich merchant, respected by all, and before he died was elected Lord Mayor of London."

"That's a pretty good story," said Dick; "but I don't believe all the cats in New York will ever make me mayor."

"No, probably not, but you may rise in some other way. A good many distinguished men have once been poor boys. There's hope for you, Dick, if you'll try."

"Nobody ever talked to me so before," said Dick. "They just called me Ragged Dick, and told me I'd grow up to be a vagabone (boys who are better educated need not be surprised at Dick's blunders) and come to the gallows."

"Telling you so won't make it turn out so, Dick. If you'll try to be somebody, and grow up into a respectable member of society, you will. You may not become rich,—it isn't everybody that becomes rich, you know—but you can obtain a good position, and be respected."

"I'll try," said Dick, earnestly. "I needn't have been Ragged Dick so long if I hadn't spent my money in goin' to the theatre, and treatin' boys to oyster-stews, and bettin' money on cards, and such like."

"Have you lost money that way?"

"Lots of it. One time I saved up five dollars to buy me a new rig-out, cos my best suit was all in rags, when Limpy Jim wanted me to play a game with him."

"Limpy Jim?" said Frank, interrogatively.

"Yes, he's lame; that's what makes us call him Limpy Jim."

"I suppose you lost?"

"Yes, I lost every penny, and had to sleep out, cos I hadn't a cent to pay for lodgin'. 'Twas a awful cold night, and I got most froze."

"Wouldn't Jim let you have any of the money he had won to pay for a lodging?"

"No; I axed him for five cents, but he wouldn't let me have it."

"Can you get lodging for five cents?" asked Frank, in surprise.

"Yes," said Dick, "but not at the Fifth Avenue Hotel.[1] That's it right out there."

CHAPTER VII: THE POCKET-BOOK

They had reached the junction of Broadway and of Fifth Avenue. Before them was a beautiful park of ten acres. On the left-hand side was a large marble building, presenting a fine appearance with its extensive white front. This was the building at which Dick pointed.

"Is that the Fifth Avenue Hotel?" asked Frank. "I've heard of it often. My Uncle William always stops there when he comes to New York."

"I once slept on the outside of it," said Dick. "They was very reasonable in their charges, and told me I might come again."

"Perhaps sometime you'll be able to sleep inside," said Frank.

"I guess that'll be when Queen Victoria goes to the Five Points[2] to live."

"It looks like a palace," said Frank. "The queen needn't be ashamed to live in such a beautiful building as that."

Though Frank did not know it, one of the queen's palaces is far from being as fine a looking building as the Fifth Avenue Hotel. St. James' Palace[3] is a very ugly-looking brick structure, and appears much more like a factory than like the home of royalty. There are few hotels in the world as fine-looking as this democratic institution.

---

1 The tony Fifth Avenue Hotel was located at 200 Fifth Avenue near Madison Square in New York.

2 Five Points was a crime-ridden slum in lower Manhattan, south of Canal Street and adjacent to the Bowery.

3 Alger had visited St. James's Palace while in London during his *Wanderjahr* in 1860.

At that moment a gentleman passed them on the sidewalk, who looked back at Dick, as if his face seemed familiar.

"I know that man," said Dick, after he had passed. "He's one of my customers."

"What is his name?"

"I don't know."

"He looked back as if he thought he knew you."

"He would have knowed me at once if it hadn't been for my new clothes," said Dick. "I don't look much like Ragged Dick now."

"I suppose your face looked familiar."

"All but the dirt," said Dick, laughing. "I don't always have the chance of washing my face and hands in the Astor House."

"You told me," said Frank, "that there was a place where you could get lodging for five cents. Where's that?"

"It's the News-boys' Lodgin' House, on Fulton Street," said Dick, "up over the 'Sun' office. It's a good place. I don't know what us boys would do without it. They give you supper for six cents, and a bed for five cents more."

"I suppose some boys don't even have the five cents to pay,—do they?"

"They'll trust the boys," said Dick. "But I don't like to get trusted. I'd be ashamed to get trusted for five cents, or ten either. One night I was comin' down Chatham Street, with fifty cents in my pocket. I was goin' to get a good oyster-stew, and then go to the lodgin' house; but somehow it slipped through a hole in my trowse[r]s-pocket, and I hadn't a cent left. If it had been summer I shouldn't have cared, but it's rather tough stayin' out winter nights."

Frank, who had always possessed a good home of his own, found it hard to realize that the boy who was walking at his side had actually walked the streets in the cold without a home, or money to procure the common comfort of a bed.

"What did you do?" he asked, his voice full of sympathy.

"I went to the 'Times' office.[1] I knowed one of the pressmen, and he let me set down in a corner, where I was warm, and I soon got fast asleep."

"Why don't you get a room somewhere, and so always have a home to go to?"

---

1 At the time, the *New York Times* editorial offices occupied a five-story building at 41 Park Row.

"I dunno," said Dick. "I never thought of it. P'rhaps I may hire a furnished house on Madison Square."[1]

"That's where Flora McFlimsey lived."

"I don't know her," said Dick, who had never read the popular poem of which she is the heroine.[2]

While this conversation was going on, they had turned into Twenty-fifth Street, and had by this time reached Third Avenue.

Just before entering it, their attention was drawn to the rather singular conduct of an individual in front of them. Stopping suddenly, he appeared to pick up something from the sidewalk, and then looked about him in rather a confused way.

"I know his game," whispered Dick. "Come along and you'll see what it is."

He hurried Frank forward until they overtook the man, who had come to a stand-still.

"Have you found anything?" asked Dick.

"Yes," said the man, "I've found this."

He exhibited a wallet which seemed stuffed with bills, to judge from its plethoric appearance.

"Whew!" exclaimed Dick; "you're in luck."

"I suppose somebody has lost it," said the man, "and will offer a handsome reward."

"Which you'll get."

"Unfortunately I am obliged to take the next train to Boston. That's where I live. I haven't time to hunt up the owner."

"Then I suppose you'll take the pocket-book with you," said Dick, with assumed simplicity.

"I should like to leave it with some honest fellow who would see it returned to the owner," said the man, glancing at the boys.

"I'm honest," said Dick.

"I've no doubt of it," said the other. "Well, young man, I'll make you an offer. You take the pocket-book—"

"All right. Hand it over, then."

"Wait a minute. There must be a large sum inside. I shouldn't wonder if there might be a thousand dollars. The owner will probably give you a hundred dollars reward."

---

1 Named for President James Madison (1751–1836), Madison Square is located between 23rd and 26th Streets and Broadway and Madison Avenue.

2 Flora McFlimsey was the heroine of the ballad "Nothing to Wear" (1857) by William Allen Butler (1825–1902). Alger parodied the poem in "Nothing to Do: A Tilt at Our Best Society" (1857).

Figure 5. The Confidence Game, *Ragged Dick* (1868), opposite p. 76. Editor's collection.

"Why don't you stay and get it?" asked Frank.

"I would, only there is sickness in my family, and I must get home as soon as possible. Just give me twenty dollars, and I'll hand you the pocket-book, and let you make whatever you can out of it. Come, that's a good offer. What do you say?"

Dick was well dressed, so that the other did not regard it as at all improbable that he might possess that sum. He was prepared, however, to let him have it for less, if necessary.

"Twenty dollars is a good deal of money," said Dick, appearing to hesitate.

"You'll get it back, and a good deal more," said the stranger, persuasively.

"I don't know but I shall. What would you do, Frank?"

"I don't know but I would," said Frank, "if you've got the money." He was not a little surprised to think that Dick had so much by him.

"I don't know but I will," said Dick, after some irresolution. "I guess I won't lose much."

"You can't lose anything," said the stranger briskly. "Only be quick, for I must be on my way to the cars. I am afraid I shall miss them now."

Dick pulled out a bill from his pocket, and handed it to the stranger, receiving the pocket-book in return. At that moment a policeman turned the corner, and the stranger, hurriedly thrusting the bill into his pocket, without looking at it, made off with rapid steps.

"What is there in the pocket-book, Dick?" asked Frank in some excitement. "I hope there's enough to pay you for the money you gave him."

Dick laughed.

"I'll risk that," said he.

"But you gave him twenty dollars. That's a good deal of money."

"If I had given him as much as that, I should deserve to be cheated out of it."

"But you did,—didn't you?"

"He thought so."

"What was it, then?"

"It was nothing but a dry-goods circular got up to imitate a bank-bill."

Frank looked sober.

"You ought not to have cheated him, Dick," he said, reproachfully.

"Didn't he want to cheat me?"

"I don't know."

"What do you s'pose there is in that pocket-book?" asked Dick, holding it up.

Frank surveyed its ample proportions, and answered sincerely enough, "Money, and a good deal of it."

"There aint stamps enough in it to buy a oyster-stew," said Dick. "If you don't believe it, just look while I open it."

So saying he opened the pocket-book, and showed Frank that it was stuffed out with pieces of blank paper, carefully folded up in the shape of bills. Frank, who was unused to city life, and had never heard anything of the "drop-game," looked amazed at this unexpected development.

"I knowed how it was all the time," said Dick. "I guess I got the best of him there. This wallet's worth somethin'. I shall use it to keep my stiffkit's of Erie stock in, and all my other papers what aint of no use to anybody but the owner."

"That's the kind of papers it's got in it now," said Frank, smiling.

"That's so!" said Dick.

"By hokey!" he exclaimed suddenly, "if there aint the old chap comin' back ag'in. He looks as if he'd heard bad news from his sick family."

By this time the pocket-book dropper had come up.

Approaching the boys, he said in an undertone to Dick, "Give me back that pocket-book, you young rascal!"

"Beg your pardon, mister," said Dick, "but was you addressin' me?"

"Yes, I was."

"'Cause you called me by the wrong name. I've knowed some rascals, but I aint the honor to belong to the family."

He looked significantly at the other as he spoke, which didn't improve the man's temper. Accustomed to swindle others, he did not fancy being practised upon in return.

"Give me back that pocket-book," he repeated in a threatening voice.

"Couldn't do it," said Dick, coolly. "I'm go'n' to restore it to the owner. The contents is so valooable that most likely the loss has made him sick, and he'll be likely to come down liberal to the honest finder."

"You gave me a bogus bill," said the man.

"It's what I use myself," said Dick.

"You've swindled me."

"I thought it was the other way."

"None of your nonsense," said the man angrily. "If you don't give up that pocket-book, I'll call a policeman."

"I wish you would," said Dick. "They'll know most likely whether it's Stewart or Astor[1] that's lost the pocket-book, and I can get 'em to return it."

The "dropper," whose object it was to recover the pocket-book, in order to try the same game on a more satisfactory customer, was irritated by Dick's refusal, and above all by the coolness he displayed. He resolved to make one more attempt.

"Do you want to pass the night in the Tombs?" he asked.

"Thank you for your very obligin' proposal," said Dick; "but it aint convenient to-day. Any other time, when you'd like to have me come and stop with you, I'm agreeable; but my two youngest children is down with the measles, and I expect I'll have to set up all night to take care of 'em. Is the Tombs, in gineral, a pleasant place of residence?"

Dick asked this question with an air of so much earnestness

---

1   William Backhouse Astor Jr. (1829–92) was the grandson of the first multi-millionaire in American history and a prominent businessman in his own right.

that Frank could scarcely forbear laughing, though it is hardly necessary to say that the "dropper" was by no means so inclined.

"You'll know sometime," he said, scowling.

"I'll make you a fair offer," said Dick. "If I get more'n fifty dollars as a reward for my honesty, I'll divide with you. But I say, aint it most time to go back to your sick family in Boston?"

Finding that nothing was to be made out of Dick, the man strode away with a muttered curse.

"You were too smart for him, Dick," said Frank.

"Yes," said Dick, "I aint knocked round the city streets all my life for nothin'."

CHAPTER VIII: DICK'S EARLY HISTORY

"Have you always lived in New York, Dick?" asked Frank, after a pause.

"Ever since I can remember."

"I wish you'd tell me a little about yourself. Have you got any father or mother?"

"I aint got no mother. She died when I wasn't but three years old. My father went to sea; but he went off before mother died, and nothin' was ever heard of him. I expect he got wrecked, or died at sea."

"And what became of you when your mother died?"

"The folks she boarded with took care of me, but they was poor, and they couldn't do much. When I was seven the woman died, and her husband went out West, and then I had to scratch for myself."

"At seven years old!" exclaimed Frank, in amazement.

"Yes," said Dick, "I was a little feller to take care of myself, but," he continued with pardonable pride, "I did it."

"What could you do?"

"Sometimes one thing, and sometimes another," said Dick. "I changed my business accordin' as I had to. Sometimes I was a newsboy, and diffused intelligence among the masses, as I heard somebody say once in a big speech he made in the Park. Them was the times when Horace Greeley and James Gordon Bennett[1] made money."

---

1   Either James Gordon Bennett Sr. (1795–1872), the founder, publisher, and editor of the *New York Herald* from 1835 until 1866, or his son James Gordon Bennett Jr. (1841–1918), who edited the *Herald* from 1866 until 1877.

"Through your enterprise?" suggested Frank.

"Yes," said Dick; "but I give it up after a while."

"What for?"

"Well, they didn't always put news enough in their papers, and people wouldn't buy 'em as fast as I wanted 'em to. So one mornin' I was stuck on a lot of Heralds, and I thought I'd make a sensation. So I called out 'GREAT NEWS! QUEEN VICTORIA ASSASSINATED!' All my Heralds went off like hot cakes, and I went off, too, but one of the gentlemen what got sold remembered me, and said he'd have me took up, and that's what made me change my business."

"That wasn't right, Dick," said Frank.

"I know it," said Dick; "but lots of boys does it."

"That don't make it any better."

"No," said Dick, "I was sort of ashamed at the time, 'specially about one poor old gentleman,—a Englishman he was. He couldn't help cryin' to think the queen was dead, and his hands shook when he handed me the money for the paper."

"What did you do next?"

"I went into the match business," said Dick; "but it was small sales and small profits. Most of the people I called on had just laid in a stock, and didn't want to buy. So one cold night, when I hadn't money enough to pay for a lodgin', I burned the last of my matches to keep me from freezin'. But it cost too much to get warm that way, and I couldn't keep it up."

"You've seen hard times, Dick," said Frank, compassionately.

"Yes," said Dick, "I've knowed what it was to be hungry and cold, with nothin' to eat or to warm me; but there's one thing I never could do," he added, proudly.

"What's that?"

"I never stole," said Dick. "It's mean and I wouldn't do it."

"Were you ever tempted to?"

"Lots of times. Once I had been goin' round all day, and hadn't sold any matches, except three cents' worth early in the mornin'. With that I bought an apple, thinkin' I should get some more bimeby. When evenin' come I was awful hungry. I went into a baker's just to look at the bread. It made me feel kind o' good just to look at the bread and cakes, and I thought maybe they would give me some. I asked 'em wouldn't they give me a loaf, and take their pay in matches. But they said they'd got enough matches to last three months; so there wasn't any chance for a trade. While I was standin' at the stove warmin' me, the baker went into a back room, and I felt so hungry I thought I would take just one loaf, and go off with it. There was such a big pile I don't think he'd have known it."

"But you didn't do it?"

"No, I didn't and I was glad of it, for when the man came in ag'in, he said he wanted some one to carry some cake to a lady in St. Mark's Place.[1] His boy was sick, and he hadn't no one to send; so he told me he'd give me ten cents if I would go. My business wasn't very pressin' just then, so I went, and when I come back, I took my pay in bread and cakes. Didn't they taste good, though?"

"So you didn't stay long in the match business, Dick?"

"No, I couldn't sell enough to make it pay. Then there was some folks that wanted me to sell cheaper to them; so I couldn't make any profit. There was one old lady—she was rich, too, for she lived in a big brick house—beat me down so, that I didn't make no profit at all; but she wouldn't buy without, and I hadn't sold none that day; so I let her have them. I don't see why rich folks should be so hard upon a poor boy that wants to make a livin'."

"There's a good deal of meanness in the world, I'm afraid, Dick."

"If everybody was like you and your uncle," said Dick, "there would be some chance for poor people. If I was rich I'd try to help 'em along."

"Perhaps you will be rich sometime, Dick."

Dick shook his head.

"I'm afraid all my wallets will be like this," said Dick, indicating the one he had received from the dropper, "and will be full of papers what aint of no use to anybody except the owner."

"That depends very much on yourself, Dick," said Frank. "Stewart wasn't always rich, you know."

"Wasn't he?"

"When he first came to New York as a young man he was a teacher, and teachers are not generally very rich. At last he went into business, starting in a small way, and worked his way up by degrees. But there was one thing he determined in the beginning: that he would be strictly honorable in all his dealings, and never overreach any one for the sake of making money. If there was a chance for him, Dick, there is a chance for you."

"He knowed enough to be a teacher, and I'm awful ignorant," said Dick.

---

1 Alger resided in the East Village at St. Mark's Place, 8th Street between Third Avenue and Avenue A, between 1866 and 1875.

"But you needn't stay so."

"How can I help it?"

"Can't you learn at school?"

"I can't go to school 'cause I've got my livin' to earn. It wouldn't do me much good if I learned to read and write, and just as I'd got learned I starved to death."

"But are there no night-schools?"

"Yes."

"Why don't you go? I suppose you don't work in the evenings."

"I never cared much about it," said Dick, "and that's the truth. But since I've got to talkin' with you, I think more about it. I guess I'll begin to go."

"I wish you would, Dick. You'll make a smart man if you only get a little education."

"Do you think so?" asked Dick, doubtfully.

"I know so. A boy who has earned his own living since he was seven years old must have something in him. I feel very much interested in you, Dick. You've had a hard time of it so far in life, but I think better times are in store. I want you to do well, and I feel sure you can if you only try."

"You're a good fellow," said Dick, gratefully. "I'm afraid I'm a pretty rough customer, but I aint as bad as some. I mean to turn over a new leaf, and try to grow up 'spectable."

"There've been a great many boys begin as low down as you, Dick, that have grown up respectable and honored. But they had to work pretty hard for it."

"I'm willin' to work hard," said Dick.

"And you must not only work hard, but work in the right way."

"What's the right way?"

"You began in the right way when you determined never to steal, or do anything mean or dishonorable, however strongly tempted to do so. That will make people have confidence in you when they come to know you. But, in order to succeed well, you must manage to get as good an education as you can. Until you do, you cannot get a position in an office or counting-room, even to run errands."

"That's so," said Dick, soberly. "I never thought how awful ignorant I was till now."

"That can be remedied with perseverance," said Frank. "A year will do a great deal for you."

"I'll go to work and see what I can do," said Dick, energetically.

CHAPTER IX: A SCENE IN A THIRD AVENUE CAR

The boys had turned into Third Avenue, a long street, which, commencing just below the Cooper Institute, runs out to Harlem.[1] A man came out of a side street, uttering at intervals a monotonous cry which sounded like "glass puddin'."

"Glass pudding!" repeated Frank, looking in surprised wonder at Dick. "What does he mean?"

"Perhaps you'd like some," said Dick.

"I never heard of it before."

"Suppose you ask him what he charges for his puddin'."

Frank looked more narrowly at the man, and soon concluded that he was a glazier.

"Oh, I understand," he said. "He means 'glass put in'."

Frank's mistake was not a singular one. The monotonous cry of these men certainly sounds more like "glass puddin'," than the words they intend to utter.

"Now," said Dick, "where shall we go?"

"I should like to see Central Park," said Frank. "Is it far off?"

"It is about a mile and a half from here," said Dick. "This is Twenty-ninth Street, and the Park begins at Fifty-ninth Street."

It may be explained, for the benefit of readers who have never visited New York, that about a mile from the City Hall the cross-streets begin to be numbered in regular order. There is a continuous line of houses as far as One Hundred and Thirtieth Street, where may be found the terminus of the Harlem line of horse-cars. When the entire island is laid out and settled, probably the numbers will reach two hundred or more. Central Park, which lies between Fifty-ninth Street on the south, and One Hundred and Tenth Street on the north, is true to its name, occupying about the centre of the island. The distance between two parallel streets is called a block, and twenty blocks make a mile. It will therefore be seen that Dick was exactly right, when he said they were a mile and a half from Central Park.

"That is too far to walk," said Frank.

"'Twon't cost but six cents to ride," said Dick.

"You mean in the horse-cars?"

"Yes."

"All right then. We'll jump aboard the next car."

---

1 Harlem was a booming neighborhood in northern Manhattan immediately after the Civil War.

The Third Avenue and Harlem line of horse-cars is better patronized than any other in New York, though not much can be said for the cars, which are usually dirty and overcrowded. Still, when it is considered that only seven cents are charged for the entire distance to Harlem, about seven miles from the City Hall, the fare can hardly be complained of. But of course most of the profit is made from the way-passengers who only ride a short distance.

A car was at that moment approaching, but it seemed pretty crowded.

"Shall we take that, or wait for another?" asked Frank.

"The next'll most likely be as bad," said Dick.

The boys accordingly signalled to the conductor to stop, and got on the front platform. They were obliged to stand up till the car reached Fortieth Street, when so many of the passengers had got off that they obtained seats.

Frank sat down beside a middle-aged woman, or lady, as she probably called herself, whose sharp visage and thin lips did not seem to promise a very pleasant disposition. When the two gentlemen who sat beside her arose, she spread her skirts in the endeavor to fill two seats. Disregarding this, the boys sat down.

"There aint room for two," she said, looking sourly at Frank.

"There were two here before."

"Well, there ought not to have been. Some people like to crowd in where they're not wanted."

"And some like to take up a double allowance of room," thought Frank; but he did not say so. He saw that the woman had a bad temper, and thought it wisest to say nothing.

Frank had never ridden up the city as far as this, and it was with much interest that he looked out of the car windows at the stores on either side. Third Avenue is a broad street, but in the character of its houses and stores it is quite inferior to Broadway, though better than some of the avenues further east. Fifth Avenue, as most of my readers already know, is the finest street in the city, being lined with splendid private residences, occupied by the wealthier classes. Many of the cross streets also boast houses which may be considered palaces, so elegant are they externally and internally. Frank caught glimpses of some of these as he was carried towards the Park.

After the first conversation, already mentioned, with the lady at his side, he supposed he should have nothing further to do with her. But in this he was mistaken. While he was busy looking out of the car window, she plunged her hand into her pocket in search of her purse, which she was unable to find. Instantly she jumped to the conclusion that it had been stolen, and her suspicions fastened upon Frank, with whom she was already provoked for "crowding her," as she termed it.

"Conductor!" she exclaimed in a sharp voice.

"What's wanted, ma'am?" returned that functionary.

"I want you to come here right off."

"What's the matter?"

"My purse has been stolen. There was four dollars and eighty cents in it. I know, because I counted it when I paid my fare."

"Who stole it?"

"That boy," she said pointing to Frank, who listened to the charge in the most intense astonishment. "He crowded in here on purpose to rob me, and I want you to search him right off."

"That's a lie!" exclaimed Dick, indignantly.

"Oh, you're in league with him, I dare say," said the woman spitefully. "You're as bad as he is, I'll be bound."

"You're a nice female, you be!" said Dick, ironically.

"Don't you dare to call me a female, sir," said the lady, furiously.

"Why, you aint a man in disguise, be you?" said Dick.

"You are very much mistaken, madam," said Frank, quietly. "The conductor may search me, if you desire it."

A charge of theft, made in a crowded car, of course made quite a sensation. Cautious passengers instinctively put their hands on their pockets, to make sure that they, too, had not been robbed. As for Frank, his face flushed, and he felt very indignant that he should even be suspected of so mean a crime. He had been carefully brought up, and been taught to regard stealing as low and wicked.

Dick, on the contrary, thought it a capital joke that such a charge should have been made against his companion. Though he had brought himself up, and known plenty of boys and men, too, who would steal, he had never done so himself. He thought it mean. But he could not be expected to regard it as Frank did. He had been too familiar with it in others to look upon it with horror.

Meanwhile the passengers rather sided with the boys. Appearances go a great ways, and Frank did not look like a thief.

"I think you must be mistaken, madam," said a gentleman sitting opposite. "The lad does not look as if he would steal."

"You can't tell by looks," said the lady, sourly. "They're deceitful; villains are generally well dressed."

"Be they?" said Dick. "You'd ought to see me with my Washington coat on. You'd think I was the biggest villain ever you saw."

"I've no doubt you are," said the lady, scowling in the direction of our hero.

"Thank you, ma'am," said Dick. "'Tisn't often I get such fine compliments."

"None of your impudence," said the lady, wrathfully. "I believe you're the worst of the two."

Meanwhile the car had been stopped.

"How long are we going to stop here?" demanded a passenger, impatiently. "I'm in a hurry, if none of the rest of you are."

"I want my pocket-book," said the lady, defiantly.

"Well, ma'am, I haven't got it, and I don't see as it's doing you any good detaining us all here."

"Conductor, will you call a policeman to search that young scamp?" continued the aggrieved lady. "You don't expect I'm going to lose my money, and do nothing about it?"

"I'll turn my pockets inside out if you want me to," said Frank, proudly. "There's no need of a policeman. The conductor, or any one else, may search me."

"Well, youngster," said the conductor, "if the lady agrees, I'll search you."

The lady signified her assent.

Frank accordingly turned his pockets inside out, but nothing was revealed except his own porte-monnaie and a penknife.

"Well, ma'am, are you satisfied?" asked the conductor.

"No, I aint," said she, decidedly.

"You don't think he's got it still?"

"No, but he's passed it over to his confederate, that boy there that's so full of impudence."

"That's me," said Dick, comically.

"He confesses it," said the lady; "I want him searched."

"All right," said Dick, "I'm ready for the operation, only, as I've got valooable property about me, be careful not to drop any of my Erie Bonds."

The conductor's hand forthwith dove into Dick's pocket, and drew out a rusty jack-knife, a battered cent, about fifty cents in change, and the capacious pocket-book which he had received from the swindler who was anxious to get back to his sick family in Boston.

"Is that yours, ma'am?" asked the conductor, holding up the

wallet which excited some amazement, by its size, among the other passengers.

"It seems to me you carry a large pocket-book for a young man of your age," said the conductor.

"That's what I carry my cash and valooable papers in," said Dick.

"I suppose that isn't yours, ma'am," said the conductor, turning to the lady.

"No," said she, scornfully. "I wouldn't carry round such a great wallet as that. Most likely he's stolen it from somebody else."

"What a prime detective you'd be!" said Dick. "P'rhaps you know who I took it from."

"I don't know but my money's in it," said the lady, sharply. "Conductor, will you open that wallet, and see what there is in it?"

"Don't disturb the valooable papers," said Dick, in a tone of pretended anxiety.

The contents of the wallet excited some amusement among the passengers.

"There don't seem to be much money here," said the conductor, taking out a roll of tissue paper cut out in the shape of bills, and rolled up.

"No," said Dick. "Didn't I tell you them were papers of no valoo to anybody but the owner? If the lady'd like to borrow, I won't charge no interest."

"Where is my money, then?" said the lady, in some discomfiture. "I shouldn't wonder if one of the young scamps had thrown it out of the window."

"You'd better search your pocket once more," said the gentleman opposite. "I don't believe either of the boys is in fault. They don't look to me as if they would steal."

"Thank you, sir," said Frank.

The lady followed out the suggestion, and, plunging her hand once more into her pocket, drew out a small porte-monnaie. She hardly knew whether to be glad or sorry at this discovery. It placed her in rather an awkward position after the fuss she had made, and the detention to which she had subjected the passengers, now, as it proved, for nothing.

"Is that the pocket-book you thought stolen?" asked the conductor.

"Yes," said she, rather confusedly.

"Then you've been keeping me waiting all this time for nothing," he said, sharply. "I wish you'd take care to be sure next time before you make such a disturbance for nothing. I've lost five minutes, and shall not be on time."

"I can't help it," was the cross reply; "I didn't know it was in my pocket."

"It seems to me you owe an apology to the boys you accused of a theft which they have not committed," said the gentleman opposite.

"I shan't apologize to anybody," said the lady, whose temper was not of the best; "least of all to such whipper-snappers as they are."

"Thank you, ma'am," said Dick, comically; "your handsome apology is accepted. It aint of no consequence, only I didn't like to expose the contents of my valooable pocket-book, for fear it might excite the envy of some of my poor neighbors."

"You're a character," said the gentleman who had already spoken, with a smile.

"A bad character!" muttered the lady.

But it was quite evident that the sympathies of those present were against the lady, and on the side of the boys who had been falsely accused, while Dick's drollery had created considerable amusement.

The cars had now reached Fifty-ninth Street, the southern boundary of the Park, and here our hero and his companion got off.

"You'd better look out for pickpockets, my lad," said the conductor, pleasantly. "That big wallet of yours might prove a great temptation."

"That's so," said Dick. "That's the misfortin' of being rich. Astor and me don't sleep much for fear of burglars breakin' in and robbin' us of our valooable treasures. Sometimes I think I'll give all my money to an Orphan Asylum, and take it out in board. I guess I'd make money by the operation."

While Dick was speaking, the car rolled away, and the boys turned up Fifty-ninth Street, for two long blocks yet separated them from the Park.

CHAPTER X: INTRODUCES A VICTIM OF MISPLACED CONFIDENCE

"What a queer chap you are, Dick!" said Frank, laughing. "You always seem to be in good spirits."

"No, I aint always. Sometimes I have the blues."

"When?"

"Well, once last winter it was awful cold, and there was big holes in my shoes, and my gloves and all my warm clothes was at the tailor's. I felt as if life was sort of tough, and I'd like it if some rich man would adopt me, and give me plenty to eat and drink and wear, without my havin' to look so sharp after it. Then agin' when I've seen boys with good homes, and fathers, and mothers, I've thought I'd like to have somebody to care for me."

Dick's tone changed as he said this, from his usual levity, and there was a touch of sadness in it. Frank, blessed with a good home and indulgent parents, could not help pitying the friendless boy who had found life such up-hill work.

"Don't say you have no one to care for you, Dick," he said, lightly laying his hand on Dick's shoulder. "I will care for you."

"Will you?"

"If you will let me."

"I wish you would," said Dick, earnestly. "I'd like to feel that I have one friend who cares for me."

Central Park was now before them, but it was far from presenting the appearance which it now exhibits. It had not been long since work had been commenced upon it, and it was still very rough and unfinished. A rough tract of land, two miles and a half from north to south, and a half a mile broad, very rocky in parts, was the material from which the Park Commissioners have made the present beautiful enclosure. There were no houses of good appearance near it, buildings being limited mainly to rude temporary huts used by the workmen who were employed in improving it. The time will undoubtedly come when the Park will be surrounded by elegant residences, and compare favorably in this respect with the most attractive parts of any city in the world. But at the time when Frank and Dick visited it, not much could be said in favor either of the Park or its neighborhood.

"If this is Central Park," said Frank, who naturally felt disappointed, "I don't think much of it. My father's got a large pasture that is much nicer."

"It'll look better some time," said Dick. "There aint much to see now but rocks. We will take a walk over it if you want to."

"No," said Frank, "I've seen as much of it as I want to. Besides, I feel tired."

"Then we'll go back. We can take the Sixth Avenue cars. They will bring us out at Vesey Street just beside the Astor House."

"All right," said Frank. "That will be the best course. I hope," he added, laughing, "our agreeable lady friend won't be there. I don't care about being accused of *stealing* again."

"She was a tough one," said Dick. "Wouldn't she make a nice wife for a man that likes to live in hot water, and didn't mind bein' scalded two or three times a day?"

"Yes, I think she'd just suit him. Is that the right car, Dick?"

"Yes, jump in, and I'll follow."

The Sixth Avenue is lined with stores, many of them of very good appearance, and would make a very respectable principal street for a good-sized city. But it is only one of several long business streets which run up the island, and illustrate the extent and importance of the city to which they belong.

No incidents worth mentioning took place during their ride down town. In about three-quarters of an hour the boys got out of the car beside the Astor House.

"Are you goin' in now, Frank?" asked Dick.

"That depends upon whether you have anything else to show me."

"Wouldn't you like to go to Wall Street?"[1]

"That's the street where there are so many bankers and brokers,—isn't it?"

"Yes, I s'pose you aint afraid of bulls and bears,—are you?"

"Bulls and bears?" repeated Frank, puzzled.

"Yes."

"What are they?"

"The bulls is what tries to make the stocks go up, and the bears is what try to growl 'em down."

"Oh, I see. Yes, I'd like to go."

Accordingly they walked down on the west side of Broadway as far as Trinity Church,[2] and then, crossing, entered a street not very wide or very long, but of very great importance. The reader would be astonished if he could know the amount of money

---

1   Wall Street, in the financial district of New York, runs from Broadway to South Street on the East River.

2   Located at 75 Broadway in lower Manhattan, the present Trinity Church was completed in 1846 and, at 284 feet, was the tallest building in New York until 1890.

involved in the transactions which take place in a single day in this street. It would be found that although Broadway is much greater in length, and lined with stores, it stands second to Wall Street in this respect.

"What is that large marble building?" asked Frank, pointing to a massive structure on the corner of Wall and Nassau Streets. It was in the form of a parallelogram, two hundred feet long by ninety wide, and about eighty feet in height, the ascent to the entrance being by eighteen granite steps.

"That's the Custom House,"[1] said Dick.

"It looks like pictures I've seen of the Parthenon at Athens,"[2] said Frank, meditatively.

"Where's Athens?" asked Dick. "It aint in York State,—is it?"

"Not the Athens I mean, at any rate. It is in Greece, and was a famous city two thousand years ago."

"That's longer than I can remember," said Dick. "I can't remember distinctly more'n about a thousand years."

"What a chap you are, Dick! Do you know if we can go in?"

The boys ascertained, after a little inquiry, that they would be allowed to do so. They accordingly entered the Custom House and made their way up to the roof, from which they had a fine view of the harbor, the wharves crowded with shipping, and the neighboring shores of Long Island and New Jersey. Towards the north they looked down for many miles upon continuous lines of streets, and thousands of roofs, with here and there a church-spire rising above its neighbors. Dick had never before been up there, and he, as well as Frank, was interested in the grand view spread before them.

At length they descended, and were going down the granite steps on the outside of the building, when they were addressed by a young man, whose appearance is worth describing.

He was tall, and rather loosely put together, with small eyes and rather a prominent nose. His clothing had evidently not been furnished by a city tailor. He wore a blue coat with brass buttons, and pantaloons of rather scanty dimensions, which were several inches too short to cover his lower limbs. He held in his hand a piece of paper, and his countenance wore a look of mingled bewilderment and anxiety.

---

1 Between 1862 and 1907 the New York Custom House was located in the Merchants' Exchange Building at 55 Wall Street.

2 A temple on the Acropolis of Athens dedicated to the goddess Athena.

"Be they a-payin' out money inside there?" he asked, indicating the interior by a motion of his hand.

"I guess so," said Dick. "Are you a-goin' in for some?"

"Wal, yes. I've got an order here for sixty dollars,—made a kind of speculation this morning."

"How was it?" asked Frank.

"Wal, you see I brought down some money to put in the bank, fifty dollars it was, and I hadn't justly made up my mind what bank to put it into, when a chap came up in a terrible hurry, and said it was very unfortunate, but the bank wasn't open, and he must have some money right off. He was obliged to go out of the city by the next train. I asked him how much he wanted. He said fifty dollars. I told him I'd got that, and he offered me a check on the bank for sixty, and I let him have it. I thought that was a pretty easy way to earn ten dollars, so I counted out the money and he went off. He told me I'd hear a bell ring when they began to pay out money. But I've waited most two hours, and I haint heard it yet. I'd ought to be goin', for I told dad I'd be home to-night. Do you think I can get the money now?"

"Will you show me the check?" asked Frank, who had listened attentively to the countryman's story, and suspected that he had been made the victim of a swindler. It was made out upon the "Washington Bank," in the sum of sixty dollars, and was signed "Ephraim Smith."

"Washington Bank!" repeated Frank. "Dick, is there such a bank in the city?"

"Not as I knows on," said Dick. "Leastways I don't own any shares in it."

"Aint this the Washington Bank?" asked the countryman, pointing to the building on the steps of which the three were now standing.

"No, it's the Custom House."

"And won't they give me any money for this?" asked the young man, the perspiration standing on his brow.

"I am afraid the man who gave it to you was a swindler," said Frank, gently.

"And won't I ever see my fifty dollars again?" asked the youth in agony.

"I am afraid not."

"What'll dad say?" ejaculated the miserable youth. "It makes me feel sick to think of it. I wish I had the feller here. I'd shake him out of his boots."

"What did he look like? I'll call a policeman and you shall

describe him. Perhaps in that way you can get track of your money."

Dick called a policeman, who listened to the description, and recognized the operator as an experienced swindler. He assured the countryman that there was very little chance of his ever seeing his money again. The boys left the miserable youth loudly bewailing his bad luck, and proceeded on their way down the street.

"He's a baby," said Dick, contemptuously. "He'd ought to know how to take care of himself and his money. A feller has to look sharp in this city, or he'll lose his eye-teeth before he knows it."

"I suppose you never got swindled out of fifty dollars, Dick?"

"No, I don't carry no such small bills. I wish I did," he added.

"So do I, Dick. What's that building there at the end of the street?"

"That's the Wall-Street Ferry to Brooklyn."

"How long does it take to go across?"

"Not more'n five minutes."

"Suppose we just ride over and back."

"All right!" said Dick. "It's rather expensive; but if you don't mind, I don't."

"Why, how much does it cost?"

"Two cents apiece."

"I guess I can stand that. Let us go."

They passed the gate, paying the fare to a man who stood at the entrance, and were soon on the ferry-boat, bound for Brooklyn.

They had scarcely entered the boat, when Dick, grasping Frank by the arm, pointed to a man just outside of the gentlemen's cabin.

"Do you see that man, Frank?" he inquired.

"Yes, what of him?"

"He's the man that cheated the country chap out of his fifty dollars."

CHAPTER XI: DICK AS A DETECTIVE

Dick's ready identification of the rogue who had cheated the countryman surprised Frank.

"What makes you think it is he?" he asked.

"Because I've seen him before, and I know he's up to them kind of tricks. When I heard how he looked, I was sure I knowed him."

"Our recognizing him won't be of much use," said Frank. "It won't give back the countryman his money."

"I don't know," said Dick, thoughtfully. "Maybe I can get it."

"How?" asked Frank, incredulously.

"Wait a minute, and you'll see."

Dick left his companion, and went up to the man whom he suspected.

"Ephraim Smith," said Dick, in a low voice.

The man turned suddenly, and looked at Dick uneasily.

"What did you say?" he asked.

"I believe your name is Ephraim Smith," continued Dick.

"You're mistaken," said the man, and was about to move off.

"Stop a minute," said Dick. "Don't you keep your money in the Washington Bank?"

"I don't know any such bank. I'm in a hurry, young man, and I can't stop to answer any foolish questions."

The boat had by this time reached the Brooklyn pier, and Mr. Ephraim Smith seemed in a hurry to land.

"Look here," said Dick, significantly; "you'd better not go on shore unless you want to jump into the arms of a policeman."

"What do you mean?" asked the man, startled.

"That little affair of yours is known to the police," said Dick; "about how you got fifty dollars out of a greenhorn on a false check, and it mayn't be safe for you to go ashore."

"I don't know what you're talking about," said the swindler with affected boldness, though Dick could see that he was ill at ease.

"Yes you do," said Dick. "There isn't but one thing to do. Just give me back that money, and I'll see that you're not touched. If you don't, I'll give you up to the first p'liceman we meet."

Dick looked so determined, and spoke so confidently, that the other, overcome by his fears, no longer hesitated, but passed a roll of bills to Dick and hastily left the boat.

All this Frank witnessed with great amazement, not understanding what influence Dick could have obtained over the swindler sufficient to compel restitution.

"How did you do it?" he asked eagerly.

"I told him I'd exert my influence with the president to have him tried by *habeas corpus*,"[1] said Dick.

"And of course that frightened him. But tell me, without joking, how you managed."

---

1 Latin: a legal motion to contest unlawful detainment.

Dick gave a truthful account of what occurred, and then said, "Now we'll go back and carry the money."

"Suppose we don't find the poor countryman?"

"Then the p'lice will take care of it."

They remained on board the boat, and in five minutes were again in New York. Going up Wall Street, they met the country-man a little distance from the Custom House. His face was marked with the traces of deep anguish; but in his case even grief could not subdue the cravings of appetite. He had purchased some cakes of one of the old women who spread out for the benefit of passers-by an array of apples and seed-cakes, and was munching them with melancholy satisfaction.

"Hilloa!" said Dick. "Have you found your money?"

"No," ejaculated the young man, with a convulsive gasp. "I shan't ever see it again. The mean skunk's cheated me out of it. Consarn his picter! It took me most six months to save it up. I was workin' for Deacon Pinkham in our place. Oh, I wish I'd never come to New York! The deacon, he told me he'd keep it for me; but I wanted to put it in the bank, and now it's all gone, boo hoo!"

And the miserable youth, having despatched his cakes, was so overcome by the thought of his loss that he burst into tears.

"I say," said Dick, "dry up, and see what I've got here."

The youth no sooner saw the roll of bills, and comprehended that it was indeed his lost treasure, than from the depths of anguish he was exalted to the most ecstatic joy. He seized Dick's hand, and shook it with so much energy that our hero began to feel rather alarmed for its safety.

"'Pears to me you take my arm for a pump-handle," said he. "Couldn't you show your gratitood some other way? It's just possible I may want to use my arm ag'in some time."

The young man desisted, but invited Dick most cordially to come up and stop a week with him at his country home, assuring him that he wouldn't charge him anything for board.

"All right!" said Dick. "If you don't mind I'll bring my wife along, too. She's delicate, and the country air might do her good."

Jonathan[1] stared at him in amazement, uncertain whether to credit the fact of his marriage. Dick walked on with Frank, leaving him in an apparent state of stupefaction, and it is possible that he has not yet settled the affair to his satisfaction.

---

1 A "Jonathan" is a country bumpkin.

"Now," said Frank, "I think I'll go back to the Astor House. Uncle has probably got through his business and returned."

"All right," said Dick.

The two boys walked up to Broadway, just where the tall steeple of Trinity faces the street of bankers and brokers, and walked leisurely to the hotel. When they arrived at the Astor House, Dick said, "Good-by, Frank."

"Not yet," said Frank; "I want you to come in with me."

Dick followed his young patron up the steps. Frank went to the reading-room, where, as he had thought probable, he found his uncle already arrived, and reading a copy of "The Evening Post,"[1] which he had just purchased outside.

"Well, boys," he said, looking up, "have you had a pleasant jaunt?"

"Yes, sir," said Frank. "Dick's a capital guide."

"So this is Dick," said Mr. Whitney, surveying him with a smile. "Upon my word, I should hardly have known him. I must congratulate him on his improved appearance."

"Frank's been very kind to me," said Dick, who, rough street-boy as he was, had a heart easily touched by kindness, of which he had never experienced much. "He's a tip-top fellow."

"I believe he is a good boy," said Mr. Whitney. "I hope, my lad, you will prosper and rise in the world. You know in this free country poverty in early life is no bar to a man's advancement. I haven't risen very high myself," he added, with a smile, "but have met with moderate success in life; yet there was a time when I was as poor as you."

"Were you, sir?" asked Dick, eagerly.

"Yes, my boy, I have known the time I have been obliged to go without my dinner because I didn't have enough money to pay for it."

"How did you get up in the world?" asked Dick, anxiously.

"I entered a printing-office as an apprentice, and worked for some years. Then my eyes gave out and I was obliged to give that up. Not knowing what else to do, I went into the country, and worked on a farm. After a while I was lucky enough to invent a machine, which has brought me in a great deal of money. But there was one thing I got while I was in the printing-office which I value more than money."

---

1 Founded in 1801 by Alexander Hamilton (c. 1755–1804), the New York *Evening Post* was edited at the time by William Cullen Bryant (1794–1878).

"What was that, sir?"

"A taste for reading and study. During my leisure hours I improved myself by study, and acquired a large part of the knowledge which I now possess. Indeed, it was one of my books that first put me on the track of the invention, which I afterwards made. So you see, my lad, that my studious habits paid me in money, as well as in another way."

"I'm awful ignorant," said Dick, soberly.

"But you are young, and, I judge, a smart boy. If you try to learn, you can, and if you ever expect to do anything in the world, you must know something of books."

"I will," said Dick, resolutely. "I aint always goin' to black boots for a livin'."

"All labor is respectable, my lad, and you have no cause to be ashamed of any honest business; yet when you can get something to do that promises better for your future prospects, I advise you to do so. Till then earn your living in the way you are accustomed to, avoid extravagance, and save up a little money if you can."

"Thank you for your advice," said our hero. "There aint many that takes an interest in Ragged Dick."

"So that's your name," said Mr. Whitney. "If I judge you rightly, it won't be long before you change it. Save your money, my lad, buy books, and determine to be somebody, and you may yet fill an honorable position."

"I'll try," said Dick. "Good-night, sir."

"Wait a minute, Dick," said Frank. "Your blacking-box and old clothes are upstairs. You may want them."

"In course," said Dick. "I couldn't get along without my best clothes, and my stock in trade."

"You may go up to the room with him, Frank," said Mr. Whitney. "The clerk will give you the key. I want to see you, Dick, before you go."

"Yes, sir," said Dick.

"Where are you going to sleep to-night, Dick?" asked Frank, as they went upstairs together.

"P'r'aps at the Fifth Avenue Hotel—on the outside," said Dick.

"Haven't you any place to sleep, then?"

"I slept in a box, last night."

"In a box?"

"Yes, on Spruce Street."

"Poor fellow!" said Frank, compassionately.

"Oh, 'twas a bully bed—full of straw! I slept like a top."

"Don't you earn enough to pay for a room, Dick?"

"Yes," said Dick; "only I spend my money foolish, goin' to the Old Bowery, and Tony Pastor's, and sometimes gamblin' in Baxter Street."

"You won't gamble any more,—will you, Dick?" said Frank, laying his hand persuasively on his companion's shoulder.

"No, I won't," said Dick.

"You'll promise?"

"Yes, and I'll keep it. You're a good feller. I wish you was goin' to be in New York."

"I am going to a boarding-school in Connecticut. The name of the town is Barnton. Will you write to me, Dick?"

"My writing would look like hens' tracks," said our hero.

"Never mind. I want you to write. When you write you can tell me how to direct, and I will send you a letter."

"I wish you would," said Dick. "I wish I was more like you."

"I hope you will make a much better boy, Dick. Now we'll go in to my uncle. He wishes to see you before you go."

They went into the reading-room. Dick had wrapped up his blacking-brush in a newspaper with which Frank had supplied him, feeling that a guest of the Astor House should hardly be seen coming out of the hotel displaying such a professional sign.

"Uncle, Dick's ready to go," said Frank.

"Good-by, my lad," said Mr. Whitney. "I hope to hear good accounts of you sometime. Don't forget what I have told you. Remember that your future position depends mainly upon yourself, and that it will be high or low as you choose to make it."

He held out his hand, in which was a five-dollar bill. Dick shrunk back.

"I don't like to take it," he said. "I haven't earned it."

"Perhaps not," said Mr. Whitney; "but I give it to you because I remember my own friendless youth. I hope it may be of service to you. Sometime when you are a prosperous man, you can repay it in the form of aid to some poor boy, who is struggling upward as you are now."

"I will, sir," said Dick, manfully.

He no longer refused the money, but took it gratefully, and, bidding Frank and his uncle good-by, went out into the street. A feeling of loneliness came over him as he left the presence of Frank, for whom he had formed a strong attachment in the few hours he had known him.

CHAPTER XII:
DICK HIRES A ROOM ON MOTT STREET

Going out into the fresh air Dick felt the pangs of hunger. He accordingly went to a restaurant and got a substantial supper. Perhaps it was the new clothes he wore, which made him feel a little more aristocratic. At all events, instead of patronizing the cheap restaurant where he usually procured his meals, he went into the refectory attached to Lovejoy's Hotel,[1] where the prices were higher and the company more select. In his ordinary dress, Dick would have been excluded, but now he had the appearance of a very respectable, gentlemanly boy, whose presence would not discredit any establishment. His orders were therefore received with attention by the waiter and in due time a good supper was placed before him.

"I wish I could come here every day," thought Dick. "It seems kind o' nice and 'spectable, side of the other place. There's a gent at that other table that I've shined boots for more'n once. He don't know me in my new clothes. Guess he don't know his boot-black patronizes the same establishment."

His supper over, Dick went up to the desk, and, presenting his check, tendered in payment his five-dollar bill, as if it were one of a large number which he possessed. Receiving back his change he went out into the street.

Two questions now arose: How should he spend the evening, and where should he pass the night? Yesterday, with such a sum of money in his possession, he would have answered both questions readily. For the evening, he would have passed it at the Old Bowery, and gone to sleep in any out-of-the-way place that offered. But he had turned over a new leaf, or resolved to do so. He meant to save his money for some useful purpose,—to aid his advancement in the world. So he could not afford the theatre. Besides, with his new clothes, he was unwilling to pass the night out of doors.

"I should spile 'em," he thought, "and that wouldn't pay."

So he determined to hunt up a room which he could occupy regularly, and consider as his own, where he could sleep nights, instead of depending on boxes and old wagons for a chance shelter. This would be the first step towards respectability, and Dick determined to take it.

He accordingly passed through the City Hall Park, and walked leisurely up Centre Street.

---

1 Lovejoy's Hotel was located on Beekman Street opposite the Astor House.

Figure 6. City Hall Park, *Student and Schoolmate* 19 (February 1867): 44. Editor's collection.

He decided that it would hardly be advisable for him to seek lodgings in Fifth Avenue, although his present cash capital consisted of nearly five dollars in money, besides the valuable papers contained in his wallet. Besides, he had reason to doubt whether any in his line of business lived on that aristocratic street. He took his way to Mott Street, which is considerably less pretentious, and halted in front of a shabby brick lodging-house kept by a Mrs. Mooney, with whose son, Tom, Dick was acquainted.

Dick rang the bell, which sent back a shrill metallic response.

The door was opened by a slatternly servant, who looked at him inquiringly, and not without curiosity. It must be remembered Dick was well dressed, and that nothing in his appearance bespoke his occupation. Being naturally a good-looking boy, he might readily be mistaken for a gentleman's son.

"Well, Queen Victoria," said Dick, "is your missus at home?"

"My name's Bridget," said the girl.

"Oh, indeed!" said Dick. "You looked so much like the queen's picter what she gave me last Christmas in exchange for mine, that I couldn't help calling you by her name."

"Oh, go along wid ye!" said Bridget. "It's makin' fun ye are."

"If you don't believe me," said Dick, gravely, "all you've got to do is to ask my partic'lar friend, the Duke of Newcastle."[1]

"Bridget!" called a shrill voice from the basement.

"The missus is calling me," said Bridget, hurriedly. "I'll tell her ye want her."

"All right!" said Dick.

The servant descended into the lower regions, and in a short time a stout, red-faced woman appeared on the scene.

"Well, sir, what's your wish?" she asked.

"Have you got a room to let?" asked Dick.

"Is it for yourself you ask?" questioned the woman, in some surprise.

Dick answered in the affirmative.

"I haven't got any very good rooms vacant. There's a small room in the third story."

"I'd like to see it," said Dick.

"I don't know as it would be good enough for you," said the woman, with a glance at Dick's clothes.

"I aint very partic'lar about accommodations," said our hero. "I guess I'll look at it."

---

1 Henry Pelham Alexander Pelham-Clinton (1834–79) was the sixth Duke of Newcastle-under-Lyne.

Dick followed the landlady up two narrow stair-cases, uncarpeted and dirty, to the third landing, where he was ushered into a room about ten feet square. It could not be considered a very desirable apartment. It had once been covered with an oilcloth carpet, but this was now very ragged, and looked worse than none. There was a single bed in the corner, covered with an indiscriminate heap of bed-clothing, rumpled and not over-clean. There was a bureau, with the veneering scratched and in some parts stripped off, and a small glass, eight inches by ten, cracked across the middle; also two chairs in rather a disjointed condition. Judging from Dick's appearance, Mrs. Mooney thought he would turn from it in disdain.

But it must be remembered that Dick's past experience had not been of a character to make him fastidious. In comparison with a box, or an empty wagon, even this little room seemed comfortable. He decided to hire it if the rent proved reasonable.

"Well, what's the tax?" asked Dick.

"I ought to have a dollar a week," said Mrs. Mooney, hesitatingly.

"Say seventy-five cents, and I'll take it," said Dick.

"Every week in advance?"

"Yes."

"Well, as times is hard,[1] and I can't afford to keep it empty, you may have it. When will you come?"

"To-night," said Dick.

"It aint lookin' very neat. I don't know as I can fix it up to-night."

"Well, I'll sleep here to-night, and you can fix it up to-morrow."

"I hope you'll excuse the looks. I'm a lone woman, and my help is so shiftless, I have to look after everything myself; so I can't keep things as straight as I want to."

"All right!" said Dick.

"Can you pay me the first week in advance?" asked the landlady, cautiously.

Dick responded by drawing seventy-five cents from his pocket, and placing it in her hand.

"What's your business, sir, if I may inquire?" said Mrs. Mooney.

"Oh, I'm professional!" said Dick.

---

1 The financial panic of 1866 had precipitated a worldwide economic recession.

"Indeed!" said the landlady, who did not feel much enlightened by this answer.

"How's Tom?" asked Dick.

"Do you know my Tom?" said Mrs. Mooney in surprise. "He's gone to sea,—to Californy. He went last week."

"Did he?" said Dick. "Yes, I knew him."

Mrs. Mooney looked upon her new lodger with increased favor, on finding that he was acquainted with her son, who, by the way, was one of the worst young scamps in Mott Street, which is saying considerable.

"I'll bring over my baggage from the Astor House this evening," said Dick in a tone of importance.

"From the Astor House!" repeated Mrs. Mooney, in fresh amazement.

"Yes, I've been stoppin' there a short time with some friends," said Dick.

Mrs. Mooney might be excused for a little amazement at finding that a guest from the Astor House was about to become one of her lodgers—such transfers not being common.

"Did you say you was purfessional?" she asked.

"Yes, ma'am," said Dick, politely.

"You aint a—a—" Mrs. Mooney paused, uncertain what conjecture to hazard.

"Oh, no, nothing of the sort," said Dick, promptly. "How could you think so, Mrs. Mooney?"

"No offence, sir," said the landlady, more perplexed than ever.

"Certainly not," said our hero. "But you must excuse me now, Mrs. Mooney, as I have business of great importance to attend to."

"You'll come round this evening?"

Dick answered in the affirmative, and turned away.

"I wonder what he is!" thought the landlady, following him with her eyes as he crossed the street. "He's got good clothes on, but he don't seem very particular about his room. Well; I've got all my rooms full now. That's one comfort."

Dick felt more comfortable now that he had taken the decisive step of hiring a lodging, and paying a week's rent in advance. For seven nights he was sure of a shelter and a bed to sleep in. The thought was a pleasant one to our young vagrant, who hitherto had seldom known when he rose in the morning where he should find a resting-place at night.

"I must bring my traps round," said Dick to himself. "I guess I'll go to bed early to-night. It'll feel kinder good to sleep in a reg'lar bed. Boxes is rather hard to the back, and aint comfortable in case of rain. I wonder what Johnny Nolan would say if he knew I'd got a room of my own."

CHAPTER XIII: MICKY MAGUIRE

About nine o'clock Dick sought his new lodgings. In his hands he carried his professional wardrobe, namely, the clothes which he had worn at the commencement of the day, and the implements of his business. These he stowed away in the bureau drawers, and by the light of a flickering candle took off his clothes and went to bed. Dick had a good digestion and a reasonably good conscience; consequently he was a good sleeper. Perhaps, too, the soft feather bed conduced to slumber. At any rate his eyes were soon closed, and he did not awake until half-past six the next morning.

He lifted himself on his elbow, and stared around him in transient bewilderment.

"Blest if I hadn't forgot where I was," he said to himself. "So this is my room, is it? Well, it seems kind of 'spectable to have a room and a bed to sleep in. I'd orter be able to afford seventy-five cents a week. I've throwed away more money than that in one evenin'. There aint no reason why I shouldn't live 'spectable. I wish I knowed as much as Frank. He's a tip-top feller. Nobody ever cared enough for me before to give me good advice. It was kicks, and cuffs, and swearin' at me all the time. I'd like to show him I can do something."

While Dick was indulging in these reflections, he had risen from bed, and, finding an accession to the furniture of his room, in the shape of an ancient wash-stand bearing a cracked bowl and broken pitcher, indulged himself in the rather unusual ceremony of a good wash. On the whole, Dick preferred to be clean, but it was not always easy to gratify his desire. Lodging in the street as he had been accustomed to do, he had had no opportunity to perform his toilet in the customary manner. Even now he found himself unable to arrange his dishevelled locks, having neither comb nor brush. He determined to purchase a comb, at least, as soon as possible, and a brush too, if he could get one cheap. Meanwhile he combed his hair with his fingers as well as he could, though the result was not quite so satisfactory as it might have been.

A question now came up for consideration. For the first time in his life Dick possessed two suits of clothes. Should he put on the clothes Frank had given him, or resume his old rags?

Now, twenty-four hours before, at the time Dick was introduced to the reader's notice, no one could have been less fastidious as to his clothing than he. Indeed, he had rather a contempt for good clothes, or at least he thought so. But now, as he surveyed the ragged and dirty coat and the patched pants, Dick felt ashamed of them. He was unwilling to appear in the streets with them. Yet, if he went to work in his new suit, he was in danger of spoiling it, and he might not have it in his power to purchase a new one. Economy dictated a return to the old garments. Dick tried them on, and surveyed himself in the cracked glass; but the reflection did not please him.

"They don't look 'spectable," he decided; and, forthwith taking them off again, he put on the new suit of the day before.

"I must try to earn a little more," he thought, "to pay for my room, and to buy some new clo'es when these is wore out."

He opened the door of his chamber, and went downstairs and into the street, carrying his blacking-box with him.

It was Dick's custom to commence his business before breakfast; generally it must be owned, because he began the day penniless, and must earn his meal before he ate it. To-day it was different. He had four dollars left in his pocket-book; but this he had previously determined not to touch. In fact he had formed the ambitious design of starting an account at a savings' bank, in order to have something to fall back upon in case of sickness or any other emergency, or at any rate as a reserve fund to expend in clothing or other necessary articles when he required them. Hitherto he had been content to live on from day to day without a penny ahead; but the new vision of respectability which now floated before Dick's mind, owing to his recent acquaintance with Frank, was beginning to exercise a powerful effect upon him.

In Dick's profession as in others there are lucky days, when everything seems to flow prosperously. As if to encourage him in his new-born resolution, our hero obtained no less than six jobs in the course of an hour and a half. This gave him sixty cents, quite abundant to purchase his breakfast, and a comb besides. His exertions made him hungry, and, entering a small eating-house he ordered a cup of coffee and a beefsteak. To this he added a couple of rolls. This was quite a luxurious breakfast for Dick, and more expensive than he was accustomed to indulge himself with. To gratify the curiosity of my young readers, I will put down the items with their cost,—

```
Coffee, . . . . . . . . . . . . .   5 cts.
Beefsteak, . . . . . . . . . . . 15
A couple of rolls, . . . . . . . 5
                    —25 cts.
```

It will thus be seen that our hero had expended nearly one-half of his morning's earnings. Some days he had been compelled to breakfast on five cents, and then he was forced to content himself with a couple of apples, or cakes. But a good breakfast is a good preparation for a busy day, and Dick sallied forth from the restaurant lively and alert, ready to do a good stroke of business.

Dick's change of costume was liable to lead to one result of which he had not thought. His brother boot-blacks might think he had grown aristocratic, and was putting on airs,—that, in fact, he was getting above his business, and desirous to outshine his associates. Dick had not dreamed of this, because in fact, in spite of his new-born ambition, he entertained no such feeling. There was nothing of what boys call "big-feeling" about him. He was a thorough democrat, using the word not politically, but in its proper sense, and was disposed to fraternize with all whom he styled "good fellows," without regard to their position. It may seem a little unnecessary to some of my readers to make this explanation; but they must remember that pride and "big-feeling" are confined to no age or class, but may be found in boys as well as men, and in boot-blacks as well as those of a higher rank.

The morning being a busy time with the boot-blacks, Dick's changed appearance had not as yet attracted much attention. But when business slackened a little, our hero was destined to be reminded of it.

Among the down-town boot-blacks was one hailing from the Five Points,—a stout, red-haired, freckled-faced boy of fourteen, bearing the name of Micky Maguire. This boy, by his boldness and recklessness, as well as by his personal strength, which was considerable, had acquired an ascendancy among his fellow professionals, and had a gang of subservient followers, whom he led on to acts of ruffianism, not unfrequently terminating in a month or two at Blackwell's Island.[1] Micky himself had served two terms there; but the confinement appeared to have had very little effect in amending his conduct, except, perhaps, in making him a little more cautious about an encounter with the "copps," as the

---

1   Blackwell's Island, today Roosevelt Island, in the East River was the site of a jail, asylum, and hospitals.

members of the city police are, for some unknown reason, styled among the Five-Point boys.

Now Micky was proud of his strength, and of the position of leader which it had secured him. Moreover he was democratic in his tastes, and had a jealous hatred of those who wore good clothes and kept their faces clean. He called it putting on airs, and resented the implied superiority. If he had been fifteen years older, and had a trifle more education, he would have interested himself in politics, and been prominent at ward meetings, and a terror to respectable voters on election day. As it was, he contented himself with being the leader of a gang of young ruffians, over whom he wielded a despotic power.

Now it is only justice to Dick to say that, so far as wearing good clothes was concerned, he had never hitherto offended the eyes of Micky Maguire. Indeed, they generally looked as if they patronized the same clothing establishment. On this particular morning it chanced that Micky had not been very fortunate in a business way, and, as a natural consequence, his temper, never very amiable, was somewhat ruffled by the fact. He had had a very frugal breakfast,—not because he felt abstemious, but owing to the low state of his finances. He was walking along with one of his particular friends, a boy nicknamed Limpy Jim, so called from a slight peculiarity in his walk, when all at once he espied our friend Dick in his new suit.

"My eyes!" he exclaimed, in astonishment; "Jim, just look at Ragged Dick. He's come into a fortun', and turned gentleman. See his new clothes."

"So he has," said Jim. "Where'd he get 'em, I wonder?"

"Hooked' em, p'raps. Let's go and stir him up a little. We don't want no gentlemen on our beat. So he's puttin' on airs,—is he? I'll give him a lesson."

So saying the two boys walked up to our hero, who had not observed them, his back being turned, and Micky Maguire gave him a smart slap on the shoulder.

Dick turned round quickly.

CHAPTER XIV: A BATTLE AND A VICTORY

"What's that for?" demanded Dick, turning round to see who had struck him.

"You're gettin' mighty fine!" said Micky Maguire, surveying Dick's new clothes with a scornful air.

There was something in his words and tone, which Dick, who was disposed to stand up for his dignity, did not at all relish.

"Well, what's the odds if I am?" he retorted. "Does it hurt you any?"

"See him put on airs, Jim," said Micky, turning to his companion. "Where'd you get them clo'es?"

"Never mind where I got 'em. Maybe the Prince of Wales[1] gave 'em to me."

"Hear him, now, Jim," said Micky. "Most likely he stole 'em."

"Stealin' aint in *my* line."

It might have been unconscious the emphasis which Dick placed on the word "my." At any rate Micky chose to take offence.

"Do you mean to say *I* steal?" he demanded, doubling up his fist, and advancing towards Dick in a threatening manner.

"I don't say anything about it," answered Dick, by no means alarmed at this hostile demonstration. "I know you've been to the Island twice. P'r'aps 'twas to make a visit along of the Mayor and Aldermen. Maybe you was a innocent victim of oppression. I aint a goin' to say."

Micky's freckled face grew red with wrath, for Dick had only stated the truth.

"Do you mean to insult me?" he demanded shaking the fist already doubled up in Dick's face. "Maybe you want a lickin'?"

"I aint partic'larly anxious to get one," said Dick, coolly. "They don't agree with my constitution which is nat'rally delicate. I'd rather have a good dinner than a lickin' any time."

"You're afraid," sneered Micky. "Isn't he, Jim?"

"In course he is."

"P'r'aps I am," said Dick, composedly, "but it don't trouble me much."

"Do you want to fight?" demanded Micky, encouraged by Dick's quietness, fancying he was afraid to encounter him.

"No, I don't," said Dick. "I aint fond of fightin'. It's a very poor amusement, and very bad for the complexion, 'specially for the eyes and nose, which is apt to turn red, white, and blue."

Micky misunderstood Dick, and judged from the tenor of his speech that he would be an easy victim. As he knew, Dick very seldom was concerned in any street fight,—not from cowardice, as he imagined, but because he had too much good sense to do

---

1 The oldest son of Queen Victoria and Prince Albert, the future King Edward VII (r. 1901–10).

so. Being quarrelsome, like all bullies, and supposing that he was more than a match for our hero, being about two inches taller, he could no longer resist an inclination to assault him, and tried to plant a blow in Dick's face which would have hurt him considerably if he had not drawn back just in time.

Now, though Dick was far from quarrelsome, he was ready to defend himself on all occasions, and it was too much to expect that he would stand quiet and allow himself to be beaten.

He dropped his blacking-box on the instant, and returned Micky's blow with such good effect that the young bully staggered back, and would have fallen, if he had not been propped up by his confederate, Limpy Jim.

"Go in, Micky!" shouted the latter, who was rather a coward on his own account, but liked to see others fight. "Polish him off, that's a good feller."

Micky was now boiling over with rage and fury, and required no urging. He was fully determined to make a terrible example of poor Dick. He threw himself upon him, and strove to bear him to the ground; but Dick, avoiding a close hug, in which he might possibly have got the worst of it, by an adroit movement, tripped up his antagonist, and stretched him on the side walk.

"Hit him, Jim!" exclaimed Micky, furiously.

Limpy Jim did not seem inclined to obey orders. There was a quiet strength and coolness about Dick, which alarmed him. He preferred that Micky should incur all the risks of battle, and accordingly set himself to raising his fallen comrade.

"Come, Micky," said Dick, quietly, "you'd better give it up. I wouldn't have touched you if you hadn't hit me first. I don't want to fight. It's low business."

"You're afraid of hurtin' your clo'es," said Micky, with a sneer.

"Maybe I am," said Dick. "I hope I haven't hurt yours."

Micky's answer to this was another attack, as violent and impetuous as the first. But his fury was in the way. He struck wildly, not measuring his blows, and Dick had no difficulty in turning aside, so that his antagonist's blow fell upon the empty air, and his momentum was such that he nearly fell forward headlong. Dick might readily have taken advantage of his unsteadiness, and knocked him down; but he was not vindictive, and chose to act on the defensive, except when he could not avoid it.

Recovering himself, Micky saw that Dick was a more formidable antagonist than he had supposed, and was meditating another assault, better planned, which by its impetuosity might bear our hero to the ground. But there was an unlooked-for interference.

"Look out for the 'copp'," said Jim, in a low voice.

Micky turned round and saw a tall policeman heading towards him, and thought it might be prudent to suspend hostilities. He accordingly picked up his black-box, and, hitching up his pants, walked off, attended by Limpy Jim.

"What's that chap been doing?" asked the policeman of Dick.

"He was amoosin' himself by pitchin' into me," replied Dick.

"What for?"

"He didn't like it 'cause I patronized a different tailor from him."

"Well, it seems to me you *are* dressed pretty smart for a boot-black," said the policeman.

"I wish I wasn't a boot-black," said Dick.

"Never mind, my lad. It's an honest business," said the policeman, who was a sensible man and a worthy citizen. "It's an honest business. Stick to it till you get something better."

"I mean to," said Dick. "It aint easy to get out of it, as the prisoner remarked, when he was asked how he liked his residence."

"I hope you don't speak from experience."

"No," said Dick; "I don't mean to get into prison if I can help it."

"Do you see that gentleman over there?" asked the officer, pointing to a well-dressed man who was walking on the other side of the street.

"Yes."

"Well, he was once a newsboy."

"And what is he now?"

"He keeps a bookstore, and is quite prosperous."

Dick looked at the gentleman with interest, wondering if he should look as respectable when he was a grown man.

It will be seen that Dick was getting ambitious. Hitherto he had thought very little of the future, but was content to get along as he could, dining as well as his means would allow, and spending the evenings in the pit of the Old Bowery, eating peanuts between the acts if he was prosperous, and if unlucky supping on dry bread or an apple, and sleeping in an old box or a wagon. Now, for the first time, he began to reflect that he could not black boots all his life. In seven years he would be a man, and, since his meeting with Frank, he felt that he would like to be a respectable man. He could see and appreciate the difference between Frank and such a boy as Micky Maguire, and it was not strange that he preferred the society of the former.

In the course of the next morning, in pursuance of his new resolutions for the future, he called at a savings bank, and held out four dollars in bills besides another dollar in change. There was a high railing, and a number of clerks busily writing at desks behind it. Dick, never having been in a bank before, did not know where to go. He went, by mistake, to the desk where money was paid out.

"Where's your book?" asked the clerk.

"I haven't got any."

"Have you any money deposited here?"

"No, sir, I want to leave some here."

"Then go to the next desk."

Dick followed directions, and presented himself before an elderly man with gray hair, who looked at him over the rims of his spectacles.

"I want you to keep that for me," said Dick, awkwardly emptying his money out on the desk.

"How much is there?"

"Five dollars."

"Have you got an account here?"

"No, sir."

"Of course you can write?"

The "of course" was said on account of Dick's neat dress.

"Have I got to do any writing?" asked our hero, a little embarrassed.

"We want you to sign your name in this book," and the old gentleman shoved round a large folio volume containing the names of depositors.

Dick surveyed the book with some awe.

"I aint much on writin'," he said.

"Very well; write as well as you can."

The pen was put into Dick's hand, and, after dipping it in the inkstand, he succeeded after a hard effort, accompanied by many contortions of the face, in inscribing upon the book of the bank the name DICK HUNTER.

"Dick!—that means Richard, I suppose," said the bank officer, who had some difficulty in making out the signature.

"No; Ragged Dick is what folks call me."

"You don't look very ragged."

"No, I've left my rags to home. They might get wore out if I used 'em too common."

"Well, my lad, I'll make out a book in the name of Dick Hunter, since you seem to prefer Dick to Richard. I hope you will save up your money and deposit more with us."

Our hero took his bank-book, and gazed on the entry "Five Dollars" with a new sense of importance. He had been accustomed to joke about Erie shares, but now, for the first time, he felt himself a capitalist; on a small scale, to be sure, but still it was no small thing for Dick to have five dollars which he could call his own. He firmly determined that he would lay by every cent he could spare from his earnings towards the fund he hoped to accumulate.

But Dick was too sensible not to know that there was something more than money needed to win a respectable position in the world. He felt that he was very ignorant. Of reading and writing he only knew the rudiments, and that, with a slight acquaintance with arithmetic, was all he did know of books. Dick knew he must study hard, and he dreaded it. He looked upon learning as attended with greater difficulties than it really possesses. But Dick had good pluck. He meant to learn, nevertheless, and resolved to buy a book with his first spare earnings.

When Dick went home at night he locked up his bank-book in one of the drawers of the bureau. It was wonderful how much more independent he felt whenever he reflected upon the contents of that drawer, and with what an important air of joint ownership he regarded the bank building in which his small savings were deposited.

CHAPTER XV: DICK SECURES A TUTOR

The next morning Dick was unusually successful, having plenty to do, and receiving for one job twenty-five cents,—the gentleman refusing to take change. Then flashed upon Dick's mind the thought that he had not yet returned the change due to the gentleman whose boots he had blacked on the morning of his introduction to the reader.

"What'll he think of me?" said Dick to himself. "I hope he won't think I'm mean enough to keep the money."

Now Dick was scrupulously honest, and though the temptation to be otherwise had often been strong, he had always resisted it. He was not willing on any account to keep money which did not belong to him, and he immediately started for 125 Fulton Street (the address which had been given him) where he found Mr. Greyson's name on the door of an office on the first floor.

The door being open, Dick walked in.

"Is Mr. Greyson in?" he asked of a clerk who sat on a high stool before a desk.

"Not just now. He'll be in soon. Will you wait?"

"Yes," said Dick.

"Very well; take a seat then."

Dick sat down and took up the morning "Tribune," but presently came to a word of four syllables, which he pronounced to himself a "sticker," and laid it down. But he had not long to wait, for five minutes later Mr. Greyson entered.

"Did you wish to speak to me, my lad?" said he to Dick, whom in his new clothes he did not recognize.

"Yes, sir," said Dick. "I owe you some money."

"Indeed!" said Mr. Greyson, pleasantly; "that's an agreeable surprise. I didn't know but you had come for some. So you are a debtor of mine, and not a creditor?"

"I b'lieve that's right," said Dick, drawing fifteen cents from his pocket, and placing in Mr. Greyson's hand.

"Fifteen cents!" repeated he, in some surprise. "How do you happen to be indebted to me in that amount?"

"You gave me a quarter for a-shinin' your boots, yesterday mornin', and couldn't wait for the change. I meant to have brought it before, but I forgot all about it till this mornin'."

"It had quite slipped my mind also. But you don't look like the boy I employed. If I remember rightly he wasn't as well dressed as you."

"No," said Dick. "I was dressed for a party, then, but the clo'es was too well ventilated to be comfortable in cold weather."

"You're an honest boy," said Mr. Greyson. "Who taught you to be honest?"

"Nobody," said Dick. "But it's mean to cheat and steal. I've always knowed that."

"Then you've got ahead of some of our business men. Do you read the Bible?"

"No," said Dick. "I've heard it's a good book, but I don't know much about it."

"You ought to go to some Sunday School. Would you be willing?"

"Yes," said Dick, promptly. "I want to grow up 'spectable. But I don't know where to go."

"Then I'll tell you. The church I attend is at the corner of Fifth Avenue and Twenty-first Street."[1]

---

1 Apparently the South Dutch Reformed Church. See Todd Postol, "Where Ragged Dick Went to Church," *Newsboy* 26 (January–February 1988): 118–19.

"I've seen it," said Dick.

"I have a class in the Sunday School there. If you'll come next Sunday, I'll take you into my class, and do what I can to help you."

"Thank you," said Dick, "but p'r'aps you'll get tired of teaching me. I'm awful ignorant."

"No, my lad," said Mr. Greyson, kindly. "You evidently have some good principles to start with, as you have shown by your scorn of dishonesty. I shall hope good things of you in the future."

"Well, Dick," said our hero, apostrophizing himself, as he left the office; "you're gettin' up in the world. You've got money invested, and are goin' to attend church, by partic'lar invitation, on Fifth Avenue. I shouldn't wonder much if you should find cards, when you get home, from the Mayor, requestin' the honor of your company to dinner, along with other distinguished guests."

Dick felt in very good spirits. He seemed to be emerging from the world in which he had hitherto lived, into a new atmosphere of respectability, and the change seemed very pleasant to him.

At six o'clock Dick went into a restaurant on Chatham Street, and got a comfortable supper. He had been so successful during the day that, after paying for this, he still had ninety cents left. While he was despatching his supper, another boy came in, smaller and slighter than Dick, and sat down beside him. Dick recognized him as a boy who three months before had entered the ranks of the boot-blacks, but who, from a natural timidity, had not been able to earn much. He was ill-fitted for the coarse companionship of the street boys, and shrank from the rude jokes of his present associates. Dick had never troubled him; for our hero had a certain chivalrous feeling which would not allow him to bully or disturb a younger and weaker boy than himself.

"How are you, Fosdick?" said Dick, as the other seated himself.

"Pretty well," said Fosdick. "I suppose you're all right."

"Oh, yes, I'm right side up with care. I've been havin' a bully supper. What are you goin' to have?"

"Some bread and butter."

"Why don't you get a cup o' coffee?"

"Why," said Fosdick, reluctantly, "I haven't got money enough to-night."

"Never mind," said Dick; "I'm in luck to-day, I'll stand treat."

"That's kind in you," said Fosdick, gratefully.

"Oh, never mind that," said Dick.

Accordingly he ordered a cup of coffee, and a plate of beef-steak, and was gratified to see that his young companion partook of both with evident relish. When the repast was over, the boys went out into the street together, Dick pausing at the desk to settle for both suppers.

"Where are you going to sleep to-night, Fosdick?" asked Dick, as they stood on the sidewalk.

"I don't know," said Fosdick, a little sadly. "In some doorway, I expect. But I'm afraid the police will find me out, and make me move on."

"I'll tell you what," said Dick, "you must go home with me. I guess my bed will hold two."

"Have you got a room?" asked the other, in surprise.

"Yes," said Dick, rather proudly, and with a little excusable exultation. "I've got a room over in Mott Street; there I can receive my friends. That'll be better than sleepin' in a door-way,—won't it?"

"Yes, indeed it will," said Fosdick. "How lucky I was to come across you! It comes hard to me living as I do. When my father was alive I had every comfort."

"That's more'n I ever had," said Dick. "But I'm goin' to try to live comfortable now. Is your father dead?"

"Yes," said Fosdick, sadly. "He was a printer; but he was drowned one dark night from a Fulton ferry-boat, and, as I had no relations in the city, and no money, I was obliged to go to work as quick as I could. But I don't get on very well."

"Didn't you have no brothers nor sisters?" asked Dick.

"No," said Fosdick; "father and I used to live alone. He was always so much company to me that I feel very lonesome without him. There's a man out West somewhere that owes him two thousand dollars. He used to live in the city, and father lent him all his money to help him go into business; but he failed, or pretended to, and went off. If father hadn't lost that money he would have left me well off; but no money would have made up his loss to me."

"What's the man's name that went off with your father's money?"

"His name is Hiram Bates."

"P'r'aps you'll get the money again, sometime."

"There isn't much chance of it," said Fosdick. "I'd sell out my chances of that for five dollars."

"Maybe I'll buy you out sometime," said Dick. "Now, come round and see what sort of a room I've got. I used to go to the theatre evenings, when I had money; but now I'd rather go to bed early, and have a good sleep."

"I don't care much about theatres," said Fosdick. "Father didn't use to let me go very often. He said it wasn't good for boys."

"I like to go to the Old Bowery sometimes. They have tip-top plays there. Can you read and write well?" he asked, as a sudden thought came to him.

"Yes," said Fosdick. "Father always kept me at school when he was alive, and I stood pretty well in my classes. I was expecting to enter at the Free Academy[1] next year."

"Then I'll tell you what," said Dick; "I'll make a bargain with you. I can't read much more'n a pig; and my writin' looks like hens' tracks. I don't want to grow up knowin' no more'n a four-year-old boy. If you'll teach me readin' and writin' evenin's, you shall sleep in my room every night. That'll be better'n door-steps or old boxes, where I've slept many a time."

"Are you in earnest?" said Fosdick, his face lighting up hopefully.

"In course I am," said Dick. "It's fashionable for young gentlemen to have private tootors to introduce 'em into the flower-beds of literatoor and science, and why shouldn't I foller the fashion? You shall be my perfessor; only you must promise not to be very hard if my writin' looks like a rail-fence on a bender."

"I'll try not to be too severe," said Fosdick, laughing. "I shall be thankful for such a chance to get a place to sleep. Have you got anything to read out of?"

"No," said Dick. "My extensive and well-selected library was lost overboard in a storm, when I was sailin' from the Sandwich Islands to the desert of Sahara. But I'll buy a paper. That'll do me a long time."

Accordingly Dick stopped at a paper-stand, and bought a copy of a weekly paper, filled with the usual variety of reading matter,—stories, sketches, poems, etc.

They soon arrived at Dick's lodging-house. Our hero, procuring a lamp from the landlady, led the way into his apartment, which he entered with the proud air of a proprietor.

"Well, how do you like it, Fosdick?" he asked, complacently.

---

1 [Alger's note:] Now the college of the city of New York.

The time was when Fosdick would have thought it untidy and not particularly attractive. But he had served a severe apprenticeship in the streets, and it was pleasant to feel himself under shelter, and he was not disposed to be critical.

"It looks very comfortable, Dick," he said.

"The bed aint very large," said Dick; "but I guess we can get along."

"Oh, yes," said Fosdick, cheerfully. "I don't take up much room."

"Then that's all right. There's two chairs, you see, one for you and one for me. In case the mayor comes in to spend the evenin' socially, he can sit on the bed."

The boys seated themselves, and five minutes later, under the guidance of his young tutor, Dick had commenced his studies.

CHAPTER XVI: THE FIRST LESSON

Fortunately for Dick, his young tutor was well qualified to instruct him. Henry Fosdick, though only twelve years old, knew as much as many boys of fourteen. He had always been studious and ambitious to excel. His father, being a printer, employed in an office where books were printed, often brought home new books in sheets, which Henry was always glad to read. Mr. Fosdick had been, besides, a subscriber to the Mechanics' Apprentices' Library,[1] which contains many thousands of well-selected and instructive books. Thus Henry had acquired an amount of general information, unusual in a boy of his age. Perhaps he had devoted too much time to study, for he was not naturally robust. All this, however, fitted him admirably for the office to which Dick had appointed him,—that of his private instructor.

The two boys drew up their chairs to the rickety table, and spread out the paper before them.

---

1 Located in Mechanics' Hall at 32 Crosby Street, the Mechanics' Apprentices' Library, or the Library of the General Society of Mechanics and Tradesmen of the City of New York, was the largest and second-oldest circulating library in the city. Mark Twain (1835–1910) frequented the library while working as a journeyman printer in New York in 1853 (*Mark Twain's Letters*, ed. Edgar Marquess Branch et al. [Berkeley: U of California P, 1988], vol. I: 10, 12). See also Tom Glynn, "Books for a Reformed Republic: The Apprentices' Library of New York City, 1820–1865," *Libraries and Culture* 34 (Fall 1999): 347–72.

"The exercises generally commence with ringin' the bell," said Dick; "but as I aint got none, we'll have to do without."

"And the teacher is generally provided with a rod," said Fosdick. "Isn't there a poker handy, that I can use in case my scholar doesn't behave well?"

"'Taint lawful to use fire-arms," said Dick.

"Now, Dick," said Fosdick, "before we begin, I must find out how much you already know. Can you read any?"

"Not enough to hurt me," said Dick. "All I know about readin' you could put in a nutshell, and there'd be room left for a small family."

"I suppose you know your letters?"

"Yes," said Dick, "I know 'em all, but not intimately. I guess I can call 'em all by name."

"Where did you learn them? Did you ever go to school?"

"Yes; I went two days."

"Why did you stop?"

"It didn't agree with my constitution."

"You don't look very delicate," said Fosdick.

"No," said Dick, "I aint troubled much that way; but I found lickins didn't agree with me."

"Did you get punished?"

"Awful," said Dick.

"What for?"

"For indulgin' in a little harmless amoosement," said Dick. "You see the boy that was sittin' next to me fell asleep, which I considered improper in school-time; so I thought I'd help the teacher a little by wakin' him up. So I took a pin and stuck into him; but I guess it went a little too far, for he screeched awful. The teacher found out what it was that made him holler, and whipped me with a ruler till I was black and blue. I thought 'twas about time to take a vacation; so that's the last time I went to school."

"You didn't learn to read in that time, of course?"

"No," said Dick; "but I was a newsboy a little while; so I learned a little, just so's to find out what the news was. Sometimes I didn't read straight and called the wrong news. One mornin' I asked another boy what the paper said, and he told me the King of Africa was dead. I thought it was all right till folks began to laugh."

"Well, Dick, if you'll only study well, you won't be liable to make such mistakes."

"I hope so," said Dick. "My friend Horace Greeley told me the other day that he'd get me to take his place now and then when he was off makin' speeches if my edication hadn't been neglected."

"I must find a good piece for you to begin on," said Fosdick, looking over the paper.

"Find an easy one," said Dick, "with words of one story."

Fosdick at length found a piece which he thought would answer. He discovered on trial that Dick had not exaggerated his deficiencies. Words of two syllables he seldom pronounced right, and was much surprised when he was told how "through" was sounded.

"Seems to me it's throwin' away letters to use all them," he said.

"How would you spell it?" asked his young teacher.

"T-h-r-u," said Dick.

"Well," said Fosdick, "there's a good many other words that are spelt with more letters than they need to have. But it's the fashion, and we must follow it."

But if Dick was ignorant, he was quick, and had an excellent capacity. Moreover he had perseverance, and was not easily discouraged. He had made up his mind he must know more, and was not disposed to complain of the difficulty of his task. Fosdick had occasion to laugh more than once at his ludicrous mistakes; but Dick laughed too, and on the whole both were quite interested in the lesson.

At the end of an hour and a half the boys stopped for the evening.

"You're learning fast, Dick," said Fosdick. "At this rate you will soon learn to read well."

"Will I?" asked Dick with an expression of satisfaction. "I'm glad of that. I don't want to be ignorant. I didn't use to care, but I do now. I want to grow up 'spectable."

"So do I, Dick. We will both help each other, and I am sure we can accomplish something. But I am beginning to feel sleepy."

"So am I," said Dick. "Them hard words make my head ache. I wonder who made 'em all?"

"That's more than I can tell. I suppose you've seen a dictionary."

"That's another of 'em. No, I can't say I have, though I may have seen him in the street without knowin' him."

"A dictionary is a book containing all the words in the language."

"How many are there?"

"I don't rightly know; but I think there are about fifty thousand."

"It's a pretty large family," said Dick. "Have I got to learn 'em all?"

"That will not be necessary. There are a large number which you would never find occasion to use."

"I'm glad of that," said Dick; "for I don't expect to live to be more'n a hundred, and by that time I wouldn't be more'n half through."

By this time the flickering lamp gave a decided hint to the boys that unless they made haste they would have to undress in the dark. They accordingly drew off their clothes, and Dick jumped into bed. But Fosdick, before doing so, knelt down by the side of the bed, and said a short prayer.

"What's that for?" asked Dick, curiously.

"I was saying my prayers," said Fosdick, as he rose from his knees. "Don't you ever do it?"

"No," said Dick. "Nobody ever taught me."

"Then I'll teach you. Shall I?"

"I don't know," said Dick, dubiously. "What's the good?"

Fosdick explained as well as he could, and perhaps his simple explanation was better adapted to Dick's comprehension than one from an older person would have been. Dick felt more free to ask questions, and the example of his new friend, for whom he was beginning to feel a warm attachment, had considerable effect upon him. When, therefore, Fosdick asked again if he should teach him a prayer, Dick consented, and his young bedfellow did so. Dick was not naturally irreligious. If he had lived without a knowledge of God and of religious things, it was scarcely to be wondered at in a lad who, from an early age, had been thrown upon his own exertions for the means of living, with no one to care for him or give him good advice. But he was so far good that he could appreciate goodness in others, and this it was that had drawn him to Frank in the first place, and now to Henry Fosdick. He did not, therefore, attempt to ridicule his companion, as some boys better brought up might have done, but was willing to follow his example in what something told him was right. Our young hero had taken an important step toward securing that genuine respectability which he was ambitious to attain.

Weary with the day's work, and Dick perhaps still more fatigued by the unusual mental effort he had made, the boys soon sank into a deep and peaceful slumber, from which they did not awaken till six o'clock the next morning. Before going out Dick sought Mrs. Mooney, and spoke to her on the subject of taking Fosdick as a room-mate. He found that she had no objection, provided he would allow her twenty-five cents a week extra, in consideration of the extra trouble which his companion might be expected to make. To this Dick assented, and the arrangement was definitely concluded.

This over, the two boys went out and took stations near each other. Dick had more of a business turn than Henry, and less shrinking from publicity, so that his earnings were greater. But he had undertaken to pay the entire expenses of the room, and needed to earn more. Sometimes, when two customers presented themselves at the same time, he was able to direct one to his friend. So at the end of the week both boys found themselves with surplus earnings. Dick had the satisfaction of adding two dollars and a half to his deposits in the Savings Bank, and Fosdick commenced an account by depositing seventy-five cents.

On Sunday morning Dick bethought himself of his promise to Mr. Greyson to come to the church on Fifth Avenue. To tell the truth, Dick recalled it with some regret. He had never been inside a church since he could remember, and he was not much attracted by the invitation he had received. But Henry, finding him wavering, urged him to go, and offered to go with him. Dick gladly accepted the offer, feeling that he required someone to lend him countenance under such unusual circumstances.

Dick dressed himself with scrupulous care, giving his shoes a "shine" so brilliant that it did him great credit in a professional point of view, and endeavored to clean his hands thoroughly; but, in spite of all he could do, they were not so white as if his business had been of a different character.

Having fully completed his preparations, he descended into the street, and, with Henry by his side, crossed over to Broadway.

The boys pursued their way up Broadway, which on Sunday presents a striking contrast in its quietness to the noise and confusion of ordinary week-days, as far as Union Square, then turned down Fourteenth Street, which brought them to Fifth Avenue.

"Suppose we dine at Delmonico's," said Fosdick, looking towards that famous restaurant.

"I'd have to sell some of my Erie shares," said Dick.

A short walk now brought them to the church of which mention has already been made. They stood outside, a little abashed, watching the fashionably attired people who were entering, and were feeling a little undecided as to whether they had better enter also, when Dick felt a light touch upon his shoulder.

Turning round, he met the smiling glance of Mr. Greyson.

"So, my young friend, you have kept your promise," he said. "And whom have you brought with you?"

"A friend of mine," said Dick. "His name is Henry Fosdick."

"I am glad you have brought him. Now follow me, and I will give you seats."

CHAPTER XVII: DICK'S FIRST APPEARANCE IN SOCIETY

It was the hour for morning service. The boys followed Mr. Greyson into the handsome church, and were assigned seats in his own pew.

There were two persons already seated in it,—a good-looking lady of middle age, and a pretty little girl of nine. They were Mrs. Greyson and her only daughter Ida. They looked pleasantly at the boys as they entered, smiling a welcome to them.

The morning service commenced. It must be acknowledged that Dick felt rather awkward. It was an unusual place for him, and it need not be wondered at that he felt like a cat in a strange garret. He would not have known when to rise if he had not taken notice of what the rest of the audience did, and followed their example. He was sitting next to Ida, and as it was the first time he had ever been near so well-dressed a young lady, he naturally felt bashful. When the hymns were announced, Ida found the place, and offered a hymn-book to our hero. Dick took it awkwardly, but his studies had not yet been pursued far enough for him to read the words readily. However, he resolved to keep up appearances, and kept his eyes fixed steadily on the hymn-book.

At length the service was over. The people began to file slowly out of church, and among them, of course, Mr. Greyson's family and the two boys. It seemed very strange to Dick to find himself in such different companionship from what he had been accustomed, and he could not help thinking, "Wonder what Johnny Nolan 'ould say if he could see me now!"

But Johnny's business engagements did not often summon him to Fifth Avenue, and Dick was not likely to be seen by any of his friends in the lower part of the city.

"We have our Sunday school in the afternoon," said Mr. Greyson. "I suppose you live at some distance from here?"

"In Mott Street, sir," answered Dick.

"That is too far to go and return. Suppose you and your friend come and dine with us, and then we can come here together in the afternoon."

Dick was as much astonished at this invitation as if he had really been invited by the Mayor to dine with him and the Board of Aldermen. Mr. Greyson was evidently a rich man, and yet he had actually invited two boot-blacks to dine with him.

"I guess we'd better go home, sir," said Dick, hesitating.

"I don't think you can have any very pressing engagements to interfere with your accepting my invitation," said Mr. Greyson, good-humoredly, for he understood the reason of Dick's hesitation. "So I take it for granted that you both accept."

Before Dick fairly knew what he intended to do, he was walking down Fifth Avenue with his new friends.

Now, our young hero was not naturally bashful; but he certainly felt so now, especially as Miss Ida Greyson chose to walk by his side, leaving Henry Fosdick to walk with her father and mother.

"What is your name?" asked Ida, pleasantly.

Our hero was about to answer "Ragged Dick," when it occurred to him that in the present company he had better forget his old nickname.

"Dick Hunter," he answered.

"Dick!" repeated Ida. "That means Richard, doesn't it?"

"Everybody calls me Dick."

"I have a cousin Dick," said the young lady, sociably. "His name is Dick Wilson. I suppose you don't know him?"

"No," said Dick.

"I like the name of Dick," said the young lady, with charming frankness.

Without being able to tell why, Dick felt rather glad she did. He plucked up courage to ask her name.

"My name is Ida," answered the young lady. "Do you like it?"

"Yes," said Dick. "It's a bully name."

Dick turned red as soon as he had said it, for he felt that he had not used the right expression.

The little girl broke into a silvery laugh.

"What a funny boy you are!" she said.

"I didn't mean it," said Dick, stammering. "I meant it's a tip-top name."

Here Ida laughed again, and Dick wished himself back in Mott Street.

"How old are you?" inquired Ida, continuing her examination.

"I'm fourteen,—goin' on fifteen," said Dick.

"You're a big boy of your age," said Ida. "My cousin Dick is a year older than you, but he isn't as large."

Dick looked pleased. Boys generally like to be told that they are large of their age.

"How old be you?" asked Dick, beginning to feel more at his ease.

"I'm nine years old," said Ida. "I go to Miss Jarvis's school. I've just begun to learn French. Do you know French?"

"Not enough to hurt me," said Dick.

Ida laughed again, and told him that he was a droll boy.

"Do you like it?" asked Dick.

"I like it pretty well, except the verbs. I can't remember them well. Do you go to school?"

"I'm studying with a private tutor," said Dick.

"Are you? So is my cousin Dick. He's going to college this year. Are you going to college?"

"Not this year."

"Because, if you did, you know you'd be in the same class with my cousin. It would be funny to have two Dicks in one class."

They turned down Twenty-fourth Street, passing the Fifth Avenue Hotel on the left, and stopped before an elegant house with a brown stone front. The bell was rung, and the door being opened, the boys, somewhat abashed, followed Mr. Greyson into a handsome hall. They were told where to hang their hats, and a moment afterwards were ushered into a comfortable dining-room, where a table was spread for dinner.

Dick took his seat on the edge of a sofa, and was tempted to rub his eyes to make sure that he was really awake. He could hardly believe that he was a guest in so fine a mansion.

Ida helped to put the boys at their ease.

"Do you like pictures?" she asked.

"Very much," answered Henry.

The little girl brought a book of handsome engravings, and, seating herself beside Dick, to whom she seemed to have taken a decided fancy, commenced showing them to him.

"There are the Pyramids of Egypt," she said, pointing to one engraving.

"What are they for?" asked Dick, puzzled. "I don't see any winders."

"No," said Ida, "I don't believe anybody lives there. Do they, papa?"

"No, my dear. They were used for the burial of the dead. The largest of them is said to be the loftiest building in the world with one exception. The spire of the Cathedral of Strasbourg[1] is twenty-four feet higher, if I remember rightly."

"Is Egypt near here?" asked Dick.

"Oh, no, it's ever so many miles off; about four or five hundred. Didn't you know?"

"No," said Dick. "I never heard."

"You don't appear to be very accurate in your information, Ida," said her mother. "Four or five thousand miles would be considerably nearer the truth."

After a little more conversation they sat down to dinner. Dick seated himself in an embarrassed way. He was very much afraid of doing or saying something which would be considered an impropriety, and had the uncomfortable feeling that everybody was looking at him, and watching his behavior.

"Where do you live, Dick?" asked Ida, familiarly.

"In Mott Street."

"Where is that?"

"More than a mile off."

"Is it a nice street?"

"Not very," said Dick. "Only poor folks live there."

"Are you poor?"

"Little girls should be seen and not heard," said her mother, gently.

"If you are," said Ida, "I'll give you the five-dollar gold-piece aunt gave me for a birthday present."

"Dick cannot be called poor, my child," said Mrs. Greyson, "since he earns his living by his own exertions."

"Do you earn your living?" asked Ida, who was a very inquisitive young lady, and not easily silenced. "What do you do?"

Dick blushed violently. At such a table, and in presence of the servant who was standing at that moment behind his chair, he did not like to say that he was a shoe-black, although he well knew that there was nothing dishonorable in the occupation.

Mr. Greyson perceived his feelings, and to spare them, said, "You are too inquisitive, Ida. Sometime Dick may tell you, but you know we don't talk of business on Sundays."

Dick in his embarrassment had swallowed a large spoonful of hot soup, which made him turn red in the face. For the second time, in spite of the prospect of the best dinner he had ever eaten, he wished himself back in Mott Street. Henry Fosdick was more

---

1 At 472 feet, the Cathedral of Strasbourg in Alsace was the tallest building in the world from 1647 until 1874.

easy and unembarrassed than Dick, not having led such a vagabond and neglected life. But it was to Dick that Ida chiefly directed her conversation, having apparently taken a fancy to his frank and handsome face. I believe I have already said that Dick was a very good-looking boy, especially now since he kept his face clean. He had a frank, honest expression, which generally won its way to the favor of those with whom he came in contact.

Dick got along pretty well at the table by dint of noticing how the rest acted, but there was one thing he could not manage, eating with his fork, which, by the way, he thought a very singular arrangement.

At length they arose from the table, somewhat to Dick's relief. Again Ida devoted herself to the boys, and exhibited a profusely illustrated Bible for their entertainment. Dick was interested in looking at the pictures, though he knew very little of their subjects. Henry Fosdick was much better informed, as might have been expected.

When the boys were about to leave the house with Mr. Greyson for the Sunday school, Ida placed her hand in Dick's, and said persuasively, "You'll come again, Dick, won't you?"

"Thank you," said Dick, "I'd like to," and he could not help thinking Ida the nicest girl he had ever seen.

"Yes," said Mrs. Greyson, hospitably, "we shall be glad to see you both here again."

"Thank you very much," said Henry Fosdick, gratefully. "We shall like very much to come."

I will not dwell upon the hour spent in Sunday school, nor upon the remarks of Mr. Greyson to his class. He found Dick's ignorance of religious subjects so great that he was obliged to begin at the beginning with him. Dick was interested in hearing the children sing, and readily promised to come again the next Sunday.

When the service was over Dick and Henry walked homewards. Dick could not help letting his thoughts rest on the sweet little girl who had given him so cordial a welcome, and hoping that he might meet her again.

"Mr. Greyson is a nice man,—isn't he, Dick?" asked Henry, as they were turning into Mott Street, and were already in sight of their lodging-house.

"Aint he, though?" said Dick. "He treated us just as if we were young gentlemen."

"Ida seemed to take a great fancy to you."

"She's a tip-top girl," said Dick, "but she asked so many questions that I didn't know what to say."

He had scarcely finished speaking, when a stone whizzed by his head, and, turning quickly, he saw Micky Maguire running round the corner of the street which they had just passed.

CHAPTER XVIII: MICKY MAGUIRE'S SECOND DEFEAT

Dick was no coward. Nor was he in the habit of submitting passively to an insult. When, therefore, he recognized Micky as his assailant, he instantly turned and gave chase. Micky anticipated pursuit, and ran at his utmost speed. It is doubtful if Dick would have overtaken him, but Micky had the ill luck to trip just as he had entered a narrow alley, and, falling with some violence, received a sharp blow from the hard stones, which made him scream with pain.

"Ow!" he whined. "Don't you hit a feller when he's down."

"What made you fire that stone at me?" demanded our hero, looking down at the fallen bully.

"Just for fun," said Micky.

"It would have been a very agreeable s'prise if it had hit me," said Dick. "S'posin' I fire a rock at you jest for fun."

"Don't!" exclaimed Micky, in alarm.

"It seems you don't like agreeable s'prises," said Dick, "any more'n the man did what got hooked by a cow one mornin', before breakfast. It didn't improve his appetite much."

"I've most broke my arm," said Micky, ruefully, rubbing the affected limb.

"If it's broke you can't fire no more stones, which is a very cheerin' reflection," said Dick. "Ef you haven't money enough to buy a wooden one I'll lend you a quarter. There's one good thing about wooden ones, they aint liable to get cold in winter, which is another cheerin' reflection."

"I don't want none of yer cheerin' reflections," said Micky, sullenly. "Yer company aint wanted here."

"Thank you for your polite invitation to leave," said Dick, bowing ceremoniously. "I'm willin' to go, but ef you throw any more stones at me, Micky Maguire, I'll hurt you worse than the stones did."

The only answer made to this warning was a scowl from his fallen opponent. It was quite evident that Dick had the best of it, and he thought it prudent to say nothing.

"As I've got a friend waitin' outside, I shall have to tear myself away," said Dick. "You'd better not throw any more stones, Micky Maguire, for it don't seem to agree with your constitution."

Micky muttered something which Dick did not stay to hear. He backed out of the alley, keeping a watchful eye on his fallen foe, and rejoined Henry Fosdick, who was awaiting his return.

"Who was it, Dick?" he asked.

"A partic'lar friend of mine, Micky Maguire," said Dick. "He playfully fired a rock at my head as a mark of his 'fection. He loves me like a brother, Micky does."

"Rather a dangerous kind of a friend, I should think," said Fosdick. "He might have killed you."

"I've warned him not to be so 'fectionate another time," said Dick.

"I know him," said Henry Fosdick. "He's at the head of a gang of boys living at the Five-Points. He threatened to whip me once because a gentleman employed me to black his boots instead of him."

"He's been at the Island two or three times for stealing," said Dick. "I guess he won't touch me again. He'd rather get hold of small boys. If he ever does anything to you, Fosdick, just let me know, and I'll give him a thrashing."

Dick was right. Micky Maguire was a bully, and like most bullies did not fancy tackling boys whose strength was equal or superior to his own. Although he hated Dick more than ever, because he thought our hero was putting on airs, he had too lively a remembrance of his strength and courage to venture upon another open attack. He contented himself, therefore, whenever he met Dick, with scowling at him. Dick took this very philosophically, remarking that, "if it was soothin' to Micky's feelings, he might go ahead, as it didn't hurt him much."

It will not be necessary to chronicle the events of the next few weeks. A new life had commenced for Dick. He no longer haunted the gallery of the Old Bowery; and even Tony Pastor's hospitable doors had lost their old attractions. He spent two hours every evening in study. His progress was astonishingly rapid. He was gifted with a natural quickness; and he was stimulated by the desire to acquire a fair education as a means of "growin' up 'spectable," as he termed it. Much was due also to the patience and perseverance of Henry Fosdick, who made a capital teacher.

"You're improving wonderfully, Dick," said his friend, one evening, when Dick had read an entire paragraph without a mistake.

"Am I?" said Dick, with satisfaction.

"Yes. If you'll buy a writing-book to-morrow, we can begin writing to-morrow evening."

"What else do you know, Henry?" asked Dick.

"Arithmetic, and geography, and grammar."

"What a lot you know!" said Dick, admiringly.

"I don't *know* any of them," said Fosdick. "I've only studied them. I wish I knew a great deal more."

"I'll be satisfied when I know as much as you," said Dick.

"It seems a great deal to you now, Dick, but in a few months you'll think differently. The more you know, the more you'll want to know."

"Then there aint any end to learnin'?" said Dick.

"No."

"Well," said Dick, "I guess I'll be as much as sixty before I know everything."

"Yes; as old as that, probably," said Fosdick, laughing.

"Anyway, you know too much to be blackin' boots. Leave that to ignorant chaps like me."

"You won't be ignorant long, Dick."

"You'd ought to get into some office or countin'-room."

"I wish I could," said Fosdick, earnestly. "I don't succeed very well at blacking boots. You make a great deal more than I do."

"That's cause I aint troubled with bashfulness," said Dick. "Bashfulness aint as natural to me as it is to you. I'm always on hand, as the cat said to the milk. You'd better give up shines, Fosdick, and give your 'tention to mercantile pursuits."

"I've thought of trying to get a place," said Fosdick; "but no one would take me with these clothes"; and he directed his glance to his well-worn suit, which he kept as neat as he could, but which, in spite of all his care, began to show decided marks of use. There was also here and there a stain of blacking upon it, which, though an advertisement of his profession, scarcely added to its good appearance.

"I almost wanted to stay at home from Sunday school last Sunday," he continued, "because I thought everybody would notice how dirty and worn my clothes had got to be."

"If my clothes wasn't two sizes too big for you," said Dick, generously, "I'd change. You'd look as if you'd got into your great-uncle's suit by mistake."

"You're very kind, Dick, to think of changing," said Fosdick, "for your suit is much better than mine; but I don't think that mine would suit you very well. The pants would show a little more of your ankles than is the fashion, and you couldn't eat a very hearty dinner without bursting the buttons off the vest."

"That wouldn't be very convenient," said Dick. "I aint fond of lacin' to show my elegant figger. But I say," he added with a sudden thought, "how much money have we got in the savings' bank?"

Fosdick took a key from his pocket, and went to the drawer in which the bank-books were kept, and, opening it, brought them out for inspection.

It was found that Dick had the sum of eighteen dollars and ninety cents placed to his credit, while Fosdick had six dollars and forty-five cents. To explain the large difference, it must be remembered that Dick had deposited five dollars before Henry deposited anything, being the amount he had received as a gift from Mr. Whitney.

"How much does that make, the lot of it?" asked Dick. "I aint much on figgers yet, you know."

"It makes twenty-five dollars and thirty-five cents, Dick," said his companion, who did not understand the thought which suggested the question.

"Take it, and buy some clothes, Henry," said Dick, shortly.

"What, your money too?"

"In course."

"No, Dick, you are too generous. I couldn't think of it. Almost three-quarters of the money is yours. You must spend it on yourself."

"I don't need it," said Dick.

"You may not need it now, but you will some time."

"I shall have some more then."

"That may be; but it wouldn't be fair for me to use your money, Dick. I thank you all the same for your kindness."

"Well, I'll lend it to you, then," persisted Dick, "and you can pay me when you get to be a rich merchant."

"But it isn't likely I ever shall be one."

"How d'you know? I went to a fortun' teller once, and she told me I was born under a lucky star with a hard name, and I should have a rich man for my particular friend, who would make my fortun'. I guess you are going to be the rich man."

Fosdick laughed, and steadily refused for some time to avail himself of Dick's generous proposal; but at length, perceiving that our hero seemed much disappointed, and would be really glad if his offer were accepted, he agreed to use as much as might be needful.

This at once brought back Dick's good-humor, and he entered with great enthusiasm into his friend's plans.

The next day they withdrew the money from the bank, and, when business got a little slack, in the afternoon set out in search of a clothing store. Dick knew enough of the city to be able to find a place where a good bargain could be obtained. He was determined that Fosdick should have a good serviceable suit, even if it took all the money they had. The result of their search was that for twenty-three dollars Fosdick obtained a very neat outfit, including a couple of shirts, a hat, and a pair of shoes, besides a dark mixed suit, which appeared stout and of good quality.

"Shall I send the bundle home?" asked the salesman, impressed by the off-hand manner in which Dick drew out the money in payment for the clothes.

"Thank you," said Dick, "you're very kind, but I'll take it home myself, and you can allow me something for my trouble."

"All right," said the clerk, laughing; "I'll allow it on your next purchase."

Proceeding to their apartment in Mott Street, Fosdick at once tried on his new suit, and it was found to be an excellent fit. Dick surveyed his new friend with much satisfaction.

"You look like a young gentleman of fortun'," he said, "and do credit to your governor."

"I suppose that means you, Dick," said Fosdick, laughing.

"In course it does."

"You should say *of* course," said Fosdick, who, in virtue of his position as Dick's tutor, ventured to correct his language from time to time.

"How dare you correct your gov'nor?" said Dick, with comic indignation. "'I'll cut you off with a shillin', you young dog,' as the Markis says to his nephew in the play at the Old Bowery."[1]

CHAPTER XIX: FOSDICK CHANGES HIS BUSINESS

Fosdick did not venture to wear his new clothes while engaged in his business. This he felt would have been wasteful extravagance. About ten o'clock in the morning, when business slackened, he went home, and dressing himself went to a hotel where he could see copies of the "Morning Herald" and "Sun," and, noting down the places where a boy was wanted, went on a round of applica-

---

1 In this bit of invented dialogue, the Marquis threatens to disinherit his nephew.

tions. But he found it no easy thing to obtain a place. Swarms of boys seemed to be out of employment, and it was not unusual to find from fifty to a hundred applicants for a single place.

There was another difficulty. It was generally desired that the boy wanted should reside with his parents. When Fosdick, on being questioned, revealed the fact of his having no parents, and being a boy of the street, this was generally sufficient of itself to insure a refusal. Merchants were afraid to trust one who had led such a vagabond life. Dick, who was always ready for an emergency, suggested borrowing a white wig, and passing himself off for Fosdick's father or grandfather. But Henry thought this might be rather a difficult character for our hero to sustain. After fifty applications and as many failures, Fosdick began to get discouraged. There seemed to be no way out of his present business, for which he felt unfitted.

"I don't know but I shall have to black boots all my life," he said, one day, despondently, to Dick.

"Keep a stiff upper lip," said Dick. "By the time you get to be a gray-headed veteran, you may get a chance to run errands for some big firm on the Bowery, which is a very cheerin' reflection."

So Dick by his drollery and perpetual good spirits kept up Fosdick's courage.

"As for me," said Dick, "I expect by that time to lay up a colossal fortun' out of shines, and live in princely style on the Avenoo."

But one morning, Fosdick, straying into French's Hotel,[1] discovered the following advertisement in the columns of "The Herald,"—

> "WANTED—A smart, capable boy to run errands, and make himself generally useful in a hat and cap store. Salary three dollars a week at first. Inquire at No. — Broadway, after ten o'clock, A.M."

He determined to make application, and, as the City Hall clock just then struck the hour indicated, lost no time in proceeding to the store, which was only a few blocks distant from the Astor House. It was easy to find the store, as from a dozen to twenty boys were already assembled in front of it. They surveyed

---

1   The seven-story luxury French's Hotel, located at the corner of Chatham and Frankfort Streets in the neighborhood of City Hall, opened in 1849.

each other askance, feeling that they were rivals, and mentally calculating each other's chances.

"There isn't much chance for me," said Fosdick to Dick, who had accompanied him. "Look at all these boys. Most of them have good homes, I suppose, and good recommendations, while I have nobody to refer to."

"Go ahead," said Dick. "Your chance is as good as anybody's."

While this was passing between Dick and his companion, one of the boys, a rather supercilious-looking young gentleman, genteelly dressed, and evidently having a very high opinion of his dress and himself turned suddenly to Dick, and remarked,—

"I've seen you before."

"Oh, have you?" said Dick, whirling round; "then p'r'aps you'd like to see me behind."

At this unexpected answer all the boys burst into a laugh with the exception of the questioner, who, evidently, considered that Dick had been disrespectful.

"I've seen you somewhere," he said, in a surly tone, correcting himself.

"Most likely you have," said Dick. "That's where I generally keep myself."

There was another laugh at the expense of Roswell Crawford, for that was the name of the young aristocrat. But he had his revenge ready. No boy relishes being an object of ridicule, and it was with a feeling of satisfaction that he retorted,—

"I know you for all your impudence. You're nothing but a boot-black."

This information took the boys who were standing around by surprise, for Dick was well-dressed, and had none of the implements of his profession with him.

"S'pose I be," said Dick. "Have you got any objection?"

"Not at all," said Roswell, curling his lip; "only you'd better stick to blacking boots, and not try to get into a store."

"Thank you for your kind advice," said Dick. "Is it gratooitous, or do you expect to be paid for it?"

"You're an impudent fellow."

"That's a very cheerin' reflection," said Dick, good-naturedly.

"Do you expect to get this place when there's gentlemen's sons applying for it? A boot-black in a store! That would be a good joke."

Boys as well as men are selfish, and, looking upon Dick as a possible rival, the boys who listened seemed disposed to take the same view of the situation.

"That's what I say," said one of them, taking sides with Roswell.

"Don't trouble yourselves," said Dick. "I aint agoin' to cut you out. I can't afford to give up a independent and loocrative purfession for a salary of three dollars a week."

"Hear him talk!" said Roswell Crawford, with an unpleasant sneer. "If you are not trying to get the place, what are you here for?"

"I came with a friend of mine," said Dick, indicating Fosdick, "who's goin' in for the situation."

"Is he a boot-black, too?" demanded Roswell, superciliously.

"He!" retorted Dick, loftily. "Didn't you know his father was a member of Congress, and intimately acquainted with all the biggest men in the State?"

The boys surveyed Fosdick as if they did not quite know whether to credit this statement, which, for the credit of Dick's veracity, it will be observed he did not assert, but only propounded in the form of a question. There was no time for comment, however, as just then the proprietor of the store came to the door, and, casting his eyes over the waiting group, singled out Roswell Crawford, and asked him to enter.

"Well, my lad, how old are you?"

"Fourteen years old," said Roswell, consequentially.

"Are your parents living?"

"Only my mother. My father is dead. He was a gentleman," he added, complacently.

"Oh, was he?" said the shop-keeper. "Do you live in the city?"

"Yes, sir. In Clinton Place."[1]

"Have you ever been in a situation before?"

"Yes, sir," said Roswell, a little reluctantly.

"Where was it?"

"In an office on Dey Street."

"How long were you there?"

"A week."

"It seems to me that was a short time. Why did you not stay longer?"

"Because," said Roswell, loftily, "the man wanted me to get to the office at eight o'clock, and make the fire. I'm a gentleman's son, and am not used to such dirty work."

---

1 8th Street between Sixth Avenue and the Bowery was named Clinton Place during most of the nineteenth century in honor of DeWitt Clinton (1769–1828), US Senator and governor of New York.

"Indeed!" said the shop-keeper. "Well, young gentleman, you may step aside a few minutes. I will speak with some of the other boys before making my selection."

Several other boys were called in and questioned. Roswell stood by and listened with an air of complacency. He could not help thinking his chances the best. "The man can see I'm a gentleman, and will do credit to his store," he thought.

At length it came to Fosdick's turn. He entered with no very sanguine anticipations of success. Unlike Roswell, he set a very low estimate upon his qualifications when compared with those of other applicants. But his modest bearing, and quiet, gentlemanly manner, entirely free from pretension, prepossessed the shop-keeper, who was a sensible man, in his favor.

"Do you reside in the city?" he asked.

"Yes, sir," said Henry.

"What is your age?"

"Twelve."

"Have you ever been in any situation?"

"No, sir."

"I should like to see a specimen of your handwriting. Here, take the pen and write your name."

Henry Fosdick had a very handsome handwriting for a boy of his age, while Roswell, who had submitted to the same test, could do little more than scrawl.

"Do you reside with your parents?"

"No, sir, they are dead."

"Where do you live, then?"

"In Mott Street."

Roswell curled his lip when this name was pronounced, for Mott Street, as my New York readers know, is in the immediate neighborhood of the Five-Points, and very far from a fashionable locality.

"Have you any testimonials to present?" asked Mr. Henderson, for that was his name.

Fosdick hesitated. This was the question which he had foreseen would give him trouble.

But at this moment it happened most opportunely that Mr. Greyson entered the shop with the intention of buying a hat.

"Yes," said Fosdick, promptly; "I will refer to this gentleman."

"How do you do, Fosdick?" asked Mr. Greyson, noticing him for the first time. "How do you happen to be here?"

"I am applying for a place, sir," said Fosdick. "May I refer the gentleman to you?"

"Certainly, I shall be glad to speak a good word for you. Mr. Henderson, this is a member of my Sunday-school class, of whose good qualities and good abilities I can speak confidently."

"That will be sufficient," said the shop-keeper, who knew Mr. Greyson's high character and position. "He could have no better recommendation. You may come to the store to-morrow morning at half past seven o'clock. The pay will be three dollars a week for the first six months. If I am satisfied with you, I shall then raise it to five dollars."

The other boys looked disappointed, but none more so than Roswell Crawford. He would have cared less if anyone else had obtained the situation; but for a boy who lived in Mott Street to be preferred to him, a gentleman's son, he considered indeed humiliating. In a spirit of petty spite, he was tempted to say, "He's a boot-black. Ask him if he isn't."

"He's an honest and intelligent lad," said Mr. Greyson. "As for you, young man, I only hope you have one-half his good qualities."

Roswell Crawford left the store in disgust, and the other unsuccessful applicants with him.

"What luck, Fosdick?" asked Dick, eagerly, as his friend came out of the store.

"I've got the place," said Fosdick, in accents of satisfaction; "but it was only because Mr. Greyson spoke up for me."

"He's a trump," said Dick, enthusiastically.

The gentleman, so denominated, came out before the boys went away, and spoke with them kindly.

Both Dick and Henry were highly pleased at the success of the application. The pay would indeed be small, but, expended economically, Fosdick thought he could get along on it, receiving his room rent, as before, in return for his services as Dick's private tutor. Dick determined, as soon as his education would permit, to follow his companion's example.

"I don't know as you'll be willin' to room with a boot-black," he said, to Henry, "now you're goin' into business."

"I couldn't room with a better friend, Dick," said Fosdick, affectionately, throwing his arm round our hero. "When we part, it'll be because you wish it."

So Fosdick entered upon a new career.

CHAPTER XX: NINE MONTHS LATER

The next morning Fosdick rose early, put on his new suit, and, after getting breakfast, set out for the Broadway store in which he had obtained a position. He left his little blacking-box in the room.

"It'll do to brush my own shoes," he said. "Who knows but I may have to come back to it again?"

"No danger," said Dick; "I'll take care of the feet, and you'll have to look after the heads, now you're in a hat-store."

"I wish you had a place too," said Fosdick.

"I don't know enough yet," said Dick. "Wait till I've gradooated."

"And can put A.B. after your name."

"What's that?"

"It stands for Bachelor of Arts. It's a degree that students get when they graduate from college."

"Oh," said Dick, "I didn't know but it meant A Boot-black. I can put that after my name now. Wouldn't Dick Hunter, A.B., sound tip-top?"

"I must be going," said Fosdick. "It won't do for me to be late the very first morning."

"That's the difference between you and me," said Dick. "I'm my own boss, and there aint no one to find fault with me if I'm late. But I might as well be goin' too. There's a gent as comes down to his store pretty early that generally wants a shine."

The two boys parted at the Park. Fosdick crossed it, and proceeded to the hat-store, while Dick, hitching up his pants, began to look about him for a customer. It was seldom that Dick had to wait long. He was always on the alert, and if there was any business to do he was always sure to get his share of it. He had now a stronger inducement than ever to attend strictly to business; his little stock of money in the savings bank having been nearly exhausted by his liberality to his room-mate. He determined to be as economical as possible, and moreover to study as hard as he could, that he might be able to follow Fosdick's example, and obtain a place in a store or counting-room. As there were no striking incidents occurring in our hero's history within the next nine months, I propose to pass over that period, and recount the progress he made in that time.

Fosdick was still at the hat-store, having succeeded in giving perfect satisfaction to Mr. Henderson. His wages had just been raised to five dollars a week. He and Dick still kept house together at Mrs. Mooney's lodging-house, and lived very frugally, so that both were able to save up money. Dick had been unusually successful in business. He had several regular patrons, who had been drawn to him by his ready wit, and quick humor, and from two of them he had received presents of clothing, which had saved him any expense on that score. His income had averaged quite seven dollars a week in addition to this. Of this amount he was now obliged to pay one dollar weekly for the room which he and Fosdick occupied, but he was still able to save one half the remainder. At the end of nine months therefore, or thirty-nine weeks, it will be seen that he had accumulated no less a sum than one hundred and seventeen dollars. Dick may be excused for feeling like a capitalist when he looked at the long row of deposits in his little bank-book. There were other boys in the same business who had earned as much money, but they had had little care for the future, and spent as they went along, so that few could boast a bank-account, however small.

"You'll be a rich man some time, Dick," said Henry Fosdick, one evening.

"And live on Fifth Avenoo," said Dick.

"Perhaps so. Stranger things have happened."

"Well," said Dick, "if such a misfortin' should come upon me I should bear it like a man. When you see a Fifth Avenoo manshun for sale for a hundred and seventeen dollars, just let me know and I'll buy it as an investment."

"Two hundred and fifty years ago you might have bought one for that price, probably. Real estate wasn't very high among the Indians."

"Just my luck," said Dick; "I was born too late. I'd orter have been an Indian, and lived in splendor on my present capital."

"I'm afraid you'd have found your present business rather unprofitable at that time."

But Dick had gained something more valuable than money. He had studied regularly every evening, and his improvement had been marvellous. He could now read well, write a fair hand, and had studied arithmetic as far as Interest. Besides this he had obtained some knowledge of grammar and geography. If some of my boy readers, who have been studying for years, and got no farther than this, should think it incredible that Dick, in less than a year, and studying evenings only, should have accomplished it, they must remember that our hero was very much in earnest in his desire to improve. He knew that, in order to grow up respectable, he must be well advanced, and he was willing to work. But then the reader must not forget that Dick was naturally a smart boy. His street education had sharpened his faculties, and taught him to rely upon himself. He knew that it would take him a long time to reach the goal which he had set before him, and he had patience to keep on trying. He knew that he had only himself to depend upon, and he determined to make the most of himself,—a resolution which is the secret of success in nine cases out of ten.

"Dick," said Fosdick, one evening, after they had completed their studies, "I think you'll have to get another teacher soon."

"Why?" asked Dick, in some surprise. "Have you been offered a more loocrative position?"

"No," said Fosdick, "but I find I have taught you all I know myself. You are now as good a scholar as I am."

"Is that true?" said Dick, eagerly, a flush of gratification coloring his brown cheek.

"Yes," said Fosdick. "You've made wonderful progress. I propose, now that evening schools have begun, that we join one, and study together through the winter."

"All right," said Dick. "I'd be willin' to go now; but when I first began to study I was ashamed to have anybody know that I was so ignorant. Do you really mean, Fosdick, that I know as much as you?"

"Yes, Dick, it's true."

"Then I've got you to thank for it," said Dick, earnestly. "You've made me what I am."

"And haven't you paid me, Dick?"

"By payin' the room-rent," said Dick, impulsively. "What's that? It isn't half enough. I wish you'd take half my money; you deserve it."

"Thank you, Dick, but you're too generous. You've more than paid me. Who was it took my part when all the other boys imposed upon me? And who gave me money to buy clothes, and so got me my situation?"

"Oh, that's nothing!" said Dick.

"It's a great deal, Dick. I shall never forget it. But now it seems to me you might try to get a situation yourself."

"Do I know enough?"

"You know as much as I do."

"Then I'll try," said Dick, decidedly.

"I wish there was a place in our store," said Fosdick. "It would be pleasant for us to be together."

"Never mind," said Dick; "there'll be plenty of other chances.

P'r'aps A. T. Stewart might like a partner. I wouldn't ask more'n a quarter of the profits."

"Which would be a very liberal proposal on your part," said Fosdick, smiling. "But perhaps Mr. Stewart might object to a partner living on Mott Street."

"I'd just as lieves move to Fifth Avenoo," said Dick. "I aint got no prejudices in favor of Mott Street."

"Nor I," said Fosdick, "and in fact I have been thinking it might be a good plan for us to move as soon as we could afford. Mrs. Mooney doesn't keep the room quite so neat as she might."

"No," said Dick. "She aint got no prejudices against dirt. Look at that towel."

Dick held up the article indicated, which had now seen service nearly a week, and hard service at that,—Dick's avocation causing him to be rather hard on towels.

"Yes," said Fosdick, "I've got about tired of it. I guess we can find some better place without having to pay much more. When we move, you must let me pay my share of the rent."

"We'll see about that," said Dick. "Do you propose to move to Fifth Avenoo?"

"Not just at present, but to some more agreeable neighborhood than this. We'll wait till you get a situation, and then we can decide."

A few days later, as Dick was looking about for customers in the neighborhood of the Park, his attention was drawn to a fellow boot-black, a boy about a year younger than himself, who appeared to have been crying.

"What's the matter, Tom?" asked Dick. "Haven't you had luck to-day?"

"Pretty good," said the boy; "but we're havin' hard times at home. Mother fell last week and broke her arm, and to-morrow we've got to pay the rent, and if we don't the landlord says he'll turn us out."

"Haven't you got anything except what you earn?" asked Dick.

"No," said Tom, "not now. Mother used to earn three or four dollars a week; but she can't do nothin' now, and my little sister and brother are too young."

Dick had quick sympathies. He had been so poor himself, and obliged to submit to so many privations that he knew from personal experience how hard it was. Tom Wilkins he knew as an excellent boy who never squandered his money, but faithfully carried it home to his mother. In the days of his own extravagance and shiftlessness he had once or twice asked Tom to accompany him to the Old Bowery or Tony Pastor's, but Tom had always steadily refused.

"I'm sorry for you, Tom," he said. "How much do you owe for rent?"

"Two weeks now," said Tom.

"How much is it a week?"

"Two dollars a week—that makes four."

"Have you got anything towards it?"

"No; I've had to spend all my money for food for mother and the rest of us. I've had pretty hard work to do that. I don't know what we'll do. I haven't any place to go to, and I'm afraid mother'll get cold in her arm."

"Can't you borrow the money somewhere?" asked Dick.

Tom shook his head despondingly.

"All the people I know are as poor as I am," said he. "They'd help me if they could, but it's hard work for them to get along themselves."

"I'll tell you what, Tom," said Dick, impulsively, "I'll stand your friend."

"Have you got any money?" asked Tom, doubtfully.

"Got any money!" repeated Dick. "Don't you know that I run a bank on my own account? How much is it you need?"

"Four dollars," said Tom. "If we don't pay that before to-morrow night, out we go. You haven't got as much as that, have you?"

"Here are three dollars," said Dick, drawing out his pocket-book. "I'll let you have the rest to-morrow, and maybe a little more."

"You're a right down good fellow, Dick," said Tom; "but won't you want it yourself?"

"Oh, I've got some more," said Dick.

"Maybe I'll never be able to pay you."

"S'pose you don't," said Dick; "I guess I won't fail."

"I won't forget it, Dick. I hope I'll be able to do somethin' for you sometime."

"All right," said Dick. "I'd ought to help you. I haven't got no mother to look out for. I wish I had."

There was a tinge of sadness in his tone, as he pronounced the last four words; but Dick's temperament was sanguine, and he never gave way to unavailing sadness. Accordingly he began to whistle as he turned away, only adding, "I'll see you to-morrow, Tom."

The three dollars which Dick had handed to Tom Wilkins were

his savings for the present week. It was now Thursday afternoon. His rent, which amounted to a dollar, he expected to save out of the earnings of Friday and Saturday. In order to give Tom the additional assistance he had promised, Dick would be obliged to have recourse to his bank-savings. He would not have ventured to trench upon it for any other reason but this. But he felt that it would be selfish to allow Tom and his mother to suffer when he had it in his power to relieve them. But Dick was destined to be surprised, and that in a disagreeable manner, when he reached home.

CHAPTER XXI: DICK LOSES HIS BANK-BOOK

It was hinted at the close of the last chapter that Dick was destined to be disagreeably surprised on reaching home.

Having agreed to give further assistance to Tom Wilkins, he was naturally led to go to the drawer where he and Fosdick kept their bank-books. To his surprise and uneasiness *the drawer proved to be empty!*

"Come here a minute, Fosdick," he said.

"What's the matter, Dick?"

"I can't find my bank-book, nor yours either. What's 'come of them?"

"I took mine with me this morning, thinking I might want to put in a little more money. I've got it in my pocket, now."

"But where's mine?" asked Dick, perplexed.

"I don't know. I saw it in the drawer when I took mine this morning."

"Are you sure?"

"Yes, positive, for I looked into it to see how much you had got."

"Did you lock it again?" asked Dick.

"Yes; didn't you have to unlock it just now?"

"So I did," said Dick. "But it's gone now. Somebody opened it with a key that fitted the lock, and then locked it ag'in."

"That must have been the way."

"It's rather hard on a feller," said Dick, who, for the first time since we became acquainted with him, began to feel downhearted.

"Don't give it up, Dick. You haven't lost the money, only the bank-book."

"Aint that the same thing?"

"No. You can go to the bank to-morrow morning, as soon as it opens, and tell them you have lost the book, and ask them not to pay the money to any one except yourself."

"So I can," said Dick, brightening up. "That is, if the thief hasn't been to the bank to-day."

"If he has, they might detect him by his handwriting."

"I'd like to get hold of the one that stole it," said Dick, indignantly. "I'd give him a good lickin'."

"It must have been somebody in the house. Suppose we go and see Mrs. Mooney. She may know whether anybody came into our room to-day."

The two boys went downstairs, and knocked at the door of a little back sitting-room where Mrs. Mooney generally spent her evenings. It was a shabby little room, with a threadbare carpet on the floor, the walls covered with a certain large-figured paper, patches of which had been stripped off here and there, exposing the plaster, the remainder being defaced by dirt and grease. But Mrs. Mooney had one of those comfortable temperaments which are tolerant of dirt, and didn't mind it in the least. She was seated beside a small pine work-table, industriously engaged in mending stockings.

"Good-evening, Mrs. Mooney," said Fosdick, politely.

"Good-evening," said the landlady. "Sit down, if you can find chairs. I'm hard at work as you see, but a poor lone widder can't afford to be idle."

"We can't stop long, Mrs. Mooney, but my friend here has had something taken from his room to-day, and we thought we'd come and see you about it."

"What is it?" asked the landlady. "You don't think I'd take anything? If I am poor, it's an honest name I've always had, as all my lodgers can testify."

"Certainly not, Mrs. Mooney; but there are others in the house that may not be honest. My friend has lost his bank-book. It was safe in the drawer this morning, but to-night it is not to be found."

"How much money was there in it?" asked Mrs. Mooney.

"Over a hundred dollars," said Fosdick.

"It was my whole fortun'," said Dick. "I was goin' to buy a house next year."

Mrs. Mooney was evidently surprised to learn the extent of Dick's wealth, and was disposed to regard him with increased respect.

"Was the drawer locked?" she asked.

"Yes."

"Then it couldn't have been Bridget. I don't think she has any keys."

"She wouldn't know what a bank-book was," said Fosdick. "You didn't see any of the lodgers go into our room to-day, did you?"

"I shouldn't wonder if it was Jim Travis," said Mrs. Mooney, suddenly.

This James Travis was a bar-tender in a low groggery in Mulberry Street, and had been for a few weeks an inmate of Mrs. Mooney's lodging-house. He was a coarse-looking fellow who, from his appearance, evidently patronized liberally the liquor he dealt out to others. He occupied a room opposite Dick's, and was often heard by the two boys reeling upstairs in a state of intoxication, uttering shocking oaths.

This Travis had made several friendly overtures to Dick and his room-mate, and had invited them to call round at the barroom where he tended, and take something. But this invitation had never been accepted, partly because the boys were better engaged in the evening, and partly because neither of them had taken a fancy to Mr. Travis; which certainly was not strange, for nature had not gifted him with many charms, either of personal appearance or manners. The rejection of his friendly proffers had caused him to take a dislike to Dick and Henry, whom he considered stiff and unsocial.

"What makes you think it was Travis?" asked Fosdick. "He isn't at home in the daytime."

"But he was to-day. He said he had got a bad cold, and had to come home for a clean handkerchief."

"Did you see him?" asked Dick.

"Yes," said Mrs. Mooney. "Bridget was hanging out clothes, and I went to the door to let him in."

"I wonder if he had a key that would fit our drawer," said Fosdick.

"Yes," said Mrs. Mooney. "The bureaus in the two rooms are just alike. I got 'em at auction, and most likely the locks is the same."

"It must have been he," said Dick, looking towards Fosdick.

"Yes," said Fosdick, "it looks like it."

"What's to be done? That's what I'd like to know," said Dick. "Of course he'll say he hasn't got it; and he won't be such a fool as to leave it in his room."

"If he hasn't been to the bank, it's all right," said Fosdick.

"You can go there the first thing to-morrow morning, and stop their paying any money on it."

"But I can't get any money on it myself," said Dick. "I told Tom Wilkins I'd let him have some more money to-morrow, or his sick mother'll have to turn out of their lodgin's."

"How much money were you going to give him?"

"I gave him three dollars to-day, and was goin' to give him two dollars to-morrow."

"I've got the money, Dick. I didn't go to the bank this morning."

"All right. I'll take it, and pay you back next week."

"No, Dick; if you've given three dollars, you must let me give two."

"No, Fosdick, I'd rather give the whole. You know I've got more money than you. No, I haven't, either," said Dick, the memory of his loss flashing upon him. "I thought I was rich this morning, but now I'm in destitoot circumstances."

"Cheer up, Dick; you'll get your money back."

"I hope so," said our hero, rather ruefully.

The fact was, that our friend Dick was beginning to feel what is so often experienced by men who do business of a more important character and on a larger scale than he, the bitterness of a reverse of circumstances. With one hundred dollars and over carefully laid away in the savings bank, he had felt quite independent. Wealth is comparative, and Dick probably felt as rich as many men who are worth a hundred thousand dollars. He was beginning to feel the advantages of his steady self-denial, and to experience the pleasures of property. Not that Dick was likely to be unduly attached to money. Let it be said to his credit that it had never given him so much satisfaction as when it enabled him to help Tom Wilkins in his trouble.

Besides this, there was another thought that troubled him. When he obtained a place he could not expect to receive as much as he was now making from blacking boots,—probably not more than three dollars a week,—while his expenses without clothing would amount to four dollars. To make up the deficiency he had confidently relied upon his savings, which would be sufficient to carry him along for a year, if necessary. If he should not recover his money, he would be compelled to continue a boot-black for at least six months longer; and this was rather a discouraging reflection. On the whole it is not to be wondered at that Dick felt unusually sober this evening, and that neither of the boys felt much like studying.

The two boys consulted as to whether it would be best to speak to Travis about it. It was not altogether easy to decide. Fosdick was opposed to it.

"It will only put him on his guard," said he, "and I don't see as it will do any good. Of course he will deny it. We'd better keep quiet, and watch him, and, by giving notice at the bank, we can make sure that he doesn't get any money on it. If he does present himself at the bank, they will know at once that he is a thief, and he can be arrested."

This view seemed reasonable, and Dick resolved to adopt it. On the whole, he began to think prospects were brighter than he had at first supposed, and his spirits rose a little.

"How'd he know I had any bank-book? That's what I can't make out," he said.

"Don't you remember?" said Fosdick, after a moment's thought, "we were speaking of our savings, two or three evenings since?"

"Yes," said Dick.

"Our door was a little open at the time, and I heard somebody come upstairs, and stop a minute in front of it. It must have been Jim Travis. In that way he probably found out about your money, and took the opportunity to-day to get hold of it."

This might or might not be the correct explanation. At all events it seemed probable.

The boys were just on the point of going to bed, later in the evening, when a knock was heard at the door, and, to their no little surprise, their neighbor, Jim Travis, proved to be the caller. He was a sallow-complexioned young man, with dark hair and bloodshot eyes.

He darted a quick glance from one to the other as he entered, which did not escape the boys' notice.

"How are ye, to-night?" he said, sinking into one of the two chairs with which the room was scantily furnished.

"Jolly," said Dick. "How are you?"

"Tired as a dog," was the reply. "Hard work and poor pay; that's the way with me. I wanted to go to the theater, to-night, but I was hard up, and couldn't raise the cash."

Here he darted another quick glance at the boys; but neither betrayed anything.

"You don't go out much, do you?" he said

"Not much," said Fosdick. "We spend our evenings in study."

"That's precious slow," said Travis, rather contemptuously. "What's the use of studying so much? You don't expect to be a lawyer, do you, or anything of that sort?"

"Maybe," said Dick. "I haven't made up my mind yet. If my feller-citizens should want me to go to Congress some time, I shouldn't want to disapp'int 'em; and then readin' and writin' might come handy."

"Well," said Travis, rather abruptly, "I'm tired and I guess I'll turn in."

"Good-night," said Fosdick.

The boys looked at each other as their visitor left the room.

"He came in to see if we'd missed the bank-book," said Dick.

"And to turn off suspicion from himself, by letting us know he had no money," added Fosdick.

"That's so," said Dick. "I'd like to have searched them pockets of his."

CHAPTER XXII: TRACKING THE THIEF

Fosdick was right in supposing that Jim Travis had stolen the bank-book. He was also right in supposing that that worthy young man had come to the knowledge of Dick's savings by what he had accidentally overheard. Now, Travis, like a very large number of young men of his class, was able to dispose of a larger amount of money than he was able to earn. Moreover, he had no great fancy for work at all, and would have been glad to find some other way of obtaining money enough to pay his expenses. He had recently received a letter from an old companion, who had strayed out to California, and going at once to the mines had been lucky enough to get possession of a very remunerative claim. He wrote to Travis that he had already realized two thousand dollars from it, and expected to make his fortune within six months.

Two thousand dollars! This seemed to Travis a very large sum, and quite dazzled his imagination. He was at once inflamed with the desire to go out to California and try his luck. In his present situation he only received thirty dollars a month, which was probably all that his services were worth, but went a very little way towards gratifying his expensive tastes. Accordingly he determined to take the next steamer to the land of gold, if he could possibly manage to get money enough to pay the passage.

The price of a steerage passage at that time was seventy-five dollars,—not a large sum, certainly,—but it might as well have been seventy-five hundred for any chance James Travis had of raising the amount at present. His available funds consisted of precisely two dollars and a quarter, of which sum, one dollar and a half, was due to his washerwoman. This, however, would not have troubled Travis much, and he would conveniently have forgotten all about it; but, even leaving this debt unpaid, the sum at his command would not help him materially towards paying his passage money.

Travis applied for help to two or three of his companions; but they were all of that kind who never keep an account with savings banks, but carry all their spare cash about with them. One of these friends offered to lend him thirty-seven cents, and another a dollar; but neither of these offers seemed to encourage him much. He was about giving up his project in despair, when he learned, accidentally, as we have already said, the extent of Dick's savings.

One hundred and seventeen dollars! Why, that would not only pay his passage, but carry him up to the mines, after he had arrived in San Francisco. He could not help thinking it over, and the result of this thinking was that he determined to borrow it of Dick without leave. Knowing that neither of the boys were in their room in the daytime, he came back in the course of the morning, and, being admitted by Mrs. Mooney herself, said, by way of accounting for his presence, that he had a cold, and had come back for a handkerchief. The landlady suspected nothing, and, returning at once to her work in the kitchen, left the coast clear.

Travis at once entered Dick's room, and, as there seemed to be no other place for depositing money, tried the bureau-drawers. They were all readily opened, except one, which proved to be locked. This he naturally concluded must contain the money, and going back to his own chamber for the key of the bureau, tried it on his return, and found to his satisfaction that it would fit. When he discovered the bank-book, his joy was mingled with disappointment. He had expected to find bank-bills instead. This would have saved all further trouble, and would have been immediately available. Obtaining money at the savings bank would involve fresh risk. Travis hesitated whether to take it or not; but finally decided that it would be worth the trouble and hazard.

He accordingly slipped the book into his pocket, locked the drawer again, and, forgetting all about the handkerchief for which he had come home went downstairs, and into the street.

There would have been time to go to the savings bank that day, but Travis had already been absent from his place of business some time, and did not venture to take the additional time required. Besides, not being very much used to savings banks, never having had occasion to use them, he thought it would be more prudent to look over the rules and regulations, and see if he could not get some information as to the way he ought to proceed. So the day passed, and Dick's money was left in safety at the bank.

In the evening, it occurred to Travis that it might be well to find out whether Dick had discovered his loss. This reflection it was that induced the visit which is recorded at the close of the last chapter. The result was that he was misled by the boys' silence on the subject, and concluded that nothing had yet been discovered.

"Good!" thought Travis, with satisfaction. "If they don't find out for twenty-four hours, it'll be too late, then, and I shall be all right."

There being a possibility of the loss being discovered before the boys went out in the morning, Travis determined to see them at that time, and judge whether such was the case. He waited, therefore, until he heard the boys come out, and then opened his own door.

"Morning, gents," said he, sociably. "Going to business?"

"Yes," said Dick. "I'm afraid my clerks'll be lazy if I aint on hand."

"Good joke!" said Travis. "If you pay good wages, I'd like to speak for a place."

"I pay all I get myself," said Dick. "How's business with you?"

"So so. Why don't you call round, some time?"

"All my evenin's is devoted to literatoor and science," said Dick. "Thank you all the same."

"Where do you hang out?" inquired Travis, in choice language, addressing Fosdick.

"At Henderson's hat and cap store, on Broadway."

"I'll look in upon you some time when I want a tile," said Travis. "I suppose you sell cheaper to your friends."

"I'll be as reasonable as I can," said Fosdick, not very cordially; for he did not much fancy having it supposed by his employer that such a disreputable-looking person as Travis was a friend of his.

However, Travis had no idea of showing himself at the Broadway store, and only said this by way of making conversation, and encouraging the boys to be social.

"You haven't any of you gents seen a pearl-handled knife, have you?" he asked.

"No," said Fosdick; "have you lost one?"

"Yes," said Travis, with unblushing falsehood. "I left it on my bureau a day or two since. I've missed one or two other little matters. Bridget don't look to me any too honest. Likely she's got 'em."

"What are you goin' to do about it?" said Dick.

"I'll keep mum unless I lose something more, and then I'll kick up a row, and haul her over the coals. Have you missed anything?"

"No," said Fosdick, answering for himself, as he could do without violating the truth.

There was a gleam of satisfaction in the eyes of Travis, as he heard this.

"They haven't found it out yet," he thought. "I'll bag the money to-day, and then they may whistle for it."

Having no further object to serve in accompanying the boys, he bade them good-morning, and turned down another street.

"He's mighty friendly all of a sudden," said Dick.

"Yes," said Fosdick; "it's very evident what it all means. He wants to find out whether you have discovered your loss or not."

"But he didn't find out."

"No; we've put him on the wrong track. He means to get his money to-day, no doubt."

"My money," suggested Dick.

"I accept the correction," said Fosdick.

"Of course, Dick, you'll be on hand as soon as the bank opens."

"In course I shall. Jim Travis'll find he's walked into the wrong shop."

"The bank opens at ten o'clock, you know."

"I'll be there on time."

The two boys separated.

"Good luck, Dick," said Fosdick, as he parted from him. "It'll all come out right, I think."

"I hope 'twill," said Dick.

He had recovered from his temporary depression, and made up his mind that the money would be recovered. He had no idea of allowing himself to be outwitted by Jim Travis, and enjoyed already, in anticipation, the pleasure of defeating his rascality.

It wanted two hours and a half yet to ten o'clock, and this time to Dick was too precious to be wasted. It was the time of his greatest harvest. He accordingly repaired to his usual place of business, succeeded in obtaining six customers, which yielded him sixty cents. He then went to a restaurant, and got some breakfast. It was now half-past nine, and Dick, feeling that it wouldn't do to be late, left his box in charge of Johnny Nolan, and made his way to the bank.

The officers had not yet arrived, and Dick lingered on the outside, waiting till they should come. He was not without a little uneasiness, fearing that Travis might be as prompt as himself, and finding him there, might suspect something, and so escape the snare. But, though looking cautiously up and down the street, he could discover no traces of the supposed thief. In due time ten o'clock struck, and immediately afterwards the doors of the bank were thrown open, and our hero entered.

As Dick had been in the habit of making a weekly visit for the last nine months, the cashier had come to know him by sight.

"You're early, this morning, my lad," he said, pleasantly. "Have you got some more money to deposit? You'll be getting rich, soon."

"I don't know about that," said Dick. "My bank-book's been stole."

"Stolen!" echoed the cashier. "That's unfortunate. Not so bad as it might be, though. The thief can't collect the money."

"That's what I came to see about," said Dick. "I was afraid he might have got it already."

"He hasn't been here yet. Even if he had, I remember you, and should have detected him. When was it taken?"

"Yesterday," said Dick. "I missed it in the evenin' when I got home."

"Have you any suspicion as to the person who took it?" asked the cashier.

Dick thereupon told all he knew as to the general character and suspicious conduct of Jim Travis, and the cashier agreed with him that he was probably the thief. Dick also gave his reason for thinking that he would visit the bank that morning, to withdraw the funds.

"Very good," said the cashier. "We'll be ready for him. What is the number of your book?"

"No. 5,678," said Dick.

"Now give me a little description of this Travis whom you suspect."

Dick accordingly furnished a brief outline sketch of Travis, not particularly complimentary to the latter.

"That will answer. I think I shall know him," said the cashier. "You may depend upon it that he shall receive no money on your account."

"Thank you," said Dick.

Considerably relieved in mind, our hero turned towards the door, thinking that there would be nothing gained by his remaining longer, while he would of course lose time.

He had just reached the doors, which were of glass, when through them he perceived James Travis himself just crossing the street, and apparently coming towards the bank. It would not do, of course, for him to be seen.

"Here he is," he exclaimed, hurrying back. "Can't you hide me somewhere? I don't want to be seen."

The cashier understood at once how the land lay. He quickly opened a little door, and admitted Dick behind the counter.

"Stoop down," he said, "so as not to be seen."

Dick had hardly done so when Jim Travis opened the outer door, and, looking about him in a little uncertainty, walked up to the cashier's desk.

CHAPTER XXIII: TRAVIS IS ARRESTED

Jim Travis advanced into the bank with a doubtful step, knowing well that he was on a dishonest errand, and heartily wishing that he were well out of it. After a little hesitation, he approached the paying-teller, and, exhibiting the bank-book, said, "I want to get my money out."

The bank-officer took the book, and, after looking at it a moment, said, "How much do you want?"

"The whole of it," said Travis.

"You can draw out any part of it, but to draw out the whole requires a week's notice."

"Then I'll take a hundred dollars."

"Are you the person to whom the book belongs?"

"Yes, sir," said Travis, without hesitation.

"Your name is—"

"Hunter."

The bank-clerk went to a large folio volume, containing the names of depositors, and began to turn over the leaves. While he was doing this, he managed to send out a young man connected with the bank for a policeman. Travis did not perceive this, or did not suspect that it had anything to do with himself. Not being used to savings banks, he supposed the delay only what was usual. After a search, which was only intended to gain time that a policeman might be summoned, the cashier came back, and,

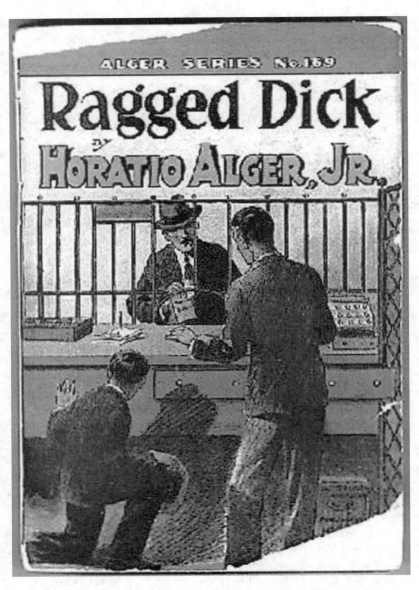

Figure 7. Cover of *Ragged Dick* reprint (Street & Smith, 1926).
Editor's collection.

sliding out a piece of paper to Travis, said, "It will be necessary for you to write an order for the money."

Travis took a pen, which he found on the ledge outside, and wrote the order, signing his name "Dick Hunter," having observed that name on the outside of the book.

"Your name is Dick Hunter, then?" said the cashier, taking the paper, and looking at the thief over his spectacles.

"Yes," said Travis, promptly.

"But," continued the cashier, "I find Hunter's age is put down on the bank-book as fourteen. Surely you must be more than that."

Travis would gladly have declared that he was only fourteen; but, being in reality twenty-three, and possessing a luxuriant pair of whiskers, this was not to be thought of. He began to feel uneasy.

"Dick Hunter's my younger brother," he said. "I'm getting out the money for him."

"I thought you said your own name was Dick Hunter," said the cashier.

"I said my name was Hunter," said Travis, ingeniously. "I didn't understand you."

"But you've signed the name of Dick Hunter to this order. How is that?" questioned the troublesome cashier.

Travis saw that he was getting himself into a tight place; but his self-possession did not desert him.

"I thought I must give my brother's name," he answered.

"What is your own name?"

"Henry Hunter."

"Can you bring any one to testify that the statement you are making is correct?"

"Yes, a dozen if you like," said Travis, boldly. "Give me the book, and I'll come back this afternoon. I didn't think there'd be such a fuss about getting out a little money."

"Wait a moment. Why don't your brother come himself?"

"Because he's sick. He's down with the measles," said Travis.

Here the cashier signed to Dick to rise and show himself. Our hero accordingly did so.

"You will be glad to find that he has recovered," said the cashier, pointing to Dick.

With an exclamation of anger and dismay, Travis, who saw the game was up, started for the door, feeling that safety made such a course prudent. But he was too late. He found himself confronted by a burly policeman, who seized him by the arm, saying,

"Not so fast, my man. I want you."

"Let me go," exclaimed Travis, struggling to free himself.

"I'm sorry I can't oblige you," said the officer. "You'd better not make a fuss, or I may have to hurt you a little."

Travis sullenly resigned himself to his fate, darting a look of rage at Dick, whom he considered the author of his present misfortune.

"This is your book," said the cashier, handing back his rightful property to our hero. "Do you wish to draw out any money?"

"Two dollars," said Dick.

"Very well. Write an order for the amount."

Before doing so, Dick, who now that he saw Travis in the power of the law began to pity him, went up to the officer, and said,—

"Won't you let him go? I've got my bank-book back, and I don't want anything done to him."

"Sorry I can't oblige you," said the officer; "but I'm not allowed to do it. He'll have to stand his trial."

"I'm sorry for you, Travis," said Dick. "I didn't want you arrested. I only wanted my bank-book back."

"Curse you!" said Travis, scowling vindictively. "Wait till I get free. See if I don't fix you."

"You needn't pity him too much," said the officer. "I know him now. He's been to the Island before."

"It's a lie," said Travis, violently.

"Don't be too noisy, my friend," said the officer. "If you've got no more business here, we'll be going."

He withdrew with the prisoner in charge, and Dick, having drawn his two dollars, left the bank. Notwithstanding the violent words the prisoner had used towards himself, and his attempted robbery, he could not help feeling sorry that he had been instrumental in causing his arrest.

"I'll keep my book a little safer hereafter," thought Dick. "Now I must go and see Tom Wilkins."

Before dismissing the subject of Travis and his theft, it may be remarked that he was duly tried, and, his guilt being clear, was sent to Blackwell's Island for nine months. At the end of that time, on his release, he got a chance to work his passage on a ship to San Francisco, where he probably arrived in due time. At any rate, nothing more has been heard of him, and probably his threat of vengence against Dick will never be carried into effect.

Returning to the City Hall Park, Dick soon fell in with Tom Wilkins.

"How are you, Tom?" he said. "How's your mother?"

"She's better, Dick, thank you. She felt worried about bein' turned out into the street; but I gave her that money from you, and now she feels a good deal easier."

"I've got some more for you, Tom," said Dick, producing a two-dollar bill from his pocket.

"I ought not to take it from you, Dick."

"Oh, it's all right, Tom. Don't be afraid."

"But you may need it yourself."

"There's plenty more where that came from."

"Any way, one dollar will be enough. With that we can pay the rent."

"You'll want the other to buy something to eat."

"You're very kind, Dick."

"I'd ought to be. I've only got myself to take care of."

"Well, I'll take it for my mother's sake. When you want anything done just call on Tom Wilkins."

"All right. Next week, if your mother doesn't get better, I'll give you some more."

Tom thanked our hero very gratefully, and Dick walked away, feeling the self-approval which always accompanies a generous and disinterested action. He was generous by nature, and, before the period at which he is introduced to the reader's notice, he frequently treated his friends to cigars and oyster-stews. Sometimes he invited them to accompany him to the theatre at his expense. But he never derived from these acts of liberality the same degree of satisfaction as from this timely gift to Tom Wilkins. He felt that his money was well bestowed, and would save an entire family from privation and discomfort. Five dollars would, to be sure, make something of a difference in the mount of his savings. It was more than he was able to save up in a week. But Dick felt fully repaid for what he had done, and he felt prepared to give as much more, if Tom's mother should continue to be sick, and should appear to him to need it.

Besides all this, Dick felt a justifiable pride in his financial ability to afford so handsome a gift. A year before, however much he might have desired to give, it would have been quite out of his power to give five dollars. His cash balance never reached that amount. It was seldom, indeed, that it equalled one dollar. In more ways than one Dick was beginning to reap the advantage of his self-denial and judicious economy.

It will be remembered that when Mr. Whitney at parting with Dick presented him with five dollars, he told him that he might repay it to some other boy who was struggling upward. Dick thought of this, and it occurred to him that after all he was only paying up an old debt.

When Fosdick came home in the evening, Dick announced his success in recovering his lost money, and described the manner it had been brought about.

"You're in luck," said Fosdick. "I guess we'd better not trust the bureau-drawer again."

"I mean to carry my book round with me," said Dick.

"So shall I, as long as we stay at Mrs. Mooney's. I wish we were in a better place."

"I must go down and tell her she needn't expect Travis back. Poor chap, I pity him!"

Travis was never more seen in Mrs. Mooney's establishment. He was owing that lady for a fortnight's rent of his room, which prevented her feeling much compassion for him. The room was soon after let to a more creditable tenant who proved a less troublesome neighbor than his predecessor.

CHAPTER XXIV: DICK RECEIVES A LETTER

It was about a week after Dick's recovery of his bank-book, that Fosdick brought home with him in the evening a copy of the "Daily Sun."[1]

"Would you like to see your name in print, Dick?" he asked.

"Yes," said Dick, who was busy at the wash-stand, endeavoring to efface the marks which his day's work had left upon his hands. "They haven't put me up for mayor, have they? 'Cause if they have, I shan't accept. It would interfere too much with my private business."

"No," said Fosdick, "they haven't put you up for office yet, though that may happen sometime. But if you want to see your name in print, here it is."

Dick was rather incredulous, but, having dried his hands on the towel, took the paper, and following the directions of

---

1 The editorial offices of the New York *Sun*, founded in 1833, were located in the same building as the Newsboys' Lodging House on Fulton Street. Alger contributed nine serials to the *Sun* between 1857 and 1860 and thirteen travel essays from Europe to the paper between 1860 and 1861.

Fosdick's finger, observed in the list of advertised letters the name of "RAGGED DICK."

"By gracious, so it is," said he. "Do you s'pose it means me?"

"I don't know of any other Ragged Dick,—do you?"

"No," said Dick, reflectively; "it must be me. But I don't know of anybody that would be likely to write to me."

"Perhaps it is Frank Whitney," suggested Fosdick, after a little reflection. "Didn't he promise to write to you?"

"Yes," said Dick, "and he wanted me to write to him."

"Where is he now?"

"He was going to a boarding-school in Connecticut, he said. The name of the town was Barnton."

"Very likely the letter is from him."

"I hope it is. Frank was a tip-top boy, and he was the first that made me ashamed of bein' so ignorant and dirty."

"You had better go to the post-office to-morrow morning, and ask for the letter."

"P'r'aps they won't give it to me."

"Suppose you wear the old clothes you used to a year ago, when Frank first saw you? They won't have any doubt of your being Ragged Dick then."

"I guess I will. I'll be sort of ashamed to be seen in 'em though," said Dick, who had considerable more pride in a neat personal appearance than when we were first introduced to him.

"It will be only for one day, or one morning," said Fosdick.

"I'd do more'n that for the sake of gettin' a letter from Frank. I'd like to see him."

The next morning, in accordance with the suggestion of Fosdick, Dick arrayed himself in the long disused Washington coat and Napoleon pants, which he had carefully preserved, for what reason he could hardly explain.

When fairly equipped, Dick surveyed himself in the mirror,— if the little seven-by-nine-inch looking-glass, with which the room was furnished, deserved the name. The result of the survey was not on the whole a pleasing one. To tell the truth, Dick was quite ashamed of his appearance, and, on opening the chamber-door, looked around to see that the coast was clear, not being willing to have any of his fellow-boarders see him in his present attire.

He managed to slip out into the street unobserved, and, after attending to two or three regular customers who came down-town early in the morning, he made his way down Nassau Street to the post-office. He passed along until he came to a compartment on which he read ADVERTISED LETTERS, and, stepping up to the little window, said,—

"There's a letter for me. I saw it advertised in the 'Sun' yesterday."

"What name?" demanded the clerk.

"Ragged Dick," answered our hero.

"That's a queer name," said the clerk, surveying him a little curiously. "Are you Ragged Dick?"

"If you don't believe me, look at my clo'es," said Dick.

"That's pretty good proof, certainly," said the clerk, laughing. "If that isn't your name, it deserves to be."

"I believe in dressin' up to your name," said Dick.

"Do you know any one in Barnton, Connecticut?" asked the clerk, who had by this time found the letter.

"Yes," said Dick. "I know a chap that's at boardin'-school there."

"It appears to be in a boy's hand. I think it must be yours."

The letter was handed to Dick through the window. He received it eagerly, and drawing back so as not to be in the way of the throng who were constantly applying for letters, or slipping them into the boxes provided for them, hastily opened it, and began to read. As the reader may be interested in the contents of the letter as well as Dick, we transcribe it below.

It was dated Barnton, Conn., and commenced thus,—

"DEAR DICK,—You must excuse my addressing this letter to 'Ragged Dick'; but the fact is, I don't know what your last name is, nor where you live. I am afraid there is not much chance of your getting this letter; but I hope you will. I have thought of you very often, and wondered how you were getting along, and I should have written to you before if I had known where to direct.

"Let me tell you a little about myself. Barnton is a very pretty country town, only about six miles from Hartford. The boarding-school which I attend is under the charge of Ezekiel Munroe, A.M. He is a man of about fifty, a graduate of Yale College, and has always been a teacher. It is a large two-story house, with an addition containing a good many small bed-chambers for the boys. There are about twenty of us, and there is one assistant teacher who teaches the English branches.

Mr. Munroe, or Old Zeke, as we call him behind his back, teaches Latin and Greek. I am studying both these languages, because father wants me to go to college.

"But you won't be interested in hearing about our studies. I will tell you how we amuse ourselves. There are about fifty acres of land belonging to Mr. Munroe; so that we have plenty of room for play. About a quarter of a mile from the house there is a good-sized pond. There is a large, round-bottomed boat, which is stout and strong. Every Wednesday and Saturday afternoon, when the weather is good, we go out rowing on the pond. Mr. Barton, the assistant teacher, goes with us, to look after us. In the summer we are allowed to go in bathing. In the winter there is splendid skating on the pond.

"Besides this, we play ball a good deal, and we have various other plays. So we have a pretty good time, although we study pretty hard too. I am getting on very well in my studies. Father has not decided yet where he will send me to college.

"I wish you were here, Dick. I should enjoy your company, and besides I should like to feel that you were getting an education. I think you are naturally a pretty smart boy; but I suppose, as you have to earn your own living, you don't get much chance to learn. I only wish I had a few hundred dollars of my own. I would have you come up here, and attend school with us. If I ever have a chance to help you in any way, you may be sure that I will.

"I shall have to wind up my letter now, as I have to hand in a composition to-morrow, on the life and character of Washington. I might say that I have a friend who wears a coat that once belonged to the general. But I suppose that coat must be worn out by this time. I don't much like writing compositions. I would a good deal rather write letters.

"I have written a longer letter than I meant to. I hope you will get it, though I am afraid not. If you do, you must be sure to answer it, as soon as possible. You needn't mind if your writing does look like 'hens-tracks,' as you told me once.

"Good-by, Dick. You must always think of me, as your very true friend,

"FRANK WHITNEY."

Dick read this letter with much satisfaction. It is always pleasant to be remembered, and Dick had so few friends that it was more to him than to boys who are better provided. Again, he felt a new sense of importance in having a letter addressed to him. It was the first letter he had ever received. If it had been sent to him a year before, he would not have been able to read it. But now, thanks to Fosdick's instructions, he could not only read writing, but he could write a very good hand himself.

There was one passage in the letter which pleased Dick. It was where Frank said that if he had the money he would pay for his education himself.

"He's a tip-top feller," said Dick. "I wish I could see him ag'in."

There were two reasons why Dick would like to have seen Frank. One was the natural pleasure he would have in meeting a friend; but he felt also that he would like to have Frank witness the improvement he had made in his studies and mode of life.

"He'd find me a little more 'spectable than when he first saw me," thought Dick.

Dick had by this time got up to Printing House Square. Standing on Spruce Street, near the "Tribune" office, was his old enemy, Micky Maguire.

It has already been said that Micky felt a natural enmity towards those in his own condition in life who wore better clothes than himself. For the last nine months, Dick's neat appearance had excited the ire of the young Philistine. To appear in neat attire and with a clean face Micky felt was a piece of presumption, and an assumption of superiority on the part of our hero, and he termed it "tryin' to be a swell."

Now his astonished eyes rested on Dick in his ancient attire, which was very similar to his own. It was a moment of triumph to him. He felt that "pride had had a fall,"[1] and he could not forbear reminding Dick of it.

"Them's nice clo'es you've got on," said he, sarcastically, as Dick came up.

---

1   Proverbs 16:18: "Pride goeth before destruction, and an haughty spirit before a fall."

"Yes," said Dick, promptly. "I've been employin' your tailor. If my face was only dirty we'd be taken for twin brothers."

"So you've give up tryin' to be a swell?"

"Only for this partic'lar occasion," said Dick. "I wanted to make a fashionable call, so I put on my regimentals."

"I don't b'lieve you've got any better clo'es," said Micky.

"All right," said Dick, "I won't charge you nothin' for what you believe."

Here a customer presented himself for Micky, and Dick went back to his room to change his clothes, before resuming business.

CHAPTER XXV: DICK WRITES HIS FIRST LETTER

When Fosdick reached home in the evening, Dick displayed his letter with some pride.

"It's a nice letter," said Fosdick, after reading it. "I should like to know Frank."

"I'll bet you would," said Dick. "He's a trump."

"When are you going to answer it?"

"I don't know," said Dick, dubiously. "I never writ a letter."

"That's no reason why you shouldn't. There's always a first time, you know."

"I don't know what to say," said Dick.

"Get some paper and sit down to it, and you'll find enough to say. You can do that this evening instead of studying."

"If you'll look it over afterwards, and shine it up a little."

"Yes, if it needs it; but I rather think Frank would like it best just as you wrote it."

Dick decided to adopt Fosdick's suggestion. He had very serious doubts as to his ability to write a letter. Like a good many other boys, he looked upon it as a very serious job, not reflecting that, after all, letter-writing is nothing but talking upon paper. Still, in spite of his misgivings, he felt that the letter ought to be answered, and he wished Frank to hear from him. After various preparations, he at last got settled down to his task, and, before the evening was over, a letter was written. As the first letter which Dick had ever produced, and because it was characteristic of him, my readers may like to read it.

Here it is,—

"DEAR FRANK,—I got your letter this mornin', and was very glad to hear you hadn't forgotten Ragged

Dick. I aint so ragged as I was. Openwork coats and trowsers has gone out of fashion. I put on the Washington coat and Napoleon pants to go to the post-office, for fear they wouldn't think I was the boy that was meant. On my way back I received the congratulations of my intimate friend, Micky Maguire, on my improved appearance.

"I've give up sleepin' in boxes, and old wagons, findin' it didn't agree with my constitution. I've hired a room in Mott Street, and have got a private tooter, who rooms with me and looks after my studies in the evenin'. Mott Street aint very fashionable; but my manshun on Fifth Avenoo isn't finished yet, and I'm afraid it won't be till I'm a gray-haired veteran. I've got a hundred dollars towards it, which I've saved up from my earnin's. I haven't forgot what you and your uncle said to me, and I'm tryin' to grow up 'spectable. I haven't been to Tony Pastor's, or the Old Bowery, for ever so long. I'd rather save up my money to support me in my old age. When my hair gets gray, I'm goin' to knock off blackin' boots, and go into some light, genteel employment, such as keepin' an apple-stand, or disseminatin' pea-nuts among the people.

"I've got so as to read pretty well, so my tooter says. I've been studyin' geography and grammar also. I've made such astonishin' progress that I can tell a noun from a conjunction as far away as I can see 'em. Tell Mr. Munroe that if he wants an accomplished teacher in his school, he can send for me, and I'll come on by the very next train. Or, if he wants to sell out for a hundred dollars, I'll buy the whole concern, and agree to teach the scholars all I know myself in less than six months. Is teachin' as good business, generally speakin', as blackin' boots? My private tooter combines both, and is makin' a fortun' with great rapidity. He'll be as rich as Astor some time, *if he only lives long enough.*

"I should think you'd have a bully time at your school. I should like to go out in the boat, or play ball with you. When are you comin' to the city? I wish you'd write and let me know when you do, and I'll call and see you. I'll leave my business in the hands of my numerous clerks, and go round with you. There's lots of things you didn't see when you was here before. They're getting on fast at the Central Park. It looks better than it did a year ago.

"I aint much used to writin' letters. As this is the first one I ever wrote, I hope you'll excuse the mistakes. I hope you'll write to me again soon. I can't write so good a letter as you; but, I'll do my best, as the man said when he was asked if he could swim over to Brooklyn backwards. Good-by, Frank. Thank you for all your kindness. Direct your next letter to No. — Mott Street.

"Your true friend,

"DICK HUNTER."

When Dick had written the last word, he leaned back in his chair, and surveyed the letter with much satisfaction.

"I didn't think I could have wrote such a long letter, Fosdick," said he.

"Written would be more grammatical, Dick," suggested his friend.

"I guess there's plenty of mistakes in it," said Dick. "Just look at it, and see."

Fosdick took the letter, and read it over carefully.

"Yes, there are some mistakes," he said; "but it sounds so much like you that I think it would be better to let it go just as it is. It will be more likely to remind Frank of what you were when he first saw you."

"Is it good enough to send?" asked Dick, anxiously.

"Yes; it seems to me to be quite a good letter. It is written just as you talk. Nobody but you could have written such a letter, Dick. I think Frank will be amused at your proposal to come up there as teacher."

"P'r'aps it would be a good idea for us to open a seleck school here in Mott Street," said Dick, humorously. "We could call it 'Professor Fosdick and Hunter's Mott Street Seminary.' Boot-blackin' taught by Professor Hunter."

The evening was so far advanced that Dick decided to postpone copying his letter till the next evening. By this time he had come to have a very fair handwriting, so that when the letter was complete it really looked quite creditable, and no one would have suspected that it was Dick's first attempt in this line. Our hero surveyed it with no little complacency. In fact, he felt rather proud of it, since it reminded him of the great progress he had made. He carried it down to the post-office, and deposited it with his own hands in the proper box. Just on the steps of the building, as he was coming out, he met Johnny Nolan, who had been sent on an errand to Wall Street by some gentleman, and was just returning.

"What are you doin' down here, Dick?" asked Johnny.

"I've been mailin' a letter."

"Who sent you?"

"Nobody."

"I mean, who writ the letter?"

"I wrote it myself."

"Can you write letters?" asked Johnny, in amazement.

"Why shouldn't I?"

"I didn't know you could write. I can't."

"Then you ought to learn."

"I went to school once; but it was too hard work, so I give it up."

"You're lazy, Johnny,—that's what's the matter. How'd you ever expect to know anything, if you don't try?"

"I can't learn."

"You can, if you want to."

Johnny Nolan was evidently of a different opinion. He was a good-natured boy, large of his age, with nothing particularly bad about him, but utterly lacking in that energy, ambition, and natural sharpness, for which Dick was distinguished. He was not adapted to succeed in the life which circumstances had forced upon him; for in the street-life of the metropolis a boy needs to be on the alert, and have all his wits about him, or he will find himself wholly distanced by his more enterprising competitors for popular favor. To succeed in his profession, humble as it is, a boot-black must depend upon the same qualities which gain success in higher walks in life. It was easy to see that Johnny, unless very much favored by circumstances, would never rise much above his present level. For Dick, we cannot help hoping much better things.

CHAPTER XXVI: AN EXCITING ADVENTURE

Dick now began to look about for a position in a store or count-ing-room. Until he should obtain one he determined to devote half the day to blacking boots, not being willing to break in upon his small capital. He found that he could earn enough in half a day to pay all his necessary expenses, including the entire rent of the room. Fosdick desired to pay his half; but Dick steadily refused, insisting upon paying so much as compensation for his friend's services as instructor.

It should be added that Dick's peculiar way of speaking and use of slang terms had been somewhat modified by his education and his intimacy with Henry Fosdick. Still he continued to indulge in them to some extent, especially when he felt like joking, and it was natural to Dick to joke, as my readers have probably found out by this time. Still his manners were consider-ably improved, so that he was more likely to obtain a situation than when first introduced to our notice.

Just now, however, business was very dull, and merchants, instead of hiring new assistants, were disposed to part with those already in their employ. After making several ineffectual applica-tions, Dick began to think he should be obliged to stick to his profession until the next season. But about this time something occurred which considerably improved his chances of prefer-ment.

This is the way it happened.

As Dick, with a balance of more than a hundred dollars in the savings bank, might fairly consider himself a young man of prop-erty, he thought himself justified in occasionally taking a half holiday from business, and going on an excursion. On Wednesday afternoon Henry Fosdick was sent by his employer on an errand to that part of Brooklyn near Greenwood Cemetery.[1] Dick hastily dressed himself in his best, and determined to accompany him.

The two boys walked down to the South Ferry, and, paying their two cents each, entered the ferry boat. They remained at the stern, and stood by the railing, watching the great city, with its crowded wharves, receding from view. Beside them was a gentle-man with two children,—a girl of eight and a little boy of six. The children were talking gayly to their father. While he was pointing

---

1 Established in rural King's County in 1838, the prestigious Green-Wood Cemetery consists of several hundred acres located between Prospect Park and Sunset Park.

out some object of interest to the little girl, the boy managed to creep, unobserved, beneath the chain that extends across the boat, for the protection of passengers, and, stepping incautiously to the edge of the boat, fell over into the foaming water.

At the child's scream, the father looked up, and, with a cry of horror, sprang to the edge of the boat. He would have plunged in, but, being unable to swim, would only have endangered his own life, without being able to save his child.

"My child!" he exclaimed in anguish,—"who will save my child? A thousand—ten thousand dollars to any one who will save him!"

There chanced to be but few passengers on board at the time, and nearly all these were either in the cabins or standing forward. Among the few who saw the child fall was our hero.

Now Dick was an expert swimmer. It was an accomplishment which he had possessed for years, and he no sooner saw the boy fall than he resolved to rescue him. His determination was formed before he heard the liberal offer made by the boy's father. Indeed, I must do Dick the justice to say that, in the excitement of the moment, he did not hear it at all, nor would it have stimulated the alacrity with which he sprang to the rescue of the little boy.

Little Johnny had already risen once, and gone under for the second time, when our hero plunged in. He was obliged to strike out for the boy, and this took time. He reached him none too soon. Just as he was sinking for the third and last time, he caught him by the jacket. Dick was stout and strong, but Johnny clung to him so tightly, that it was with great difficulty he was able to sustain himself.

"Put your arms round my neck," said Dick.

The little boy mechanically obeyed, and clung with a grasp strengthened by his terror. In this position Dick could bear his weight better. But the ferry-boat was receding fast. It was quite impossible to reach it. The father, his face pale with terror and anguish, and his hands clasped in suspense, saw the brave boy's struggles, and prayed with agonizing fervor that he might be successful. But it is probable, for they were now midway of the river, that both Dick and the little boy whom he had bravely undertaken to rescue would have been drowned, had not a row-boat been fortunately near. The two men who were in it witnessed the accident, and hastened to the rescue of our hero.

"Keep up a little longer," they shouted, bending to their oars, "and we will save you."

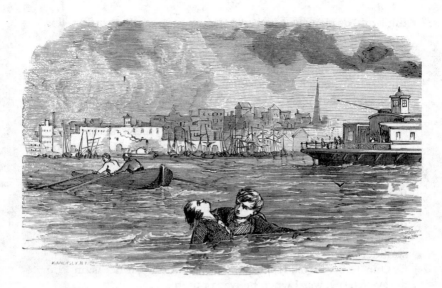

Figure 8. The Rescue, *Ragged Dick* (1868), opposite p. 284.
Editor's collection.

Dick heard the shout, and it put fresh strength into him. He battled manfully with the treacherous sea, his eyes fixed longingly upon the approaching boat.

"Hold on tight, little boy," he said. "There's a boat coming."

The little boy did not see the boat. His eyes were closed to shut out the fearful water, but he clung the closer to his young preserver. Six long, steady strokes, and the boat dashed along side. Strong hands seized Dick and his youthful burden, and drew them into the boat, both dripping with water.

"God be thanked!" exclaimed the father, as from the steamer he saw the child's rescue. "That brave boy shall be rewarded, if I sacrifice my whole fortune to compass it."

"You've had a pretty narrow escape, young chap," said one of the boatmen to Dick. "It was a pretty tough job you undertook."

"Yes," said Dick. "That's what I thought when I was in the water. If it hadn't been for you, I don't know what would have 'come of us."

"Anyhow you're a plucky boy, or you wouldn't have dared to jump into the water after this little chap. It was a risky thing to do."

"I'm used to the water," said Dick, modestly. "I didn't stop to think of the danger, but I wasn't going to see that little fellow drown without tryin' to save him."

The boat at once headed for the ferry wharf on the Brooklyn side. The captain of the ferry-boat, seeing the rescue, did not think it necessary to stop his boat, but kept on his way. The whole occurrence took place in less time than I have occupied in telling it.

The father was waiting on the wharf to receive his little boy, with what feelings of gratitude and joy can be easily understood. With a burst of happy tears he clasped him to his arms. Dick was about to withdraw modestly, but the gentleman perceived the movement, and, putting down the child, came forward, and, clasping his hand, said with emotion, "My brave boy, I owe you a debt I can never repay. But for your timely service I should now be plunged into an anguish which I cannot think of without a shudder."

Our hero was ready enough to speak on most occasions, but always felt awkward when he was praised.

"It wasn't any trouble," he said, modestly. "I can swim like a top."

"But not many boys would have risked their lives for a stranger," said the gentleman. "But," he added with a sudden thought, as his glance rested on Dick's dripping garments, "both you and my little boy will take cold in wet clothes. Fortunately I have a friend living close at hand, at whose house you will have an opportunity of taking off your clothes, and having them dried."

Dick protested that he never took cold; but Fosdick, who had now joined them, and who, it is needless to say, had been greatly alarmed at Dick's danger, joined in urging compliance with the gentleman's proposal, and in the end our hero had to yield. His new friend secured a hack, the driver of which agreed for extra recompense to receive the dripping boys into his carriage, and they were whirled rapidly to a pleasant house in a side street, where matters were quickly explained, and both boys were put to bed.

"I aint used to goin' to bed quite so early," thought Dick. "This is the queerest excursion I ever took."

Like most active boys Dick did not enjoy the prospect of spending half a day in bed; but his confinement did not last as long as he anticipated.

In about an hour the door of his chamber was opened, and a servant appeared, bringing a new and handsome suit of clothes throughout.

"You are to put on these," said the servant to Dick; "but you needn't get up till you feel like it."

"Whose clothes are they?" asked Dick.

"They are yours."

"Mine! Where did they come from?"

"Mr. Rockwell sent out and bought them for you. They are the same size as your wet ones."

"Is he here now?"

"No. He bought another suit for the little boy, and has gone back to New York. Here's a note he asked me to give you."

Dick opened the paper, and read as follows,—

"Please accept this outfit of clothes as the first instalment of a debt which I can never repay. I have asked to have your wet suit dried, when you can reclaim it. Will you oblige me by calling to-morrow at my counting room, No. —, Pearl Street.

"Your friend,

"JAMES ROCKWELL."

CHAPTER XXVII: CONCLUSION

When Dick was dressed in his new suit, he surveyed his figure with pardonable complacency. It was the best he had ever worn, and fitted him as well as if it had been made expressly for him.

"He's done the handsome thing," said Dick to himself; "but there wasn't no 'casion for his givin' me these clothes. My lucky stars are shinin' pretty bright now. Jumpin' into the water pays better than shinin' boots; but I don't think I'd like to try it more'n once a week."

About eleven o'clock the next morning Dick repaired to Mr. Rockwell's counting-room on Pearl Street. He found himself in front of a large and handsome warehouse. The counting-room was on the lower floor. Our hero entered, and found Mr. Rockwell sitting at a desk. No sooner did that gentleman see him than he arose, and, advancing, shook Dick by the hand in the most friendly manner.

"My young friend," he said, "you have done me so great service that I wish to be of some service to you in return. Tell me about yourself, and what plans or wishes you have formed for the future."

Dick frankly related his past history, and told Mr. Rockwell of his desire to get into a store or counting-room, and of the failure of all his applications thus far. The merchant listened attentively to Dick's statement, and, when he had finished, placed a sheet of paper before him, and, handing him a pen, said, "Will you write your name on this piece of paper?"

Dick wrote in a free, bold hand, the name Richard Hunter. He had very much improved in his penmanship, as has already been mentioned, and now had no cause to be ashamed of it.

Mr. Rockwell surveyed it approvingly.

"How would you like to enter my counting-room as clerk, Richard?" he asked.

Dick was about to say "Bully," when he recollected himself, and answered, "Very much."

"I suppose you know something of arithmetic, do you not?"

"Yes, sir."

"Then you may consider yourself engaged at a salary of ten dollars a week. You may come next Monday morning."

"Ten dollars!" repeated Dick, thinking he must have misunderstood.

"Yes; will that be sufficient?"

"It's more than I can earn," said Dick, honestly.

"Perhaps it is at first," said Mr. Rockwell, smiling; "but I am willing to pay you that. I will besides advance you as fast as your progress will justify it."

Dick was so elated that he hardly restrained himself from some demonstration which would have astonished the merchant; but he exercised self-control, and only said, "I'll try to serve you so faithfully, sir, that you won't repent having taken me into your service."

"And I think you will succeed," said Mr. Rockwell, encouragingly. "I will not detain you any longer, for I have some important business to attend to. I shall expect to see you on Monday morning."

Dick left the counting-room, hardly knowing whether he stood on his head or his heels, so overjoyed was he at the sudden change in his fortunes. Ten dollars a week was to him a fortune, and three times as much as he had expected to obtain at first. Indeed he would have been glad, only the day before, to get a place at three dollars a week. He reflected that with the stock of clothes which he had now on hand, he could save up at least half of it, and even then live better than he had been accustomed to do; so that his little fund in the savings bank, instead of being diminished, would be steadily increasing. Then he was to be advanced if he deserved it. It was indeed a bright prospect for a boy who, only a year before, could neither read nor write, and depended for a night's lodging upon the chance hospitality of an alley-way or old wagon. Dick's great ambition to "grow up 'spectable" seemed likely to be accomplished after all.

"I wish Fosdick was as well off as I am," he thought generously. But he determined to help his less fortunate friend, and assist him up the ladder as he advanced himself.

When Dick entered his room on Mott Street, he discovered that some one else had been there before him, and two articles of wearing apparel had disappeared.

"By gracious!" he exclaimed; "somebody's stole my Washington coat and Napoleon pants. Maybe it's an agent of Barnum's, who expects to make a fortun' by exhibitin' the valooable wardrobe of a gentleman of fashion."

Dick did not shed many tears over his loss, as, in his present circumstances, he never expected to have any further use for the well-worn garments. It may be stated that he afterwards saw them adorning the figure of Micky Maguire; but whether that estimable young man stole them himself, he never ascertained. As to the loss, Dick was rather pleased that it had occurred. It seemed to cut him off from the old vagabond life which he hoped never to resume. Henceforward he meant to press onward, and rise as high as possible.

Although it was yet only noon, Dick did not go out again with his brush. He felt that it was time to retire from business. He would leave his share of the public patronage to other boys less fortunate than himself. That evening Dick and Fosdick had a long conversation. Fosdick rejoiced heartily in his friend's success, and on his side had the pleasant news to communicate that his pay had been advanced to six dollars a week.

"I think we can afford to leave Mott Street now," he continued. "This house isn't as neat as it might be, and I shall like to live in a nicer quarter of the city."

"All right," said Dick. "We'll hunt up a new room to-morrow. I shall have plenty of time, having retired from business. I'll try to get my reg'lar customers to take Johnny Nolan in my place. That boy hasn't any enterprise. He needs some body to look out for him."

"You might give him your box and brush, too, Dick."

"No," said Dick; "I'll give him some new ones, but mine I want to keep, to remind me of the hard times I've had, when I was an ignorant boot-black, and never expected to be anything better."

"When, in short, you were 'Ragged Dick.' You must drop that name, and think of yourself now as"—

"Richard Hunter, Esq.," said our hero, smiling.

"A young gentleman on the way to fame and fortune," added Fosdick.

★★★

Here ends the story of Ragged Dick. As Fosdick said, he is Ragged Dick no longer. He has taken a step upward, and is determined to mount still higher. There are fresh adventures in store for him, and for others who have been introduced in these pages. Those who have felt interested in his early life will find his history continued in a new volume, forming the second of the series, to be called,—

Fame and Fortune; or, The Progress of Richard Hunter.

RISEN FROM THE RANKS; OR, HARRY WALTON'S SUCCESS

Contents

PREFACE

"Risen from the Ranks" contains the further history of Harry Walton, who was first introduced to the public in the pages of "Bound to Rise." Those who are interested in learning how far he made good the promise of his boyhood, may here find their curiosity gratified. For the benefit of those who may only read the present volume, a synopsis of Harry's previous life is given in the first chapter.

In describing Harry's rise from the ranks I have studiously avoided the extraordinary incidents and pieces of good luck, which the story writer has always at command, being desirous of presenting my hero's career as one which may be imitated by the thousands of boys similarly placed, who, like him, are anxious to rise from the ranks. It is my hope that this story, suggested in part by the career of an eminent American editor,[1] may afford encouragement to such boys, and teach them that "where there is a will there is always a way."

New York, October 1874.

---

1 Apparently Horace Greeley (1811–72). See Chapter V of *Ragged Dick*, p. 74, note 1.

CHAPTER I: HARRY WALTON

"I am sorry to part with you, Harry," said Professor Henderson. "You have been a very satisfactory and efficient assistant, and I shall miss you."

"Thank you, sir," said Harry. "I have tried to be faithful to your interests."

"You have been so," said the Professor emphatically. "I have had perfect confidence in you, and this has relieved me of a great deal of anxiety. It would have been very easy for one in your position to cheat me out of a considerable sum of money."

"It was no credit to me to resist such a temptation as that," said Harry.

"I am glad to hear you say so, but it shows your inexperience nevertheless. Money is the great tempter nowadays. Consider how many defalcations and breaches of trust we read of daily in confidential positions, and we are forced to conclude that honesty is a rarer virtue than we like to think it. I have every reason to believe that my assistant last winter purloined, at the least, a hundred dollars, but I was unable to prove it, and submitted to the loss. It may be the same next winter. Can't I induce you to change your resolution, and remain in my employ? I will advance your pay."

"Thank you, Professor Henderson," said Harry gratefully. "I appreciate your offer, even if I do not accept it. But I have made up my mind to learn the printing business."

"You are to enter the office of the 'Centreville Gazette,' I believe."

"Yes, sir."

"How much pay will you get?"

"I shall receive my board the first month, and for the next six months have agreed to take two dollars a week and board."

"That won't pay your expenses."

"It *must*," said Harry, firmly.

"You have laid up some money while with me, haven't you!"

"Yes, sir; I have fifty dollars in my pocket-book, besides having given eighty dollars at home."

"That is doing well, but you won't be able to lay up anything for the next year."

"Perhaps not in money, but I shall be gaining the knowledge of a good trade."

"And you like that better than remaining with me, and learning my business?"

"Yes, sir."

"Well, perhaps you are right. I don't fancy being a magician myself; but I am too old to change. I like moving round, and I make a good living for my family. Besides I contribute to the innocent amusement of the public, and earn my money fairly."

"I agree with you, sir," said Harry. "I think yours is a useful employment, but it would not suit everybody. Ever since I read the life of Benjamin Franklin,[1] I have wanted to learn to be a printer."

"It is an excellent business, no doubt, and if you have made up your mind I will not dissuade you. When you have a paper of your own, you can give your old friend, Professor Henderson, an occasional puff."[2]

"I shall be glad to do that," said Harry, smiling, "but I shall have to wait some time first."

"How old are you now?"

"Sixteen."

"Then you may qualify yourself for an editor in five or six years. I advise you to try it at any rate. The editor in America is a man of influence."

"I do look forward to it," said Harry, seriously. "I should not be satisfied to remain a journeyman[3] all my life, nor even the half of it."

"I sympathize with your ambition, Harry," said the Professor, earnestly, "and I wish you the best success. Let me hear from you occasionally."

"I should be very glad to write you, sir."

"I see the stage is at the door, and I must bid you good-by. When you have a vacation, if you get a chance to come our way, Mrs. Henderson and myself will be glad to receive a visit from you. Good-by!" And with a hearty shake of the hand, Professor Henderson bade farewell to his late assistant.

Those who have read "Bound to Rise," and are thus familiar with Harry Walton's early history, will need no explanation of the

---

1 Benjamin Franklin (1706–90), one of the most eminent scientists and philosophers of his time, began to write his autobiography in 1771. It was published posthumously, and the first complete edition in English appeared in 1868.

2 An advertising blurb.

3 Printers were ranked as apprentices or "printer's devils," entry-level interns who performed much of the drudge work in the print shop; journeymen or "jour" printers, temporary or itinerant employees; and full-fledged printers, often proprietors of the print shop.

preceding conversation. But for the benefit of new readers, I will recapitulate briefly the leading events in the history of the boy of sixteen who is to be our hero.

Harry Walton was the oldest son of a poor New Hampshire farmer, who found great difficulty is wresting from his few sterile acres a living for his family. Nearly a year before, he had lost his only cow by a prevalent disease, and being without money, was compelled to buy another of Squire Green, a rich but mean neighbor, on a six months' note, on very unfavorable terms. As it required great economy to make both ends meet, there seemed no possible chance of his being able to meet the note at maturity. Beside, Mr. Walton was to forfeit ten dollars if he did not have the principal and interest ready for Squire Green. The hard-hearted creditor was mean enough to take advantage of his poor neighbor's necessities, and there was not the slightest chance of his receding from his unreasonable demand. Under these circumstances Harry, the oldest boy, asked his father's permission to go out into the world and earn his own living. He hoped not only to do this, but to save something toward paying his father's note. His ambition had been kindled by reading the life of Benjamin Franklin, which had been awarded to him as a school prize. He did not expect to emulate Franklin, but he thought that by imitating him he might attain an honorable position in the community.

Harry's request was not at first favorably received. To send a boy out into the world to earn his own living is a hazardous experiment, and fathers are less sanguine than their sons. Their experience suggests difficulties and obstacles of which the inexperienced youth knows and possesses nothing. But in the present case Mr. Walton reflected that the little farming town in which he lived offered small inducements for a boy to remain there, unless he was content to be a farmer, and this required capital. His farm was too small for himself, and of course he could not give Harry a part when he came of age. On the whole, therefore, Harry's plan of becoming a mechanic seemed not so bad a one after all. So permission was accorded, and our hero, with his little bundle of clothes, left the paternal roof, and went out in quest of employment.

After some adventures Harry obtained employment in a shoe-shop as pegger.[1] A few weeks sufficed to make him a good workman, and he was then able to earn three dollars a week and

---

1 A manual laborer who assembles shoes with wooden pegs.

board. Out of this sum be hoped to save enough to pay the note held by Squire Green against his father, but there were two unforeseen obstacles. He had the misfortune to lose his pocket-book, which was picked up by an unprincipled young man, by name Luke Harrison, also a shoemaker, who was always in pecuniary difficulties, though he earned much higher wages than Harry. Luke was unable to resist the temptation, and appropriated the money to his own use. This Harry ascertained after a while, but thus far had succeeded in obtaining the restitution of but a small portion of his hard-earned savings. The second obstacle was a sudden depression in the shoe trade which threw him out of work. More than most occupations the shoe business is liable to these sudden fluctuations and suspensions, and the most industrious and ambitious workman is often compelled to spend in his enforced weeks of idleness all that he had been able to save when employed, and thus at the end of the year finds himself, through no fault of his own, no better off than at the beginning. Finding himself out of work, our hero visited other shoe establishments in the hope of employment. But his search was in vain. Chance in this emergency made him acquainted with Professor Henderson, a well-known magician and conjurer, whose custom it was to travel, through the fall and winter, from town to town, giving public exhibitions of his skill. He was in want of an assistant, to sell tickets and help him generally, and he offered the position to our hero, at a salary of five dollars a week. It is needless to say that the position was gladly accepted. It was not the business that Harry preferred, but he reasoned justly that it was honorable, and was far better than remaining idle. He found Professor Henderson as he called himself, a considerate and agreeable employer, and as may be inferred from the conversation with which this chapter begins, his services were very satisfactory. At the close of the six months, he had the satisfaction of paying the note which his father had given, and so of disappointing the selfish schemes of the grasping creditor.

This was not all. He met with an adventure while travelling for the Professor, in which a highwayman who undertook to rob him, came off second best, and he was thus enabled to add fifty dollars to his savings. His financial condition at the opening of the present story has already been set forth.

Though I have necessarily omitted many interesting details, to be found in "Bound to Rise," I have given the reader all the information required to enable him to understand the narrative of Harry's subsequent fortunes.

CHAPTER II: THE PRINTING OFFICE

Jotham Anderson, editor and publisher of the "Centreville Gazette," was sitting at his desk penning an editorial paragraph, when the office door opened, and Harry Walton entered.

"Good-morning, Mr. Anderson," said our hero, removing his hat.

"Good-morning, my friend. I believe you have the advantage of me," replied the editor.

Our hero was taken aback. It didn't occur to him that the engagement was a far less important event to the publisher than to himself. He began to be afraid that the place had not been kept open for him.

"My name is Harry Walton," he explained. "I was travelling with Prof. Henderson last winter, and called here to get some bills printed."

"Oh yes, I remember you now. I agreed to take you into the office," said the editor, to Harry's great relief.

"Yes, sir."

"You haven't changed your mind, then?—You still want to be a printer?"

"Yes, sir."

"You have left the Professor, I suppose."

"I left him yesterday."

"What did he pay you?"

"Five dollars a week. He offered me six, if I would stay with him."

"Of course you know that I can't pay you any such wages at present."

"Yes, sir. You agreed to give me my board the first month, and two dollars a week for six months afterward."

"That is all you will be worth to me at first. It is a good deal less than you would earn with Professor Henderson."

"I know that, sir; but I am willing to come for that."

"Good. I see you are in earnest about printing, and that is a good sign. I wanted you to understand just what you had to expect, so that you need not be disappointed."

"I sha'n't be disappointed, sir," said Harry confidently. "I have made up my mind to be a printer, and if you didn't receive me into your office, I would try to get in somewhere else."

"Then no more need be said. When do you want to begin?"

"I am ready any time."

"Where is your trunk?"

ALGER SERIES No. 38

RISEN FROM THE RANKS

by **HORATIO ALGER, JR.**

Figure 9. Cover of *Risen from the Ranks* (Street & Smith, 1917). Editor's collection.

"At the tavern."

"You can have it brought over to my house whenever you please. The hotel-keeper will send it over for you. He is our expressman. Come into the house now, and I will introduce you to my wife."

The editor's home was just across the street from his printing office. Followed by Harry he crossed the street, opened the front door, and led the way into the sitting-room, where a pleasant-looking lady of middle age was seated.

"My dear," he said, "I bring you a new boarder."

She looked at Harry inquiringly.

"This young man," her husband explained, "is going into the office to learn printing. I have taken a contract to make a second Benjamin Franklin of him."

"Then you'll do more for him than you have been able to do for yourself," said Mrs. Anderson, smiling.

"You are inclined to be severe, Mrs. Anderson, but I fear you are correct. However, I can be like a guide-post, which points the way which it does not travel. Can you show Harry Walton—for that is his name—where you propose to put him?"

"I am afraid I must give you a room in the attic," said Mrs. Anderson. "Our house is small, and all the chambers on the second floor are occupied."

"I am not at all particular," said Harry. "I have not been accustomed to elegant accommodations."

"If you will follow me upstairs, I will show you your room."

Pausing on the third landing, Mrs. Anderson found the door of a small but comfortable bed-room. There was no carpet on the floor, but it was painted yellow, and scrupulously clean. A bed, two chairs, a bureau and wash-stand completed the list of furniture.

"I shall like this room very well," said our hero.

"There is a closet," said the lady, pointing to a door in the corner. "It is large enough to contain your trunk, if you choose to put it in there. I hope you don't smoke."

"Oh, no, indeed," said Harry, laughing. "I haven't got so far along as that."

"Mr. Anderson's last apprentice—he is a journeyman now—was a smoker. He not only scented up the room, but as he was very careless about lights, I was continually alarmed lest he should set the house on fire. Finally, I got so nervous that I asked him to board somewhere else."

"Is he working for Mr. Anderson now?"

"Yes; you probably saw him in the office."

"I saw two young men at the case."[1]

"The one I speak of is the youngest. His name is John Clapp."

"There is no danger of my smoking. I don't think it would do me any good. Besides, it is expensive, and I can't afford it."

"I see we think alike," said Mrs. Anderson, smiling. "I am sure we will get along well together."

"I shall try not to give you any trouble," said our hero, and his tone, which was evidently sincere, impressed Mrs. Anderson still more favorably.

"You won't find me very hard to suit, I hope. I suppose you will be here to supper?"

"If it will be quite convenient. My trunk is at the tavern, and I could stay there till morning, if you wished."

"Oh, no, come at once. Take possession of the room now, if you like, and leave an order to have your trunk brought here."

"Thank you. What is your hour for supper?"

"Half-past five."

"Thank you. I will go over and speak to Mr. Anderson a minute."

The editor looked up as Harry reappeared.

"Well, have you settled arrangements with Mrs. Anderson?" he asked.

"Yes, sir, I believe so."

"I hope you like your room."

"It is very comfortable. It won't take me long to feel at home there."

"Did she ask you whether you smoked?"

"Yes, sir."

"I thought she would. That's where Clapp and she fell out."

Harry's attention was drawn to a thin, sallow young man of about twenty, who stood at a case on the opposite side of the room.

"Mrs. Anderson was afraid I would set the house on fire," said the young man thus referred to.

"Yes, she felt nervous about it. However, it is not surprising. An uncle of hers lost his house in that way. I suppose you don't smoke, Walton?"

"No, sir."

---

1   A type case is a box containing moveable type used by a printer.

"Clapp smokes for his health. You see how stout and robust he is," said the editor, a little satirically.

"It doesn't do me any harm," said Clapp, a little testily.

"Oh, well, I don't interfere with you, though I think you would be better off if you should give up the habit. Ferguson don't smoke."

This was the other compositor,[1] a man of thirty, whose case was not far distant from Clapp's.

"I can't afford it," said Ferguson; "nor could Clapp, if he had a wife and two young children to support."

"Smoking doesn't cost much," said the younger journeyman.

"So you think; but did you ever reckon it up?"

"No."

"Don't you keep any accounts?"

"No; I spend when I need to, and I can always tell how much I have left. What's the use of keeping accounts?"

"You can tell how you stand."

"I can tell that without taking so much trouble."

"You see we must all agree to disagree," said Mr. Anderson. "I am afraid Clapp isn't going to be a second Benjamin Franklin."

"Who is?" asked Clapp.

"Our young friend here," said the editor.

"Oh, is he?" queried the other with a sneer. "It'll be a great honor, I'm sure, to have him in the office."

"Come, no chaffing, Clapp," said Mr. Anderson.

Harry hastened to disclaim the charge, for Clapp's sneer affected him disagreeably.

"I admire Franklin," he said, "but there isn't much danger of my turning out a second edition of him."

"Professional already, I see, Walton," said the editor.

"When shall I go to work, Mr. Anderson?"

"Whenever you are ready."

"I am ready now."

"You are prompt."

"You won't be in such a hurry to go to work a week hence," said Clapp.

"I think I shall," said Harry. "I am anxious to learn as fast as possible."

"Oh, I forgot. You want to become a second Franklin."

---

1 The typesetter or printer who set type by hand prior to the introduction, in the late nineteenth century, of various automated typesetting machines.

"I sha'n't like him," thought our hero. "He seems to try to make himself disagreeable."

"Mr. Ferguson will give you some instruction, and set you to work," said his employer.

Harry was glad that it was from the older journeyman that he was to receive his first lesson, and not from the younger.

CHAPTER III:
HARRY STUMBLES UPON AN ACQUAINTANCE

After supper Harry went round to the tavern to see about his trunk. A group of young men were in the bar-room, some of whom looked up as he entered. Among these was Luke Harrison, who was surprised and by no means pleased to see his creditor. Harry recognized him at the same instant, and said, "How are you, Luke?"

"Is that you, Walton?" said Luke. "What brings you to Centreville? Professor Henderson isn't here, is he?"

"No; I have left him."

"Oh, you're out of a job, are you?" asked Luke, in a tone of satisfaction, for we are apt to dislike those whom we have injured, and for this reason he felt by no means friendly.

"No, I'm not," said Harry, quietly. "I've found work in Centreville."

"Gone back to pegging, have you? Whose shop are you in?"

"I am in a different business."

"You don't say! What is it?" asked Luke, with some curiosity.

"I'm in the office of the 'Centreville Gazette.' I'm going to learn the printing business."

"You are? Why, I've got a friend in the office,—John Clapp. He never told me about your being there."

"He didn't know I was coming. I only went to work this afternoon."

"So you are the printer's devil?"[1] said Luke, with a slight sneer.

"I believe so," answered our hero, quietly.

"Do you get good pay?"

"Not much at first. However, I can get along with what money I have, *and what is due me.*"

1   See Chapter I, p. 192, note 3.

Luke Harrison understood the last allusion, and turned away abruptly.

He had no wish to pay up the money which he owed Harry, and for this reason was sorry to see him in the village. He feared, if the conversation were continued, Harry would be asking for the money, and this would be disagreeable.

At this moment John Clapp entered the bar-room. He nodded slightly to Harry, but walked up to Luke, and greeted him cordially. There were many points of resemblance between them, and this drew them into habits of intimacy.

"Will you have something to drink, Harrison?" said Clapp.

"I don't mind if I do," answered Luke, with alacrity.

They walked up to the bar, and they were soon pledging each other in a fiery fluid which was not very likely to benefit either of them. Meanwhile Harry gave directions about his trunk, and left the room.

"So you've got a new 'devil' in your office," said Luke, after draining his glass.

"Yes. He came this afternoon. How did you hear?"

"He told me."

"Do you know him?" asked Clapp, in some surprise.

"Yes. I know him as well as I want to."

"What sort of a fellow is he?"

"Oh, he's a sneak—one of your pious chaps, that 'wants to be an angel, and with the angels stand.'"[1]

"Then he's made a mistake in turning 'devil,'" said Clapp.

"Good for you!" said Luke, laughing. "You're unusually brilliant to-night, Clapp."

"So he's a saint, is he?"

"He set up for one; but I don't like his style myself. He's as mean as dirt. Why I knew him several months, and he never offered to treat in all that time. He's as much afraid of spending a cent as if it were a dollar."

"He won't have many dollars to spend just at present. He's working for his board."

"Oh, he's got money saved up," said Luke. "Fellows like him hang on to a cent when they get it. I once asked him to lend me a few dollars, just for a day or two, but he wouldn't do it. I hate such mean fellows."

"So do I. Will you have a cigar?"

---

1 A line in a popular mid-nineteenth-century Christian hymn by Urania Locke Bailey (1820–82).

"I'll treat this time," said Luke, who thought it polite to take his turn in treating once to his companion's four or five times.

"Thank you. From what you say, I am sorry Anderson has taken the fellow into the office."

"You needn't have much to say to him."

"I shan't trouble myself much about him. I didn't like his looks when I first set eyes on him. I suppose old Mother Anderson will like him. She couldn't abide my smoking, and he won't trouble her that way."

"So; he's too mean to buy the cigars."

"He said he couldn't afford it."

"That's what it comes to. By the way, Clapp, when shall we take another ride?"

"I can get away next Monday afternoon, at three."

"All right. I'll manage to get off at the same time. We'll go to Winston and take supper at the hotel. It does a fellow good to get off now and then. It won't cost more than five dollars apiece altogether."

"We'll get the carriage charged. The fact is, I'm little low on funds."

"So am I, but it won't matter. Griffin will wait for his pay."

While Harry's character was being so unfavorably discussed, he was taking a walk by himself, observing with interest the main features of his new home. He had been here before with Professor Henderson, but had been too much occupied at that time to get a very clear idea of Centreville, nor had it then the interest for him which it had acquired since. He went upon a hill overlooking the village, and obtained an excellent view from its summit. It was a pleasant, well-built village of perhaps three thousand inhabitants, with outlying farms and farm-houses. Along the principal streets the dwellings and stores were closely built, so as to make it seem quite city-like. It was the shire town of the county, and being the largest place in the neighborhood, country people for miles around traded at its stores. Farmers' wives came to Centreville to make purchases, just as ladies living within a radius of thirty miles visit New York and Boston, for a similar purpose. Altogether, therefore, Centreville was quite a lively place, and a town of considerable local importance. The fact that it had a weekly paper of its own, contributed to bring it into notice. Nor was that all. Situated on a little hillock was a building with a belfry, which might have been taken for a church but for a play-ground near by, which indicated that it had a different character. It was in fact the Prescott Academy, so called from the name of its founder, who had endowed it with a fund of ten thousand dollars, besides erecting the building at his own expense on land bought for the purpose. This academy also had a local reputation, and its benefits were not confined to the children of Centreville. There were about twenty pupils from other towns who boarded with the Principal or elsewhere in the town, and made up the whole number of students in attendance—about eighty on an average.

Standing on the eminence referred to, Harry's attention was drawn to the Academy, and he could not help forming the wish that he, too, might share in its advantages.

"There is so much to learn, and I know so little," he thought.

But he did not brood over the poverty which prevented him from gratifying his desire. He knew it would do no good, and he also reflected that knowledge may be acquired in a printing office as well as within the walls of an academy or college.

"As soon as I get well settled," he said to himself, "I mean to get some books and study a little every day. That is the way Franklin did. I never can be an editor, that's certain, without knowing more than I do now. Before I am qualified to teach others, I must know something myself."

Looking at the village which lay below him, Harry was disposed to congratulate himself on his new residence.

"It looks like a pleasant place," he said to himself, "and when I get a little acquainted, I shall enjoy myself very well, I am sure. Of course I shall feel rather lonely just at first."

He was so engrossed by his thoughts that he did not take heed to his steps, and was only reminded of his abstraction by his foot suddenly coming in contact with a boy who was lying under a tree, and pitching headfirst over him.

"Holloa!" exclaimed the latter, "what are you about? You didn't take me for a foot-ball, did you?"

"I beg your pardon," said Harry, jumping up in some confusion. "I was so busy thinking that I didn't see you. I hope I didn't hurt you."

"Nothing serious. Didn't you hurt yourself?"

"I bumped my head a little, but it only struck the earth. If it had been a stone, it might have been different. I had no idea there was any one up here except myself."

"It was very kind of you to bow so low to a perfect stranger," said the other, his eyes twinkling humorously. "I suppose it would only be polite for me to follow your example."

"I'll excuse you," said Harry laughing.

"Thank you. That takes a great burden off my mind. I don't like to be outdone in politeness, but really I shouldn't like to tumble over you. My head may be softer than yours. There's one thing clear. We ought to know each other. As you've taken the trouble to come up here, and stumble over me, I really feel as if we ought to strike up a friendship. What do you say?"

"With all my heart," said our hero.

CHAPTER IV: OSCAR VINCENT

"Allow me to introduce myself," said the stranger boy. "My name is Oscar Vincent, from Boston, at present a student at the Prescott Academy, at your service."

As he spoke, he doffed his hat and bowed, showing a profusion of chestnut hair, a broad, open brow, and an attractive face, lighted up by a pleasant smile.

Harry felt drawn to him by a feeling which was not long in ripening into friendship.

Imitating the other's frankness, he also took off his hat and replied,—

"Let me introduce myself, in turn, as Harry Walton, junior apprentice in the office of the 'Centreville Gazette,' sometimes profanely called 'printer's devil.'"

"Good!" said Oscar, laughing. "How do you like the business?"

"I think I shall like it, but I have only just started in it. I went into the office for the first time to-day."

"I have an uncle who started as you are doing," said Oscar. "He is now chief editor of a daily paper in Boston."

"Is he?" said Harry, with interest. "Did he find it hard to rise?"

"He is a hard worker. I have heard him say that he used to sit up late of nights during his apprenticeship, studying and improving himself."

"That is what I mean to do," said Harry.

"I don't think he was as lazy as his nephew," said Oscar. "I am afraid if I had been in his place I should have remained in it."

"Are you lazy?" asked Harry, smiling at the other's frankness.

"A little so; that is, I don't improve my opportunities as I might. Father wants to make a lawyer of me so he has put me here, and I am preparing for Harvard."

"I envy you," said Harry. "There is nothing I should like so much as entering college."

"I daresay I shall like it tolerably well," said Oscar; "but I don't *hanker* after it, as the boy said after swallowing a dose of castor oil. I'll tell you what I should like better—"

"What?" asked Harry, as the other paused.

"I should like to enter the Naval Academy,[1] and qualify myself for the naval service. I always liked the sea."

"Doesn't your father approve of your doing this?"

"He wouldn't mind my entering the navy as an officer, but he is not willing to have me enter the merchant service."

"Then why doesn't he send you to the Naval Academy?"

"Because I can't enter without receiving the appointment from a member of Congress. Our member can only appoint one, and there is no vacancy. So, as I can't go where I want to, I am preparing for Harvard."

"Are you studying Latin and Greek?"

"Yes."

"Have you studied them long?"

"About two years. I was looking over my Greek lesson when you playfully tumbled over me."

"Will you let me look at your book? I never saw a Greek book."

"I sometimes wish I never had," said Oscar; "but that's when I am lazy."

Harry opened the book—a Greek reader—in the middle of an extract from Xenophon,[2] and looked with some awe at the unintelligible letters.

"Can you read it? Can you understand what it means?" he asked, looking up from the book.

"So-so."

"You must know a great deal."

Oscar laughed.

"I wonder what Dr. Burton would say if he heard you," he said.

"Who is he?"

"Principal of our Academy. He gave me a blowing up for my ignorance to-day, because I missed an irregular Greek verb. I'm not exactly a dunce, but I don't think I shall ever be a Greek professor."

---

1 The US Naval Academy was founded in Annapolis, Maryland, in 1845. Applicants for admission usually required a nomination from a member of Congress.
2 Greek historian and soldier (430–354 BCE).

"If you speak of yourself that way, what will you think of me? I don't know a word of Latin, of Greek, or any language except my own."

"Because you have had no chance to learn. There's one language I know more about than Latin or Greek."

"English?"

"I mean French; I spent a year at a French boarding-school, three years since."

"What! Have you been in France?"

"Yes; an uncle of mine—in fact, the editor—was going over, and urged father to send me. I learned considerable French, but not much else. I can speak and understand it pretty well."

"How I wish I had had your advantages," said Harry. "How did you like your French schoolmates?"

"They wouldn't come near me at first. Because I was an American they thought I carried a revolver and a dirk-knife, and was dangerous. That is their idea of American boys. When they found I was tame, and carried no deadly weapons, they ventured to speak with me, and after that we got along pretty well."

"How soon do you expect to go to college?"

"A year from next summer. I suppose I shall be ready by that time. You are going to stay in town, I suppose?"

"Yes, if I keep my place."

"Oh, you'll do that. Then we can see something of each other. You must come up to my room, and see me. Come almost any evening."

"I should like to. Do you live in Dr. Barton's family?"

"No, I hope not."

"Why not?"

"Oh, the Doctor has a way of looking after the fellows that room in the house, and of keeping them at work all the time. That would-n't suit me. I board at Mrs. Greyson's, at the south-east corner of the church common. Have you got anything to do this evening?"

"Nothing in particular."

"Then come round and take a look at my den, or sanctum I ought to call it; as I am talking to a member of the editorial profession."

"Not quite yet," said Harry, smiling.

"Oh, well that'll come in due time. Will you come?"

"Sha'n't I be disturbing you?"

"Not a bit. My Greek lesson is about finished, and that's all I've got to do this evening. Come round, and we will sit over the fire, and chat like old friends."

"Thank you, Oscar," said Harry, irresistibly attracted by his bright and lively acquaintance, "I shall enjoy calling. I have made no acquaintances yet, and I feel lonely."

"I have got over that," said Oscar. "I am used to being away from home and don't mind it."

The two boys walked together to Oscar's boarding-place. It was a large house, of considerable pretension for a village, and Oscar's room was large and handsomely furnished. But what attracted Harry's attention was not the furniture, but a collection of over a hundred books, ranged on shelves at one end of the room. In his father's house it had always been so difficult to obtain the necessaries of life that books had necessarily been regarded as superfluities, and beyond a dozen volumes which Harry had read and re-read, he was compelled to depend on such as he could borrow. Here again his privileges were scanty, for most of the neighbors were as poorly supplied as his father.

"What a fine library you have, Oscar!" he exclaimed.

"I have a few books," said Oscar. "My father filled a couple of boxes, and sent me. He has a large library."

"This seems a large library to me," said Harry. "My father likes reading, but he is poor, and cannot afford to buy books."

He said that in a matter-of-fact tone, without the least attempt to conceal what many boys would have been tempted to hide. Oscar noted this, and liked his new friend the better for it.

"Yes," he said, "books cost money, and one hasn't always the money to spare."

"Have you read all these books?"

"Not more than half of them. I like reading better than studying, I am afraid. I am reading the Waverley novels[1] now. Have you read any of them?"

"So [sic]; I never saw any of them before."

"If you see anything you would like to read, I will lend it to you with pleasure," said Oscar, noticing the interest with which Harry regarded the books.

"Will you?" said Harry, eagerly. "I can't tell you how much obliged I am. I will take good care of it."

---

1 Among the Waverley novels by Sir Walter Scott (1771–1832) were *Guy Mannering* (1815), *Rob Roy* (1818), *Ivanhoe* (1819), and *Kenilworth* (1821). See also Alger, "The Novel—Its Scope and Place in Literature," *New York Railroad Men* 9 (March 1896): 141: "Had the Waverley novels never had any worthy successors, they alone would have won for the novel a high place in literature."

"Oh, I am sure of that. Here, try *Ivanhoe*. I've just read it, and it's tip-top."

"Thank you; I will take it on your recommendation. What a nice room you have!"

"Yes, it's pretty comfortable. Father told me to fix it up to suit me. He said he wouldn't mind the expense if I would only study."

"I should think anybody might study in such a room as this, and with such a fine collection of books."

"I'm rather lazy sometimes," said Oscar, "but I shall turn over a new leaf some of these days, and astonish everybody. To-night, as I have no studying to do, I'll tell you what we'll do. Did you ever pop corn?"

"Sometimes."

"I've got some corn here, and Ma'am Greyson has a popper. Stay here alone a minute, and I'll run down and get it."

Oscar ran down stairs, and speedily returned with a corn-popper.

"Now we'll have a jolly time," said he. "Draw up that arm-chair, and make yourself at home. If Xenophon, or Virgil,[1] or any of those Greek and Latin chaps call, we'll tell 'em we are transacting important business and can't be disturbed. What do you say?"

"They won't be apt to call on me," said Harry. "I haven't the pleasure of knowing them."

"It isn't always a pleasure, I can assure you, Harry. Pass over the corn-popper."

CHAPTER V: A YOUNG F. F. B.[2]

As the two boys sat in front of the fire, popping and eating the corn, and chatting of one thing and another, their acquaintance improved rapidly. Harry learned that Oscar's father was a Boston merchant, in the Calcutta trade, with a counting-room on Long Wharf. Oscar was a year older than himself, and the oldest child. He had a sister of thirteen, named Florence, and a younger brother, Charlie, now ten. They lived on Beacon Street, opposite the Common.[3] Though Harry had never lived in Boston, he knew

---

1 The Roman poet Virgil (70–19 BCE) was the author of the epic *Aeneid* (29–19 BCE).

2 A member of a First Family of Boston.

3 Beacon Street, located south of Beacon Hill and north of the Common in central Boston, is the most prestigious address in the city.

that this was a fashionable street, and he had no difficulty in inferring that Mr. Vincent was a rich man. He felt what a wide gulf there was socially between himself and Oscar; one the son of a very poor country farmer, the other the son of a merchant prince. But nothing in Oscar's manner indicated the faintest feeling of superiority, and this pleased Harry. I may as well say, however, that our hero was not one to show any foolish subserviency to a richer boy; he thought mainly of Oscar's superiority in knowledge; and although the latter was far ahead of Harry on this score, he was not one to boast of it.

Harry, in return for Oscar's confidence, acquainted him with his own adventures since he had started out to earn his own living. Oscar was most interested in his apprenticeship to the ventriloquist.

"It must have been jolly fun," he said. "I shouldn't mind travelling round with him myself. Can you perform any tricks?"

"A few," said Harry.

"Show me some, that's a good fellow."

"If you won't show others. Professor Henderson wouldn't like to have his tricks generally known. I could show more if I had the articles he uses. But I can do some without."

"Go ahead, Professor. I'm all attention."

Not having served an apprenticeship to a magician, as Harry did, I will not undertake to describe the few simple tricks which he had picked up, and now exhibited for the entertainment of his companion. It is enough to say that they were quite satisfactory, and that Oscar professed his intention to puzzle his Boston friends with them, when his vacation arrived.

About half-past eight, a knock was heard at the door.

"Come in!" called out Oscar.

The door was opened, and a boy about his own age entered. His name was Fitzgerald Fletcher. He was also a Boston boy, and the son of a retail merchant, doing business on Washington street. His father lived handsomely, and was supposed to be rich. At any rate Fitzgerald supposed him to be so, and was very proud of the fact. He generally let any new acquaintances understand very speedily that his father was a man of property, and that his family moved in the first circles of Boston Society. He cultivated the acquaintance of those boys who belonged to rich families, and did not fail to show the superiority which he felt to those of less abundant means. For example, he liked to be considered intimate with Oscar, as the social position of Mr. Vincent was higher than that of his own family. It gave him an excuse also for calling on

Oscar in Boston. He had tried to ingratiate himself also with Oscar's sister Florence, but had only disgusted her with his airs, so that he could not flatter himself with his success in this direction. Oscar had very little liking for him, but as school-fellows they often met, and Fitzgerald often called upon him. On such occasions he treated him politely enough, for it was not in his nature to be rude without cause.

Fitz was elaborately dressed, feeling that handsome clothes would help convey the impression of wealth, which he was anxious to establish. In particular he paid attention to his neckties, of which he boasted a greater variety than any of his schoolmates. It was not a lofty ambition, but, such as it was, he was able to gratify it.

"How are you, Fitz?" said Oscar, when he saw who was his visitor.

"Draw up a chair to the fire, and make yourself comfortable."

"Thank you, Oscar," said Fitzgerald, leisurely drawing off a pair of kid gloves; "I thought I would drop in and see you."

"All right! Will you have some popped corn?"

"No, thank you," answered Fitzgerald, shrugging his shoulders. "I don't fancy the article."

"Don't you? Then you don't know what's good."

"Fancy passing round popped corn at a party in Boston," said the other. "How people would stare!"

"Would they? I don't know about that. I think some would be more sensible and eat. But, I beg your pardon, I haven't introduced you to my friend, Harry Walton. Harry, this is a classmate of mine. Fitzgerald Fletcher, Esq., of Boston."

Fitzgerald did not appear to perceive that the title Esq. was sportively added to his name. He took it seriously, and was pleased with it, as a recognition of his social superiority. He bowed ceremoniously to our hero, and said, formally, "I am pleased to make your acquaintance, Mr. Walton."

"Thank you, Mr. Fletcher," replied Harry, bowing in turn.

"I wonder who he is," thought Fitzgerald.

He had no idea of the true position of our young hero, or he would not have wasted so much politeness upon him. The fact was, that Harry was well dressed, having on the suit which had been given him by a friend from the city. It was therefore fashionably cut, and had been so well kept as still to be in very good condition. It occurred to Fitz—to give him the short name he received from his school-fellows—that it might be a Boston friend of Oscar's, just entering the Academy. This might account for his not having met him before. Perhaps he was from an aristocratic Boston family. His intimacy with Oscar rendered it probable, and it might be well to cultivate his acquaintance. On this hint he spoke.

"Are you about to enter the Academy, Mr. Walton?"

"No; I should like to do so, but cannot."

"You are one of Oscar's friends from the city, I suppose, then?"

"Oh no; I am living in Centreville."

"Who can he be?" thought Fitz. With considerable less cordiality in his manner, he continued, impelled by curiosity,—

"I don't think I have met you before."

"No: I have only just come to the village."

Oscar understood thoroughly the bewilderment of his visitor, and enjoyed it. He knew the weakness of Fitz, and he could imagine how his feelings would change when be ascertained the real position of Harry.

"My friend," he explained, "is connected with the 'Centreville Gazette.'"

"In what capacity?" asked Fitz, in surprise.

"He is profanely termed the 'printer's devil.' Isn't that so, Harry?"

"I believe you are right," said our hero, smiling. He had a suspicion that this relation would shock his new acquaintance.

"Indeed!" ejaculated Fitz, pursing up his lips, and, I was about to say, turning up his nose, but nature had saved him the little trouble of doing that.

"What in the world brings him here, then?" he thought; but there was no need of saying it, for both Oscar and Harry read it in his manner. "Strange that Oscar Vincent, from one of the first families of Boston, should demean himself by keeping company with a low printer boy!"

"Harry and I have had a jolly time popping corn this evening!" said Oscar, choosing to ignore his school-mate's changed manner.

"Indeed! I can't see what fun there is in it."

"Oh, you've got no taste. Has he, Harry?"

"His taste differs from ours," said our hero, politely.

"I should think so," remarked Fitz, with significant emphasis. "Was that all you had to amuse yourself?"

In using the singular pronoun, he expressly ignored the presence of the young printer.

"No, that wasn't all. My friend Harry has been amusing me

with some tricks which he learned while he was travelling round with Professor Henderson, the ventriloquist and magician."

"Really, he is quite accomplished," said Fitz, with a covert sneer.

"Pretty company Oscar has taken up with!" he thought. "How long were you in the circus business?" he asked, turning to Harry.

"I never was in the circus business."

"Excuse me. I should say, travelling about with the ventriloquist."

"About three months. I was with him when he performed here last winter."

"Ah! indeed. I didn't go. My father doesn't approve of my attending such common performances. I only attend first-class theatres, and the Italian opera."

"That's foolish," said Oscar. "You miss a good deal of fun, then. I went to Professor Henderson's entertainment, and I now remember seeing you there, Harry. You took money at the door, didn't you?"

"Yes."

"Now I understand what made your face seem so familiar to me, when I saw it this afternoon. By the way, I have never been into a printing office. If I come round to yours, will you show me round?"

"I should be very glad to, Oscar, but perhaps you had better wait till I have been there a little while, and learned the ropes. I know very little about it yet."

"Won't you come too, Fitz?" asked Oscar.

"You must really excuse me," drawled Fitz. "I have heard that a printing office is a very dirty place. I should be afraid of soiling my clothes."

"Especially that stunning cravat."

"Do you like it? I flatter myself it's something a little extra," said Fitz, who was always gratified by a compliment to his cravats.

"Then you won't go?"

"I haven't the slightest curiosity about such a place, I assure you."

"Then I shall have to go alone. Let me know when you are ready to receive me, Harry."

"I won't forget, Oscar."

"I wonder he allows such a low fellow to call him by his first name," thought Fitz. "Really, he has no proper pride."

"Well," he said, rising, "I must be going."

"What's your hurry, Fitz?"

"I've got to write a letter home this evening. Besides, I haven't finished my Greek. Good-evening, Oscar."

"Good-evening, Fitz."

"Good-evening, Mr. Fletcher," said Harry.

"Evening!" ejaculated Fitz, briefly; and without a look at the low "printer-boy," he closed the door and went down stairs.

CHAPTER VI: OSCAR BECOMES A PROFESSOR

"I am afraid your friend won't thank you for introducing me to him," said Harry, after Fitz had left the room.

"Fitz is a snob," said Oscar. "He makes himself ridiculous by putting on airs, and assuming to be more than he is. His father is in a good business, and may be rich—I don't know about that— but that isn't much to boast of."

"I don't think we shall be very intimate," said Harry, smiling. "Evidently a printer's apprentice is something very low in his eyes."

"When you are an influential editor he will be willing to recognize you. Let that stimulate your ambition."

"It isn't easy for a half-educated boy to rise to such a position. I feel that I know very little."

"If I can help you any, Harry, I shall be very glad to do it. I'm not much of a scholar, but I can help you a little. For instance, if you wanted to learn French, I could hear your lessons, and correct your exercises."

"Will you?" said Harry, eagerly. "There is nothing I should like better."

"Then I'll tell you what I'll do. You shall buy a French grammar, and come to my room two evenings a week, and recite what you get time to study at home."

"Won't it give you a great deal of trouble, Oscar?"

"Not a bit of it; I shall rather like it. Until you can buy a grammar, I will lend you mine. I'll set you a lesson out of it now."

He took from the book-shelves a French grammar, and inviting Harry to sit down beside him, gave him some necessary explanations as to the pronunciation of words according to the first lesson.

"It seems easy," said Harry. "I can take more than that."

"It is the easiest of the modern languages, to us at least, on account of its having so many words similar to ours."

"What evening shall I come, Oscar?"

"Tuesday and Friday will suit me as well as any. And remember, Harry, I mean to be very strict in discipline. And, by the way, how will it do to call myself Professor?"

"I'll call you Professor if you want me to."

"We'll leave all high titles to Fitz, and I won't use the rod any oftener than it is absolutely necessary."

"All right, Professor Vincent," said Harry laughing, "I'll endeavor to behave with propriety."

"I wonder what they would say at home," said Oscar, "if they knew I had taken up the profession of teacher. Strange as it may seem to you, Harry, I have the reputation in the home-circle of being decidedly lazy. How do you account for it?"

"Great men are seldom appreciated."

"You hit the nail on the head that time—glad I am not the nail, by the way. Henceforth I will submit with resignation to injustice and misconstruction, since I am only meeting with the common fate of great men."

"What time is it, Oscar?"

"Nearly ten."

"Then I will bid you good-night," and Harry rose to go. "I can't tell how much I am obliged to you for your kind offer."

"Just postpone thanks till you find out whether I am a good teacher or not."

"I am sure of that."

"I am not so sure, but I will do what I can for you. Good-night. I'll expect you Friday evening. I shall see Fitz to-morrow. Shall I give him your love?"

"Never mind!" said Harry, smiling. "I'm afraid it wouldn't be appreciated."

"Perhaps not."

As Harry left his lively companion, he felt that he had been most fortunate in securing his friendship—not only that he found him very agreeable and attractive, but he was likely to be of great use to him in promoting his plans of self-education. He had too much good sense not to perceive that the only chance he had of rising to an influential position lay in qualifying himself for it, by enlarging his limited knowledge and improving his mind.

"I have made a good beginning," he thought. "After I have learned something of French, I will take up Latin, and I think Oscar will be willing to help me in that too."

The next morning he commenced work in the printing office.

With a few hints from Ferguson, he soon comprehended what he had to do, and made very rapid progress.

"You're getting on fast, Harry," said Ferguson approvingly.

"I like it," said our hero. "I am glad I decided to be a printer."

"I wish I wasn't one," grumbled Clapp, the younger journeyman.

"Don't you like it?"

"Not much. It's hard work and poor pay. I just wish I was in my brother's shoes. He is a bookkeeper in Boston, with a salary of twelve hundred a year, while I am plodding along on fifteen dollars week."

"You may do better some day," said Ferguson.

"Don't see any chance of it."

"If I were in your place, I would save up part of my salary, and by and by have an office, and perhaps a paper of my own."

"Why don't you do it, then?" sneered Clapp.

"Because I have a family to support from my earnings—you have only yourself."

"It doesn't help me any; I can't save anything out of fifteen dollars a week."

"You mean you won't," said Ferguson quietly.

"No I don't. I mean I can't."

"How do you expect I get along, then? I have a wife and two children to support, and only get two dollars a week more than you."

"Perhaps you get into debt."

"No; I owe no man a dollar," said Ferguson emphatically. "That isn't all. I save two dollars a week; so that I actually support four on fifteen dollars a week—your salary. What do you say to that?"

"I don't want to be mean," said Clapp.

"Nor I. I mean to live comfortably, but of course I have to be economical."

"Oh, hang economy!" said Clapp impatiently. "The old man used to lecture me about economy till I got sick of hearing the word."

"It is a good thing, for all that," persisted Ferguson. "You'll think so some day, even if you don't now."

"I guess you mean to run opposition to young Franklin, over there," sneered Clapp, indicating Harry, who had listened to the discussion with not a little interest.

"I think he and I will agree together pretty well," said Ferguson, smiling. "Franklin's a good man to imitate."

"If there are going to be two Franklins in the office, it will be time for me to clear out," returned Clapp.

"You can do better."

"How is that?"

"Become Franklin No. 3."

"You don't catch me imitating any old fogy like that. As far as I know anything about him, he was a mean, stingy old curmudgeon!" exclaimed Clapp with irritation.

"That's rather strong language, Clapp," said Mr. Anderson, looking up from his desk with a smile. "It doesn't correspond with the general estimate of Franklin's character."

"I don't care," said Clapp doggedly, "I wouldn't be like Franklin if I could. I have too much self-respect."

Ferguson laughed, and Harry wanted to, but feared he should offend the younger journeyman, who evidently had worked himself into a bad humor.

"I don't think you're in any danger," said Ferguson, who did not mind his fellow-workman's little ebullitions of temper.

Clapp scowled, but did not deign to reply, partly, perhaps, because he knew that there was nothing to say.

From the outset Ferguson took a fancy to the young apprentice.

"He's got good, solid ideas," said he to Mr. Anderson, when Harry was absent. "He isn't so thoughtless as most boys of his age. He looks ahead."

"I think you are right in your judgment of him," said Mr. Anderson. "He promises to be a faithful workman."

"He promises more than that," said Ferguson. "Mark my words, Mr. Anderson; that boy is going to make his mark some day."

"It is a little too soon to say that, isn't it?"

"No; I judge from what I see. He is industrious and ambitious, and is bound to succeed. The world will hear of him yet."

Mr. Anderson smiled. He liked what he had seen of his new apprentice, but he thought Ferguson altogether too sanguine.

"He's a good, faithful boy," he admitted, "but it takes more than that to rise to distinction. If all the smart boys turned out smart men, they'd be a drug in the market."

But Ferguson held to his own opinion, notwithstanding. Time will show which was right.

The next day Ferguson said, "Harry, come round to my house, and take tea to-night. I've spoken to my wife about you, and she wants to see you."

"Thank you, Mr. Ferguson," said Harry. "I shall be very glad to come."

"I'll wait till you are ready, and you can walk along with me."

"All right; I will be ready in five minutes."

They set out together for Ferguson's modest home, which was about half a mile distant. As they passed up the village street Harry's attention was drawn to two boys who were approaching them. One he recognized at once as Fitzgerald Fletcher. He had an even more stunning necktie than when Harry first met him, and sported a jaunty little cane, which he swung in his neatly gloved hand.

"I wonder if he'll notice me," thought Harry. "At any rate, I won't be wanting in politeness."

"Good-afternoon, Mr. Fletcher," he said, as they met.

Fitzgerald stared at him superciliously, and made the slightest possible nod.

"Who is that?" asked Ferguson.

"It is a boy who has great contempt for printers' devils and low apprentices," answered Harry. "I was introduced to him two evenings ago, but he evidently doesn't care about keeping up the acquaintance."

"Who is that, Fitz?" asked his companion in turn.

"It's a low fellow—a printer's devil," answered Fitz, shortly.

"How do you happen to know him?"

"Oscar Vincent introduced him to me. Oscar's a queer fellow. He belongs to one of the first families in Boston—one of my set, you know, and yet he actually invited that boy to his room."

"He's rather a good-looking boy—the printer."

"Think so?" drawled Fitz. "He's low—all apprentices are. I mean to keep him at a distance."

CHAPTER VII: A PLEASANT EVENING

"This is my house," said Ferguson, pausing at the gate.

Harry looked at it with interest.

It was a cottage, containing four rooms, and a kitchen in the ell part.[1] There was a plot of about a quarter of an acre connected

---

1 New England houses were often designed to resemble the letter "L," with the kitchen and pantry in a wing perpendicular to the front living quarters.

with it. Everything about it was neat, though very unpretentious.

"It isn't a palace," said Ferguson, "but," he added cheerfully, "it's a happy home, and from all I've read, that is more than can be said of some palaces. Step right in and make yourself at home."

They entered a tiny entry, and Mrs. Ferguson opened the door of the sitting-room. She was a pleasant-looking woman, and her face wore a smile of welcome.

"Hannah," said Ferguson, "this is our new apprentice, Harry Walton."

"I am glad to see you," she said, offering her hand. "My husband has spoken of you. You are quite welcome, if you can put up with humble fare."

"That is what I have always been accustomed to," said Harry, beginning to feel quite at home.

"Where are the children, Hannah?"

Two children, a boy and a girl, of six and four years respectively, bounded into the room and answered for themselves. They looked shyly at Harry, but before many minutes their shyness had worn off, and the little girl was sitting on his knee, while the boy stood beside him. Harry was fond of children, and readily adapted himself to his young acquaintances.

Supper was soon ready—a plain meal, but one that Harry enjoyed. He could not help comparing Ferguson's plain, but pleasant home, with Clapp's mode of life.

The latter spent on himself as much as sufficed his fellow-workman to support a wife and two children, yet it was easy to see which found the best enjoyment in life.

"How do you like your new business?" asked Mrs. Ferguson, as she handed Harry a cup of tea.

"I like all but the name," said our hero, smiling.

"I wonder how the name came to be applied to a printer's apprentice any more than to any other apprentice," said Mrs. Ferguson.

"I never heard," said her husband. "It seems to me to be a libel upon our trade. But there is one comfort. If you stick to the business, you'll outgrow the name."

"That is lucky; I shouldn't like to be called the wife of a ——. I won't pronounce the word lest the children should catch it."

"What is it, mother?" asked Willie, with his mouth full.

"It isn't necessary for you to know, my boy."

"Do you know Mr. Clapp?" asked Harry.

"I have seen him, but never spoke with him."

"I never asked him round to tea," said Ferguson. "I don't think he would enjoy it any better than I. His tastes are very different from mine, and his views of life are equally different."

"I should think so," said Harry.

"Now I think you and I would agree very well. Clapp dislikes the business, and only sticks to it because he must get his living in some way. As for me, if I had a sum of money, say five thousand dollars, I would still remain a printer, but in that case I would probably buy out a paper, or start one, and be a publisher, as well as a printer."

"That's just what I should like," said Harry.

"Who knows but we may be able to go into partnership some day, and carry out our plan."

"I would like it," said Harry; "but I am afraid it will be a good while before we can raise the five thousand dollars."

"We don't need as much. Mr. Anderson started on a capital of a thousand dollars, and now he is in comfortable circumstances."

"Then there's hopes for us."

"At any rate I cherish hopes of doing better some day. I shouldn't like always to be a journeyman. I manage to save up a hundred dollars a year. How much have we in the savings bank, Hannah?"

"Between four and five hundred dollars, with interest."

"It has taken me four years to save it up. In five more, if nothing happens, I should be worth a thousand dollars. Journeymen printers don't get rich very fast."

"I hope to have saved up something myself, in five years," said Harry.

"Then our plan may come to pass, after all. You shall be editor, and I publisher."

"I should think you would prefer to be an editor," said his wife.

"I am diffident of my powers in the line of composition," said Ferguson. "I shouldn't be afraid to undertake local items, but when it comes to an elaborate editorial, I should rather leave it in other hands."

"I always liked writing," said Harry. "Of course I have only had a school-boy's practice, but I mean to practise more in my leisure hours."

"Suppose you write a poem for the 'Gazette,' Walton."

Harry smiled.

"I am not ambitious enough for that," he replied. "I will try plain prose."

"Do so," said Ferguson, earnestly. "Our plan may come to something after all, if we wait patiently. It will do no harm to prepare yourself as well as you can. After a while you might write something for the 'Gazette.' I think Mr. Anderson would put it in."

"Shall I sign it P. D.?" asked Harry.

"P. D. stands for Doctor of Philosophy."

"I don't aspire to such a learned title. P. D. also stands for Printer's Devil."

"I see. Well, joking aside, I advise you to improve yourself in writing."

"I will. That is the way Franklin did."

"I remember. He wrote an article, and slipped it under the door of the printing office, not caring to have it known that he was the author.[1]

"Shall I give you a piece of pie, Mr. Walton?" said Mrs. Ferguson.

"Thank you."

"Me too," said Willie, extending his plate.

"Willie is always fond of pie," said his father. "In a printing office *pi* is not such a favorite."

When supper was over, Mr. Ferguson showed Harry a small collection of books, about twenty-five in number, neatly arranged on shelves.

"It isn't much of a library," he said, "but a few books are better than none. I should like to buy as many every year; but books are expensive, and the outlay would make too great an inroad upon my small surplus."

"I always thought I should like a library," said Harry, "but my father is very poor, and has fewer books than you. As for me, I have but one book besides the school-books I studied, and that I gained as a school prize—The Life of Franklin."

"If one has few books he is apt to prize them more," said Ferguson, "and is apt to profit by them more."

"Have you read the History of China?" asked Harry, who had been looking over his friend's books.

"No; I have never seen it."

"Why, there it is," said our hero, "in two volumes."

"Take it down," said Ferguson, laughing.

---

1 At the age of 16, Franklin contributed the "Silence Dogood letters" to his brother James's *New England Courant*.

Harry did so, and to his surprise it opened in his hands, and revealed a checker-board.

"You see appearances are deceitful. Can you play checkers?"

"I never tried."

"You will easily learn. Shall I teach you the game?"

"I wish you would."

They sat down; and Harry soon became interested in the game, which requires a certain degree of thought and foresight.

"You will make a good player after a while," said his companion. "You must come in often and play with me."

"Thank you, I should like to do so. It may not be often, for I am taking lessons in French, and I want to get on as fast as possible."

"I did not know there was any one in the village who gave lessons in French."

"Oh, he's not a professional teacher. Oscar Vincent, one of the Academy boys, is teaching me. I am to take two lessons a week, on Tuesday and Friday evenings."

"Indeed, that is a good arrangement. How did it come about?"

Harry related the particulars of his meeting with Oscar.

"He's a capital fellow," he concluded. "Very different from another boy I met in his room. I pointed him out to you in the street. Oscar seems to be rich, but he doesn't put on any airs, and he treated me very kindly."

"That is to his credit. It's the sham aristocrats that put on most airs. I believe you will make somebody, Walton. You have lost no time in getting to work."

"I have no time to lose. I wish I was in Oscar's place. He is preparing for Harvard, and has nothing to do but to learn."

"I heard a lecturer once who said that the printing office is the poor man's college,[1] and he gave a great many instances of printers who had risen high in the world, particularly in our own country."

"Well, that is encouraging. I should like to have heard the lecture."

"I begin to think, Harry, that I should have done well to follow your example. When I was in your position, I might have studied too, but I didn't realize the importance as I do now. I read some useful books, to be sure, but that isn't like studying."

"It isn't too late now."

Ferguson shook his head.

---

1   This quotation is often attributed to Abraham Lincoln (1809–65).

"Now I have a wife and children," he said. "I am away from them during the day, and the evening I like to pass socially with them."

"Perhaps you would like to be divorced," said his wife, smiling. "Then you would get time for study."

"I doubt if that would make me as happy, Hannah. I am not ready to part with you just yet. But our young friend here is not quite old enough to be married, and there is nothing to prevent his pursuing his studies. So, Harry, go on, and prepare yourself for your editorial duties."

Harry smiled thoughtfully. For the first time he had formed definite plans for his future. Why should not Ferguson's plans be realized?

"If I live long enough," he said to himself, "I will be an editor, and exert some influence in the world."

At ten o'clock he bade good-night to Mr. and Mrs. Ferguson, feeling that he had passed a pleasant and what might prove a profitable evening.

CHAPTER VIII:
FLETCHER'S VIEWS ON SOCIAL POSITION

"You are getting on finely, Harry," said Oscar Vincent, a fortnight later. "You do credit to my teaching. As you have been over all the regular verbs now, I will give you a lesson in translating."

"I shall find that interesting," said Harry, with satisfaction.

"Here is a French Reader," said Oscar, taking one down from the shelves. "It has a dictionary at the end. I won't give you a lesson. You may take as much as you have time for, and at the same time three or four of the irregular verbs. You are going about three times as fast as I did when I commenced French."

"Perhaps I have a better teacher than you had," said Harry, smiling.

"I shouldn't wonder," said Oscar. "That explains it to my satisfaction. Well, now the lesson is over, sit down and we'll have a chat. Oh, by the way, there's one thing I want to speak to you about. We've got a debating society at our school. It is called 'The Clionian Society.'[1] Most of the students belong to it. How would you like to join?"

---

1 Alger obliquely refers to the "Junto," a club of young Philadelphia intellectuals that Franklin organized in 1727.

"I should like it very much. Do you think they would admit me?"

"I don't see why not. I'll propose you at the next meeting, Thursday evening. Then the nomination will lie over a week, and be acted upon at the next meeting."

"I wish you would. I never belonged to a debating society, but I should like to learn to speak."

"It's nothing when you're used to it. It's only the first time, you know, that troubles you. By Jove! I remember how my knees trembled when I first got up and said Mr. President. I felt as if all eyes were upon me, and I wanted to sink through the floor. Now I can get up and chatter with the best of them. I don't mean that I can make an eloquent speech or anything of that kind, but I can talk at a minute's notice on almost any subject."

"I wish I could."

"Oh, you can, after you've tried a few times. Well, then, it's settled. I'll propose you at the next meeting."

"How lucky I am to have fallen in with you, Oscar."

"I know what you mean. I'm your guide, philosopher, and friend, and all that sort of thing. I hope you'll have proper veneration for me. It's rather a new character for me. Would you believe it, Harry,—at home I am regarded as a rattle-brained chap, instead of the dignified Professor that you know me to be. Isn't it a shame?"

"Great men are seldom appreciated at home, Oscar."

"I know that. I shall have to get a certificate from you, certifying to my being a steady and erudite young man."

"I'll give it with the greatest pleasure."

"Holloa, there's a knock. Come in!" shouted Oscar.

The door opened, and Fitzgerald Fletcher entered the room.

"How are you, Fitz?" said Oscar. "Sit down and make yourself comfortable. You know my friend, Harry Walton, I believe?"

"I believe I had the honor to meet him here one evening," said Fitzgerald stiffly, slightly emphasizing the word "honor."

"I hope you are well, Mr. Fletcher," said Harry, more amused than disturbed by the manner of the aristocratic visitor.

"Thank you, my health is good," said Fitzgerald with equal stiffness, and forthwith turned to Oscar, not deigning to devote any more attention to Harry.

Our hero had intended to remain a short time longer, but, under the circumstances, as Oscar's attention would be occupied by Fletcher, with whom he was not on intimate terms, he thought he might spend the evening more profitably at home in study.

"If you'll excuse me, Oscar," he said, rising, "I will leave you now, as I have something to do this evening."

"If you insist upon it, Harry, I will excuse you. Come round Friday evening."

"Thank you."

"Do you have to work at the printing office in the evening?" Fletcher deigned to inquire.

"No; I have some studying to do."

"Reading and spelling, I suppose," sneered Fletcher.

"I am studying French."

"Indeed!" returned Fletcher, rather surprised. "How can you study it without a teacher?"

"I have a teacher."

"Who is it?"

"Professor Vincent," said Harry, smiling.

"You didn't know that I had developed into a French Professor, did you, Fitz? Well, it's so, and whether it's the superior teaching or not, I can't say, but my scholar is getting on famously."

"It must be a great bore to teach," said Fletcher.

"Not at all. I like it."

"Every one to his taste," said Fitzgerald unpleasantly.

"Good-night, Oscar. Good-night, Mr. Fletcher," said Harry, and made his exit.

"You're a strange fellow, Oscar," said Fletcher, after Harry's departure.

"Very likely, but what particular strangeness do you refer to now?"

"No one but you would think of giving lessons to a printer's devil."

"I don't know about that."

"No one, I mean, that holds your position in society."

"I don't know that I hold any particular position in society."

"Your family live on Beacon Street, and move in the first circles. I am sure my mother would be disgusted if I should demean myself so far as to give lessons to any vulgar apprentice."

"I don't propose to give lessons to any vulgar apprentice."

"You know whom I mean. This Walton is only a printer's devil."

"I don't know that that is any objection to him. It isn't morally wrong to be a printer's devil, is it?"

"What a queer fellow you are, Oscar. Of course I don't mean that. I daresay he's well enough in his place, though he seems to be very forward and presuming, but you know that he's not your equal."

"He is not my equal in knowledge, but I shouldn't be surprised if he would be some time. You'd be astonished to see how fast he gets on."

"I daresay. But I mean in social position."

"It seems to me you can't think of anything but social position."

"Well, it's worth thinking about."

"No doubt, as far as it is deserved. But when it is founded on nothing but money, I wouldn't give much for it."

"Of course we all know that the higher classes are more refined—"

"Than printers' devils and vulgar apprentices, I suppose," put in Oscar, laughing,

"Yes."

"Well, if refinement consists in wearing kid gloves and stunning neckties, I suppose the higher classes, as you call them, are more refined."

"Do you mean me?" demanded Fletcher, who was noted for the character of his neckties.

"Well, I can't say I don't. I suppose you regard yourself as a representative of the higher classes, don't you?"

"To be sure I do," said Fletcher, complacently.

"So I supposed. Then you see I had a right to refer to you. Now listen to my prediction. Twenty-five years from now, the boy whom you look down upon as a vulgar apprentice will occupy a high position, and you will be glad to number him among your acquaintances."

"Speak for yourself, Oscar," said Fletcher, scornfully.

"I speak for both of us."

"Then I say I hope I can command better associates than this friend of yours."

"You may, but I doubt it."

"You seem to be carried away by him," said Fitzgerald, pettishly. "I don't see anything very wonderful about him, except dirty hands."

"Then you have seen more than I have."

"Of course a fellow who meddles with printer's ink must have dirty hands. Faugh!" said Fletcher, turning up his nose.

At the same time he regarded complacently his own fingers, which he carefully kept aloof from anything that would soil or mar their aristocratic whiteness.

"The fact is, Fitz," said Oscar, argumentatively, "'our upper ten'[1] as we call them, spring from just such beginnings as my friend Harry Walton. My own father commenced life in a printing office. But, as you say, he occupies a high position at present."

"Really!" said Fletcher, a little taken aback, for he knew that Vincent's father ranked higher than his own.

"I daresay your own ancestors were not always patricians."[2]

Fletcher winced. He knew well enough that his father commenced life as a boy in a country grocery, but in the mutations of fortune had risen to be the proprietor of a large dry-goods store on Washington Street. None of the family cared to look back to the beginning of his career. They overlooked the fact that it was creditable to him to have risen from the ranks, though the rise was only in wealth, for Mr. Fletcher was a purse-proud parvenu, who owed all the consideration he enjoyed to his commercial position. Fitz liked to have it understood that he was of patrician lineage, and carefully ignored the little grocery, and certain country relations who occasionally paid a visit to their wealthy relatives, in spite of the rather frigid welcome they received.

"Oh, I suppose there are exceptions," Fletcher admitted reluctantly. "Your father was smart."

"So is Harry Walton. I know what he is aiming at, and I predict that he will be an influential editor some day."

"Have you got your Greek lesson?" asked Fletcher, abruptly, who did not relish the course the conversation had taken.

"Yes."

"Then I want you to translate a passage for me. I couldn't make it out."

"All right."

Half an hour later Fletcher left Vincent's room.

"What a snob he is!" thought Oscar.

And Oscar was right.

CHAPTER IX: THE CLIONIAN SOCIETY

On Thursday evening the main school of the Academy building was lighted up, and groups of boys, varying in age from thirteen to nineteen, were standing in different parts of the room. These

---

1 The upper ten thousand people, used to describe the New York upper crust.

2 Aristocrats or nobility.

were members of the Clionian Society, whose weekly meeting was about to take place.

At eight o'clock precisely the President took his place at the teacher's desk, with the Secretary at his side, and rapped for order. The presiding officer was Alfred DeWitt, a member of the Senior Class, and now nearly ready for college. The Secretary was a member of the same class, by name George Sanborn.

"The Secretary will read the minutes of the last meeting," said the President, when order had been obtained.

George Sanborn rose and read his report, which was accepted.

"Are any committees prepared to report?" asked the President.

The Finance Committee reported through its chairman, recommending that the fee for admission be established at one dollar, and that each member be assessed twenty-five cents monthly.

"Mr. President," said Fitzgerald Fletcher, rising to his feet, "I would like to say a word in reference to this report."

"Mr. Fletcher has the floor."

"Then, Mr. President, I wish to say that I disagree with the Report of the Committee. I think a dollar is altogether too small. It ought to be at least three dollars, and I myself should prefer five dollars. Again, sir, the Committee has recommended for the monthly assessment the ridiculously small sum of twenty-five cents. I think it ought to be a dollar."

"Mr. President, I should like to ask the gentleman his reason," said Henry Fairbanks, Chairman of the Finance Committee. "Why should we tax the members to such an extent, when the sums reported are sufficient to defray the ordinary expenses of the Society, and to leave a small surplus besides?"

"Mr. President," returned Fletcher, "I will answer the gentleman. We don't want to throw open the Society to every one that can raise a dollar. We want to have an exclusive society."

"Mr. President," said Oscar Vincent, rising, "I should like to ask the gentleman for how many he is speaking. He certainly is not speaking for me. I don't want the Society to be exclusive. There are not many who can afford to pay the exorbitant sums which he desires fixed for admission fee and for monthly assessments, and I for one am not willing to exclude any good fellow who desires to become one of us, but does not boast as heavy a purse as the gentleman who has just spoken."

These remarks of Oscar were greeted with applause, general enough to show that the opinions of nearly all were with him.

"Mr. President," said Henry Fairbanks, "though I am opposed to the gentleman's suggestion, (does he offer it as an amendment?) I have no possible objection to his individually paying the increased rates which he recommends, and I am sure the Treasurer will gladly receive them."

Laughter and applause greeted this hit, and Fletcher once more arose, somewhat vexed at the reception of his suggestion.

"I don't choose—" he commenced.

"The gentleman will address the chair," interrupted the President.

"Mr. President, I don't choose to pay more than the other members, though I can do it without inconvenience. But, as I said, I don't believe in being too democratic. I am not in favor of admitting anybody and everybody into the Society."

"Mr. President," said James Hooper, "I congratulate the gentleman on the flourishing state of his finances. For my own part, I am not ashamed to say that I cannot afford to pay a dollar a month assessment, and, were it required, I should be obliged to offer my resignation."

"So much the better," thought Fitzgerald, for, as Hooper was poor, and went coarsely clothed, he looked down upon him. Fortunately for himself he did not give utterance to his thought.

"Does Mr. Fletcher put his recommendation into the form of an amendment?" asked, the President.

"I do."

"Be kind enough to state it, then."

Fletcher did so, but as no one seconded it, no action was of course taken.

"Nominations for membership are now in order," said the President.

"I should like to propose my friend Henry Walton."

"Who is Henry Walton?" asked a member.

"Mr. President, may I answer the gentleman?" asked Fitzgerald Fletcher, rising to his feet.

"As the nominee is not to be voted upon this evening, it is not in order."

"Mr. President," said Oscar, "I should be glad to have the gentleman report his information."

"Mr. Fletcher may speak if he desires it, but as the name will be referred to the Committee on Nominations, it is hardly necessary."

"Mr. President, I merely wish to inform the Society, that Mr.

Walton occupies the dignified position of printer's devil in the office of the 'Centreville Gazette.'"

"Mr. President," said Oscar, "may I ask the indulgence of the Society long enough to say that I am quite aware of the fact. I will add that Mr. Walton is a young man of excellent abilities, and I am confident will prove an accession to the Society."

"I cannot permit further remarks on a matter which will come in due course before the Committee on Nominations," said the President.

"The next business in order is the debate."

Of the debate, and the further proceedings, I shall not speak, as they are of no special interest. But after the meeting was over, groups of members discussed matters which had come up during the evening. Fletcher approached Oscar Vincent, and said, "I can't see, Oscar, why you are trying to get that printer's devil into our Society."

"Because he's a good fellow, and smart enough to do us credit."

"If there were any bootblacks in Centreville I suppose you'd be proposing them?" said Fletcher with a sneer.

"I might, if they were as smart as my friend Walton."

"You are not very particular about your friends," said Fletcher in the same tone.

"I don't ask them to open their pocket-books, and show me how much money they have."

"I prefer to associate with gentlemen."

"So do I."

"Yet you associate with that printer's devil."

"I consider him a gentleman."

Fletcher laughed scornfully.

"You have strange ideas of a gentleman," he said.

"I hold the same," said James Hooper, who had come up in time to hear the last portion of the conversation. "I don't think a full purse is the only or the chief qualification of a gentleman. If labor is to be a disqualification, then I must resign all claims to be considered a gentleman, as I worked on a farm for two years before coming to school, and in that way earned the money to pay my expenses here."

Fletcher turned up his nose, but did not reply.

Hooper was a good scholar and influential in the Society, but in Fletcher's eyes he was unworthy of consideration.

"Look here, Fletcher,—what makes you so confoundedly exclusive is your ideas?" asked Henry Fairbanks.

"Because I respect myself," said Fletcher in rather a surly tone.

"Then you have one admirer," said Fairbanks.

"What do you mean by that?" asked Fletcher, suspiciously.

"Nothing out of the way. I believe in self-respect, but I don't see how it is going to be endangered by the admission of Oscar's friend to the Society."

"Am I expected to associate on equal terms with a printer's devil?"

"I can't answer for you. As for me, if he is a good fellow, I shall welcome him to our ranks. Some of our most eminent men have been apprenticed to the trade of printer. I believe, after all, it is the name that has prejudiced you."

"No it isn't. I have seen him."

"Henry Walton?"

"Yes."

"Where?"

"In Oscar's room."

"Well?"

"I don't like his appearance."

"What's the matter with his appearance?" asked Oscar.

"He looks low."

"That's where I must decidedly contradict you, Fitz, and I shall appeal confidently to the members of the Society when they come to know him, as they soon will, for I am sure no one else shares your ridiculous prejudices. Harry Walton, in my opinion, is a true gentleman, without reference to his purse, and he is bound to rise hereafter, take my word for it."

"There's plenty of room for him to rise," said Fletcher with a sneer.

"That is true not only of him, but of all of us, I take it."

"Do you refer to me?"

"Oh no," said Oscar with sarcasm. "I am quite aware that you are at the pinnacle of eminence, even if you do flunk in Greek occasionally."

Fitzgerald had failed in the Greek recitation during the day, and that in school parlance is sometimes termed a "flunk." He bit his lip in mortification at this reference, and walked away, leaving Oscar master of the situation.

"You had the best of him there, Vincent," said George Sanborn. "He has gone off in disgust."

"I like to see Fletcher taken down," said Henry Fairbanks. "I never saw a fellow put on so many airs. He is altogether too aristocratic to associate with ordinary people."

"Yes," said Oscar, "he has a foolish pride, which I hope he will some time get rid of."

"He ought to have been born in England, and not in a republic."

"If he had been born in England, he would have been unhappy unless he had belonged to the nobility," said Alfred DeWitt.

"Look here, boys," said Tom Carver, "what do you say to mortifying Fitz's pride?"

"Have you got a plan in view, Tom? If so, out with it."

"Yes: you know the pedler that comes into town about once a month to buy up rags, and sell his tinwares."

"I have seen him. Well, what of him?"

"He is coming early next week. Some of us will see him privately, and post him up as to Fitz's relations and position, and hire him to come up to school, and inquire for Fitz, representing himself as his cousin. Of course Fitz will deny it indignantly, but he will persist and show that he knows all about the family."

"Good! Splendid!" exclaimed the boys laughing. "Won't Fitz be raving?"

"There's no doubt about that. Well, boys, I'll arrange it all, if you'll authorize me."

"Go ahead, Tom. You can draw upon us for the necessary funds."

Fletcher had retired to his room, angry at the opposition his proposal had received, and without any warning of the humiliation which awaited him.

CHAPTER X: THE TIN-PEDLER

Those of my readers who live in large cities are probably not familiar with the travelling tin-pedler, who makes his appearance at frequent intervals in the country towns and villages of New England.

His stock of tinware embraces a large variety of articles for culinary purposes, ranging from milk-pans to nutmeg-graters. These are contained in a wagon of large capacity, in shape like a box, on which he sits enthroned a merchant prince. Unlike most traders, he receives little money, most of his transactions being in the form of a barter, whereby he exchanges his merchandise for rags, white and colored, which have accumulated in the household, and are gladly traded off for bright tinware. Behind the cart usually depend two immense bags, one for white, the other for colored rags, which, in time, are sold to paper manufacturers. It may be that the very paper on which this description is printed, was manufactured from rags so collected.

Abner Bickford was the proprietor of such an establishment as I have described. No one, at first sight, would have hesitated to class him as a Yankee. He was long in the limbs, and long in the face, with a shrewd twinkle in the eye, a long nose, and the expression of a man who respected himself and feared nobody. He was unpolished, in his manners, and knew little of books, but he belonged to the same resolute and hardy type of men who in years past sprang to arms, and fought bravely for an idea. He was strong in his manhood, and would have stood unabashed before a king. Such was the man who was to mortify the pride of Fitzgerald Fletcher.

Tom Carver watched for his arrival in Centreville, and walking up to his cart, accosted him.

"Good-morning, Mr. Bickford."

"Good-mornin', young man. You've got the advantage of me. I never saw you before as I know of."

"I am Tom Carver, at your service."

"Glad to know you. Where do you live? Maybe your wife would like some tinware this mornin'?" said Abner, relaxing his gaunt features into a smile.

"She didn't say anything about it when I came out," said Tom, entering into the joke.

"Maybe you'd like a tin-dipper for your youngest boy?"

"Maybe I would, if you've got any to give away."

"I see you've cut your eye-teeth. Is there anything else I can do for you? I'm in for a trade."

"I don't know, unless I sell myself for rags."

"Anything for a trade. I'll give you two cents a pound."

"That's too cheap. I came to ask your help in a trick we boys want to play on one of our number."

"Sho! you don't say so. That aint exactly in my line."

"I'll tell you all about it. There's a chap at our school—the Academy, you know—who's awfully stuck up. He's all the time bragging about belonging to a first family in Boston, and turning up his nose at poorer boys. We want to mortify him."

"Just so!" said Abner, nodding. "Drive ahead!"

"Well, we thought if you'd call at the school and ask after him, and pretend he was a cousin of yours, and all that, it would make him mad."

"Oh, I see," said Abner, nodding, "he wouldn't like to own a tin-pedler for his cousin."

"No," said Tom; "he wants us to think all his relations are rich. I wouldn't mind at all myself," he added, it suddenly occurring to him that Abner's feelings might be hurt.

"Good!" said Abner, "I see you aint one of the stuck-up kind. I've got some relations in Boston myself, that are rich and stuck up. I never go near 'em. What's the name of this chap you're talkin' about?"

"Fletcher—Fitzgerald Fletcher."

"Fletcher!" repeated Abner. "Whew! well, that's a joke!"

"What's a joke?" asked Tom, rather surprised.

"Why, he *is* my relation—a sort of second cousin. Why, my mother and his father are own cousins. So, don't you see we're second cousins?"

"That's splendid!" exclaimed Tom. "I can hardly believe it."

"It's so. My mother's name was Fletcher—Roxanna Fletcher —afore she married. Jim Fletcher—this boy's father—used to work in my grandfather's store, up to Hampton, but he got kinder discontented, and went off to Boston, where he's been lucky, and they do say he's mighty rich now. I never go nigh him, 'cause I know he looks down on his country cousins, and I don't believe in pokin' my nose in where I aint wanted."

"Then you are really and truly Fitz's cousin?"

"If that's the boy's name. Seems to me it's a kinder queer one. I s'pose it's a fust-class name. Sounds rather stuck up."

"Won't the boys roar when they hear about it! Are you willing to enter into our plan?"

"Well," said Abner, "I'll do it. I can't abide folks that's stuck up. I'd rather own a cousin like you."

"Thank you, Mr. Bickford."

"When do you want me to come round?"

"How long do you stay in town?"

"Well, I expect to stop overnight at the tavern; I can't get through in one day."

"Then come round to the Academy to-morrow morning, about half-past eight. School don't begin till nine, but the boys will be playing ball alongside. Then we'll give you an introduction to your cousin."

"That'll suit me well enough. I'll come."

Tom Carver returned in triumph, and communicated to the other boys the arrangement he had made with Mr. Bickford, and his unexpected discovery of the genuine relationship that existed between Fitz and the tin-pedler. His communication was listened to with great delight, and no little hilarity, and the boys discussed the probable effect of the projected meeting.

"Fitz will be perfectly raving," said Henry Fairbanks. "There's nothing that will take down his pride so much."

"He'll deny the relationship, probably," said Oscar.

"How can he?"

"He'll do it. See if he don't. It would be death to all his aristocratic claims to admit it."

"Suppose it were yourself, Oscar?"

"I'd say, 'How are you, cousin? How's the tin business?'" answered Oscar, promptly.

"I believe you would, Oscar. There's nothing of the snob about you."

"I hope not."

"Yet your family stands as high as Fletcher's."

"That's a point I leave to others to discuss," said Oscar. "My father is universally respected, I am sure, but he rose from the ranks. He was once a printer's devil, like my friend Harry Walton. Wouldn't it be ridiculous in me to turn up my nose at Walton, just because be stands now where my father did thirty years ago? It would be the same thing as sneering at father."

"Give us your hand, Oscar," said Henry Fairbanks. "You've got no nonsense about you—I like you."

"I'm not sure whether your compliment is deserved, Henry," said Oscar, "but if I have any nonsense it isn't of that kind."

"Do you believe Fitz has any suspicion that he has a cousin in the tin business?"

"No; I don't believe he has. He must know he has poor relations, living in the country, but he probably thinks as little as possible about them. As long as they don't intrude themselves upon his greatness, I suppose he is satisfied."

"And as long as no one suspects that he has any connection with such plebeians."

"Of course."

"What sort of a man is this tin-pedler, Tom?" asked Oscar.

"He's a pretty sharp fellow—not educated, or polished, you know, but he seems to have some sensible ideas. He said he had never seen the Fletchers; because he didn't want to poke his nose in where he wasn't wanted. He showed his good sense also by saying that he had rather have me for a cousin than Fitz."

"That isn't a very high compliment—I'd say the same myself."

"Thank you, Oscar. Your compliment exalts me. You won't mind my strutting a little."

And Tom humorously threw back his head, and strutted about with mock pride.

"To be sure," said Oscar, "you don't belong to one of the first families of Boston, like our friend, Fitz."

"No, I belong to one of the second families. You can't blame me, for I can't help it."

"No, I won't blame you, but of course I consider you low."

"I am afraid, Tom, I haven't got any cousins in the tin trade, like Fitz."

"Poor Fitz! he little dreams of his impending trial. If he did, I am afraid he wouldn't sleep a wink to-night."

"I wish I thought as much of myself as Fitz does," said Henry Fairbanks. "You can see by his dignified pace, and the way he tosses his head, how well satisfied he is with being Fitzgerald Fletcher, Esq."

"I'll bet five cents he won't strut round so much to-morrow afternoon," said Tom, "after his interview with his new cousin. But hush, boys! Not a word more of this. There's Fitz coming up the hill. I wouldn't have him suspect what's going on, or he might defeat our plans by staying away."

CHAPTER XI: FITZ AND HIS COUSIN

The next morning at eight the boys began to gather in the field beside the Seminary. They began to play ball, but took little interest in the game, compared with the "tragedy in real life," as Tom jocosely called it, which was expected soon to come off.

Fitz appeared upon the scene early. In fact one of the boys called for him, and induced him to come round to school earlier than usual. Significant glances were exchanged when he made his appearance, but Fitz suspected nothing, and was quite unaware that he was attracting more attention than usual.

Punctually at half-past eight, Abner Bickford with his tin-cart appeared in the street, and with a twitch of the rein began to ascend the Academy Hill.

"Look there," said Tom Carver, "the tin-pedler's coming up the hill. Wonder if he expects to sell any of his wares to us boys. Do you know him, Fitz?"

"I!" answered Fitzgerald with a scornful look, "what should I know of a tin-pedler?"

Tom's mouth twitched, and his eyes danced with the anticipation of fun.

By this time Mr. Bickford had brought his horse to a halt, and jumping from his box, approached the group of boys, who suspended their game.

"We don't want any tinware," said one of the boys, who was not in the secret.

"Want to know! Perhaps you haven't got tin enough to pay for it. Never mind, I'll buy you for old rags, at two cents a pound."

"He has you there, Harvey," said Tom Carver. "Can I do anything for you, sir?"

"Is your name Fletcher?" asked Abner, not appearing to recognize Tom.

"Why, he wants you, Fitz!" said Harvey, in surprise.

"This gentleman's name is Fletcher," said Tom, placing his hand on the shoulder of the astonished Fitzgerald.

"Not Fitz Fletcher?" said Abner, interrogatively.

"My name is Fitzgerald Fletcher," said the young Bostonian, haughtily, "but I am at a loss to understand why you should desire to see me."

Abner advanced with hand extended, his face lighted up with an expansive grin.

"Why, Cousin Fitz," he said heartily, "do you mean to say you don't know me?"

"Sir," said Fitzgerald, drawing back, "you are entirely mistaken in the person. I don't know you."

"I guess it's you that are mistaken, Fitz," said the pedler, familiarly; "why, don't you remember Cousin Abner, that used to trot you on his knee when you was a baby? Give us your hand, in memory of old times."

"You must be crazy," said Fitzgerald, his cheeks red with indignation, and all the more exasperated because he saw significant smiles on the faces of his school-companions.

"I s'pose you was too young to remember me," said Abner. "I haint seen you for ten years."

"Sir," said Fitz, wrathfully, "you are trying to impose upon me. I am a native of Boston."

"Of course you be," said the imperturbable pedler. "Cousin Jim—that's your father—went to Boston when he was a boy, and they do say he's worked his way up to be a mighty rich man. Your father *is* rich, aint he?"

"My father is wealthy, and always was," said Fitzgerald.

"No he wasn't, Cousin Fitz," said Abner. "When he was a boy, he used to work in grandfather's store up to Hampton; but he got sort of discontented and went to Boston. Did you ever hear him tell of his cousin Roxanna? That's my mother."

"I see that you mean to insult me, fellow," said Fitz, pale with passion. "I don't know what your object is, in pretending that I am your relation. If you want any pecuniary help—"

"Hear the boy talk!" said the pedler, bursting into a horse laugh. "Abner Bickford don't want no pecuniary help, as you call it. My tin-cart'll keep me, I guess."

"You needn't claim relationship with me," said Fitzgerald, scornfully; "I haven't any low relations."

"That's so," said Abner, emphatically; "but I aint sure whether I can say that for myself."

"Do you mean to insult me?"

"How can I? I was talkin' of my relations. You say you aint one of 'em."

"I am not."

"Then you needn't go for to put on the coat.[1] But you're out of your reckoning, I guess. I remember your mother very well. She was Susan Baker."

"Is that true, Fitz?"

"Ye—es," answered Fitz, reluctantly.

"I told you so," said the pedler, triumphantly.

"Perhaps he is your cousin, after all," said Henry Fairbanks.

"I tell you he isn't," said Fletcher, impetuously.

"How should he know your mother's name, then, Fitz?" asked Tom.

"Some of you fellows told him," said Fitzgerald.

"I can say, for one, that I never knew it," said Tom.

"Nor I."

"Nor I."

"We used to call her Sukey Baker," said Abner. "She used to go to the deestrict school along of Mother. They was in the same class. I haven't seen your mother since you was a baby. How many children has she got?"

"I must decline answering your impertinent questions," said Fitzgerald, desperately. He began to entertain, for the first time, the horrible suspicion that the pedler's story might be true—that he might after all be his cousin. But he resolved that he never would admit it—NEVER! Where would be his pretentious claims to aristocracy—where his pride—if this humiliating discovery

---

1 To change identities.

were made? Judging of his school-fellows and himself, he feared that they would look down upon him.

"You seem kind o' riled to find that I am your cousin," said Abner. "Now, Fitz, that's foolish. I aint rich, to be sure, but I'm respectable. I don't drink nor chew,[1] and I've got five hundred dollars laid away in the bank."

"You're welcome to your five hundred dollars," said Fitz, in what was meant to be a tone of withering sarcasm.

"Am I? Well, I'd orter be, considerin' I earned it by hard work. Seems to me you've got high notions, Fitz. Your mother was kind of flighty, and I've heard mine say Cousin Jim—that's your father—was mighty sot up by gettin' rich. But seems to me you ought not to deny your own flesh and blood."

"I don't know who you refer to, sir."

"Why, you don't seem to want to own me as your cousin."

"Of course not. You're only a common tin-pedler."

"Well, I know I'm a tin-pedler, but that don't change my bein' your cousin."

"I wish my father was here to expose your falsehood."

"Hold on there!" said Abner. "You're goin' a leetle too far. I don't let no man, nor boy neither, charge me with lyin', if he *is* my cousin, I don't stand that, nohow."

There was something in Abner's tone which convinced Fitzgerald that he was in earnest, and that he himself must take care not to go too far.

"I don't wish to have anything more to say to you," said Fitz.

"I say, boys," said Abner, turning to the crowd who had now formed a circle around the cousins, "I leave it to you if it aint mean for Fitz to treat me in that way. If he was to come to my house, that aint the way I'd treat him."

"Come, Fitz," said Tom, "you are not behaving right. I would not treat my cousin that way."

"He isn't my cousin, and you know it," said Fitz, stamping with rage.

"I wish I wasn't," said Abner. "If I could have my pick, I'd rather have him," indicating Tom. "But blood can't be wiped out. We're cousins, even if we don't like it."

"Are you quite sure you are right about this relationship?" asked Henry Fairbanks, gravely. "Fitz, here, says he belongs to one of the first families of Boston."

---

1   Refrain from both liquor and chewing tobacco.

"Well, I belong to one of the first families of Hampton," said Abner, with a grin. "Nobody don't look down on me, I guess."

"You hear that, Fitz," said Oscar. "Be sensible, and shake hands with your cousin."

"Yes, shake hands with your cousin!" echoed the boys.

"You all seem to want to insult me," said Fitz, sullenly.

"Not I," said Oscar, "and I'll prove it—will you shake hands with me, sir?"

"That I will," said Abner, heartily. "I can see that you're a young gentleman, and I wish I could say as much for my cousin, Fitz."

Oscar's example was followed by the rest of the boys, who advanced in turn, and shook hands with the tin-pedler.

"Now Fitz, it's your turn," said Tom.

"I decline," said Fitz, holding his hands behind his back.

"How much he looks like his marm did when she was young," said Abner. "Well, boys, I can't stop no longer. I didn't think Cousin Fitz would be so stuck up, just because his father's made some money. Good-mornin'!"

"Three cheers for Fitz's cousin!" shouted Tom.

They were given with a will, and Mr. Bickford made acknowledgment by a nod and a grin.

"Remember me to your mother when you write, Cousin Fitz," he said at parting.

Fitz was too angry to reply. He walked off sullenly, deeply mortified and humiliated, and for weeks afterward nothing would more surely throw him into a rage than any allusion to his cousin the tin-pedler. One good effect, however, followed. He did not venture to allude to the social position of his family in presence of his school-mates, and found it politic to lay aside some of his airs of superiority.

CHAPTER XII:
HARRY JOINS THE CLIONIAN SOCIETY

A week later Harry Walton received the following note:—

> "Centreville, May 16th, 18—,
> "Dear Sir: At the last meeting of the Clionian Society
> you were elected a member. The next meeting will be
> held on Thursday evening, in the Academy building.
> "Yours truly,
> "GEORGE SANBORN,
> "Secretary.
> "MR. HARRY WALTON."

Our hero read this letter with satisfaction. It would be pleasant for him to become acquainted with the Academy students, but he thought most of the advantages which his membership would afford him in the way of writing and speaking. He had never attempted to debate, and dreaded attempting it for the first time; but he knew that nothing desirable would be accomplished without effort, and he was willing to make that effort.

"What have you there, Walton?" asked Clapp, noticing the letter which he held in his hand.

"You can read it if you like," said Harry.

"Humph!" said Clapp; "so you are getting in with the Academy boys?"

"Why shouldn't he?" said Ferguson.

"Oh, they're a stuck-up set."

"I don't find them so—that is, with one exception," said Harry.

"They are mostly the sons of rich men, and look down on those who have to work for a living." Clapp was of a jealous and envious disposition, and he was always fancying slights where they were not intended.

"If I thought so," said Harry, "I would not join the Society, but as they have elected me, I shall become a member, and see how things turn out."

"It is a good plan, Harry," said Ferguson. "It will be a great advantage to you."

"I wish I had a chance to attend the Academy for a couple of years," said our hero, thoughtfully.

"I don't," said Clapp. "What's the good of studying Latin and Greek, and all that rigmarole? It won't bring you money, will it?"

"Yes," said Ferguson. "Education will make a man more competent to earn money, at any rate in many cases. I have a cousin, who used to go to school with me, but his father was able to send him to college. He is now a lawyer in Boston, making four or five times my income. But it isn't for the money alone that an education is worth having. There is a pleasure in being educated."

"So I think," said Harry.

"I don't see it," said Clapp. "I wouldn't be a bookworm for anybody. There's Walton learning French. What good is it ever going to do him?"

"I can tell you better by and by, when I know a little more," said Harry. "I am only a beginner now."

"Dr. Franklin would never have become distinguished if he had been satisfied with what he knew as an apprentice," said Ferguson.

"Oh, if you're going to bring up Franklin again, I've got through," said Clapp with a sneer. "I forgot that Walton was trying to be a second Franklin."

"I don't see much chance of it," said Harry, good-humoredly. "I should like to be if I could."

Clapp seemed to be in an ill-humor, and the conversation was not continued. He had been up late the night before with Luke Harrison, and both had drank more than was good for them. In consequence, Clapp had a severe headache, and this did not improve his temper.

"Come round Thursday evening, Harry," said Oscar Vincent, "and go to the Society with me. I will introduce you to the fellows. It will be less awkward, you know."

"Thank you, Oscar. I shall be glad to accept your escort."

When Thursday evening came, Oscar and Harry entered the Society hall arm in arm. Oscar led his companion up to the Secretary and introduced him.

"I am glad to see you, Mr. Walton," said he. "Will you sign your name to the Constitution? That is all the formality we require."

"Except a slight pecuniary disbursement," added Oscar.

"How much is the entrance fee?" asked Harry.

"One dollar. You will pay that to the Treasurer."

Oscar next introduced our hero to the President, and some of the leading members, all of whom welcomed him cordially.

"Good-evening, Mr. Fletcher," said Harry, observing that young gentleman near him.

"Good-evening, sir," said Fletcher stiffly, and turned on his heel without offering his hand.

"Fletcher don't feel well," whispered Oscar. "He had a visit from a poor relation the other day—a tin-pedler—and it gave such a shock to his sensitive system that he hasn't recovered from it yet."

"I didn't imagine Mr. Fletcher had such a plebeian relative," said Harry.

"Nor did any of us. The interview was rich. It amused us all, but what was sport to us was death to poor Fitz. You have only to make the most distant allusion to a tin-pedler in his hearing, and he will become furious."

"Then I will be careful."

"Oh, it won't do any harm. The fact was, the boy was getting too overbearing, and putting on altogether too many airs. The lesson will do him good, or ought to."

Here the Society was called to order, and Oscar and Harry took their seats.

The exercises proceeded in regular order until the President announced a declamation by Fitzgerald Fletcher.

"Mr. President," said Fletcher, rising, "I must ask to be excused. I have not had time to prepare a declamation."

"Mr. President," said Tom Carver, "under the circumstances I hope you will excuse Mr. Fletcher, as during the last week he has had an addition to his family."

There was a chorus of laughter, loud and long, at this sally. All were amused except Fletcher himself, who looked flushed and provoked.

"Mr. Fletcher is excused," said the President, unable to refrain from smiling. "Will any member volunteer to speak in his place? It will be a pity to have our exercises incomplete."

Fletcher was angry, and wanted to be revenged on somebody. A bright idea came to him. He would place the "printer's devil," whose admission to the Society he resented, in an awkward position. He rose with a malicious smile upon his face.

"Mr. President," he said, "doubtless Mr. Walton, the new member who has done us the *honor* to join our society, will be willing to supply my place."

"We shall certainly be glad to hear a declamation from Mr. Walton, though it is hardly fair to call upon him at such short notice."

"Can't you speak something, Harry?" whispered Oscar. "Don't do it, unless you are sure you can get through."

Harry started in surprise when his name was first mentioned, but he quickly resolved to accept his duty. He had a high reputation at home for speaking, and he had recently learned a spirited poem, familiar, no doubt, to many of my young readers, called "Shamus O'Brien."[1] It is the story of an Irish volunteer, who was arrested for participating in the Irish rebellion of '98,[2] and is by turns spirited and pathetic. Harry had rehearsed it to himself only the night before, and he had confidence in a strong and retentive memory. At the President's invitation he rose to his feet, and said, "Mr. President, I will do as well as I can, but I hope the members of the Society will make allowance for me, as I have had no time for special preparation."

All eyes were fixed with interest upon our hero, as he advanced to the platform, and, bowing composedly, commenced his declamation. It was not long before that interest increased, as Harry proceeded in his recitation. He lost all diffidence, forgot the audience, and entered thoroughly into the spirit of the piece. Especially when, in the trial scene, Shamus is called upon to plead guilty or not guilty, Harry surpassed himself, and spoke with a spirit and fire which brought down the house. This is the passage:—

"My lord, if you ask me, if in my life-time
I thought any treason, or did any crime,
That should call to my cheek, as I stand alone here,
The hot blush of shame, or the coldness of fear,
Though I stood by the grave to receive my death-blow,
Before God and the world I would answer you, no!
But if you would ask me, as I think it like,
If in the rebellion I carried a pike,
An' fought for ould Ireland from the first to the close,
An' shed the heart's blood of her bitterest foes,
I answer you, *yes*; and I tell you again,
Though I stand here to perish, it's my glory that then
In her cause I was willing my veins should run dhry,
An' that now for her sake I am ready to die."

After the applause had subsided, Harry proceeded, and at the conclusion of the declamation, when he bowed modestly and left the platform, the hall fairly shook with the stamping, in which all

---

1   The ballad "Shamus O'Brien" (1850) by Joseph Sheridan Le Fanu (1814–73).

2   A rebellion against British rule in Ireland during the spring and summer of 1798.

joined except Fletcher, who sat scowling with dissatisfaction at a result so different from his hopes. He had expected to bring discomfiture to our hero. Instead, he had given him an opportunity to achieve a memorable triumph.

"You did yourself credit, old boy!" said Oscar, seizing and wringing the hand of Harry, as the latter resumed his seat. "Why, you ought to go on the stage!"

"Thank you," said Harry; "I am glad I got through well."

"Isn't Fitz mad, though? He thought you'd break down. Look at him!"

Harry looked over to Fletcher, who, with a sour expression, was sitting upright, and looking straight before him.

"He don't look happy, does he?" whispered Oscar, comically.

Harry came near laughing aloud, but luckily for Fletcher's peace of mind, succeeded in restraining himself.

"He won't call you up again in a hurry; see if he does," continued Oscar.

"I am sure we have all been gratified by Mr. Walton's spirited declamation," said the President, rising. "We congratulate ourselves upon adding so fine a speaker to our society, and hope often to have the pleasure of hearing him declaim."

There was a fresh outbreak of applause, after which the other exercises followed. When the meeting was over the members of the Society crowded around Harry, and congratulated him on his success. These congratulations he received so modestly, as to confirm the favorable impression he had made by his declamation.

"By Jove! old fellow," said Oscar, as they were walking home, "I am beginning to be proud of you. You are doing great credit to your teacher."

"Thank you, Professor," said Harry. "Don't compliment me too much, or I may become vain, and put on airs."

"If you do, I'll get Fitz to call, and remind you that you are only a printer's devil, after all."

CHAPTER XIII:
VACATION BEGINS AT THE ACADEMY

Not long after his election as a member of the Clionian Society, the summer term of the Prescott Academy closed. The examination took place about the tenth of June, and a vacation followed, lasting till the first day of September. Of course, the Clionian

Society, which was composed of Academy students, suspended its meetings for the same length of time. Indeed, the last meeting for the season took place during the first week in June, as the evenings were too short and too warm, and the weather was not favorable to oratory. At the last meeting, an election was held of officers to serve for the following term. The same President and Vice-President were chosen; but as the Secretary declined to serve another term, Harry Walton, considerably to his surprise, found himself elected in his place.

Fitzgerald Fletcher did not vote for him. Indeed, he expressed it as his opinion that it was a shame to elect a "printer's devil" Secretary of the Society.

"Why is it?" said Oscar. "Printing is a department of literature, and the Clionian is a literary society, isn't it?"

"Of course it is a literary society, but a printer's devil is not literary."

"He's as literary as a tin-pedler," said Tom Carver, maliciously.

Fletcher turned red, but managed to say, "And what does that prove?"

"We don't object to you because you are connected with the tin business."

"Do you mean to insult me?" demanded Fletcher, angrily. "What have I to do with the tin business?"

"Oh, I beg pardon, it's your cousin that's in it."

"I deny the relationship," said Fletcher, "and I will thank you not to refer again to that vulgar pedler."

"Really, Fitz, you speak rather roughly, considering he's your cousin. But as to Harry Walton, he's a fine fellow, and he has an excellent handwriting, and I was very glad to vote for him."

Fitzgerald walked away, not a little disgusted, as well at the allusion to the tin-pedler, as at the success of Harry Walton in obtaining an office to which he had himself secretly aspired. He had fancied that it would sound well to put "Secretary of the Clionian Society" after his name, and would give him increased consequence at home. As to the tin-pedler, it would have relieved his mind to hear that Mr. Bickford had been carried off suddenly by an apoplectic fit, and notwithstanding the tie of kindred, he would not have taken the trouble to put on mourning in his honor.

Harry Walton sat in Oscar Vincent's room, on the last evening of the term. He had just finished reciting the last French lesson in which he would have Oscar's assistance for some time to come.

"You have made excellent progress," said Oscar. "It is only two months since you began French, and now you take a long lesson in translation."

"That is because I have so good a teacher. But do you think I can get along without help during the summer?"

"No doubt of it. You may find some difficulties, but those you can mark, and I will explain when I come back. Or I'll tell you what is still better. Write to me, and I'll answer. Shall I write in French?"

"I wish you would, Oscar."

"Then I will. I'm rather lazy with the pen, but I can find time for you. Besides, it will be a good way for me to keep up my French."

"Shall you be in Boston all summer, Oscar?"

"No; our family has a summer residence at Nahant,[1] a sea-shore place twelve miles from Boston. Then I hope father will let me travel about a little on my own account. I want to go to Saratoga and Lake George."

"That would be splendid."

"I wish you could go with me, Harry."

"Thank you, Oscar, but perhaps you can secure Fletcher's company. That will be much better than that of a 'printer's devil' like myself."

"It may show bad taste, but I should prefer your company, notwithstanding your low employment."

"Thank you, Oscar. I am much obliged."

"Fitz has been hinting to me how nice it would be for us to go off somewhere together, but I don't see it in that light. I asked him why he didn't secure board with his cousin, the tin-pedler, but that made him angry, and he walked away in disgust. But I can't help pitying you a little, Harry."

"Why? On account of my occupation?"

"Partly. All these warm summer days, you have got to be working at the case, while I can lounge in the shade, or travel for pleasure. Sha'n't you have a vacation?"

"I don't expect any. I don't think I could well be spared. However, I don't mind it. I hope to do a good deal of studying while you are gone."

"And I sha'n't do any."

"Neither would I, perhaps, in your position. But there's a good deal of difference between us. You are a Latin and Greek scholar,

---

1   The village of Nahant, Massachusetts, was located northeast of Boston. Alger taught there one summer early in the 1860s.

and can talk French, while I am at the bottom of the ladder. I have no time to lose."

"You have begun to mount the ladder, Harry. Don't be discouraged. You can climb up."

"But I must work for it. I haven't got high enough up to stop and rest. But there is one question I want to ask you, before you go."

"What is it?"

"What French book would you recommend after I have finished this Reader? I am nearly through now."

"Télémaque[1] will be a good book to take next. It is easy and interesting. Have you got a French dictionary?"

"No; but I can buy one."

"You can use mine while I am gone. You may as well have it as not. I have no copy of Télémaque, but I will send you one from Boston."

"Agreed, provided you will let me pay you for it."

"So I would, if I had to buy one. But I have got an old copy, not very ornamental, but complete. I will send it through the mail."

"Thank you, Oscar. How kind you are!"

"Don't flatter me, Harry. The favors you refer to are but trifles. I will ask a favor of you in return."

"I wish you would."

"Then help me pack my trunk. There's nothing I detest so much. Generally I tumble things in helter-skelter, and get a good scolding from mother for doing it, when she inspects my trunk."

"I'll save you the trouble, then. Bring what you want to carry home, and pile it on the floor, and I'll do the packing."

"A thousand thanks, as the French say. It takes a load off my mind. By the way, here's a lot of my photographs. Would you like one to remember your professor by?"

"Very much, Oscar."

"Then take your choice. They don't do justice to my beauty, which is of a stunning description, as you are aware, nor do they convey an idea of the lofty intellect which sits enthroned behind my classic brow; but such as they are, you are welcome to one."

"Any one would think, to hear you, that you had no end of self-conceit, Oscar," said Harry, laughing.

---

1 *Les aventures de Télémaque* (*The Adventures of Telemachus*) was a 1699 didactic novel by the French archbishop François Fénelon (1651–1715).

"How do you know that I haven't? Most people think they are beautiful. A photographer told my sister that he was once visited by a frightfully homely man from the country, who wanted his 'picter took.' When the result was placed before him, he seemed dissatisfied. 'Don't you think it like?' said the artist.—'Well, yes,' he answered slowly, 'but it hasn't got my sweet expression about the mouth'!"

"Very good," said Harry, laughing; "that's what's the matter with your picture."

"Precisely. I am glad your artistic eye detects what is wanting. But, hold! there's a knock. It's Fitz, I'll bet a hat."

"Come in!" he cried, and Fletcher walked in.

"Good-evening, Fletcher," said Oscar. "You see I'm packing, or rather Walton is packing. He's a capital packer."

"Indeed!" sneered Fletcher. "I was not aware that Mr. Walton was in that line of business. What are his terms?"

"I refer you to him."

"What do you charge for packing trunks, Mr. Walton?"

"I think fifty cents would be about right," answered Harry, with perfect gravity. "Can you give me a job, Mr. Fletcher?"

"I might, if I had known it in time, though I am particular who handles my things."

"Walton is careful, and I can vouch for his honesty," said Oscar, carrying out the joke. "His wages in the printing office are not large, and he would be glad to make a little extra money."

"It must be very inconvenient to be poor," said Fletcher, with a supercilious glance at our hero, who was kneeling before Oscar's trunk.

"It is," answered Harry, quietly, "but as long as work is to be had I shall not complain."

"To be sure!" said Fletcher. "My father is wealthy, and I shall not have to work."

"Suppose he should fail?" suggested Oscar.

"That is a very improbable supposition," said Fletcher, loftily.

"But not impossible?"

"Nothing is impossible."

"Of course. I say, Fitz, if such a thing should happen, you've got something to fall back upon."

"To what do you refer?"

"Mr. Bickford could give you an interest in the tin business."

"Good-evening!" said Fletcher, not relishing the allusion.

"Good-evening! Of course I shall see you in the city."

"I suppose I ought not to tease Fitz," said Oscar, after his visitor had departed, "but I enjoy seeing how disgusted he looks."

In due time the trunk was packed, and Harry, not without regret, took leave of his friend for the summer.

CHAPTER XIV: HARRY BECOMES AN AUTHOR

The closing of the Academy made quite a difference in the life of Centreville. The number of boarding scholars was about thirty, and these, though few in number, were often seen in the street and at the post-office, and their withdrawal left a vacancy. Harry Walton felt quite lonely at first; but there is no cure for loneliness like occupation, and he had plenty of that. The greater part of the day was spent in the printing office, while his evenings and early mornings were occupied in study and reading. He had become very much interested in French, in which he found himself advancing rapidly. Occasionally he took tea at Mr. Ferguson's, and this he always enjoyed; for, as I have already said, he and Ferguson held very similar views on many important subjects. One evening, at the house of the latter, he saw a file of weekly papers, which proved, on examination, to be back numbers of the "Weekly Standard," a literary paper issued in Boston.

"I take the paper for my family," said Ferguson. "It contains quite a variety of reading matter, stories, sketches and essays."

"It seems quite interesting," said Harry.

"Yes, it is. I will lend you some of the back numbers, if you like."

"I would like it. My father never took a literary paper; his means were so limited that he could not afford it."

"I think it is a good investment. There are few papers from which you cannot obtain in a year more than the worth of the subscription. Besides, if you are going to be an editor, it will be useful for you to become familiar with the manner in which such papers are conducted."

When Harry went home he took a dozen copies of the paper, and sat up late reading them. While thus engaged an idea struck him. It was this: Could not he write something which would be accepted for publication in the "Standard"? It was his great ambition to learn to write for the press, and he felt that he was old enough to commence.

"If I don't succeed the first time, I can try again," he reflected. The more he thought of it, the more he liked the plan. It is very possible that he was influenced by the example of Franklin, who, while yet a boy in his teens, contributed articles to his brother's paper though at the time the authorship was not suspected. Finally he decided to commence writing as soon as he could think of a suitable subject. This he found was not easy. He could think of plenty of subjects of which he was not qualified to write, or in which he felt little interest; but he rightly decided that he could succeed better with something that had a bearing upon his own experience or hopes for the future.

Finally he decided to write on Ambition.

I do not propose to introduce Harry's essay in these pages, but will give a general idea of it, as tending to show his views of life.

He began by defining ambition as a desire for superiority, by which most men were more or less affected, though it manifested itself in very different ways, according to the character of him with whom it was found. Here I will quote a passage, as a specimen of Harry's style and mode of expression.

"There are some who denounce ambition as wholly bad and to be avoided by all; but I think we ought to make a distinction between true and false ambition. The desire of superiority is an honorable motive, if it leads to honorable exertion. I will mention Napoleon as an illustration of false ambition, which is selfish in itself, and has brought misery and ruin, to prosperous nations. Again, there are some who are ambitious to dress better than their neighbors, and their principal thoughts are centred upon the tie of their cravat, or the cut of their coat, if young men; or upon the richness and style of their dresses, if they belong to the other sex. Beau Brummel[1] is a noted instance of this kind of ambition. It is said that fully half of his time was devoted to his toilet, and the other half to displaying it in the streets, or in society. Now this is a very low form of ambition, and it is wrong to indulge it, because it is a waste of time which could be much better employed."

Harry now proceeded to describe what he regarded as a true and praiseworthy ambition. He defined it as a desire to excel in what would be of service to the human race, and he instanced his old Franklin, who, induced by an honorable ambition, worked his way up to a high civil station, as well as a commanding position in the scientific world. He mentioned Columbus[2] as ambitious to

---

1   George Bryan "Beau" Brummell (1778–1840) was a dandy and an arbiter of fashion in Regency England.
2   Christopher Columbus (1451–1506) completed four voyages to the Americas between 1492 and 1502.

extend the limits of geographical knowledge, and made a brief reference to the difficulties and discouragements over which he triumphed on the way to success. He closed by an appeal to boys and young men to direct their ambition into worthy channels, so that even if they could not leave behind a great name, they might at least lead useful lives, and in dying have the satisfaction of thinking that they done some service to the race.

This will give a very fair idea of Harry's essay. There was nothing remarkable about it, and no striking originality in the ideas, but it was very creditably expressed for a boy of his years, and did even more credit to his good judgment, since it was an unfolding of the principles by which he meant to guide his own life.

It must not be supposed that our hero was a genius, and that he wrote his essay without difficulty. It occupied him two evenings to write it, and he employed the third in revising and copying it. It covered about five pages of manuscript, and, according to his estimate, would fill about two-thirds of a long column in the "Standard."

After preparing it, the next thing was to find a *nom de plume*, for he shrank from signing his own name. After long consideration, he at last decided upon Franklin, and this was the name he signed to his maiden contribution to the press.

He carried it to the post-office one afternoon, after his work in the printing office was over, and dropped it unobserved into the letter-box. He did not want the postmaster to learn his secret, as he would have done had he received it directly from him, and noted the address on the envelope.

For the rest of the week, Harry went about his work weighed down with his important secret—a secret which he had not even shared with Ferguson. If the essay was declined, as he thought it might very possibly be, he did not want any one to know it. If it were accepted, and printed, it would be time enough then to make it known.

But there were few minutes in which his mind was not on his literary venture. His preoccupation was observed by his fellow-workmen in the office, and he was rallied upon it, good-naturedly, by Ferguson, but in a different spirit by Clapp.

"It seems to me you are unusually silent, Harry," said Ferguson. "You're not in love, are you?"

"Not that I know of," said Harry, smiling. "It's rather too early yet."

"I've known boys of your age to fancy themselves in love."

"He is is [*sic*] more likely thinking up some great discovery," said Clapp, sneering. "You know he's a second Franklin."

"Thank you for the compliment," said our hero, good-humoredly, "but I don't deserve it. I don't expect to make any great discovery at present."

"I suppose you expect to set the river on fire, some day," said Clapp, sarcastically.

"I am afraid it wouldn't do much good to try," said Harry, who was too sensible to take offence. "It isn't so easily done."

"I suppose some day we shall be proud of having been in the same office with so great a man," pursued Clapp.

"Really, Clapp, you're rather hard on our young friend," said Ferguson. "He doesn't put on any airs of superiority, or pretend to anything uncommon."

"He's very kind—such an intellect as he's got, too!" said Clapp.

"I'm glad you found it out," said Harry. "I haven't a very high idea of my intellect yet. I wish I had more reason to do so."

Finding that he had failed in his attempt to provoke Harry by his ridicule, Clapp desisted, but he disliked him none the less.

The fact was, that Clapp was getting into a bad way. He had no high aim in life, and cared chiefly for the pleasure of the present moment. He had found Luke Harrison a congenial companion, and they had been associated in more than one excess. The morning previous, Clapp had entered the printing office so evidently under the influence of liquor, that he had been sharply reprimanded by Mr. Anderson.

"I don't choose to interfere with your mode of life, unwise and ruinous as I may consider it," he said, "as long as it does not interfere with your discharge of duty. But to-day you are clearly incapacitated for labor, and I have a right to complain. If it happens again, I shall be obliged to look for another journeyman."

Clapp did not care to leave his place just at present, for he had no money saved up, and was even somewhat in debt, and it might be some time before he got another place. So he rather sullenly agreed to be more careful in future, and did not go to work till the afternoon.

But though circumstances compelled him to submit, it put him in bad humor, and made him more disposed to sneer than ever. He had an unreasoning prejudice against Harry, which was stimulated by Luke Harrison, who had this very sufficient reason for hating our hero, that he had succeeded in injuring him. As an old proverb has it "We are slow to forgive those whom we have injured."[1]

CHAPTER XV: A LITERARY DEBUT

Harry waited eagerly for the next issue of the "Weekly Standard." It was received by Mr. Anderson in exchange for the "Centreville Gazette," and usually came to hand on Saturday morning. Harry was likely to obtain the first chance of examining the paper, as he was ordinarily sent to the post-office on the arrival of the morning mail.

His hands trembled as he unfolded the paper and hurriedly scanned the contents. But he looked in vain for his essay on Ambition. There was not even a reference to it. He was disappointed, but he soon became hopeful again.

"I couldn't expect it to appear so soon," he reflected. "These city weeklies have to be printed some days in advance. It may appear yet."

So he was left in suspense another week, hopeful and doubtful by turns of the success of his first offering for the press. He was rallied from time to time on his silence in the office, but he continued to keep his secret. If his contribution was slighted, no one should know it but himself.

At last another Saturday morning came around and again he set out for the post-office. Again he opened the paper with trembling fingers, and eagerly scanned the well-filled columns. This time his search was rewarded. There, on the first column of the last page, in all the glory of print, was his treasured essay!

A flash of pleasure tinged his cheek, and his heart beat rapidly, as he read his first printed production. It is a great event in the life of a literary novice, when he first sees himself [in print]. Even Byron says,—

"'Tis pleasant, sure, to see one's self in print."[2]

To our young hero the essay read remarkably well—better than he had expected; but then, very likely he was prejudiced in its favor. He read it through three times on his way back to the printing office, and each time felt better satisfied.

---

1 An ironic corruption of one of the rules of St. Augustine (354–430 CE).
2 Line 51 in *English Bards and Scotch Reviewers* (1809) by the poet George Gordon, Lord Byron (1788–1824).

"I wonder if any of the readers will think it was written by a boy?" thought Harry. Probably many did so suspect, for, as I have said, though the thoughts were good and sensible, the article was only moderately well expressed. A practised critic would readily have detected marks of immaturity, although it was a very creditable production for a boy of sixteen.

"Shall I tell Ferguson?" thought Harry.

On the whole he concluded to remain silent just at present. He knew Ferguson took the paper, and waited to see if he would make any remark about it.

"I should like to hear him speak of it, without knowing that I was the writer," thought our hero.

Just before he reached the office, he discovered with satisfaction the following editorial reference to his article:—

"We print in another column an essay on 'ambition' by a new contributor. It contains some good ideas, and we especially commend it to the perusal of our young readers. We hope to hear from 'Franklin' again."

"That's good," thought Harry. "I am glad the editor likes it. I shall write again as soon as possible."

"What makes you look so bright, Harry?" asked Ferguson, as he re-entered the office. "Has any one left you a fortune?"

"Not that I know of," said Harry. "Do I look happier than usual?"

"So it seems to me."

Harry was spared answering this question, for Clapp struck in, grumbling, as usual: "I wish somebody'd leave me a fortune. You wouldn't see me here long."

"What would you do?" asked his fellow-workman.

"Cut work to begin with. I'd go to Europe and have a jolly time."

"You can do that without a fortune."

"I should like to know how?"

"Be economical, and you can save enough in three years to pay for a short trip. Bayard Taylor was gone two years, and only spent five hundred dollars."

"Oh, hang economy!" drawled Clapp. "It don't suit me. I should like to know how a feller's going to economize on fifteen dollars a week."

"I could."

"Oh, no doubt," sneered Clapp, "but a man can't starve."

"Come round and take supper with me, some night," said Ferguson, good-humoredly, "and you can judge for yourself whether I believe in starving."

Clapp didn't reply to this invitation. He would not have enjoyed a quiet evening with his fellow-workman. An evening at billiards or cards, accompanied by bets on the games, would have been much more to his mind.

"Who is Bayard Taylor, that made such a cheap tour in Europe?" asked Harry, soon afterward.

"A young journalist who had a great desire to travel. He has lately published an account of his tour.[1] I don't buy many books, but I bought that. Would you like to read it?"

"Very much."

"You can have it any time."

"Thank you."

On Monday, a very agreeable surprise awaited Harry.

"I am out of copy," he said, going up to Mr. Anderson's table.

"Here's a selection for the first page," said Mr. Anderson. "Cut it in two, and give part of it to Clapp."

Could Harry believe his eyes! It was his own article on ambition, and it was to be reproduced in the "Gazette." Next to the delight of seeing one's self in print for the first time, is the delight of seeing that first article copied. It is a mark of appreciation which cannot be mistaken.

Still Harry said nothing, but, with a manner as unconcerned as possible, handed the lower half of the essay to Clapp to set up. The signature "Franklin" had been cut off, and the name of the paper from which the essay had been cut was substituted.

"Wouldn't Clapp feel disgusted," thought Harry, "if he knew that he was setting up an article of mine. I believe he would have a fit."

He was too considerate to expose his fellow-workman to such a contingency, and went about his work in silence.

That evening he wrote to the publisher of the "Standard," inclosing the price of two copies of the last number, which he desired should be sent to him by mail. He wished to keep one himself, and the other he intended to forward to his father, who, he knew, would sympathize with him in his success as well as his aspirations. He accompanied the paper by a letter in which he said,—

"I want to improve in writing as much as I can. I want to be something more than a printer, sometime. I shall try to qualify

---

1   The travel writer and novelist Bayard Taylor (1825–78) was the author of *By-Ways of Europe*, serialized in the *Atlantic Monthly* between August 1867 and May 1868 and issued as a hardcover volume in 1869.

myself for an editor; for an editor can exert a good deal of influence in the community. I hope you will approve my plans."

In due time Harry received the following reply,—

"My dear son:—I am indeed pleased and proud to hear of your success, not that it is a great matter in itself, but because I think it shows that you are in earnest in your determination to win an honorable position by honorable labor. I am sorry that my narrow means have not permitted me to give you those advantages which wealthy fathers can bestow upon their sons. I should like to have sent you to college and given you an opportunity afterward of studying for a profession. I think your natural abilities would have justified such an outlay. But, alas! poverty has always held me back. It shuts out you, as it has shut out me, from the chance of culture. Your college, my boy, must be the printing office. If you make the best of that, you will find that it is no mean instructor. Not Franklin alone, but many of our most eminent and influential men have graduated from it.

"You will be glad to hear that we are all well. I have sold the cow which I bought of Squire Green, and got another in her place that proves to be much better. We all send much love, and your mother wishes me to say that she misses you very much, as indeed we all do. But we know that you are better off in Centreville than you would be at home, and that helps to make us contented. Don't forget to write every week.

"Your affectionate father,
"HIRAM WALTON.
"P. S.—If you print any more articles, we shall be interested to read them."

Harry read this letter with eager interest. He felt glad that his father was pleased with him, and it stimulated him to increased exertions.

"Poor father!" he said to himself. "He has led a hard life, cultivating that rocky little farm. It has been hard work and poor pay with him. I hope there is something better in store for him. If I ever get rich, or even well off, I will take care that he has an easier time."

After the next issue of the "Gazette" had appeared, Harry

informed Ferguson in confidence that he was the author of the article on Ambition.

"I congratulate you, Harry," said his friend. "It is an excellent essay, well thought out, and well expressed. I don't wonder, now you tell me of it. It sounds like you. Without knowing the authorship, I asked Clapp his opinion of it."

"What did he say?"

"Are you sure it won't hurt your feelings?"

"It may; but I shall get over it. Go ahead."

"He said it was rubbish."

Harry laughed.

"He would be confirmed in his decision, if he knew that I wrote it," he said.

"No doubt. But don't let that discourage you. Keep on writing by all means, and you'll become an editor in time."

CHAPTER XVI: FERDINAND B. KENSINGTON

It has already been mentioned that John Clapp and Luke Harrison were intimate. Though their occupations differed, one being a printer and the other a shoemaker, they had similar tastes, and took similar views of life. Both were discontented with the lot which Fortune had assigned them. To work at the case, or the shoe-bench, seemed equally irksome, and they often lamented to each other the hard necessity which compelled them to it. Suppose we listen to their conversation, as they walked up the village street, one evening about this time, smoking cigars.

"I say, Luke," said John Clapp, "I've got tired of this kind of life. Here I've been in the office a year, and I'm not a cent richer than when I entered it, besides working like a dog all the while."

"Just my case," said Luke. "I've been shoe-makin' ever since I was fourteen, and I'll be blest if I can show five dollars, to save my life."

"What's worse," said Clapp, "there isn't any prospect of anything better in my case. What's a feller to do on fifteen dollars a week?"

"Won't old Anderson raise your wages?"

"Not he! He thinks I ought to get rich on what he pays me now," and Clapp laughed scornfully. "If I were like Ferguson, I might. He never spends a cent without taking twenty-four hours to think it over beforehand."

My readers, who are familiar with Mr. Ferguson's views and

ways of life, will at once see that this was unjust, but justice cannot be expected from an angry and discontented man.

"Just so," said Luke. "If a feller was to live on bread and water, and get along with one suit of clothes a year, he might save something, but that aint *my* style."

"Nor mine."

"It's strange how lucky some men are," said Luke. "They get rich without tryin'. I never was lucky. I bought a ticket in a lottery once, but of course I didn't draw anything. Just my luck!"

"So did I," said Clapp, "but I fared no better. It seemed as if Fortune had a spite against me. Here I am twenty-five years old, and all I'm worth is two dollars and a half, and I owe more than that to the tailor."

"You're as rich as I am," said Luke. "I only get fourteen dollars a week. That's less than you do."

"A dollar more or less don't amount to much," said Clapp. "I'll tell you what it is, Luke," he resumed after a pause, "I'm getting sick of Centreville."

"So am I," said Luke, "but it don't make much difference. If I had fifty dollars, I'd go off and try my luck somewhere else, but I'll have to wait till I'm gray-headed before I get as much as that."

"Can't you borrow it?"

"Who'd lend it to me?"

"I don't know. If I did, I'd go in for borrowing myself. I wish there was some way of my getting to California."

"California!" repeated Luke with interest. "What would you do there?"

"I'd go to the mines."

"Do you think there's money to be made there?"

"I know there is," said Clapp, emphatically.

"How do you know it?"

"There's an old school-mate of mine—Ralph Smith—went out there two years ago. Last week he returned home—I heard it in a letter—and how much do you think he brought with him?"

"How much?"

"Eight thousand dollars!"

"Eight thousand dollars! He didn't make it all at the mines, did he?"

"Yes, he did. When he went out there, he had just money enough to pay his passage. Now, after only two years, he can lay off and live like a gentleman."

"He's been lucky, and no mistake."

"You bet he has. But we might be as lucky if we were only out there."

"Ay, there's the rub. A fellow can't travel for nothing."

At this point in their conversation, a well-dressed young man, evidently a stranger in the village, met them, and stopping, asked politely for a light.

This Clapp afforded him.

"You are a stranger in the village?" he said, with some curiosity.

"Yes, I was never here before. I come from New York."

"Indeed! If I lived in New York I'd stay there, and not come to such a beastly place as Centreville."

"Do you live here?" asked the stranger.

"Yes."

"I wonder you live in such a beastly place," he said, with a smile.

"You wouldn't, if you knew the reason."

"What is the reason?"

"I can't get away."

The stranger laughed.

"Cruel parents?" he asked.

"Not much," said Clapp. "The plain reason is, that I haven't got money enough to get me out of town."

"It's the same with me," said Luke Harrison.

"Gentlemen, we are well met," said the stranger. "I'm hard up myself."

"You don't look like it," said Luke, glancing at his rather flashy attire.

"These clothes are not paid for," said the stranger, laughing; "and what's more, I don't think they are likely to be. But, I take it, you gentlemen are better off than I in one respect. You've got situations—something to do."

"Yes, but on starvation pay," said Clapp. "I'm in the office of the 'Centreville Gazette.'"

"And I'm in a shoemaker's shop. It's a beastly business for a young man of spirit," said Luke.

"Well, I'm a gentleman at large, living on my wits, and pretty poor living it is sometimes," said the stranger. "As I think we'll agree together pretty well, I'm glad I've met you. We ought to know each other better. There's my card."

He drew from his pocket a highly glazed piece of pasteboard, bearing the name,

FREDERICK B. KENSINGTON.

"I haven't any cards with me," said Clapp, "but my name is John Clapp."

"And mine is Luke Harrison," said the bearer of that appellation.

"I'm proud to know you, gentlemen. If you have no objection, we'll walk on together."

To this Clapp and Luke acceded readily. Indeed, they were rather proud of being seen in company with a young man so dashing in manner, and fashionably dressed, though in a pecuniary way their new acquaintance, by his own confession, was scarcely as well off as themselves.

"Where are you staying, Mr. Kensington?" said Clapp.

"At the hotel. It's a poor place. No style."

"Of course not. I can't help wondering, Mr. Kensington, what can bring you to such a one-horse place as this."

"I don't mind telling you, then. The fact is, I've got an old aunt living about two miles from here. She's alone in the world—got neither chick nor child—and is worth at least ten thousand dollars. Do you see?"

"I think I do," said Clapp. "You want to come in for a share of the stamps."

"Yes; I want to see if I can't get something out of the old girl," said Kensington, carelessly.

"Do you think the chance is good?"

"I don't know. I hear she's pretty tight-fisted. But I've run on here on the chance of doing something. If she will only make me her heir, and give me five hundred dollars in hand, I'll go to California, and see what'll turn up."

"California!" repeated John Clapp and Luke in unison.

"Yes; were you ever there?"

"No; but we were talking of going there just as you came up," said John. "An old school-mate of mine has just returned from there with eight thousand dollars in gold."

"Lucky fellow! That's the kind of haul I'd like to make."

"Do you know how much it costs to go out there?"

"The prices are down just at present. You can go for a hundred dollars—second cabin."

"It might as well be a thousand!" said Luke. "Clapp and I can't raise a hundred dollars apiece to save our lives."

"I'll tell you what," said Kensington. "You two fellows are just the company I'd like. If I can raise five hundred dollars out of the old girl, I'll take you along with me, and you can pay me after you get out there."

John Clapp and Luke Harrison were astounded at this liberal offer from a perfect stranger, but they had no motives of delicacy about accepting it. They grasped the hand of their new friend, and assured him that nothing would suit them so well.

"All right!" said Kensington. "Then it's agreed. Now, boys, suppose we go round to the tavern, and ratify our compact by a drink."

"I say amen to that," answered Clapp, "but I insist on standing treat."

"Just as you say," said Kensington. "Come along."

It was late when the three parted company. Luke and John Clapp were delighted with their new friend, and, as they staggered home with uncertain steps, they indulged in bright visions of future prosperity.

CHAPTER XVII: AUNT DEBORAH

Miss Deborah Kensington sat in an old-fashioned rocking-chair covered with a cheap print, industriously engaged in footing a stocking.[1] She was a maiden lady of about sixty, with a thin face, thick seamed with wrinkles, a prominent nose, bridged by spectacles, sharp gray eyes, and thin lips. She was a shrewd New England woman, who knew very well how to take care of and increase the property which she had inherited. Her nephew had been correctly informed as to her being close-fisted. All her establishment was carried on with due regard to economy, and though her income in the eyes of a city man would be counted small, she saved half of it every year, thus increasing her accumulations.

As she sat placidly knitting, an interruption came in the shape of a knock at the front door.

"I'll go myself," she said, rising, and laying down the stocking. "Hannah's out in the back room, and won't hear. I hope it aint Mrs. Smith, come to borrow some butter. She aint returned that last half-pound she borrowed. She seems to think her neighbors have got to support her."

These thoughts were in her mind as she opened the door. But no Mrs. Smith presented her figure to the old lady's gaze. She saw instead, with considerable surprise, a stylish young man with a book under his arm. She jumped to the conclusion that he was

---

1 Darning or knitting a sock.

a book-pedler, having been annoyed by several persistent specimens of that class of travelling merchants.

"If you've got books to sell," she said, opening the attack, "you may as well go away. I aint got no money to throw away."

Mr. Ferdinand B. Kensington—for he was the young man in question—laughed heartily, while the old lady stared at him half amazed, half angry.

"I don't see what there is to laugh at," said she, offended.

"I was laughing at the idea of my being taken for a book-pedler."

"Well, aint you one?" she retorted. "If you aint, what be you?"

"Aunt Deborah, don't you know me?" asked the young man, familiarly.

"Who are you that calls me aunt?" demanded the old lady, puzzled.

"I'm your brother Henry's son. My name is Ferdinand."

"You don't say so!" ejaculated the old lady. "Why, I'd never 'ave thought it. I aint seen you since you was a little boy."

"This don't look as if I was a little boy, aunt," said the young man, touching his luxuriant whiskers.

"How time passes, I do declare!" said Deborah. "Well, come in, and we'll talk over old times. Where did you come from?"

"From the city of New York. That's where I've been living for some time."

"You don't say! Well, what brings you this way?"

"To see you, Aunt Deborah. It's so long since I've seen you that I thought I'd like to come."

"I'm glad to see you, Ferdinand," said the old lady, flattered by such a degree of dutiful attention from a fine-looking young man. "So your poor father's dead?"

"Yes, aunt, he's been dead three years."

"I suppose he didn't leave much. He wasn't very forehanded."

"No, aunt; he left next to nothing."

"Well, it didn't matter much, seein' as you was the only child, and big enough to take care of yourself."

"Still, aunt, it would have been comfortable if he had left me a few thousand dollars."

"Aint you doin' well? You look as if you was," said Deborah, surveying critically her nephew's good clothes.

"Well, I've been earning a fair salary, but it's very expensive living in a great city like New York."

"Humph! that's accordin' as you manage. If you live snug, you can get along there cheap as well as anywhere, I reckon. What was you doin'?"

"I was a salesman for A. T. Stewart, our leading dry-goods merchant."

"What pay did you get?"

"A thousand dollars a year."

"Why, that's a fine salary. You'd ought to save up a good deal."

"You don't realize how much it costs to live in New York, aunt. Of course, if I lived here, I could live on half the sum, but I have to pay high prices for everything in New York."

"You don't need to spend such a sight on dress," said Deborah, disapprovingly.

"I beg your pardon, Aunt Deborah; that's where you are mistaken. The store-keepers in New York expect you to dress tip-top and look genteel, so as to do credit to them. If it hadn't been for that, I shouldn't have spent half so much for dress. Then, board's very expensive."

"You can get boarded here for two dollars and a half a week," said Aunt Deborah.

"Two dollars and a half! Why, I never paid less than eight dollars a week in the city, and you can only get poor board for that."

"The boarding-houses must make a great deal of money," said Deborah. "If I was younger, I'd maybe go to New York, and keep one myself."

"You're rich, aunt. You don't need to do that."

"Who told you I was rich?" said the old lady, quickly.

"Why, you've only got yourself to take care of, and you own this farm, don't you?"

"Yes, but farmin' don't pay much."

"I always heard you were pretty comfortable."

"So I am," said the old lady, "and maybe I save something; but my income aint as great as yours."

"You have only yourself to look after, and it is cheap living in Centreville."

"I don't fling money away. I don't spend quarter as much as you on dress."

Looking at the old lady's faded bombazine dress, Ferdinand was very ready to believe this.

"You don't have to dress here, I suppose," he answered. "But, aunt, we won't talk about money matters just yet. It was funny you took me for a book-pedler."

"It was that book you had, that made me think so."

"It's a book I brought as a present to you, Aunt Deborah."

"You don't say!" said the old lady, gratified. "What is it? Let me look at it."

"It's a copy of 'Pilgrim's Progress,' illustrated.[1] I knew you wouldn't like the trashy books they write nowadays, so I brought you this."

"Really, Ferdinand, you're very considerate," said Aunt Deborah, turning over the leaves with manifest pleasure. "It's a good book, and I shall be glad to have it. Where are you stoppin'?"

"At the hotel in the village."

"You must come and stay here. You can get 'em to send round your things any time."

"Thank you, aunt, I shall be delighted to do so. It seems so pleasant to see you again after so many years. You don't look any older than when I saw you last."

Miss Deborah knew very well that she did look older, but still she was pleased by the compliment. Is there any one who does not like to receive the same assurance?

"I'm afraid your eyes aint very sharp, Ferdinand," she said. "I feel I'm gettin' old. Why, I'm sixty-one, come October."

"Are you? I shouldn't call you over fifty, from your looks, aunt. Really I shouldn't."

"I'm afraid you tell fibs sometimes," said Aunt Deborah, but she said it very graciously, and surveyed her nephew very kindly. "Heigh ho! it's a good while since your poor father and I were children together, and went to the school-house on the hill. Now he's gone, and I'm left alone."

"Not alone, aunt. If he is dead, you have got a nephew."

"Well, Ferdinand, I'm glad to see you, and I shall be glad to have you pay me a good long visit. But how can you be away from your place so long? Did Mr. Stewart give you a vacation?"

"No, aunt; I left him."

"For good?"

"Yes."

"Left a place where you was gettin' a thousand dollars a year!" said the old lady in accents of strong disapproval.

"Yes, aunt."

---

1 John Bunyan's (1628–88) Christian-allegorical *Pilgrim's Progress* (1678) was one of the standard devotional works found in nineteenth-century American homes.

"Then I think you was very foolish," said Deborah with emphasis.

"Perhaps you won't, when you know why I left it."

"Why did you?"

"Because I could do better."

"Better than a thousand dollars a year!" said Deborah with surprise.

"Yes, I am offered two thousand dollars in San Francisco."

"You don't say!" ejaculated Deborah, letting her stocking drop in sheer amazement.

"Yes, I do. It's a positive fact."

"You must be a smart clerk!"

"Well, it isn't for me to say," said Ferdinand, laughing.

"When be you goin' out?"

"In a week, but I thought I must come and bid you good-by first."

"I'm real glad to see you, Ferdinand," said Aunt Deborah, the more warmly because she considered him so prosperous that she would have no call to help him. But here she was destined to find herself mistaken.

CHAPTER XVIII: AUNT AND NEPHEW

"I don't think I can come here till to-morrow, Aunt Deborah," said Ferdinand, a little later. "I'll stay at the hotel to-night, and come round with my baggage in the morning."

"Very well, nephew, but now you're here, you must stay to tea."

"Thank you, aunt, I will."

"I little thought this mornin', I should have Henry's son to tea," said Aunt Deborah, half to herself. "You don't look any like him, Ferdinand."

"No, I don't think I do."

"It's curis too, for you was his very picter when you was a boy."

"I've changed a good deal since then, Aunt Deborah," said her nephew, a little uneasily.

"So you have, to be sure. Now there's your hair used to be almost black, now it's brown. Railly I can't account for it," and Aunt Deborah surveyed the young man over her spectacles.

"You've got a good memory, aunt," said Ferdinand with a forced laugh.

"Now ef your hair had grown darker, I shouldn't have wondered," pursued Aunt Deborah; "but it aint often black turns to brown."

"That's so, aunt, but I can explain it," said Ferdinand, after a slight pause.

"How was it?"

"You know the French barbers can change your hair to any shade you want."

"Can they?"

"Yes, to be sure. Now—don't laugh at me, aunt—a young lady I used to like didn't fancy dark hair, so I went to a French barber, and he changed the color for me in three months."

"You don't say!"

"Fact, aunt; but he made me pay him well too."

"How much did you give him?"

"Fifty dollars, aunt."

"That's what I call wasteful," said Aunt Deborah, disapprovingly.

"Couldn't you be satisfied with the nat'ral color of your hair? To my mind black's handsomer than brown."

"You're right, aunt. I wouldn't have done it if it hadn't been for Miss Percival."

"Are you engaged to her?"

"No, Aunt Deborah. The fact was, I found she wasn't domestic, and didn't know anything about keeping house, but only cared for dress, so I drew off, and she's married to somebody else now."

"I'm glad to hear it," said Deborah, emphatically. "The jade![1] She wouldn't have been a proper wife for you. You want some good girl that's willin' to go into the kitchen, and look after things, and not carry all she's worth on her back."

"I agree with you, aunt," said Ferdinand, who thought it politic, in view of the request he meant to make by and by, to agree with his aunt in her views of what a wife should be.

Aunt Deborah began to regard her nephew as quite a sensible young man, and to look upon him with complacency.

"I wish, Ferdinand," she said, "you liked farmin'."

"Why, aunt?"

"You could stay here, and manage my farm for me."

"Heaven forbid!" thought the young man with a shudder. "I should be bored to death. Does the old lady think I would put on a frock and overalls, and go out and plough, or hoe potatoes?"

---

1 A derogatory term for a worn-out woman.

"It's a good, healthy business," pursued Aunt Deborah, unconscious of the thoughts which were passing through her nephew's mind, "and you wouldn't have to spend much for dress. Then I'm gittin' old, and though I don't want to make no promises, I'd very likely will it to you, ef I was satisfied with the way you managed."

"You're very kind, aunt," said Ferdinand, "but I'm afraid I wasn't cut out for farming. You know I never lived in the country."

"Why, yes, you did," said the old lady. "You was born in the country, and lived there till you was ten years old."

"To be sure," said Ferdinand, hastily, "but I was too young then to take notice of farming. What does a boy of ten know of such things?"

"To be sure. You're right there."

"The fact is, Aunt Deborah, some men are born to be farmers, and some are born to be traders. Now, I've got a talent for trading. That's the reason I've got such a good offer from San Francisco."

"How did you get it? Did you know the man?"

"He used to be in business in New York. He was the first man I worked for, and he knew what I was. San Francisco is full of money, and traders make more than they do here. That's the reason he can afford to offer me so large a salary."

"When did he send for you?"

"I got the letter last week."

"Have you got it with you?"

"No, aunt; I may have it at the hotel," said the young man, hesitating, "but I am not certain."

"Well, it's a good offer. There isn't nobody in Centreville gets so large a salary."

"No, I suppose not. They don't need it, as it is cheap living here."

"I hope when you get out there, Ferdinand, you'll save up money. You'd ought to save two-thirds of your pay."

"I will try to, aunt."

"You'll be wantin' to get married bimeby, and then it'll be convenient to have some money to begin with."

"To be sure, aunt. I see you know how to manage."

"I was always considered a good manager," said Deborah, complacently. "Ef your poor father had had *my* faculty, he wouldn't have died as poor as he did, I can tell you."

"What a conceited old woman she is, with her faculty!" thought Ferdinand, but what he said was quite different.

"I wish he had had, aunt. It would have been better for me."

"Well, you ought to get along, with your prospects."

"Little the old woman knows what my real prospects are!" thought the young man.

"Of course I ought," he said.

"Excuse me a few minutes, nephew," said Aunt Deborah, gathering up her knitting and rising from her chair. "I must go out and see about tea. Maybe you'd like to read that nice book you brought."

"No, I thank you, aunt. I think I'll take a little walk round your place, if you'll allow me."

"Sartin, Ferdinand. Only come back in half an hour; tea'll be ready then."

"Yes, aunt, I'll remember."

So while Deborah was in the kitchen, Ferdinand took a walk in the fields, laughing to himself from time to time, as if something amused him.

He returned in due time, and sat down to supper. Aunt Deborah had provided her best, and, though the dishes were plain, they were quite palatable.

When supper was over, the young man said,—

"Now, aunt, I think I will be getting back to the hotel."

"You'll come over in the morning, Ferdinand, and fetch your trunk?"

"Yes, aunt. Good-night."

"Good-night."

"Well," thought the young man, as he tramped back to the hotel. "I've opened the campaign, and made, I believe, a favorable impression. But what a pack of lies I have had to tell, to be sure! The old lady came near catching me once or twice, particularly about the color of my hair. It was a lucky thought, that about the French barber. It deceived the poor old soul. I don't think she could ever have been very handsome. If she was she must have changed fearfully."

In the evening, John Clapp and Luke Harrison came round to the hotel to see him.

"Have you been to see your aunt?" asked Clapp.

"Yes, I took tea there."

"Have a good time?"

"Oh, I played the dutiful nephew to perfection. The old lady thinks a sight of me."

"How did you do it?"

"I agreed with all she said, told her how young she looked, and humbugged her generally."

Clapp laughed.

"The best part of the joke is—will you promise to keep dark?"

"Of course."

"Don't breathe it to a living soul, you two fellows. *She isn't my aunt of all!*"

"Isn't your aunt?"

"No, her true nephew is in New York—I know him—but I know enough of family matters to gull the old lady, and, I hope, raise a few hundred dollars out of her."

This was a joke which Luke and Clapp could appreciate, and they laughed heartily at the deception which was being practised on simple Aunt Deborah, particularly when Ferdinand explained how he got over the difficulty of having different colored hair from the real owner of the name he assumed.

"We must have a drink on that," said Luke. "Walk up, gentlemen."

"I'm agreeable," said Ferdinand.

"And I," said Clapp. "Never refuse a good offer, say I."

Poor Aunt Deborah! She little dreamed that she was the dupe of a designing adventurer who bore no relationship to her.

CHAPTER XIX: THE ROMANCE OF A RING

Ferdinand B. Kensington, as he called himself, removed the next morning to the house of Aunt Deborah. The latter received him very cordially, partly because it was a pleasant relief to her solitude to have a lively and active young man in the house, partly because she was not forced to look upon him as a poor relation in need of pecuniary assistance. She even felt considerable respect for the prospective recipient of an income of two thousand dollars, which in her eyes was a magnificent salary.

Ferdinand, on his part, spared no pains to make himself agreeable to the old lady, whom he had a mercenary object in pleasing. Finding that she was curious to hear about the great city, which to her was as unknown as London or Paris, he gratified her by long accounts, chiefly of as imaginative character, to which she listened greedily. These included some personal adventures, in all of which he figured very creditably.

Here is a specimen.

"By the way, Aunt Deborah," he said, casually, "have you noticed this ring on my middle finger?"

"No, I didn't notice it before, Ferdinand. It's very handsome."

"I should think it ought to be, Aunt Deborah," said the young man.

"Why?"

"It cost enough to be handsome."

"How much did it cost?" asked the old lady, not without curiosity.

"Guess."

"I aint no judge of such things; I've only got this plain gold ring. Yours has got some sort of a stone in it."

"That stone is a diamond, Aunt Deborah!"

"You don't say so! Let me look at it. It aint got no color. Looks like glass."

"It's very expensive, though. How much do you think it cost?"

"Well, maybe five dollars."

"Five dollars!" ejaculated the young man. "Why, what can you be thinking of, Aunt Deborah?"

"I shouldn't have guessed so much," said the old lady, misunderstanding him, "only you said it was expensive."

"So it is. Five dollars would be nothing at all."

"You don't say it cost more?"

"A great deal more."

"Did it cost ten dollars?"

"More."

"Fifteen?"

"I see, aunt, you have no idea of the cost of diamond rings! You may believe me or not, but that ring cost six hundred and fifty dollars."

"What!" almost screamed Aunt Deborah, letting fall her knitting in her surprise.

"It's true."

"Six hundred and fifty dollars for a little piece of gold and glass!" ejaculated the old lady.

"Diamond, aunt, not glass."

"Well, it don't look a bit better'n glass, and I do say," proceeded Deborah, with energy, "that it's a sin and a shame to pay so much money for a ring. Why, it was more than half your year's salary, Ferdinand."

"I agree with you, aunt; it would have been very foolish and wrong for a young man on a small salary like mine to buy so expensive a ring as this. I hope, Aunt Deborah, I have inherited too much of your good sense to do that."

"Then where did you get it?" asked the old lady, moderating her tone.

"It was given to me."

"Given to you! Who would give you such a costly present?"

"A rich man whose life I once saved, Aunt Deborah."

"You don't say so, Ferdinand!" said Aunt Deborah, interested. "Tell me all about it."

"So I will, aunt, though I don't often speak of it," said Ferdinand, modestly. "It seems like boasting, you know, and I never like to do that. But this is the way it happened."

"Now for a good tough lie!" said Ferdinand to himself, as the old lady suspended her work, and bent forward with eager attention.

"You know, of course, that New York and Brooklyn are on opposite sides of the river, and that people have to go across in ferry-boats."

"Yes, I've heard that, Ferdinand."

"I'm glad of that, because now you'll know that my story is correct. Well, one summer I boarded over in Brooklyn—on the Heights—and used to cross the ferry morning and night. It was the Wall street ferry, and a great many bankers and rich merchants used to cross daily also. One of these was a Mr. Clayton, a wholesale dry-goods merchant, immensely rich, whom I knew by sight, though I had never spoken to him. It was one Thursday morning—I remember even the day of the week—when the boat was unusually full. Mr. Clayton was leaning against the side-railing talking to a friend, when all at once the railing gave way, and he fell backward into the water, which immediately swallowed him up."

"Merciful man!" ejaculated Aunt Deborah, intensely interested. "Go on, Ferdinand."

"Of course there was a scene of confusion and excitement," continued Ferdinand, dramatically. "'Man overboard! Who will save him?' said more than one. 'I will,' I exclaimed, and in an instant I had sprang over the railing into the boiling current."

"Weren't you frightened to death?" asked the old lady. "Could you swim?"

"Of course I could. More than once I have swum all the way from New York to Brooklyn. I caught Mr. Clayton by the collar, as he was sinking for the third time, and shouted to a boatman near by to come to my help. Well, there isn't much more to tell. We were taken on board the boat, and rowed to shore. Mr. Clayton recovered his senses so far as to realize that I had saved his life.

"'What is your name, young man?' he asked, grasping my hand.

"'Ferdinand B. Kensington,' I answered modestly.

"'You have saved my life,' he said warmly.

"'I am very glad of it,' said I.

"'You have shown wonderful bravery.'

"'Oh no,' I answered. 'I know how to swim, and I wasn't going to see you drown before my eyes.'

"'I shall never cease to be grateful to you.'

"'Oh, don't think of it,' said I.

"'But I must think of it,' he answered. 'But for you I should now be a senseless corpse lying in the bottom of the river,' and he shuddered.

"'Mr. Clayton,' said I, 'let me advise you to get home as soon as possible, or you will catch your death of cold.'

"'So will you,' he said. 'You must come with me.'

"He insisted, so I went, and was handsomely treated, you may depend. Mr. Clayton gave me a new suit of clothes, and the next morning he took me to Tiffany's—that's the best jeweller in New York—and bought me this diamond ring. He first offered me money, but I felt delicate about taking money for such a service, and told him so. So he bought me this ring."

"Well, I declare!" ejaculated Aunt Deborah. "That was an adventure. But it seems to me, Ferdinand, I would have taken the money."

"As to that, aunt, I can sell this ring, if ever I get hard up, but I hope I sha'n't be obliged to."

"You certainly behaved very well, Ferdinand. Do you ever see Mr. Clayton now?"

"Sometimes, but I don't seek his society, for fear he would think I wanted to get something more out of him."

"How much money do you think he'd have given you?" asked Aunt Deborah, who was of a practical nature.

"A thousand dollars, perhaps more."

"Seems to me I would have taken it."

"If I had, people would have said that's why I jumped into the water, whereas I wasn't thinking anything about getting a reward. So now, aunt, you won't think it very strange that I wear such an expensive ring."

"Of course it makes a difference, as you didn't buy it yourself. I don't see how folks can be such fools as to throw away hundreds of dollars for such a trifle."

"Well, aunt, everybody isn't as sensible and practical as you. Now I agree with you; I think it's very foolish. Still I'm glad I've got the ring, because I can turn it into money when I need to.

Only, you see, I don't like to part with a gift, although I don't think Mr. Clayton would blame me."

"Of course he wouldn't, Ferdinand. But I don't see why you should need money when you're goin' to get such a handsome salary in San Francisco."

"To be sure, aunt, but there's something else. However, I won't speak of it to-day. To-morrow I may want to ask your advice on a matter of business."

"I'll advise you the best I can, Ferdinand," said the flattered spinster.

"You see, aunt, you're so clear-headed, I shall place great dependence on your advice. But I think I'll take a little walk now, just to stretch my limbs."

"I've made good progress," said the young man to himself, as he lounged over the farm. "The old lady swallows it all. To-morrow must come my grand stroke. I thought I wouldn't propose it to-day, for fear she'd suspect the ring story."

CHAPTER XX: A BUSINESS TRANSACTION

Ferdinand found life at the farm-house rather slow, nor did he particularly enjoy the society of the spinster whom he called aunt. But he was playing for a valuable stake, and meant to play out his game.

"Strike while the iron is hot!" said he to himself; "That's a good rule; but how shall I know when it is hot? However, I must risk something, and take my chances with the old lady."

Aunt Deborah herself hastened his action. Her curiosity had been aroused by Ferdinand's intimation that he wished her advice on a matter of business, and the next morning, after breakfast, she said, "Ferdinand, what was that you wanted to consult me about? You may as well tell me now as any time."

"Here goes, then!" thought the young man. "I'll tell you, aunt. You know I am offered a large salary in San Francisco?"

"Yes, you told me so."

"And, as you said the other day, I can lay up half my salary, and in time become a rich man."

"To be sure you can."

"But there is one difficulty in the way."

"What is that?"

"I must go out there."

"Of course you must," said the old lady, who did not yet see the point.

"And unfortunately it costs considerable money."

"Haven't you got enough money to pay your fare out there?"

"No, aunt; it is very expensive living in New York, and I was unable to save anything from my salary."

"How much does it cost to go out there?"

"About two hundred and fifty dollars."

"That's a good deal of money."

"So it is; but it will be a great deal better to pay it than to lose so good a place."

"I hope," said the old lady, sharply, "you don't expect me to pay your expenses out there."

"My dear aunt," said Ferdinand, hastily, "how can you suspect such a thing?"

"Then what do you propose to do?" asked the spinster, somewhat relieved.

"I wanted to ask your advice."

"Sell your ring. It's worth over six hundred dollars."

"Very true; but I should hardly like to part with it. I'll tell you what I have thought of. It cost six hundred and fifty dollars. I will give it as security to any one who will lend me five hundred dollars, with permission to sell it if I fail to pay up the note in six months. By the way, aunt, why can't you accommodate me in this matter? You will lose nothing, and I will pay handsome interest."

"How do you know I have the money?"

"I don't know; but I think you must have. But, although I am your nephew, I wouldn't think of asking you to lend me money without security. Business is business, so I say."

"Very true, Ferdinand."

"I ask nothing on the score of relationship, but I will make a business proposal."

"I don't believe the ring would fetch over six hundred dollars."

"It would bring just about that. The other fifty dollars represent the profit. Now, aunt, I'll make you a regular business proposal. If you'll lend me five hundred dollars, I'll give you my note for five hundred and fifty, bearing interest at six per cent., payable in six months, or, to make all sure, say in a year. I place the ring in your hands, with leave to sell it at the end of that time if I fail to carry out my agreement. But I sha'n't if I keep my health."

The old lady was attracted by the idea of making a bonus of fifty dollars, but she was cautious, and averse to parting with her money.

"I don't know what to say, Ferdinand," she replied. "Five hundred dollars is a good deal of money."

"So it is, aunt. Well, I don't know but I can offer you a little better terms. Give me four hundred and seventy-five, and I'll give you a note for five hundred and fifty. You can't make as much interest anywhere else."

"I'd like to accommodate you," said the old lady, hesitating, for, like most avaricious persons, she was captivated by the prospect of making extra-legal interest.

"I know you would, Aunt Deborah, but I don't want to ask the money as a favor. It is a strictly business transaction."

"I am afraid I couldn't spare more than four hundred and fifty."

"Very well, I won't dispute about the extra twenty-five dollars. Considering how much income I'm going to get, it isn't of any great importance."

"And you'll give me a note for five hundred and fifty?"

"Yes, certainly."

"I don't know as I ought to take so much interest."

"It's worth that to me, for though, of course, I could raise it by selling the ring, I don't like to do that."

"Well, I don't know but I'll do it. I'll get some ink, and you can write me the due bill."

"Why, Aunt Deborah, you haven't got the money here, have you?"

"Yes, I've got it in the house. A man paid up a mortgage last week, and I haven't yet invested the money. I meant to put it in the savings bank."

"You wouldn't get but six per cent. there. Now the bonus I offer you will be equal to about twenty per cent."

"And you really feel able to pay so much?"

"Yes, aunt; as I told you, it will be worth more than that to me."

"Well, Ferdinand, we'll settle the matter now. I'll go and get the money, and you shall give me the note and the ring."

"Triumph!" said the young man to himself, when the old lady had left the room. "You're badly sold, Aunt Deborah, but it's a good job for me. I didn't think I would have so little trouble."

Within fifteen minutes the money was handed over, and Aunt Deborah took charge of the note and the valuable diamond ring.

"Be careful of the ring, Aunt Deborah," said Ferdinand. "Remember, I expect to redeem it again."

"I'll take good care of it, nephew, never fear!"

"If it were a little smaller, you could wear it, yourself."

"How would Deborah Kensington look with a diamond ring?

The neighbors would think I was crazy. No: I'll keep it in a safe place, but I won't wear it."

"Now, Aunt Deborah, I must speak about other arrangements. Don't you think it would be well to start for San Francisco as soon as possible? You know I enter upon my duties as soon as I get there."

"Yes, Ferdinand, I think you ought to."

"I wish I could spare the time to spend a week with you, aunt; but business is business, and my motto is, business before pleasure."

"And very proper, too, Ferdinand," said the old lady, approvingly.

"So I think I had better leave Centreville tomorrow."

"Maybe you had. You must write and let me know when you get there, and how you like your place."

"So I will, and I shall be glad to know that you take an interest in me. Now, aunt, as I have some errands to do, I will walk to the village and come back about the middle of the afternoon."

"Won't you be back to dinner?"

"No, I think not, aunt."

"Very well, Ferdinand. Come as soon as you can."

Half an hour later, Ferdinand entered the office of the "Centreville Gazette."

"How do you do, Mr. Kensington?" said Clapp, eagerly. "Anything new?"

"I should like to speak with you a moment in private, Mr. Clapp."

"All right!"

Clapp put on his coat, and went outside, shutting the door behind him.

"Well," said Ferdinand, "I've succeeded."

"Have you got the money?"

"Yes, but not quite as much as I anticipated."

"Can't you carry out your plan?" asked Clapp, soberly, fearing he was to be left out in the cold.

"I've formed a new one. Instead of going to California, which is very expensive, we'll go out West, say to St. Louis, and try our fortune there. What do you say?"

"I'm agreed. Can Luke go too?"

"Yes. I'll take you both out there, and lend you fifty dollars each besides, and you shall pay me back as soon as you are able. Will you let your friend know?"

"Yes, I'll undertake that; but when do you propose to start?"

"To-morrow morning."

"Whew! That's short notice."

"I want to get away as soon as possible, for fear the old lady should change her mind, and want her money back."

"That's where you're right."

"Of course you must give up your situation at once, as there is short time to get ready."

"No trouble about that," said Clapp. "I've hated the business for a long time, and shall be only too glad to leave. It's the same with Luke. He won't shed many tears at leaving Centreville."

"Well, we'll all meet this evening at the hotel. I depend upon your both being ready to start in the morning."

"All right, I'll let Luke know."

It may be thought singular that Ferdinand should have made so liberal an offer to two comparative strangers; but, to do the young man justice, though he had plenty of faults, he was disposed to be generous when he had money, though he was not particular how he obtained it. Clapp and Luke Harrison he recognized as congenial spirits, and he was willing to sacrifice something to obtain their companionship. How long his fancy was likely to last was perhaps doubtful; but for the present he was eager to associate them with his own plans.

CHAPTER XXI: HARRY IS PROMOTED

Clapp re-entered the printing office highly elated.

"Mr. Anderson," said he to the editor, "I am going to leave you."

Ferguson and Harry Walton looked up in surprise, and Mr. Anderson asked,—

"Have you got another place?"

"No; I am going West."

"Indeed! How long have you had that in view?"

"Not long. I am going with Mr. Kensington."

"The one who just called on you?"

"Yes."

"How soon do you want to leave?"

"Now."

"That is rather short notice."

"I know it, but I leave town to-morrow morning."

"Well, I wish you success. Here is the money I owe you."

"Sha'n't we see you again, Clapp?" asked Ferguson.

"Yes; I'll just look in and say good-by. Now I must go home and get ready."

"Well, Ferguson," said Mr. Anderson, after Clapp's departure, "that is rather sudden."

"So I think."

"How can we get along with only two hands?"

"Very well, sir. I'm willing to work a little longer, and Harry here is a pretty quick compositor now. The fact is, there isn't enough work for three."

"Then you think I needn't hire another journeyman?"

"No."

"If you both work harder I must increase your wages, and then I shall save money."

"I sha'n't object to that," said Ferguson, smiling.

"Nor I," said Harry.

"I was intending at any rate to raise Harry's wages, as I find he does nearly as much as a journeyman. Hereafter I will give you five dollars a week besides your board."

"Oh, thank you, sir!" said Harry, overjoyed at his good fortune.

"As for you, Ferguson, if you will give me an hour more daily, I will add three dollars a week to your pay."

"Thank you, sir. I think I can afford now to give Mrs. Ferguson the new bonnet she was asking for this morning."

"I don't want to overwork you two, but if that arrangement proves satisfactory, we will continue it."

"I suppose you will be buying your wife a new bonnet too; eh, Harry?" said Ferguson.

"I may buy myself a new hat. Luke Harrison turned up his nose at my old one the other day."

"What will Luke do without Clapp? They were always together."

"Perhaps he is going too."

"I don't know where he will raise the money, nor Clapp either, for that matter."

"Perhaps their new friend furnishes the money."

"If he does, he is indeed a friend."

"Well, it has turned out to our advantage, at any rate, Harry. Suppose you celebrate it by coming round and taking supper with me?"

"With the greatest pleasure."

Harry was indeed made happy by his promotion. Having been employed for some months on board-wages, he had been compelled to trench upon the small stock of money which he had saved up when in the employ of Prof. Henderson, and he had been unable to send any money to his father, whose circumstances were straitened, and who found it very hard to make both ends meet. That evening he wrote a letter to his father, in which he inclosed ten dollars remaining to him from his fund of savings, at the same time informing him of his promotion. A few days later, he received the following reply:—

"MY DEAR SON:

"Your letter has given me great satisfaction, for I conclude from your promotion that you have done your duty faithfully, and won the approbation of your employer. The wages you now earn will amply pay your expenses, while you may reasonably hope that they will be still further increased, as you become more skilful and experienced. I am glad to hear that you are using your leisure hours to such good purpose, and are trying daily to improve your education. In this way you may hope in time to qualify yourself for the position of an editor, which is an honorable and influential profession, to which I should be proud to have you belong.

"The money which you so considerately inclose comes at the right time. Your brother needs some new clothes, and this will enable me to provide them. We all send love, and hope to hear from you often.

"Your affectionate father,
"HIRAM WALTON."

Harry's promotion took place just before the beginning of September. During the next week the fall term of the Prescott Academy commenced, and the village streets again became lively with returning students. Harry was busy at the case, when Oscar Vincent entered the printing office, and greeted him warmly.

"How are you, Oscar?" said Harry, his face lighting up with pleasure.

"I am glad to see you back. I would shake hands, but I am afraid you wouldn't like it," and Harry displayed his hands soiled with printer's ink.

"Well, we'll shake hands in spirit, then, Harry. How have you passed the time?"

"I have been very busy, Oscar."

"And I have been very lazy. I have scarcely opened a book, that is, a study-book, during the vacation. How much have you done in French?"

"I have nearly finished Telemachus."

"You have! Then you have done splendidly. By the way, Harry, I received the paper you sent, containing your essay. It does you credit, my boy."

Mr. Anderson, who was sitting at his desk, caught the last words.

"What is that, Harry?" he asked. "Have you been writing for the papers?"

Harry blushed.

"Yes, sir," he replied. "I have written two or three articles for the 'Boston Weekly Standard.'"

"Indeed! I should like to see them."

"You republished one of them in the 'Gazette,' Mr. Anderson," said Ferguson.

"What do you refer to?"

"Don't you remember an article on 'Ambition,' which you inserted some weeks ago?"

"Yes, it was a good article. Did you write it, Walton?"

"Yes, sir."

"Why didn't you tell me of it?"

"He was too bashful," said Ferguson.

"I am glad to know that you can write," said the editor. "I shall call upon you for assistance, in getting up paragraphs occasionally."

"I shall be very glad to do what I can," said Harry, gratified.

"Harry is learning to be an editor," said Ferguson.

"I will give him a chance for practice, then," and Mr. Anderson returned to his exchanges.

"By the way, Oscar," said Harry, "I am not a printer's devil any longer. I am promoted to be a journeyman."

"I congratulate you, Harry, but what will Fitz do now? He used to take so much pleasure in speaking of you as a printer's devil."

"I am sorry to deprive him of that pleasure. Did you see much of him in vacation, Oscar?"

"I used to meet him almost every day walking down Washington Street, swinging a light cane, and wearing a stunning necktie, as usual."

"Is he coming back this term?"

"Yes, he came on the same train with me. Hasn't he called to pay his respects to you?"

"No," answered Harry, with a smile. "He hasn't done me that honor. He probably expects me to make the first call."

"Well, Harry, I suppose you will be on hand next week, when the Clionian holds its first meeting?"

"Yes, I will be there."

"And don't forget to call at my room before that time. I want to examine you in French, and see how much progress you have made."

"Thank you, Oscar."

"Now I must be going. I have got a tough Greek lesson to prepare for to-morrow. I suppose it will take me twice as long as usual. It is always hard to get to work again after a long vacation. So good-morning, and don't forget to call at my room soon—say to-morrow evening."

"I will come."

"What a gentlemanly fellow your friend is!" said Ferguson.

"What is his name, Harry?" asked Mr. Anderson.

"Oscar Vincent. His father is an editor in Boston."

"What! the son of John Vincent?" said Mr. Anderson, surprised.

"Yes, sir; do you know his father?"

"Only by reputation. He is a man of great ability."

"Oscar is a smart fellow, too, but not a hard student."

"I shall be glad to have you bring him round to the house some evening, Harry. I shall be glad to become better acquainted with him."

"Thank you, sir. I will give him the invitation."

It is very possible that Harry rose in the estimation of his employer, from his intimacy with the son of a man who stood so high in his own profession. At all events, Harry found himself from this time treated with greater respect and consideration than before, and Mr. Anderson often called upon him to write paragraphs upon local matters, so that his position might be regarded except as to pay, as that of an assistant editor.

CHAPTER XXII:
MISS DEBORAH'S EYES ARE OPENED

Aunt Deborah felt that she had done a good stroke of business. She had lent Ferdinand four hundred and fifty dollars, and received in return a note for five hundred and fifty, secured by a diamond ring worth even more. She plumed herself on her shrewdness, though at times she felt a little twinge at the idea of the exorbitant interest which she had exacted from so near a relative.

"But he said the money was worth that to him," she said to herself in extenuation, "and he's goin' to get two thousand dollars a year. I didn't want to lend the money, I'd rather have had it in the savings' bank, but I did it to obleege him."

By such casuistry Aunt Deborah quieted her conscience, and carefully put the ring away among her bonds and mortgages.

"Who'd think a little ring like that should be worth so much?" she said to herself. "It's clear waste of money. But then Ferdinand didn't buy it. It was give to him, and a very foolish gift it was too. Railly, it makes me nervous to have it to take care of. It's so little it might get lost easy."

Aunt Deborah plumed herself upon her shrewdness. It was not easy to get the advantage of her in a bargain, and yet she had accepted the ring as security for a considerable loan without once questioning its genuineness. She relied implicitly upon her nephew's assurance of its genuineness, just as she had relied upon his assertion of relationship. But the time was soon coming when she was to be undeceived.

One day, a neighbor stopped his horse in front of her house, and jumping out of his wagon, walked up to the door and knocked.

"Good-morning, Mr. Simpson," said the old lady, answering the knock herself; "won't you come in?"

"Thank you, Miss Deborah, I can't stop this morning. I was at the post-office just now, when I saw there was a letter for you, and thought I'd bring it along."

"A letter for me!" said Aunt Deborah in some surprise, for her correspondence was very limited. "Who's it from?"

"It is post-marked New York," said Mr. Simpson.

"I don't know no one in New York," said the old lady, fumbling in her pockets for her spectacles.

"Maybe it's one of your old beaux," said Mr. Simpson, humorously, a joke which brought a grim smile to the face of the old spinster. "But I must be goin'. If it's an offer of marriage, don't forget to invite me to the wedding."

Aunt Deborah went into the house, and seating herself in her accustomed place, carefully opened the letter. She turned over the page, and glanced at the signature. To her astonishment it was signed,

"Your affectionate nephew,
        "FERDINAND B. KENSINGTON."

"Ferdinand!" she exclaimed in surprise. "Why, I thought he was in Californy by this time. How could he write from New York? I s'pose he'll explain. I hope he didn't lose the money I lent him."

The first sentence in the letter was destined to surprise Miss Deborah yet more.

"Dear aunt," it commenced, "it is so many years since we have met, that I am afraid you have forgotten me."

"So many years!" repeated Miss Deborah in bewilderment. "What on earth can Ferdinand mean? Why, it's only five weeks yesterday since he was here. He must be crazy."

She resumed reading.

"I have often had it in mind to make you a little visit, but I have been so engrossed by business that I have been unable to get away. I am a salesman for A. T. Stewart, whom you must have heard of, as he is the largest retail dealer in the city. I have been three years in his employ, and have been promoted by degrees, till I now receive quite a good salary, until—and that is the news I have to write you—I have felt justified in getting married. My wedding is fixed for next week, Thursday. I should be very glad if you could attend, though I suppose you would consider it a long journey. But at any rate I can assure you that I should be delighted to see you present on the occasion, and so would Maria. If you can't come, write to me, at any rate, in memory of old times. It is just possible that during our bridal tour—we are to go to the White Mountains for a week—we shall call on you. Let me know if it will be convenient for you to receive us for a day.
        "Your affectionate nephew,
        "FERDINAND B. KENSINGTON."

Miss Deborah read this letter like one dazed. She had to read it a second time before she could comprehend its purport.

"Ferdinand going to be married! He never said a word about it when he was here. And he don't say a word about Californy. Then again he says he hasn't seen me for years. Merciful man! I see it now—the other fellow was an impostor!" exclaimed Miss Deborah, jumping to her feet in excitement. "What did he want to deceive an old woman for?"

It flashed upon her at once. He came after money, and he had succeeded only too well. He had carried away four hundred and fifty dollars with him. True, he had left a note, and security. But another terrible suspicion had entered the old lady's mind; the ring might not be genuine.

"I must know at once," exclaimed the disturbed spinster. "I'll go over to Brandon, to the jeweller's, and inquire. If it's paste, then, Deborah Kensington, you're the biggest fool in Centreville."

Miss Deborah summoned Abner, her farm servant from the field, and ordered him instantly to harness the horse, as she wanted to go to Brandon.

"Do you want me to go with you?" asked Abner.

"To be sure, I can't drive so fur, and take care of the horse."

"It'll interrupt the work," objected Abner.

"Never mind about the work," said Deborah, impatiently. "I must go right off. It's on very important business."

"Wouldn't it be best to go after dinner?"

"No, we'll get some dinner over there, at the tavern."

"What's got into the old woman?" thought Abner. "It isn't like her to spend money at a tavern for dinner, when she might as well dine at home. Interruptin' the work, too! However, it's her business!"

Deborah was ready and waiting when the horse drove up the door. She got in, and they set out. Abner tried to open a conversation, but he found Miss Deborah strangely unsocial. She appeared to take no interest in the details of farm work of which he spoke.

"Something's on her mind, I guess," thought Abner; and, as we know, he was right.

In her hand Deborah clutched the ring, of whose genuineness she had come to entertain such painful doubts. It might be genuine, she tried to hope, even if it came from an impostor; but her hope was small. She felt a presentiment that it would prove as false as the man from whom she received it. As for the story of the manner in which he became possessed of it, doubtless that was as false as the rest.

"How blind I was!" groaned Deborah in secret. "I saw he didn't look like the family. What a goose I was to believe that story about his changin' the color of his hair! I was an old fool, and that's all about it."

"Drive to the jeweller's," said Miss Deborah, when they reached Brandon.

In some surprise, Abner complied.

Deborah got out of the wagon hastily and entered the store.

"What can I do for you, Miss Kensington?" asked the jeweller, who recognized the old lady.

"I want to show you a ring," said Aunt Deborah, abruptly. "Tell me what it's worth."

She produced the ring which the false Ferdinand had intrusted to her.

The jeweller scanned it closely.

"It's a good imitation of a diamond ring," he said.

"Imitation!" gasped Deborah.

"Yes; you didn't think it was genuine?"

"What's it worth?"

"The value of the gold. That appears to be genuine. It may be worth three dollars."

"Three dollars!" ejaculated Deborah. "He told me it cost six hundred and fifty."

"Whoever told you that was trying to deceive you."

"You're sure about its being imitation, are you?"

"There can be no doubt about it."

"That's what I thought," muttered the old lady, her face pale and rigid. "Is there anything to pay?"

"Oh, no; I am glad to be of service to you."

"Good-afternoon, then," said Deborah, abruptly, and she left the store.

"Drive home, Abner, as quick as you can," she said.

"I haven't had any dinner," Abner remarked. "You said you'd get some at the tavern."

"Did I? Well, drive over there. I'm not hungry myself, but I'll pay for some dinner for you."

Poor Aunt Deborah! it was not the loss alone that troubled her, though she was fond of money; but it was humiliating to think that she had fallen such an easy prey to a designing adventurer. In her present bitter mood, she would gladly have ridden fifty miles to see the false Ferdinand hanged.

CHAPTER XXIII: THE PLOT AGAINST FLETCHER

The intimacy between Harry and Oscar Vincent continued, and, as during the former term, the latter volunteered to continue giving French lessons to our hero. These were now partly of a conversational character, and, as Harry was thoroughly in earnest, it was not long before he was able to speak quite creditably.

About the first of November, Fitzgerald Fletcher left the Prescott Academy, and returned to his home in Boston. It was not because he had finished his education, but because he felt that he was not appreciated by his fellow-students. He had been ambitious to be elected to an official position in the Clionian Society, but his aspirations were not gratified. He might have accepted this disappointment, and borne it as well as he could, had it not been aggravated by the elevation of Harry Walton to the presidency. To be only a common member, while a boy so far his social inferior was President, was more than Fitzgerald could stand. He was so incensed that upon the announcement of the vote he immediately rose to a point of order.

"Mr. President," he said warmly, "I must protest against this election. Walton is not a member of the Prescott Academy, and it is unconstitutional to elect him President."

"Will the gentleman point out the constitutional clause which has been violated by Walton's election?" said Oscar Vincent.

"Mr. President," said Fletcher, "this Society was founded by students of the Prescott Academy; and the offices should be confined to the members of the school."

Harry Walton rose and said: "Mr. President, my election has been a great surprise to myself. I had no idea that any one had thought of me for the position. I feel highly complimented by your kindness, and deeply grateful for it; but there is something in what Mr. Fletcher says. You have kindly allowed me to share in the benefits of the Society, and that satisfies me. I think it will be well for you to make another choice as President."

"I will put it to vote," said the presiding officer. "Those who are ready to accept Mr. Walton's resignation will signify it in the usual way."

Fletcher raised his hand, but he was alone.

"Those who are opposed," said the President.

Every other hand except Harry's was now raised.

"Mr. Walton, your resignation is not accepted," said the presiding officer. "I call upon you to assume the duties of your new position."

Harry rose, and, modestly advanced to the chair. "I have already thanked you, gentlemen," he said, "for the honor you have conferred upon me in selecting me as your presiding officer.

I have only to add that I will discharge its duties to the best of my ability."

All applauded except Fletcher. He sat with an unpleasant scowl upon his face, and waited for the result of the balloting for Vice-President and Secretary. Had he been elected to either position, the Clionian would probably have retained his illustrious name upon its roll. But as these honors were conferred upon other members, he formed the heroic resolution no longer to remain a member.

"Mr. President," he said, when the last vote was announced, "I desire to terminate my connection with this Society."

"I hope Mr. Fletcher will reconsider his determination," said Harry from the chair.

"I would like to inquire the gentleman's reasons," said Tom Carver.

"I don't like the way in which the Society is managed," said Fletcher. "I predict that it will soon disband."

"I don't see any signs of it," said Oscar. "If the gentleman is really sincere, he should not desert the Clionian in the hour of danger."

"I insist upon my resignation," said Fletcher.

"I move that it be accepted," said Tom Carver.

"Second the motion," said the boy who sat next him.

The resignation was unanimously accepted. Fletcher ought to have felt gratified at the prompt granting of his request, but he was not. He had intended to strike dismay into the Society by his proposal to withdraw, but there was no consternation visible. Apparently they were willing to let him go.

He rose from his seat mortified and wrathful.

"Gentlemen," he said, "you have complied with my request, and I am deeply grateful. I no longer consider it an honor to belong to the Clionian. I trust your new President may succeed as well in his new office as he has in the capacity of a printer's devil."

Fletcher was unable to proceed, being interrupted by a storm of hisses, in the midst of which he hurriedly made his exit.

"He wanted to be President himself—that's what's the matter," said Tom Carver in a whisper to his neighbor. "But he couldn't blame us for not wanting to have him."

Other members of the Society came to the same conclusion, and it was generally said that Fletcher had done himself no good by his undignified resentment. His parting taunt levelled at Harry was regarded as mean and ungenerous, and only strengthened the sentiment in favor of our hero[,] who bore his honors modestly. In fact Tom Carver, who was fond of fun, conceived a project for mortifying Fletcher, and readily obtained the co-operation of his classmates.

It must be premised that Fitz was vain of his reading and declamation. He had a secret suspicion that, if he should choose to devote his talents to the stage, he would make a second Booth.[1] This self-conceit of his made it the more easy to play off the following joke upon him.

A fortnight later, the young ladies of the village proposed to hold a Fair to raise funds for some public object. At the head of the committee of arrangements was a sister of the doctor's wife, named Pauline Clinton. This will explain the following letter, which Fletcher received the succeeding day:—

> "FITZGERALD FLETCHER, ESQ.—Dear Sir:
> Understanding that you are a superior reader, we
> should be glad of your assistance in lending *éclat*[2] to
> the Fair which we propose to hold on the evening of
> the 29th. Will you be kind enough to occupy twenty
> minutes by reading such selections as in your opinion
> will be of popular interest? It is desirable that you
> should let me know as soon as possible what pieces you
> have selected, that they may be printed on the pro-
> gramme.
> 　　　"Yours respectfully,
> 　　　　"PAULINE CLINTON,
> 　　　　　"(*for the Committee*)."

This note reached Fletcher at a time when he was still smarting from his disappointment in obtaining promotion from the Clionian Society. He read it with a flushed and triumphant face. He never thought of questioning its genuineness. Was it not true that he was a superior reader? What more natural than that he should be invited to give *éclat* to the Fair by the exercise of his talents! He felt it to be a deserved compliment. It was a greater honor to be solicited to give a public reading than to be elected President of the Clionian Society.

1　The tragedian Edwin Booth (1833–93), brother of Abraham Lincoln's
　assassin John Wilkes Booth, was one of the stars of the late-nineteenth-
　century American stage.
2　A brilliant effect (French).

"They won't laugh at me now," thought Fletcher.

He immediately started for Oscar's room to make known his new honors.

"How are you, Fitz?" said Oscar, who was in [on] the secret, and guessed the errand on which he came.

"Very well, thank you, Oscar," answered Fletcher, in a stately manner.

"Anything new with you?" asked Oscar, carelessly.

"Not much," said Fletcher. "There's a note I just received."

"Whew!" exclaimed Oscar, in affected astonishment. "Are you going to accept?"

"I suppose I ought to oblige them," said Fletcher. "It won't be much trouble to me, you know."

"To be sure; it's in a good cause. But how did they hear of your reading?"

"Oh, there are no secrets in a small village like this," said Fletcher.

"It's certainly a great compliment. Has anybody else been invited to read?"

"I think not," said Fletcher, proudly. "They rely upon me."

"Couldn't you get a chance for me? It would be quite an honor, and I should like it for the sake of the family."

"I shouldn't feel at liberty to interfere with their arrangements," said Fletcher, who didn't wish to share the glory with any one. "Besides, you don't read well enough."

"Well, I suppose I must give it up," said Oscar, in a tone of resignation. "By the way, what have you decided to read?"

"I haven't quite made up my mind," said Fletcher, in a tone of importance. "I have only just received the invitation, you know."

"Haven't you answered it yet?"

"No; but I shall as soon as I go home. Good-night, Oscar."

"Good-night, Fitz."

"How mad Fitz will be when he finds he has been sold!" said Oscar to himself. "But he deserves it for treating Harry so meanly."

CHAPTER XXIV: READING UNDER DIFFICULTIES

On reaching home, Fletcher looked over his "Speaker," and selected three poems which he thought he could read with best effect. The selection made, he sat down to his desk, and wrote a reply to the invitation, as follows:—

"MISS PAULINE CLINTON: I hasten to acknowledge your polite invitation to occupy twenty minutes in reading choice selections at your approaching Fair. I have paid much attention to reading, and hope to be able to give pleasure to the large numbers who will doubtless honor the occasion with their presence. I have selected three poems,—Poe's Raven, the Battle of Ivry, by Macaulay, and Marco Bozarris, by Halleck.[1] I shall be much pleased if my humble efforts add *éclat* to the occasion.

"Yours, very respectfully,

"FITZGERALD FLETCHER."

"There," said Fletcher, reading his letter through with satisfaction. "I think that will do. It is high-toned and dignified, and shows that I am highly cultured and refined. I will copy it off, and mail it."

Fletcher saw his letter deposited in the post-office, and returned to his room.

"I ought to practise reading these poems, so as to do it up handsomely," he said. "I suppose I shall get a good notice in the 'Gazette.' If I do, I will buy a dozen papers, and send to my friends. They will see that I am a person of consequence in Centreville, even if I didn't get elected to any office in the high and mighty Clionian Society."

I am sorry that I cannot reproduce the withering sarcasm which Fletcher put into his tone in the last sentence.

When Demosthenes[2] was practising oratory, he sought the sea-shore; but Fitzgerald repaired instead to a piece of woods about half a mile distant. It was rather an unfortunate selection, as will appear.

It so happened that Tom Carver and Hiram Huntley were strolling about the woods, when they espied Fletcher approaching with an open book in his hand.

"Hiram," said Tom, "there's fun coming. There's Fitz Fletcher with his 'Speaker' in his hand. He's going to practise reading in the woods. Let us hide, and hear the fun."

---

1 Edgar Allan Poe's "The Raven," Thomas Babington Macaulay's "The Battle of Ivry," and Fitz-Greene Halleck's "Marco Bozarris" were popular declamation pieces.

2 Prominent Greek statesman, rhetorician, and orator (384–322 BCE).

"I'm in for it," said Hiram, "but where will be the best place to hide?"

"Here in this hollow tree. He'll be very apt to halt here."

"All right! Go ahead, I'll follow."

They quickly concealed themselves in the tree, unobserved by Fletcher, whose eyes were on his book.

About ten feet from the tree he paused.

"I guess this'll be a good place," he said aloud. "There's no one to disturb me here. Now, which shall I begin with? I think I'll try The Raven. But first it may be well to practise an appropriate little speech. Something like this":—

Fletcher made a low bow to the assembled trees, cleared his throat, and commenced,—

"Ladies and Gentlemen: It gives me great pleasure to appear before you this evening, in compliance with the request of the committee, who have thought that my humble efforts would give *éclat* to the fair. I am not a professional reader, but I have ever found pleasure in reciting the noble productions of our best authors, and I hope to give you pleasure."

"That'll do, I think," said Fletcher, complacently. "Now I'll try The Raven."

In a deep, sepulchral tone, Fletcher read the first verse, which is quoted below:—

"Once upon a midnight dreary, while I pondered weak and
    weary,
 Over many a quaint and curious volume of forgotten lore,
While I nodded, nearly napping, suddenly there came a
    tapping,
As of some one gently rapping, rapping at my chamber
    door.
''Tis some visitor,' I muttered, 'tapping at my chamber
    door—
Only this and nothing more.'"

Was it fancy, or did Fletcher really hear a slow, measured tapping near him—upon one of the trees, as it seemed? He started, and looked nervously; but the noise stopped, and he decided that he had been deceived, since no one was visible.

The boys within the tree made no other demonstration till Fletcher had read the following verse:—

"Back into the chamber turning, all my soul within me
      burning,
Soon again I heard a tapping, something louder than before.
'Surely,' said I, 'surely that is something at my window
      lattice;
Let me see then what thereat is, and this mystery explore—
Let my heart be still a moment, and this mystery explore;
'Tis the wind, and nothing more.'"

Here an indescribable, unearthly noise was heard from the interior of the tree, like the wailing of some discontented ghost.

"Good heavens! what's that?" ejaculated Fletcher, turning pale, and looking nervously around him.

It was growing late, and the branches above him, partially stripped of their leaves, rustled in the wind. Fletcher was somewhat nervous, and the weird character of the poem probably increased this feeling, and made him very uncomfortable. He summoned up courage enough, however, to go on, though his voice shook a little. He was permitted to go on without interruption to the end. Those who are familiar with the poem, know that it becomes more and more wild and weird as it draws to the conclusion. This, with his gloomy surroundings, had its effect upon the mind of Fletcher. Scarcely had he uttered the last words, when a burst of wild and sepulchral laughter was heard within a few feet of him. A cry of fear proceeded from Fletcher, and, clutching his book, he ran at wild speed from the enchanted spot, not daring to look behind him. Indeed, he never stopped running till he passed out of the shadow of the woods, and was well on his way homeward.

Tom Carver and Hiram crept out from their place of concealment. They threw themselves on the ground, and roared with laughter.

"I never had such fun in my life," said Tom.

"Nor I."

"I wonder what Fitz thought."

"That the wood was enchanted, probably; he left in a hurry."

"Yes; he stood not on the order of his going, but went at once."

"I wish I could have seen him. We must have made a fearful noise."

"I was almost frightened myself. He must be almost home by this time."

"When do you think he'll find out about the trick?"

"About the invitation? Not till he gets a letter from Miss

Clinton, telling him it is all a mistake. He will be terribly mortified."

Meanwhile Fletcher reached home, tired and out of breath. His temporary fear was over, but he was quite at sea as to the cause of the noises he had heard. He could not suspect any of his school-fellows, for no one was visible, nor had he any idea that any were in the wood at the time.

"I wonder if it was an animal," he reflected. "It was a fearful noise. I must find some other place to practise reading in. I wouldn't go to that wood again for fifty dollars."

But Fletcher's readings were not destined to be long continued. When he got home from school the next day, he found the following note, which had been left for him during the forenoon:—

> "MR. FITZGERALD FLETCHER,—Dear Sir: I beg to thank you for your kind proposal to read at our Fair; but I think there must be some mistake in the matter, as we have never contemplated having any readings, nor have I written to you on the subject, as you intimate. I fear that we shall not have time to spare for such a feature, though, under other circumstances, it might be attractive. In behalf of the committee, I beg to tender thanks for your kind proposal.
>
> "Yours respectfully,
> "PAULINE CLINTON."

Fletcher read this letter with feelings which can better be imagined than described. He had already written home in the most boastful manner about the invitation he had received, and he knew that before he could contradict it, it would have been generally reported by his gratified parents to his city friends. And now he would be compelled to explain that he had been duped, besides enduring the jeers of those who had planned the trick.

This was more than he could endure. He formed a sudden resolution. He would feign illness, and go home the next day. He could let it be inferred that it was sickness alone which had compelled him to give up the idea of appearing as a public reader.

Fitz immediately acted upon his decision, and the next day found him on the way to Boston. He never returned to the Prescott Academy as a student.

CHAPTER XXV: AN INVITATION TO BOSTON

Harry was doubly glad that he was now in receipt of a moderate salary. He welcomed it as an evidence that he was rising in the estimation of his employer, which was of itself satisfactory, and also because in his circumstances the money was likely to be useful.

"Five dollars a week!" said Harry to himself. "Half of that ought to be enough to pay for my clothes and miscellaneous expenses, and the rest I will give to father. It will help him take care of the rest of the family."

Our hero at once made this proposal by letter. This is a paragraph from his father's letter in reply:—

> "I am glad, my dear son, to find you so considerate and dutiful, as your offer indicates. I have indeed had a hard time in supporting my family, and have not always been able to give them the comforts I desired. Perhaps it is my own fault in part. I am afraid I have not the faculty of getting along and making money that many others have. But I have had an unexpected stroke of good fortune. Last evening a letter reached your mother, stating that her cousin Nancy had recently died at St. Albans, Vermont, and that, in accordance with her will, your mother is to receive a legacy of four thousand dollars. With your mother's consent, one-fourth of this is to be devoted to the purchase of the ten acres adjoining my little farm, and the balance will be so invested as to yield us an annual income of one hundred and eighty dollars. Many would think this a small addition to an income, but it will enable us to live much more comfortably. You remember the ten-acre lot to the east of us, belonging to the heirs of Reuben Todd. It is excellent land, well adapted for cultivation, and will fully double the value of my farm.
>
> "You see, therefore, my dear son, that a new era of prosperity has opened for us. I am now relieved from the care and anxiety which for years have oppressed me, and feel sure of a comfortable support. Instead of accepting the half of your salary, I desire you, if possible, to save it, depositing in some reliable savings institution. If you do this every year till you are twenty-one, you will have a little capital to start you in business,

and will be able to lead a more prosperous career than your father. Knowing you as well as I do, I do not feel it necessary to caution you against unnecessary expenditures. I will only remind you that extravagance is comparative, and that what would be only reasonable expenditure for one richer than yourself would be imprudent in you."

Harry read this letter with great joy. He was warmly attached to the little home circle, and the thought that they were comparatively provided for gave him fresh courage. He decided to adopt his father's suggestion, and the very next week deposited three dollars in the savings bank.

"That is to begin an account," he thought. "If I can only keep that up, I shall feel quite rich at the end of a year."

Several weeks rolled by, and Thanksgiving approached.

Harry was toiling at his case one day, when Oscar Vincent entered the office.

"Hard at work, I see, Harry," he said.

"Yes," said Harry; "I can't afford to be idle."

"I want you to be idle for three days," said Oscar.

Harry looked up in surprise.

"How is that?" he asked.

"You know we have a vacation from Wednesday to Monday at the Academy."

"Over Thanksgiving?"

"Yes."

"Well, I am going home to spend that time, and I want you to go with me."

"What, to Boston?" asked Harry, startled, for to him, inexperienced as he was, that seemed a very long journey.

"Yes. Father and mother gave me permission to invite you. Shall I show you the letter?"

"I'll take it for granted, Oscar, but I am afraid I can't go."

"Nonsense! What's to prevent?"

"In the first place, Mr. Anderson can't spare me."

"Ask him."

"What's that?" asked the editor, hearing his name mentioned.

"I have invited Harry to spend the Thanksgiving vacation with me in Boston, and he is afraid you can't spare him?"

"Does your father sanction your invitation?"

"Yes, he wrote me this morning—that is, I got the letter this morning—telling me to ask Harry to come."

Now the country editor had a great respect for the city editor, who was indeed known by reputation throughout New England as a man of influence and ability, and he felt disposed to accede to any request of his.

So he said pleasantly, "Of course, Harry, we shall miss you, but if Mr. Ferguson is disposed to do a little additional work, we will get along till Monday. What do you say, Mr. Ferguson?"

"I shall be very glad to oblige Harry," said the older workman, "and I hope he will have a good time."

"That settles the question, Harry," said Oscar, joyfully. "So all you've got to do is to pack up and be ready to start to-morrow morning. It's Tuesday, you know, already."

Harry hesitated, and Oscar observed it.

"Well, what's the matter now?" he said; "out with it."

"I'll tell you, Oscar," said Harry, coloring a little. "Your father is a rich man, and lives handsomely. I haven't any clothes good enough to wear on a visit to your house."

"Oh, hang your clothes!" said Oscar, impetuously. "It isn't your clothes we invite. It's yourself."

"Still, Oscar—"

"Come, I see you think I am like Fitz Fletcher, after all. Say you think me a snob, and done with it."

"But I don't," said Harry, smiling.

"Then don't make any more ridiculous objections. Don't you think they are ridiculous, Mr. Ferguson?"

"They wouldn't be in some places," said Ferguson, "but here I think they are out of place. I feel sure you are right, and that you value Harry more than the clothes he wears."

"Well, Harry, do you surrender at discretion?" said Oscar. "You see Ferguson is on my side."

"I suppose I shall have to," said Harry, "as long as you are not ashamed of me."

"None of that, Harry."

"I'll go."

"The first sensible words you've spoken this morning."

"I want to tell you how much I appreciate your kindness, Oscar," said Harry, earnestly.

"Why shouldn't I be kind to my friend?"

"Even if he was once a printer's devil."

"Very true. It is a great objection, but still I will overlook it. By the way, there is one inducement I didn't mention."

"What is that?"

"We may very likely see Fitz in the city. He is studying at home now, I hear. Who knows but he may get up a great party in your honor?"

"Do you think it likely?" asked Harry, smiling.

"It might not happen to occur to him, I admit. Still, if we made him a ceremonious call—"

"I am afraid he might send word that he was not at home."

"That would be a loss to him, no doubt. However, we will leave time to settle that question. Be sure to be on hand in time for the morning train."

"All right, Oscar."

Harry had all the love of new scenes natural to a boy of sixteen. He had heard so much of Boston that he felt a strong curiosity to see it. Besides, was not that the city where the "Weekly Standard" was printed, the paper in which he had already appeared as an author? In connection with this, I must here divulge a secret of Harry's. He was ambitious not only to contribute to the literary papers, but to be paid for his contributions. He judged that essays were not very marketable, and he had therefore in his leisure moments written a humorous sketch, entitled "The Tin Pedler's Daughter." I shall not give any idea of the plot here; I will only say that it was really humorous, and did not betray as much of the novice as might have been expected. Harry had copied it out in his best hand, and resolved to carry it to Boston, and offer it in person to the editor of the "Standard" with an effort, if accepted, to obtain compensation for it.

CHAPTER XXVI: THE VINCENTS AT HOME

When Harry rather bashfully imparted to Oscar his plans respecting the manuscript, the latter entered enthusiastically into them, and at once requested the privilege of reading the story. Harry awaited his judgment with some anxiety.

"Why, Harry, this is capital," said Oscar, looking up from the perusal.

"Do you really think so, Oscar?"

"If I didn't think so, I wouldn't say so."

"I thought you might say so out of friendship."

"I don't say it is the best I ever read, mind you, but I have read a good many that are worse. I think you managed the *denoue-*

ment[1] (you're a French scholar, so I'll venture on the word) admirably."

"I only hope the editor of the 'Standard' will think so."

"If he doesn't, there are other papers in Boston; the 'Argus' for instance."

"I'll try the 'Standard' first, because I have already written for it."

"All right. Don't you want me to go to the office with you?"

"I wish you would. I shall be bashful."

"I am not troubled that way. Besides, my father's name is well known, and I'll take care to mention it. Sometimes influence goes farther than merit, you know."

"I should like to increase my income by writing for the city papers. Even if I only made fifty dollars a year, it would all be clear gain."

Harry's desire was natural. He had no idea how many shared it. Every editor of a successful weekly could give information on this subject. Certainly there is no dearth of aspiring young writers—Scotts and Shakspeares in embryo—in our country, and if all that were written for publication succeeded in getting into print, the world would scarcely contain the books and papers which would pour in uncounted thousands from the groaning press.

When the two boys arrived in Boston they took a carriage to Oscar's house. It was situated on Beacon Street, not far from the Common,—a handsome brick house with a swell front, such as they used to build in Boston. No one of the family was in, and Oscar and Harry went up at once to the room of the former, which they were to share together. It was luxuriously furnished, so Harry thought, but then our hero had been always accustomed to the plainness of a country home.

"Now, old fellow, make yourself at home," said Oscar. "You can get yourself up for dinner. There's water and towels, and a brush."

"I don't expect to look very magnificent," said Harry. "You must tell your mother I am from the country."

"I would make you an offer if I dared," said Oscar.

"I am always open to a good offer."

"It's this: I'm one size larger than you, and my last year's suits are in that wardrobe. If any will fit you, they are yours."

---

1 The climax of a narrative.

"Thank you, Oscar," said Harry; "I'll accept your offer to-morrow."

"Why not to-day?"

"You may not understand me, but when I first appear before your family, I don't want to wear false colors."

"I understand," said Oscar, with instinctive delicacy.

An hour later, the bell rang for dinner.

Harry went down, and was introduced to his friend's mother and sister. The former was a true lady, refined and kindly, and her smile made our hero feel quite at home.

"I am glad to meet you, Mr. Walton," she said. "Oscar has spoken of you frequently."

With Oscar's sister Maud—a beautiful girl two years younger than himself—Harry felt a little more bashful; but the young lady soon entered into an animated conversation with him.

"Do you often come to Boston, Mr. Walton?" she asked.

"This is my first visit," said Harry.

"Then I dare say Oscar will play all sorts of tricks upon you. We had a cousin visit us from the country, and the poor fellow had a hard time."

"Yes," said Oscar, laughing, "I used to leave him at a street corner, and dodge into a doorway. It was amusing to see his perplexity when he looked about, and couldn't find me."

"Shall you try that on me?" asked Harry.

"Very likely."

"Then I'll be prepared."

"You might tie him with a rope, Mr. Walton," said Maud, "and keep firm hold."

"I will, if Oscar consents."

"I will see about it. But here is my father. Father, this is my friend, Harry Walton."

"I am glad to see you, Mr. Walton," said Mr. Vincent. "Then you belong to my profession?"

"I hope to, some time, sir; but I am only a printer as yet."

"You are yet to rise from the ranks. I know all about that. I was once a compositor."

Harry looked at the editor with great respect. He was stout, squarely built, with a massive head and a thoughtful expression. His appearance was up to Harry's anticipations. He felt that he would be prouder to be Mr. Vincent than any man in Boston. He could hardly believe that this man, who controlled so influential an organ, and was so honored in the community, was once a printer boy like himself.

"What paper are you connected with?" asked Mr. Vincent.

"The 'Centreville Gazette.'"

"I have seen it. It is quite a respectable paper."

"But how different," thought Harry, "from a great city daily!"

"Let us go out to dinner," said Mr. Vincent, consulting his watch. "I have an engagement immediately afterward."

At table Harry sat between Maud and Oscar. If at first he felt a little bashful, the feeling soon wore away. The dinner hour passed very pleasantly. Mr. Vincent chatted very agreeably about men and things. There is no one better qualified to shine in this kind of conversation than the editor of a city daily, who is compelled to be exceptionally well informed. Harry listened with such interest that he almost forgot to eat, till Oscar charged him with want of appetite.

"I must leave in haste," said Mr. Vincent, when dinner was over. "Oscar, I take it for granted that you will take care of your friend."

"Certainly, father. I shall look upon myself as his guardian, adviser and friend."

"You are not very well fitted to be a mentor, Oscar," said Maud.

"Why not, young lady?"

"You need a guardian yourself. You are young and frivolous."

"And you, I suppose, are old and judicious."

"Thank you. I will own to the last, and the first will come in time."

"Isn't it singular, Harry, that my sister should have so much conceit, whereas I am remarkably modest?"

"I never discovered it, Oscar," said Harry, smiling.

"That is right, Mr. Walton," said Maud. "I see you are on my side. Look after my brother, Mr. Walton. He needs an experienced friend."

"I am afraid I don't answer the description, Miss Maud."

"I don't doubt you will prove competent. I wish you a pleasant walk."

"My sister's a jolly girl, don't you think so?" asked Oscar, as Maud left the room.

"That isn't exactly what I should say of her, but I can describe her as even more attractive than her brother."

"You couldn't pay her a higher compliment. But come; we'll take a walk on the Common."

They were soon on the Common, dear to every Bostonian, and sauntered along the walks, under the pleasant shade of the stately elms.

"Look there," said Oscar, suddenly; "isn't that Fitz Fletcher?"

"Yes," said Harry, "but he doesn't see us."

"We'll join him. How are you, Fitz?"

"Glad to see you, Oscar," said Fletcher, extending a gloved band, while in the other he tossed a light cane. "When did you arrive?"

"Only this morning; but you don't see Harry Walton."

Fletcher arched his brows in surprise, and said coldly, "Indeed, I was not aware Mr. Walton was in the city."

"He is visiting me," said Oscar.

Fletcher looked surprised. He knew the Vincents stood high socially, and it seemed extraordinary that they should receive a printer's devil as a guest.

"Have you given up the printing business?" he asked superciliously.

"No; I only have a little vacation from it."

"Ah, indeed! It's a very dirty business. I would as soon be a chimney-sweep."

"Each to his taste, Fitz," said Oscar. "If you have a taste for chimneys, I hope your father won't interfere."

"I haven't a taste for such a low business," said Fletcher, haughtily. "I should like it as well as being a printer's devil though."

"Would you? At any rate, if you take it up, you'll be sure to be well *sooted*."

Fletcher did not laugh at the joke. He never could see any wit in jokes directed at himself.

"How long are you going to stay at that beastly school?" he asked.

"I am not staying at any beastly school."

"I mean the Academy."

"Till I am ready for college. Where are you studying?"

"I recite to a private tutor."

"Well, we shall meet at 'Harvard' if we are lucky enough to get in."

Fletcher rather hoped Oscar would invite him to call at his house, for he liked to visit a family of high social position; but he waited in vain.

"What a fool Oscar makes of himself about that country clod-hopper!" thought the stylish young man, as he walked away. "The idea of associating with a printer's devil! I hope I know what is due to myself better."

CHAPTER XXVII:
THE OFFICE OF THE "STANDARD"

On the day after Thanksgiving, Harry brought out from his carpet-bag his manuscript story, and started with Oscar for the office of the "Weekly Standard." He bought the last copy of the paper, and thus ascertained the location of the office.

Oscar turned the last page, and ran through a sketch of about the same length as Harry's. "Yours is fully as good as this, Harry," he said.

"The editor may not think so."

"Then he ought to."

"This story is by one of his regular contributors, Kenella Kent."

"You'll have to take a name yourself,—a *nom de plume*, I mean."

"I have written so far over the name of Franklin."

"That will do very well for essays, but is not appropriate for stories."

"Suppose you suggest a name, Oscar."

"How will 'Fitz Fletcher' do?"

"Mr. Fletcher would not permit me to take such a liberty."

"And you wouldn't want to take it."

"Not much."

"Let me see. I suppose I must task my invention, then. How will Old Nick do?"

"People would think you wrote the story."

"A fair hit. Hold on, I've got just the name. Frank Lynn."

"I thought you objected to that name."

"You don't understand me. I mean two names, not one. Frank Lynn! Don't you see?"

"Yes, it's a good plan. I'll adopt it."

"Who knows but you may make the name illustrious, Harry?"

"If I do, I'll dedicate my first book to Oscar Vincent."

"Shake hands on that. I accept the dedication with mingled feelings of gratitude and pleasure."

"Better wait till you get it," said Harry, laughing. "Don't count your chickens before they're hatched."

"The first egg is laid, and that's something. But here we are at the office."

It was a building containing a large number of offices. The names of the respective occupants were printed on slips of black tin at the entrance. From this, Harry found that the office of the "Weekly Standard" was located at No. 6.

"My heart begins to beat, Oscar," said Harry, naturally excited in anticipation of an interview with one who could open the gates of authorship to him.

"Does it?" asked Oscar. "Mine has been beating for a number of years."

"You are too matter-of-fact for me, Oscar. If it was your own story, you might feel differently."

"Shall I pass it off as my own, and make the negotiation?"

Harry was half tempted to say yes, but it occurred to him that this might prove an embarrassment in the future, and he declined the proposal.

They climbed rather a dark, and not very elegant staircase, and found themselves before No. 6.

Harry knocked, or was about to do so, when a young lady with long ringlets, and a roll of manuscript in her hand, who had followed them upstairs advanced confidently, and, opening the door, went in. The two boys followed, thinking the ceremony of knocking needless.

They found themselves in a large room, one corner of which was partitioned off for the editor's sanctum. A middle-aged man was directing papers in the larger room, while piles of papers were ranged on shelves at the sides of the apartment.

The two boys hesitated to advance, but the young lady in ringlets went on, and entered the office through the open door.

"We'll wait till she is through," said Harry.

It was easy to hear the conversation that passed between the young lady and the editor, whom they could not see.

"Good-morning, Mr. Houghton," she said.

"Good-morning. Take a seat, please," said the editor, pleasantly. "Are you one of our contributors?"

"No, sir, not yet," answered the young lady, "but I would become so."

"We are not engaging any new contributors at present, but still if you have brought anything for examination you may leave it."

"I am not wholly unknown to fame," said the young lady, with an air of consequence. "You have probably heard of Prunella Prune."

"Possibly, but I don't at present recall it. We editors meet with so many names, you know. What is the character of your articles?"

"I am a poetess, sir, and I also write stories."

"Poetry is a drug in the market. We have twice as much offered us as we can accept. Still we are always glad to welcome really meritorious poems."

"I trust my humble efforts will please you," said Prunella. "I have here some lines to a nightingale, which have been very much praised in our village. Shall I read them?"

"If you wish," said the editor, by no means cheerfully.

Miss Prune raised her voice, and commenced:—

"O star-eyed Nightingale,
How nobly thou dost sail
Through the air!
No other bird can compare
With the tuneful song
Which to thee doth belong.
I sit and hear thee sing,
While with tireless wing
Thou dost fly.
And it makes me feel so sad,
It makes me feel so bad,
I know not why,
And I heave so many sighs,
O warbler of the skies!"

"Is there much more?" asked the editor.

"That is the first verse. There are fifteen more," said Prunella.

"Then I think I shall not have time at present to hear you read it all. You may leave it, and I will look it over at my leisure."

"If it suits you," said Prunella, "how much will it be worth?"

"I don't understand."

"How much would you be willing to pay for it?"

"Oh, we never pay for poems," said Mr. Houghton.

"Why not?" asked Miss Prune, evidently disappointed.

"Our contributors are kind enough to send them gratuitously."

"Is that fostering American talent?" demanded Prunella, indignantly.

"American poetical talent doesn't require fostering, judging from the loads of poems which are sent in to us."

"You pay for stories, I presume?"

"Yes, we pay for good, popular stories."

"I have one here," said Prunella, untying her manuscript, "which I should like to read to you."

"You may read the first paragraph, if you please. I haven't time to hear more. What is the title?"

"'The Bandit's Bride.' This is the way it opens:—

> "'The night was tempestuous. Lightnings [*sic*] flashed in the cerulean sky, and the deep-voiced thunder rolled from one end of the firmament to the other. It was a landscape in Spain. From a rocky defile gayly pranced forth a masked cavalier, Roderigo di Lima, a famous bandit chief.
>
> "'"Ha! ha!" he laughed in demoniac glee, "the night is well fitted to my purpose. Ere it passes, Isabella Gomez shall be mine."'"

"I think that will do," said Mr. Houghton, hastily. "I am afraid that style won't suit our readers."

"Why not?" demanded Prunella, sharply. "I can assure you, sir, that it has been praised by *excellent* judges in our village."

"It is too exciting for our readers. You had better carry it to 'The Weekly Corsair.'"

"Do they pay well for contributions?"

"I really can't say. How much do you expect?"

"This story will make about five columns. I think twenty-five dollars will be about right."

"I am afraid you will be disappointed. We can't afford to pay such prices, and the 'Corsair' has a smaller circulation than our paper."

"How much do you pay?"

"Two dollars a column."

"I expected more," said Prunella, "but I will write for you at that price."

"Send us something suited to our paper, and we will pay for it at that price."

"I will write you a story to-morrow. Good-morning, sir."

"Good-morning, Miss Prune."

The young lady with ringlets sailed out of the editor's room, and Oscar, nudging Harry, said, "Now it is our turn. Come along. Follow me, and don't be frightened."

CHAPTER XXVIII: ACCEPTED

The editor of the "Standard" looked with some surprise at the two boys. As editor, he was not accustomed to receive such young visitors. He was courteous, however, and said, pleasantly:—

"What can I do for you, young gentlemen?"

"Are you the editor of the 'Standard'?" asked Harry, diffidently.

"I am. Do you wish to subscribe?"

"I have already written something for your paper," Harry continued.

"Indeed!" said the editor. "Was it poetry or prose?"

Harry felt flattered by the question. To be mistaken for a poet he felt to be very complimentary. If he had known how much trash weekly found its way to the "Standard" office, under the guise of poetry, he would have felt less flattered.

"I have written some essays over the name of 'Franklin,'" he hastened to say.

"Ah, yes, I remember, and very sensible essays too. You are young to write."

"Yes, sir; I hope to improve as I grow older."

By this time Oscar felt impelled to speak for his friend. It seemed to him that Harry was too modest.

"My friend is assistant editor of a New Hampshire paper:— 'The Centreville Gazette,'" he announced.

"Indeed!" said the editor, looking surprised. "He is certainly young for an editor."

"My friend is not quite right," said Harry, hastily. "I am one of the compositors on that paper."

"But you write editorial paragraphs," said Oscar.

"Yes, unimportant ones."

"And are you, too, an editor?" asked the editor of the "Standard," addressing Oscar with a smile.

"Not exactly," said Oscar; "but I am an editor's son. Perhaps you are acquainted with my father,—John Vincent of this city."

"Are you his son?" said the editor, respectfully. "I know your father slightly. He is one of our ablest journalists."

"Thank you, sir."

"I am very glad to receive a visit from you, and should be glad to print anything from your pen."

"I am not sure about that," said Oscar, smiling. "If I have a talent for writing, it hasn't developed itself yet. But my friend here takes to it as naturally as a duck takes to water."

"Have you brought me another essay, Mr. 'Franklin'?" asked the editor, turning to Harry. "I address you by your *nom de plume*, not knowing your real name."

"Permit me to introduce my friend, Harry Walton," said Oscar. "Harry, where is your story?"

"I have brought you in a story," said Harry, blushing. "It is my first attempt, and may not suit you, but I shall be glad if you will take the trouble to examine it."

"With pleasure," said the editor. "Is it long?"

"About two columns. It is of a humorous character."

The editor reached out his hand, and, taking the manuscript, unrolled it. He read the first few lines, and they seemed to strike his attention.

"If you will amuse yourselves for a few minutes, I will read it at once," he said. "I don't often do it, but I will break over my custom this time."

"Thank you, sir," said Harry.

"There are some of my exchanges," said the editor, pointing to a pile on the floor. "You may find something to interest you in some of them."

They picked up some papers, and began to read. But Harry could not help thinking of the verdict that was to be pronounced on his manuscript. Upon that a great deal hinged. If he could feel that he was able to produce anything that would command compensation, however small, it would make him proud and happy. He tried, as he gazed furtively over his paper at the editor's face, to anticipate his decision, but the latter was too much accustomed to reading manuscript to show the impression made upon him.

Fifteen minutes passed, and he looked up.

"Well, Mr. Walton," he said, "your first attempt is a success."

Harry's face brightened.

"May I ask if the plot is original?"

"It is so far as I know, sir. I don't think I ever read anything like it."

"Of course there are some faults in the construction, and the dialogue might be amended here and there. But it is very creditable, and I will use it in the 'Standard' if you desire it."

"I do, sir."

"And how much are you willing to pay for it?" Oscar struck in.

The editor hesitated.

"It is not our custom to pay novices just at first," he said. "If Mr. Walton keeps on writing, he would soon command compensation."

Harry would not have dared to press the matter, but Oscar was not so diffident. Indeed, it is easier to be bold in a friend's cause than one's own.

"Don't you think it is worth being paid for, if it is worth printing?" he persisted.

"Upon that principle, we should feel obliged to pay for poetry," said the editor.

"Oh," said Oscar, "poets don't need money. They live on flowers and dew-drops."

The editor smiled.

"You think prose-writers require something more substantial?"

"Yes, sir."

"I will tell you how the matter stands," said the editor. "Mr. Walton is a beginner. He has his reputation to make. When it is made he will be worth a fair price to me, or any of my brother editors."

"I see," said Oscar; "but his story must be worth something. It will fill up two columns. If you didn't print it, you would have to pay somebody for writing these two columns."

"You have some reason in what you say. Still our ordinary rule is based on justice. A distinction should be made between new contributors and old favorites."

"Yes, sir. Pay the first smaller sums."

If the speaker had not been John Vincent's son, it would have been doubtful if his reasoning would have prevailed. As it was, the editor yielded.

"I may break over my rule in the case of your friend," said the editor; "but he must be satisfied with a very small sum for the present."

"Anything will satisfy me, sir," said Harry, eagerly.

"Your story will fill two columns. I commonly pay two dollars a column for such articles, if by practised writers. I will give you half that."

"Thank you, sir. I accept it," said Harry, promptly.

"In a year or so I may see my way clear to paying you more, Mr. Walton; but you must consider that I give you the opportunity of winning popularity, and regard this as part of your compensation, at present."

"I am quite satisfied, sir," said Harry, his heart fluttering with joy and triumph. "May I write you some more sketches?"

"I shall be happy to receive and examine them; but you must not be disappointed if from time to time I reject your manuscripts."

"No, sir; I will take it as a hint that they need improving."

"I will revise my friend's stories, sir," said Oscar, humorously, "and give him such hints as my knowledge of the world may suggest."

"No doubt such suggestions from so mature a friend will materially benefit them," said the editor, smiling.

He opened his pocket-book, and, drawing out a two-dollar bill, handed it to Harry.

"I shall hope to pay you often," he said, "for similar contributions."

"Thank you, sir," said Harry.

Feeling that their business was at an end, the boys withdrew. As they reached the foot of the stairs, Oscar took off his cap, and bowed low.

"Mr. Lynn, I congratulate you," he said.

"I can't tell you how glad I feel, Oscar," said Harry, his face radiant.

"Let me suggest that you owe me a commission for impressing upon the editor the propriety of paying you."

"How much do you ask?"

"An ice-cream will be satisfactory."

"All right."

"Come round to Copeland's then. We'll celebrate your success in a becoming manner."

CHAPTER XXIX: MRS. CLINTON'S PARTY

When Oscar and Harry reached home they were met by Maud, who flourished in her hand what appeared to be a note.

"What is it, Maud?" asked Oscar. "A love-letter for me?"

"Don't flatter yourself, Oscar. No girl would be so foolish as to write you a love-letter. It is an invitation to a party on Saturday evening."

"Where?"

"At Mrs. Clinton's."

"I think I will decline," said Oscar. "I wouldn't like to leave Harry alone."

"Oh, he is included too. Mrs. Clinton heard of his being here, and expressly included him in the invitation."

"That alters the case. You'll go, Harry, won't you?"

"I am afraid I shouldn't know how to behave at a fashionable party," said Harry.

"Oh, you've only got to make me your model," said Oscar, "and you'll be all right."

"Did you ever see such conceit, Mr. Walton?" said Maud.

"It reminds me of Fletcher," said Harry.

"Fitz Fletcher? By the way, he will probably be there. His family are acquainted with the Clintons."

"Yes, he is invited," said Maud.

"Good! Then there's promise of fun," said Oscar. "You'll see Fitz with his best company manners on."

"I am afraid he won't enjoy meeting me there," said Harry.

"Probably not."

"I don't see why," said Maud.

"Shall I tell, Harry?"

"Certainly."

"To begin with, Fletcher regards himself as infinitely superior to Walton here, because his father is rich, and Walton's poor. Again, Harry is a printer, and works for a living, which Fitz considers degrading. Besides all this, Harry was elected President of our Debating Society,—an office which Fitz wanted."

"I hope," said Maud, "that Mr. Fletcher's dislike does not affect your peace of mind, Mr. Walton."

"Not materially," said Harry, laughing.

"By the way, Maud," said Oscar, "did I ever tell you how Fletcher's pride was mortified at school by our discovering his relationship to a tin-pedler?"

"No, tell me about it."

The story, already familiar to the reader, was graphically told by Oscar, and served to amuse his sister.

"He deserved the mortification," she said. "I shall remember it if he shows any of his arrogance at the party."

"Fletcher rather admires Maud," said Oscar, after his sister had gone out of the room; "but the favor isn't reciprocated. If he undertakes to say anything to her against you, she will take him down, depend upon it."

Saturday evening came, and Harry, with Oscar and his sister, started for the party. Our hero, having confessed his inability to dance, had been diligently instructed in the Lancers by Oscar, so that he felt some confidence in being able to get through without any serious blunder.

"Of course you must dance, Harry," he said. "You don't want to be a wall-flower."

"I may have to be," said Harry. "I shall know none of the young ladies except your sister."

"Maud will dance the first Lancers[1] with you, and I will get you a partner for the second."

"You may dispose of me as you like, Oscar."

"Wisely said. Don't forget that I am your Mentor."

When they entered the brilliantly lighted parlors, they were already half full. Oscar introduced his friend to Mrs. Clinton.

"I am glad to see you here, Mr. Walton," said the hostess, graciously. "Oscar, I depend upon you to introduce your friend to some of the young ladies."

"You forget my diffidence, Mrs. Clinton."

"I didn't know you were troubled in that way."

"See how I am misjudged. I am painfully bashful."

"You hide it well," said the hostess, with a smile.

"Escort my sister to a seat, Harry," said Oscar. "By the way, you two will dance in the first Lancers."

"If Miss Maud will accept so awkward a partner," said Harry.

"Oh, yes, Mr. Walton. I'll give you a hint if you are going wrong."

Five minutes later Fletcher touched Oscar on the shoulder.

"Oscar, where is your sister?" he asked.

"There," said Oscar, pointing her out.

Fletcher, who was rather near-sighted, did not at first notice that Harry Walton was sitting beside the young lady.

He advanced, and made a magnificent bow, on which he rather prided himself.

"Good-evening, Miss Vincent," he said.

"Good-evening, Mr. Fletcher."

"I am very glad you have favored the party with your presence."

"Thank you, Mr. Fletcher. Don't turn my head with your compliments."

"May I hope you will favor me with your hand in the first Lancers?"

"I am sorry, Mr. Fletcher, but I am engaged to Mr. Walton. I believe you are acquainted with him."

Fletcher for the first time observed our hero, and his face wore a look of mingled annoyance and scorn.

"I have met the gentleman," he said, haughtily.

"Mr. Fletcher and I have met frequently," said Harry, pleasantly.

---

1 A variation of the quadrille, a popular dance in high society in the nineteenth century.

"I didn't expect to meet you *here*," said Fletcher with marked emphasis.

"Probably not," said Harry. "My invitation is due to my being a friend of Oscar's."

"I was not aware that you danced," said Fletcher who was rather curious on the subject.

"I don't—much."

"Where did you learn—in the printing office?"

"No, in the city."

"Ah! Indeed!"

Fletcher thought he had wasted time enough on our hero, and turned again to Maud.

"May I have the pleasure of your hand in the second dance?" he asked.

"I will put you down for that, if you desire it."

"Thank you."

It so happened that when Harry and Maud took the floor, they found Fletcher their *vis-à-vis*. Perhaps it was this that made Harry more emulous to get through without making any blunders. At any rate, he succeeded, and no one in the set suspected that it was his first appearance in public as a dancer.

Fletcher was puzzled. He had hoped that Harry would make himself ridiculous, and throw the set into confusion. But the dance passed off smoothly, and in due time Fletcher led out Maud. If he had known his own interest, he would have kept silent about Harry, but he had little discretion.

"I was rather surprised to see Walton here," he began.

"Didn't you know he was in the city?

"Yes, I met him with Oscar."

"Then why were you surprised?"

"Because his social position does not entitle him to appear in such a company. When I first knew him, he was only a printer's apprentice."

Fletcher wanted to say printer's devil, but did not venture to do so in presence of a young lady.

"He will rise higher than that."

"I dare say," said Fletcher, with a sneer, "he will rise in time to be a journeyman with a salary of fifteen dollars a week."

"If I am not mistaken in Mr. Walton, he will rise much higher than that. Many of our prominent men have sprung from beginnings like his."

"It must be rather a trial to him to come here. His father is a day-laborer, I believe, and of course he has never been accustomed to any refinement or polish."

"I don't detect the absence of either," said Maud, quietly.

"Do you believe in throwing down all social distinctions, and meeting the sons of laborers on equal terms?"

"As to that," said Maud, meeting her partner's glance, "I am rather democratic. I could even meet the son of a tin-pedler on equal terms, provided he were a gentleman."

The blood rushed to Fletcher's cheeks.

"A tin-pedler!" he ejaculated.

"Yes! Suppose you were the son, or relation, of a tin-pedler, why should I consider that? It would make you neither better nor worse."

"I have no connection with tin-pedlers," said Fletcher, hastily. "Who told you I had?"

"I only made a supposition, Mr. Fletcher."

But Fletcher thought otherwise. He was sure that Maud had heard of his mortification at school, and it disturbed him not a little, for, in spite of her assurance, he felt that she believed the story, and it annoyed him so much that he did not venture to make any other reference to Harry.

"Poor Fitz!" said Oscar, when on their way home Maud gave an account of their conversation, "I am afraid he will murder the tin-pedler some time, to get rid of such an odious relationship."

CHAPTER XXX: TWO LETTERS FROM THE WEST

The vacation was over all too soon, yet, brief as it was, Harry looked back upon it with great satisfaction. He had been kindly received in the family of a man who stood high in the profession which he was ambitious to enter; he had gratified his curiosity to see the chief city of New England; and, by no means least, he had secured a position as paid contributor for the "Standard."

"I suppose you will be writing another story soon," said Oscar.

"Yes," said Harry, "I have got the plan of one already."

"If you should write more than you can get into the 'Standard,' you had better send something to the 'Weekly Argus.'"

"I will; but I will wait till the 'Standard' prints my first sketch, so that I can refer to that in writing to the 'Argus.'"

"Perhaps you are right. There's one advantage to not presenting yourself. They won't know you're only a boy."

"Unless they judge so from my style."

"I don't think they would infer it from that. By the way, Harry, suppose my father could find an opening for you as a reporter on his paper,—would you be willing to accept it?"

"I am not sure whether it would be best for me," said Harry, slowly, "even if I were qualified."

"There is more chance to rise on a city paper."

"I don't know. If I stay here I may before many years control a paper of my own. Then, if I want to go into politics, there would be more chance in the country than in the city."

"Would you like to go into politics?"

"I am rather too young to decide about that; but if I could be of service in that way, I don't see why I should not desire it."

"Well, Harry, I think you are going the right way to work."

"I hope so. I don't want to be promoted till I am fit for it. I am going to work hard for the next two or three years."

"I wish I were as industrious as you are, Harry."

"And I wish I knew as much as you do, Oscar."

"Say no more, or we shall be forming a Mutual Admiration Society," said Oscar, laughing.

Harry received a cordial welcome back to the printing office. Mr. Anderson asked him many questions about Mr. Vincent; and our hero felt that his employer regarded him with increased consideration, on account of his acquaintance with the great city editor. This consideration was still farther increased when Mr. Anderson learned our hero's engagement by the "Weekly Standard."

Three weeks later, the "Standard" published Harry's sketch, and accepted another, at the same price. Before this latter was printed, Harry wrote a third sketch, which he called "Phineas Popkin's Engagement." This he inclosed to the "Weekly Argus," with a letter in which he referred to his engagement by the "Standard." In reply he received the following letter:—

> "BOSTON, Jan., 18—,
> "MR. FRANK LYNN,—Dear Sir: We enclose three
> dollars for your sketch,—'Phineas Popkin's Engage-
> ment.' We shall be glad to receive other sketches, of
> similar character and length, and, if accepted, we will
> pay the same price therefor.
> "I. B. FITCH & Co."

This was highly satisfactory to Harry. He was now an accepted contributor to two weekly papers, and the addition to his income would be likely to reach a hundred dollars a year. All this he would be able to lay up, and as much or more from his salary on the "Gazette." He felt on the high road to success. Seeing that his young compositor was meeting with success and appreciation abroad, Mr. Anderson called upon him more frequently to write paragraphs for the "Gazette." Though this work was gratuitous, Harry willingly undertook it. He felt that in this way he was preparing himself for the career to which he steadily looked forward. Present compensation, he justly reasoned, was of small importance, compared with the chance of improvement. In this view, Ferguson, who proved to be a very judicious friend, fully concurred. Indeed Harry and he became more intimate than before, if that were possible, and they felt that Clapp's departure was by no means to be regretted. They were remarking this one day, when Mr. Anderson, who had been examining his mail, looked up suddenly, and said, "What do you think, Mr. Ferguson? I've got a letter from Clapp."

"A letter from Clapp? Where is he?" inquired Ferguson, with interest.

"This letter is dated at St. Louis. He doesn't appear to be doing very well."

"I thought he was going to California."

"So he represented. But here is the letter." Ferguson took it, and, after reading, handed it to Harry.

It ran thus:—

"ST. LOUIS, April 4, 18—.
"JOTHAM ANDERSON, ESQ.,—Dear Sir: Perhaps you will be surprised to hear from me, but I feel as if I would like to hear from Centreville, where I worked so long. The man that induced me and Harrison to come out here left us in the lurch three days after we reached St. Louis. He said he was going on to San Francisco, and he had only money enough to pay his own expenses. As Luke and I were not provided with money, we had a pretty hard time at first, and had to pawn some of our clothes, or we should have starved. Finally I got a job in the 'Democrat' office, and a week after, Luke got something to do, though it didn't pay very well. So we scratched along as well as we could. Part of the time since we have been out of work, and we haven't found 'coming West' all that it was cracked up to be.

"Are Ferguson and Harry Walton still working for you? I should like to come back to the 'Gazette' office, and take my old place; but haven't got five dollars ahead to pay my travelling expenses. If you will send me out thirty dollars, I will come right on, and work it out after I come back. Hoping for an early reply, I am,

"Yours respectfully,
"HENRY CLAPP."

"Are you going to send out the money, Mr. Anderson?" asked Ferguson.

"Not I. Now that Walton has got well learnt, I don't need another workman. I shall respectfully decline his offer."

Both Harry and Ferguson were glad to hear this, for they felt that Clapp's presence would be far from making the office more agreeable.

"Here's a letter for you, Walton, also post-marked St. Louis," said Mr. Anderson, just afterward.

Harry took it with surprise, and opened it at once.

"It's from Luke Harrison," he said, looking at the signature.

"Does he want you to send him thirty dollars?" asked Ferguson.

"Listen and I will read the letter."

"DEAR HARRY," it commenced; "you will perhaps think it strange that I have written to you; but we used to be good friends. I write to tell you that I don't like this place. I haven't got along well, and I want to get back. Now I am going to ask of you a favor. Will you lend me thirty or forty dollars, to pay my fare home? I will pay you back in a month or two months sure, after I get to work. I will also pay you the few dollars which I borrowed some time ago. I ought to have done it before, but I was thoughtless, and I kept putting it off. Now, Harry, I know you have the money, and you can lend it to me just as well as not, and I'll be sure to pay it back before you need it. Just get a post-office order, and send it to Luke Harrison, 17 R—— Street, St. Louis, and I'll be sure to get it. Give my respects to Mr. Anderson, and also to Mr. Ferguson.

"Your friend,
"LUKE HARRISON."

"There is a chance for a first-class investment, Harry," said Ferguson.

"Do you want to join me in it?"

"No, I would rather pay the money to have 'your friend' keep away."

"I don't want to be unkind or disobliging," said Harry, "but I don't feel like giving Luke this money. I know he would never pay me back."

"Say no, then."

"I will. Luke will be mad, but I can't help it."

So both Mr. Anderson and Harry wrote declining to lend. The latter, in return, received a letter from Luke, denouncing him as a "mean, miserly hunks"; but even this did not cause him to regret his decision.

CHAPTER XXXI: ONE STEP UPWARD

In real life the incidents that call for notice do not occur daily. Months and years pass, sometimes, where the course of life is quiet and uneventful. So it was with Harry Walton. He went to his daily work with unfailing regularity, devoted a large part of his leisure to reading and study, or writing sketches for the Boston papers, and found himself growing steadily wiser and better informed. His account in the savings-bank grew slowly, but steadily; and on his nineteenth birthday, when we propose to look in upon him again, he was worth five hundred dollars.

Some of my readers who are favored by fortune may regard this as a small sum. It is small in itself, but it was not small for a youth in Harry's position to have saved from his small earnings. But of greater value than the sum itself was the habit of self-denial and saving which our hero had formed. He had started in the right way, and made a beginning which was likely to lead to prosperity in the end. It had not been altogether easy to save this sum. Harry's income had always been small, and he might, without incurring the charge of excessive extravagance, have spent the whole. He had denied himself on many occasions, where most boys of his age would have yielded to the temptation of spending money for pleasure or personal gratification; but he had been rewarded by the thought that he was getting on in the world.

"This is my birthday, Mr. Ferguson," he said, as he entered the printing-office on that particular morning.

"Is it?" asked Ferguson, looking up from his case with interest. "How venerable are you, may I ask?"

"I don't feel very venerable as yet," said Harry, with a smile. "I am nineteen."

"You were sixteen when you entered the office."

"As printer's devil—yes."

"You have learned the business pretty thoroughly. You are as good a workman as I now, though I am fifteen years older."

"You are too modest, Mr. Ferguson."

"No, it is quite true. You are as rapid and accurate as I am, and you ought to receive as high pay."

"That will come in time. You know I make something by writing for the papers."

"That's extra work. How much did you make in that way last year?"

"I can tell you, because I figured it up last night. It was one hundred and twenty-five dollars, and I put every cent into the savings-bank."

"That is quite an addition to your income."

"I shall make more this year. I am to receive two dollars a column, hereafter, for my sketches."

"I congratulate you, Harry,—the more heartily, because I think you deserve it. Your recent sketches show quite an improvement over those you wrote a year ago."

"Do you really think so?" said Harry, with evident pleasure.

"I have no hesitation in saying so. You write with greater ease than formerly, and your style is less that of a novice."

"So I have hoped and thought; but of course I was prejudiced in my own favor."

"You may rely upon it. Indeed, your increased pay is proof of it. Did you ask it?"

"The increase? No, the editor of the 'Standard' wrote me voluntarily that he considered my contributions worth the additional amount."

"That must be very pleasant. I tell you what, Harry, I've a great mind to set up opposition to you in the story line."

"Do so," said Harry, smiling.

"I would if I had the slightest particle of imagination; but the fact is, I'm too practical and matter-of-fact. Besides, I never had any talent for writing of any kind. Sometime I may become publisher of a village paper like this; but farther than that I don't aspire."

"We are to be partners in that, you know, Ferguson."

"That may be, for a time; but you will rise higher than that, Harry."

"I am afraid you overrate me."

"No; I have observed you closely in the time we have been together, and I have long felt that you are destined to rise from the ranks in which I am content to remain. Haven't you ever felt so, yourself, Harry?"

Harry's cheek flushed, and his eye lighted up.

"I won't deny that I have such thoughts sometimes," he said; "but it may end in that."

"It often does end in that; but it is only where ambition is not accompanied by faithful work. Now you are always at work. You are doing what you can to help fortune, and the end will be that fortune will help you."

"I hope so, at any rate," said Harry, thoughtfully. "I should like to fill an honorable position, and do some work by which I might be known in after years."

"Why not? The boys and young men of to-day are hereafter to fill the highest positions in the community and State. Why may not the lot fall to you?"

"I will try, at any rate, to qualify myself. Then if responsibilities come, I will try to discharge them."

The conversation was here interrupted by the entrance of Mr. Anderson, the editor of the "Gazette." He was not as well or strong as when we first made his acquaintance. Then he seemed robust enough, but now he was thinner, and moved with slower gait. It was not easy to say what had undermined his strength, for he had had no severe fit of sickness; but certainly he was in appearance several years older than when Harry entered the office.

"How do you feel this morning, Mr. Anderson?" asked Ferguson.

"I feel weak and languid, and indisposed to exertion of any kind."

"You need some change."

"That is precisely what I have thought myself. The doctor advises change of scene, and this very morning I had a letter from a brother in Wisconsin, asking me to come out and visit him."

"I have no doubt it would do you good."

"So it would. But how can I go? I can't take the paper with me," said Mr. Anderson, rather despondently.

"No; but you can leave Harry to edit it in your absence."

"Mr. Ferguson!" exclaimed Harry, startled by the proposition.

"Harry as editor!" repeated Mr. Anderson.

"Yes; why not? He is a practised writer. For more than two years he has written for two Boston papers."

"But he is so young. How old are you, Harry?" asked the editor.

"Nineteen to-day, sir."

"Nineteen. That's very young for an editor."

"Very true; but, after all, it isn't so much the age as the qualifications, is it, Mr. Anderson?"

"True," said the editor, meditatively. "Harry, do you think you could edit the paper for two or three months?"

"I think I could," said Harry, with modest confidence. His heart beat high at the thought of the important position which was likely to be opened to him; and plans of what he would do to make the paper interesting already began to be formed in his mind.

"It never occurred to me before, but I really think you could," said the editor, "and that would remove every obstacle to my going. By the way, Harry, you would have to find a new boarding-place, for Mrs. Anderson would accompany me, and we should shut up the house."

"Perhaps Ferguson would take me in?" said Harry.

"I should be glad to do so; but I don't know that my humble fare would be good enough for an editor."

Harry smiled. "I won't put on airs," he said, "till my commission is made out."

"I am afraid that I can't offer high pay for your services in that capacity," said Mr. Anderson.

"I shall charge nothing, sir," said Harry, "but thank you for the opportunity of entering, if only for a short time, a profession to which it is my ambition to belong."

After a brief consultation with his wife, Mr. Anderson appointed Harry editor pro tem., and began to make arrangements for his journey. Harry's weekly wages were raised to fifteen dollars, out of which he was to pay Ferguson four dollars a week for board.

So our hero found himself, at nineteen, the editor of an old established paper, which, though published in a country village, was not without its share of influence in the county and State.

CHAPTER XXXII: THE YOUNG EDITOR

The next number of the Centreville "Gazette" contained the following notice from the pen of Mr. Anderson:—

"For the first time since our connection with the 'Gazette,' we purpose taking a brief respite from our duties. The state of our health renders a vacation desirable, and an opportune invitation from a brother at the West has been accepted. Our absence may extend to two or three months. In the interim we have committed the editorial management to Mr. Harry Walton, who has been connected with the paper, in a different capacity, for nearly three years. Though Mr. Walton is a very young man, he has already acquired a reputation, as contributor to papers of high standing in Boston, and we feel assured that our subscribers will have no reason to complain of the temporary change in the editorship."

"The old man has given you quite a handsome notice, Harry," said Ferguson.

"I hope I shall deserve it," said Harry; "but I begin now to realize that I am young to assume such responsible duties. It would have seemed more appropriate for you to undertake them."

"I can't write well enough, Harry. I like to read, but I can't produce. In regard to the business management I feel competent to advise."

"I shall certainly be guided by your advice, Ferguson."

As it may interest the reader, we will raise the curtain and show our young hero in the capacity of editor. The time is ten days after Mr. Anderson's absence. Harry was accustomed to do his work as compositor in the forenoon and the early part of the afternoon. From three to five he occupied the editorial chair, read letters, wrote paragraphs, and saw visitors. He had just seated himself, when a man entered the office and looked about him inquisitively.

"I would like to see the editor," he said.

"I am the editor," said Harry, with dignity.

The visitor looked surprised.

"You are the youngest-looking editor I have met," he said. "Have you filled the office long?"

"Not long," said Harry. "Can I do anything for you?"

"Yes, sir, you can. First let me introduce myself. I am Dr. Theophilus Peabody."

"Will you be seated, Dr. Peabody?"

"You have probably heard of me before," said the visitor.

"I can't say that I have."

"I am surprised at that," said the doctor, rather disgusted to find himself unknown. "You must have heard of Peabody's Unfailing Panacea."

"I am afraid I have not."

"You are young," said Dr. Peabody, compassionately; "that accounts for it. Peabody's Panacea, let me tell you, sir, is the great remedy of the age. It has effected more cures, relieved more pain, soothed more aching bosoms, and done more good, than any other medicine in existence."

"It must be a satisfaction to you to have conferred such a blessing on mankind," said Harry, inclined to laugh at the doctor's magniloquent style.

"It is. I consider myself one of the benefactors of mankind; but, sir, the medicine has not yet been fully introduced. There are thousands, who groan on beds of pain, who are ignorant that for the small sum of fifty cents they could be restored to health and activity."

"That's a pity."

"It is a pity, Mr.——"

"Walton."

"Mr. Walton,—I have called, sir, to ask you to co-operate with me in making it known to the world, so far as your influence extends."

"Is your medicine a liquid?"

"No, sir; it is in the form of pills, twenty-four in a box. Let me show you."

The doctor opened a wooden box, and displayed a collection of very unwholesome-looking brown pills.

"Try one, sir; it won't do you any harm."

"Thank you; I would rather not. I don't like pills. What will they cure?"

"What won't they cure? I've got a list of fifty-nine diseases in my circular, all of which are relieved by Peabody's Panacea. They may cure more; in fact, I've been told of a consumptive patient who was considerably relieved by a single box. You won't try one?"

"I would rather not."

"Well, here is my circular, containing accounts of remarkable cures performed. Permit me to present you a box."

"Thank you," said Harry, dubiously.

"You'll probably be sick before long," said the doctor, cheerfully, "and then the pills will come handy."

"Doctor," said Ferguson, gravely, "I find my hair getting thin on top of the head. Do you think the panacea would restore it?"

"Yes," said the doctor, unexpectedly. "I had a case, in Portsmouth, of a gentleman whose head was as smooth as a billiard-ball. He took the pills for another complaint, and was surprised, in the course of three weeks, to find young hair sprouting all over the bald spot. Can't I sell you half-a-dozen boxes? You may have half a dozen for two dollars and a half."

Ferguson, who of course had been in jest, found it hard to forbear laughing, especially when Harry joined the doctor in urging him to purchase.

"Not to-day," he answered. "I can try Mr. Walton's box, and if it helps me I can order some more."

"You may not be able to get it, then," said the doctor, persuasively. "I may not be in Centreville."

"If the panacea is well known, I can surely get it without difficulty."

"Not so cheap as I will sell it."

"I won't take any to-day," said Ferguson, decisively.

"You haven't told me what I can do for you," said Harry, who found the doctor's call rather long.

"I would like you to insert my circular to your paper. It won't take more than two columns."

"We shall be happy to insert it at regular advertising rates."

"I thought," said Dr. Peabody, disappointed, "that you might do it gratuitously, as I had given you a box."

"We don't do business on such terms," said Harry. "I think I had better return the box."

"No, keep it," said the doctor. "You will be willing to notice it, doubtless."

Harry rapidly penned this paragraph, and read it aloud:—

"Dr. Theophilus Peabody has left with us a box of his Unfailing Panacea, which he claims will cure a large variety of diseases."

"Couldn't you give a list of the diseases?" insinuated the doctor.

"There are fifty-nine, you said?"

"Yes, sir."

"Then I am afraid we must decline."

Harry resumed his writing, and the doctor took his leave, looking far from satisfied.

"Here, Ferguson," said Harry, after the visitor had retired, "take the pills, and much good may they do you. Better take one now for the growth of your hair."

It was fortunate that Dr. Peabody did not hear the merriment that followed, or he would have given up the editorial staff of the Centreville "Gazette" as maliciously disposed to underrate his favorite medicine.

"Who wouldn't be an editor?" said Harry.

"I notice," said Ferguson, "that pill-tenders and blacking manufacturers are most liberal to the editorial profession. I only wish jewellers and piano manufacturers were as free with their manufactures. I would like a good gold watch, and I shall soon want a piano for my daughter."

"You may depend upon it, Ferguson, when such gifts come in, that I shall claim them as editorial perquisites."

"We won't quarrel about them till they come, Harry."

Our hero here opened a bulky communication.

"What is that?" asked Ferguson.

"An essay on 'The Immortality of the Soul,'—covers fifteen pages foolscap. What shall I do with it?"

"Publish it in a supplement with Dr. Peabody's circular."

"I am not sure but the circular would be more interesting reading."

"From whom does the essay come?"

"It is signed 'L. S.'"

"Then it is by Lemuel Snodgrass, a retired schoolteacher, who fancies himself a great writer."

"He'll be offended if I don't print it, won't he?"

"I'll tell you how to get over that. Say, in an editorial paragraph, 'We have received a thoughtful essay from 'L. S.', on 'The Immortality of the Soul.' We regret that its length precludes our publishing it in the 'Gazette.' We would suggest to the author to print it in a pamphlet.' That suggestion will be regarded as complimentary, and we may get the job of printing it."

"I see you are shrewd, Ferguson. I will follow your advice."

CHAPTER XXXIII: AN UNEXPECTED PROPOSAL

During his temporary editorship, Harry did not feel at liberty to make any decided changes in the character or arrangement of the paper; but he was ambitious to improve it, as far as he was able, in its different departments. Mr. Anderson had become rather indolent in the collection of local news, merely publishing such items as were voluntarily contributed. Harry, after his day's work was over, made a little tour of the village, gathering any news that he thought would be of interest to the public. Moreover he made arrangements to obtain news of a similar nature from neighboring villages, and the result was, that in the course of a month he made the "Gazette" much more readable.

"Really, the 'Gazette' gives a good deal more news than it used to," was a common remark.

It was probably in consequence of this improvement that new subscriptions began to come in, not from Centreville alone, but from towns in the neighborhood. This gratified and encouraged Harry, who now felt that he was on the right tack.

There was another department to which he devoted considerable attention. This was a condensed summary of news from all parts of the world, giving the preference and the largest space, of course, to American news. He aimed to supply those who did not take a daily paper with a brief record of events, such as they would not be likely, otherwise, to hear of. Of course all this work added to his labors as compositor; and his occasional sketches for Boston papers absorbed a large share of his time. Indeed, he had very little left at his disposal for rest and recreation.

"I am afraid you are working too hard, Harry," said Ferguson. "You are doing Mr. Anderson's work better than he ever did it, and your own too."

"I enjoy it," said Harry. "I work hard I know, but I feel paid by the satisfaction of finding that my labors are appreciated."

"When Mr. Anderson gets back, he will find it necessary to employ you as assistant editor, for it won't do to let the paper get back to its former dulness."

"I will accept," said Harry, "if he makes the offer. I feel more and more that I must be an editor."

"You are certainly showing yourself competent for the position."

"I have only made a beginning," said our hero, modestly. "In time I think I could make a satisfactory paper."

One day, about two months after Mr. Anderson's departure, Ferguson and Harry were surprised, and not altogether agreeably, by the entrance of John Clapp and Luke Harrison. They looked far from prosperous. In fact, both of them were decidedly seedy. Going West had not effected an improvement in their fortunes.

"Is that you, Clapp?" asked Ferguson. "Where did you come from?"

"From St. Louis."

"Then you didn't feel inclined to stay there?"

"Not I. It's a beastly place. I came near starving."

Clapp would have found any place beastly where a fair day's work was required for fair wages, and my young readers in St. Louis, therefore, need not heed his disparaging remarks.

"How was it with you, Luke?" asked Harry. "Do you like the West no better than Clapp?"

"You don't catch me out there again," said Luke. "It isn't what it's cracked up to be. We had the hardest work in getting money enough to get us back."

As Luke did not mention the kind of hard work by which the money was obtained, I may state here that an evening's luck at the faro[1] table had supplied them with money enough to pay the fare to Boston by railway; otherwise another year might have found them still in St. Louis.

"Hard work doesn't suit your constitution, does it?" said Ferguson, slyly.

"I can work as well as anybody," said Luke; "but I haven't had the luck of some people."

"You were lucky enough to have your fare paid to the West for you."

"Yes, and when we got there, the rascal left us to shift for ourselves. That aint much luck."

"I've always had to shift for myself, and always expect to," was the reply.

"Oh, you're a model!" sneered Clapp. "You always were as sober and steady as a deacon. I wonder they didn't make you one."

"And Walton there is one of the same sort," said Luke. "I say, Harry, it was real mean in you not to send me the money I wrote for. You hadn't it, had you?"

"Yes," said Harry, firmly; "but I worked hard for it, and I didn't feel like giving it away."

"Who asked you to give it away? I only wanted to borrow it."

"That's the same thing—with you. You were not likely to repay it again."

"Do you mean to insult me?" blustered Luke.

"No, I never insult anybody. I only tell the truth. You know, Luke Harrison, whether I have reason for what I say."

"I wouldn't leave a friend to suffer when I had plenty of money in my pocket," said Luke, with an injured air. "If you had been a different sort of fellow I would have asked you for five dollars to

---

1 A popular gambling card game.

keep me along till I can get work. I've come back with empty pockets."

"I'll lend you five dollars if you need it," said Harry, who judged from Luke's appearance that he told the truth.

"Will you?" said Luke, brightening up. "That's a good fellow. I'll pay you just as soon as I can."

Harry did not place much reliance on this assurance; but he felt that he could afford the loss of five dollars, if loss it should prove, and it might prevent Luke's obtaining the money in a more questionable way.

"Where's Mr. Anderson?" asked Clapp, looking round the office.

"He's been in Michigan[1] for a couple of months."

"You don't say so! Why, who runs the paper?"

"Ferguson and I," said Harry.

"I mean who edits it?"

"Harry does that," said his fellow-workman.

"Whew!" ejaculated Clapp, in surprise. "Why, but two years ago you was only a printer's devil!"

"He's risen from the ranks," said Ferguson, "and I can say with truth that the 'Gazette' has never been better than since it has been under his charge."

"How much does old Anderson pay you for taking his place?" asked Luke, who was quite as much surprised as Clapp.

"I don't ask anything extra. He pays me fifteen dollars a week as compositor."

"You're doing well," said Luke, enviously. "Got a big pile of money laid up, haven't you?"

"I have something in the bank."

"Harry writes stories for the Boston papers, also," said Ferguson. "He makes a hundred or two that way."

"Some folks are born to luck," said Clapp, discontentedly. "Here am I, six or eight years older, out of a place, and without a cent to fall back upon. I wish I was one of your lucky ones."

"You might have had a few hundred dollars, at any rate," said Ferguson, "if you hadn't chosen to spend all your money when you were earning good wages."

"A man must have a little enjoyment. We can't drudge all the time."

"It's better to do that than to be where you are now."

---

1   Alger has apparently forgotten that in Chapter XXXI, Jotham Anderson's brother lives in Wisconsin, not Michigan.

But Clapp was not to be convinced that he was himself to blame for his present disagreeable position. He laid the blame on fortune, like thousands of others. He could not see that Harry's good luck was the legitimate consequence of industry and frugality.

After a while the two left the office. They decided to seek their old boarding-house, and remain there for a week, waiting for something to turn up.

The next day Harry received the following letter from Mr. Anderson:—

"DEAR WALTON: My brother urges me to settle permanently at the West. I am offered a partnership in a paper in this vicinity, and my health has much improved here. The West seems the place for me. My only embarrassment is the paper. If I could dispose of the 'Gazette' for two thousand dollars cash, I could see my way clear to remove. Why can't you and Ferguson buy it? The numbers which you have sent me show that you are quite capable of filling the post of editor; and you and Ferguson can do the mechanical part. I think it will be a good chance for you. Write me at once whether there is any likelihood of your purchasing.
"Your friend,
"JOTHAM ANDERSON."

Harry's face flushed eagerly as he read this letter. Nothing would suit him better than to make this arrangement, if only he could provide the purchase money. But this was likely to present a difficulty.

CHAPTER XXXIV: A FRIEND IN NEED

Harry at once showed Ferguson the letter he had received.

"What are you going to do about it?" asked his friend.

"I should like to buy the paper, but I don't see how I can. Mr. Anderson wants two thousand dollars cash."

"How much have you got?"

"Only five hundred."

"I have seven hundred and fifty," said Ferguson, thoughtfully.

Harry's face brightened.

"Why can't we go into partnership?" he asked.

"That is what we spoke of once," said Ferguson, "and it would suit me perfectly; but there is a difficulty. Your money and mine added together will not be enough."

"Perhaps Mr. Anderson would take a mortgage on the establishment for the balance."

"I don't think so. He says expressly that he wants cash."

Harry looked disturbed.

"Do you think any one would lend us the money on the same terms?" he asked, after a while.

"Squire Trevor is the only man in the village likely to have money to lend. There he is in the street now. Run down, Harry, and ask him to step in a minute."

Our hero seized his hat, and did as requested. He returned immediately, followed by Squire Trevor, a stout, puffy little man, reputed shrewd and a capitalist.

"Excuse our calling you in, Squire Trevor," said Ferguson, "but we want to consult you on a matter of business. Harry, just show the squire Mr. Anderson's letter."

The squire read it deliberately.

"Do you want my advice?" he said, looking up from the perusal. "Buy the paper. It is worth what Anderson asks for it."

"So I think, but there is a difficulty. Harry and I can only raise twelve hundred dollars or so between us."

"Give a note for the balance. You'll be able to pay it off in two years, if you prosper."

"I am afraid that won't do. Mr. Anderson wants cash. Can't you lend us the money, Squire Trevor?" continued Ferguson, bluntly.

The village capitalist shook his head.

"If you had asked me last week I could have obliged you," he said; "but I was in Boston day before yesterday, and bought some railway stock which is likely to enhance in value. That leaves me short."

"Then you couldn't manage it?" said Ferguson, soberly.

"Not at present," said the squire, decidedly.

"Then we must write to Mr. Anderson, offering what we have, and a mortgage to secure the rest."

"That will be your best course."

"He may agree to our terms," said Harry, hopefully, after their visitor had left the office.

"We will hope so, at all events."

A letter was at once despatched, and in a week the answer was received.

"I am sorry," Mr. Anderson wrote, "to decline your proposals, but, I have immediate need of the whole sum which I ask for the paper. If I cannot obtain it, I shall come back to Centreville, though I would prefer to remain here."

Upon the receipt of this letter, Ferguson gave up his work for the forenoon, and made a tour of the Village, calling upon all who he thought were likely to have money to lend. He had small expectation of success, but felt that he ought to try everywhere before giving up so good a chance.

While he was absent, Harry had a welcome visitor. It was no other than Professor Henderson, the magician, in whose employ he had spent three months some years before, as related in "Bound to Rise."

"Take a seat, professor," said Harry, cordially. "I am delighted to see you."

"How you have grown, Harry!" said the professor. "Why, I should hardly have known you!"

"We haven't met since I left you to enter this office."

"No; it is nearly three years. How do you like the business?"

"Very much indeed."

"Are you doing well?"

"I receive fifteen dollars a week."

"That is good. What are your prospects for the future?"

"They would be excellent if I had a little more capital."

"I don't see how you need capital, as a journeyman printer."

"I have a chance to buy out the paper."

"But who would edit it?"

"I would."

"You!" said the magician, rather incredulously.

"I have been the editor for the last two months."

"You—a boy!"

"I am nineteen, professor."

"I shouldn't have dreamed of editing a paper at nineteen; or, indeed, as old as I am now."

Harry laughed.

"You are too modest, professor. Let me show you our last two issues."

The professor took out his glasses, and sat down, not without considerable curiosity, to read a paper edited by one who only three years before had been his assistant.

"Did you write this article?" he asked, after a pause, pointing to the leader in the last issue of the "Gazette."

"Yes, sir."

"Then, by Jove, you can write. Why, it's worthy of a man of twice your age!"

"Thank you, professor," said Harry, gratified.

"Where did you learn to write?"

Harry gave his old employer some account of his literary experiences, mentioning his connection with the two Boston weekly papers.

"You ought to be an editor," said the professor. "If you can do as much at nineteen, you have a bright future before you."

"That depends a little on circumstances. If I only could buy this paper, I would try to win reputation as well as money."

"What is your difficulty?"

"The want of money."

"How much do you need?"

"Eight hundred dollars."

"Is that all the price such a paper commands?"

"No. The price is two thousand dollars; but Ferguson and I can raise twelve hundred between us."

"Do you consider it good property?"

"Mr. Anderson made a comfortable living out of it, besides paying for office work. We should have this advantage, that we should be our own compositors."

"That would give you considerable to do, if you were editor also."

"I shouldn't mind," said Harry, "if I only had a paper of my own. I think I should be willing to work night and day."

"What are your chances of raising the sum you need?"

"Very small. Ferguson has gone out at this moment to see if he can find any one willing to lend; but we don't expect success."

"Why don't you apply to me?" asked the professor.

"I didn't know if you had the money to spare."

"I might conjure up some. Presto!—change!—you know. We professors of magic can find money anywhere."

"But you need some to work with. I have been behind the scenes," said Harry, smiling.

"But you don't know all my secrets, for all that. In sober earnest, I haven't been practising magic these twenty-five years for nothing. I can lend you the money you want, and I will."

Harry seized his hand, and shook it with delight.

"How can I express my gratitude?" he said.

"By sending me your paper gratis, and paying me seven per cent. interest on my money."

"Agreed. Anything more?"

"Yes. I am to give an exhibition in the village to-morrow night. You must give me a good puff."

"With the greatest pleasure. I'll write it now."

"Before it takes place? I see you are following the example of some of the city dailies."

"And I'll print you some handbills for nothing."

"Good. When do you want the money? Will next week do?"

"Yes. Mr. Anderson won't expect the money before."

Here Ferguson entered the office. Harry made a signal of silence to the professor, whom he introduced. Then he said:—

"Well, Ferguson, what luck?"

"None at all," answered his fellow-compositor, evidently dispirited. "Nobody seems to have any money. We shall have to give up our plan."

"I don't mean to give it up."

"Then perhaps you'll tell me where to find the money."

"I will."

"You don't mean to say—" began Ferguson, eagerly.

"Yes, I do. I mean to say that the money is found."

"Where?"

"Prof. Henderson has agreed to let us have it."

"Is that true?" said Ferguson, bewildered.

"I believe so," said the professor, smiling. "Harry has juggled the money out of me,—you know he used to be in the business,—and you can make your bargain as soon as you like."

It is hardly necessary to say that Prof. Henderson got an excellent notice in the next number of the Centreville "Gazette"; and it is my opinion that he deserved it.

CHAPTER XXXV:
FLETCHER'S OPINION OF HARRY WALTON

In two weeks all the business arrangements were completed, and Ferguson and Harry became joint proprietors of the "Centreville Gazette," the latter being sole editor. The change was received with favor in the village, as Harry had, as editor pro tem. for two months, shown his competence for the position. It gave him prominence also in town, and, though only nineteen, he already was classed with the minister, the doctor and the lawyer. It helped him also with the weekly papers to which he contributed in Boston, and his pay was once more raised, while his sketches were more frequently printed. Now this was all very pleasant, but it was not long before our hero found himself overburdened with work.

"What is the matter Harry? You look pale," said Ferguson, one morning.

"I have a bad headache, and am feeling out of sorts."

"I don't wonder at it. You are working too hard."

"I don't know about that."

"I do. You do nearly as much as I, as a compositor. Then you do all the editorial work, besides writing sketches for the Boston papers."

"How can I get along with less? The paper must be edited, and I shouldn't like giving up writing for the Boston papers."

"I'll tell you what to do. Take a boy and train him up as a printer. After a while he will relieve you almost wholly, while, by the time he commands good wages, we shall be able to pay them."

"It is a good idea, Ferguson. Do you know of any boy that wants to learn printing?"

"Haven't you got a younger brother?"

"The very thing," said Harry, briskly. "Father wrote to me last week that he should like to get something for——."

"Better write and offer him a place in the office."

"I will."

The letter was written at once. An immediate answer was received, of a favorable nature. The boy was glad to leave home, and the father was pleased to have him under the charge of his older brother.

After he had become editor, and part proprietor of the "Gazette," Harry wrote to Oscar Vincent to announce his promotion. Though Oscar had been in college now nearly two years, and they seldom met, the two were as warm friends as ever, and from time to time exchanged letters.

This was Oscar's reply:—

"HARVARD COLLEGE, June 10.
"DEAR MR. EDITOR: I suppose that's the proper way to address you now. I congratulate you with all my heart on your brilliant success and rapid advancement. Here you are at nineteen, while I am only a rattle-brained sophomore. I don't mind being called that, by the way, for at least it credits me with the possession of brains. Not that I am doing so very badly. I am probably in the first third of the class, and that implies respectable scholarship here.

"But you—I can hardly realize that you, whom I knew only two or three years since as a printer's apprentice (I won't use Fletcher's word), have lifted yourself to the responsible position of sole editor. Truly you have risen from the ranks!

"Speaking of Fletcher, by the way, you know he is my classmate. He occupies an honorable position somewhere near the foot of the class, where he is likely to stay, unless he receives from the faculty leave of absence for an unlimited period. I met him yesterday, swinging his little cane, and looking as dandified as he used to.

"'Hallo! Fletcher,' said I, 'I've just got a letter from a friend of yours.'

"'Who is it?' he asked.

"'Harry Walton.'

"'He never was a friend of mine,' said Fitz, turning up his delicately chiselled nose—'the beggarly printer's devil!'

"I hope you won't feel sensitive about the manner in which Fitz spoke of you.

"'You've made two mistakes,' said I. 'He's neither a beggar nor a printer's devil.'

"'He used to be,' retorted Fitz.

"'The last, not the first. You'll be glad to hear that he's getting on well.'

"'Has he had his wages raised twenty-five cents a week?' sneered Fitz.

"'He has lost his place,' said I.

"Fletcher actually looked happy, but I dashed his happiness by adding, 'but he's got a better one.'

"'What's that?' he snarled.

"'He has bought out the paper of Mr. Anderson, and is now sole editor and part proprietor.'

"'A boy like him buy a paper, without a cent of money and no education!'

"'You are mistaken. He had several hundred dollars, and as a writer he is considerably ahead of either of us.'

"'He'll run the paper into the ground,' said Fitz, prophetically.

"'If he does, it'll only be to give it firmer root.'

"'You are crazy about that country lout,' said Fitz. 'It isn't much to edit a little village paper like that, after all.'

"So you see what your friend Fitz thinks about it. As you may be in danger of having your vanity fed by compliments from other sources, I thought I would offset them by the candid opinion of a disinterested and impartial scholar like Fitz.

"I told my father of the step you have taken. 'Oscar,' said he, 'that boy is going to succeed. He shows the right spirit. I would have given him a place on my paper, but very likely he does better to stay where he is.'

"Perhaps you noticed the handsome notice he gave you in his paper yesterday. I really think he has a higher opinion of your talents than of mine; which, of course, shows singular lack of discrimination. However, you're my friend, and I won't make a fuss about it.

"I am cramming for the summer examinations and hot work I find it, I can tell you. This summer I am going to Niagara, and shall return by way of the St. Lawrence and Montreal, seeing the Thousand Islands, the rapids, and so on.[1] I may send you a letter or two for the 'Gazette,' if you will give me a puff in your editorial columns."

These letters were actually written, and, being very lively and readable, Harry felt quite justified in referring to them in a complimentary way. Fletcher's depreciation of him troubled him very little.

"It will make me neither worse nor better," he reflected. "The time will come, I hope, when I shall have risen high enough to be wholly indifferent to such ill-natured sneers."

His brother arrived in due time, and was set to work as Harry himself had been three years before. He was not as smart as Harry, nor was he ever likely to rise as high; but he worked satisfactorily, and made good progress, so that in six months he was able to relieve Harry of half his labors as compositor. This enabled

---

1 Alger similarly traveled to Niagara Falls and Montreal in the summers of 1858 and 1859 (Gary Scharnhorst with Jack Bales, *The Lost Life of Horatio Alger, Jr.* [Bloomington: Indiana UP, 1985], 40–41).

him to give more time to his editorial duties. Both boarded at Ferguson's, where they had a comfortable home and good, plain fare.

Meanwhile, Harry was acknowledged by all to have improved the paper, and the most satisfactory evidence of the popular approval of his efforts came in an increased subscription list, and this, of course, made the paper more profitable. At the end of twelve months, the two partners had paid off the money borrowed from Professor Henderson, and owned the paper without incumbrance.

"A pretty good year's work, Harry," said Ferguson, cheerfully.

"Yes," said Harry; "but we'll do still better next year."

CHAPTER XXXVI: CONCLUSION

I have thus traced in detail the steps by which Harry Walton ascended from the condition of a poor farmer's son to the influential position of editor of a weekly newspaper. I call to mind now, however, that he is no longer a boy, and his future career will be of less interest to my young readers. Yet I hope they may be interested to hear, though not in detail, by what successive steps he rose still higher in position and influence.

Harry was approaching his twenty-first birthday when he was waited upon by a deputation of citizens from a neighboring town, inviting him to deliver a Fourth of July oration. He was at first disposed, out of modesty, to decline; but, on consultation with Ferguson, decided to accept and do his best. He was ambitious to produce a good impression, and his experience in the Debating Society gave him a moderate degree of confidence and self-reliance. When the time came he fully satisfied public expectation. I do not say that his oration was a model of eloquence, for that could not have been expected of one whose advantages had been limited, and one for whom I have never claimed extraordinary genius. But it certainly was well written and well delivered, and very creditable to the young orator. The favor with which it was received may have had something to do in influencing the people of Centreville to nominate and elect him, to the New Hampshire Legislature a few months later.

He entered that body, the youngest member in it. But his long connection with a Debating Society, and the experience he had gained in parliamentary proceedings, enabled him at once to become a useful working Member. He was successively re-elected for several years, during which he showed such practical ability that he obtained a State reputation. At twenty-eight he received a nomination for Congress, and was elected by a close vote. During all this time he remained in charge of the Centreville "Gazette," but of course had long relinquished the task of a compositor into his brother's hands. He had no foolish ideas about this work being beneath him; but he felt that he could employ his time more profitably in other ways. Under his judicious management, the "Gazette" attained a circulation and influence that it had never before reached. The income derived from it was double that which it yielded in the days of his predecessor; and both he and Ferguson were enabled to lay by a few hundred dollars every year. But Harry had never sought wealth. He was content with a comfortable support and a competence. He liked influence and the popular respect, and he was gratified by the important trusts which he received. He was ambitious, but it was a creditable and honorable ambition. He sought to promote the public welfare, and advance the public interests, both as a speaker and as a writer; and though sometimes misrepresented, the people on the whole did him justice.

A few weeks after he had taken his seat in Congress, a young man was ushered into his private room. Looking up, he saw a man of about his own age, dressed with some attempt at style, but on the whole wearing a look of faded gentility.

"Mr. Walton," said the visitor, with some hesitation.

"That is my name. Won't you take a seat?"

The visitor sat down, but appeared ill at ease. He nervously fumbled at his hat, and did not speak.

"Can I do anything for you?" asked Harry, at length.

"I see you don't know me," said the stranger.

"I can't say I recall your features; but then I see a great many persons."

"I went to school at the Prescott Academy, when you were in the office of the Centreville 'Gazette.'"

Harry looked more closely, and exclaimed, in astonished recognition,

"Fitzgerald Fletcher!"

"Yes," said the other, flushing with mortification, "I am Fitzgerald Fletcher."

"I am glad to see you," said Harry, cordially, forgetting the old antagonism that had existed between them.

He rose and offered his hand, which Fletcher took with an air of relief, for he had felt uncertain of his reception.

"You have prospered wonderfully," said Fletcher, with a shade of envy.

"Yes," said Harry, smiling. "I was a printer's devil when you knew me; but I never meant to stay in that position. I have risen from the ranks."

"I haven't," said Fletcher, bitterly.

"Have you been unfortunate? Tell me about it, if you don't mind," said Harry, sympathetically.

"My father failed three years ago," said Fletcher, "and I found myself adrift with nothing to do, and no money to fall back upon. I have drifted about since then; but now I am out of employment. I came to you to-day to see if you will exert your influence to get me a government clerkship, even of the lowest class. You may rest assured, Mr. Walton, that I need it."

Was this the proud Fitzgerald Fletcher, suing, for the means of supporting himself, to one whom, as a boy, he had despised and looked down upon? Surely, the world is full of strange changes and mutations of fortune. Here was a chance for Harry to triumph over his old enemy; but he never thought of doing it. Instead, he was filled with sympathy for one who, unlike himself, had gone down in the social scale, and he cordially promised to see what he could do for Fletcher, and that without delay.

On inquiry, he found that Fletcher was qualified to discharge the duties of a clerk, and secured his appointment to a clerkship in the Treasury Department, on a salary of twelve hundred dollars a year. It was an income which Fletcher would once have regarded as wholly insufficient for his needs; but adversity had made him humble, and he thankfully accepted it. He holds the position still, discharging the duties satisfactorily. He is glad to claim the Hon. Harry Walton among his acquaintances, and never sneers at him now as a "printer's devil."

Oscar Vincent spent several years abroad, after graduation, acting as foreign correspondent of his father's paper. He is now his father's junior partner, and is not only respected for his ability, but a general favorite in society, on account of his sunny disposition and cordial good nature. He keeps up his intimacy with Harry Walton. Indeed, there is good reason for this, since Harry, four years since, married his sister Maud, and the two friends are brothers-in-law.

Harry's parents are still living, no longer weighed down by poverty, as when we first made their acquaintance. The legacy which came so opportunely improved their condition, and provided them with comforts to which they had long been strangers. But their chief satisfaction comes from Harry's unlooked-for success in life. Their past life of poverty and privation is all forgotten in their gratitude for this great happiness.

Appendix A: Alger on Children and the Novel

[In addition to his fiction for and about juveniles, Alger occasionally discussed the plight of the homeless street children of New York and the cultural work of the novel in ameliorating their condition. Two of the pieces in this appendix—Alger's essays "The Newsboys' Lodging-House" and "The Novel—Its Scope and Place in Literature"—have never been reprinted from their original sources.]

1. "The Newsboys' Lodging-House," *Liberal Christian* (20 April 1867): 6

At the corner of Nassau and Fulton streets stands a building of six stories, the lower part occupied by the daily *Sun*, while the upper two stories are devoted to the Newsboys' Lodging-House. One evening I climbed the narrow winding staircase until I found myself at the door of the school-room. Entering, I found a broad, low room, with about one hundred and fifty newsboys and book-blacks. They were arranged on benches facing a raised platform surrounded by a railing, and were listening with every appearance of attention to an exposition of Scripture. This was the Sunday evening exercise. On other evenings instruction is given in the ordinary English branches.

The boys differed largely in personal appearance. Some were apparently seventeen or eighteen; others not more than six or seven. Their faces were not all clean, nor as may be imagined, was the toilet irreproachable. The garments of many presented a curious mosaic of many-colored patching. Some were clad merely in shirts and pants, with the addition of a fragmentary vest, while in other cases the shirt was wanting. A few were quite decently dressed. But, generally speaking, they were ill and insufficiently clad. But in spite of this external disadvantage, the boys looked bright and intelligent; their faces were marked by a certain sharpness produced by the circumstances of their condition. Thrown upon the world almost in infancy, compelled to depend upon their own energy for a living, there was about them an air of self-reliance and calculation which usually comes much later. But this advantage had been gained at the expense of exposure to temptations of various kinds, and more or less ignorance of books.

After the exercises I was shown the dormitory by the obliging superintendent, Mr. [Charles] O'Connor.[1] This occupies the fifth

---

1   See the Preface to *Ragged Dick*, p. 53, note 2.

story. Here are one hundred and forty neat beds, which must seem luxurious to the weary newsboy, who not unfrequently finds a less comfortable bed in an empty box or old wagon, or on the hard pavement in some arched passage. Indeed, I could sleep upon one of the beds myself without any diminution of my usual comfort. For a night's lodging the charge is but five cents, and the same for a plain meal of coffee and bread, sometimes with soup. But one meal daily is furnished, and that at night. During the day, the young patrons of this establishment can be provided for elsewhere. The charges, of course, are much below what would be required if it was the design to make the institution self-supporting. But for its existence the least sum at which a newsboy could procure a lodging outside, would be twenty-five cents, and that probably in some miserable locality.

There is a newsboys' savings-bank in the school-room, or a table with over a hundred closed boxes appropriated to different boys; through slits in the top they drop such sums as they can spare. In the course of a month this amounts in the aggregate to several hundred dollars. Compartments are also assigned for the custody of such spare clothing as boys may possess, though this is seldom used. Few own a change of underclothing, and the possessor of two suits is regarded as a patrician among these young plebeians.

Opposite the school-room is a room fitted up with a few simple appliances, and used as a gymnasium. This the boys enjoy greatly. "Are they fond of reading?" I asked the superintendent. "Some of them very much so," he answered; "but we have no library to speak of. Some time since Mrs. Astor[1] gave a dozen volumes of the London Illustrated News,[2] and one gentleman gave some Patent Office Reports, but besides these we have little or nothing. Good boys' books they would gladly receive, and read eagerly."

I could not help thinking that some of our Sunday-schools might afford to make up a parcel of books that had been read, no matter if they were worn, and do more good than they imagined, by sending them to this Newsboys' Lodging-House. Will not some of our public-spirited superintendents and teachers take this hint?

The expense of this institution for the last year was $11,000. This year it will probably be more, as the rent has been raised from $1500 to $5300. But the present accommodations are insufficient. Sometimes two hundred boys are crowded into the hundred and forty single beds, and oftentimes even more are provided for somehow.

---

1   Caroline Webster Schermerhorn (1830–1908), the socialite wife of plutocrat William Backhouse Astor (1829–92).

2   The first illustrated newspaper, *The Illustrated London News*, was published from 1842 until 2003.

The doors are kept open until twelve at night. From nine o'clock until that time boys straggle in. Some have invested a portion of their scanty earning in a ticket to the Old Bowery Theatre or Tony Pastor's Minstrels[1] and that has kept them out till a late hour. Some perhaps have been less innocently engaged at low gambling-houses on Baxter street, where they have staked small sums, and perhaps imbibed a villainous mixture of gin which is sold at these places at two cents a glass. One evening a descent was made upon one of these establishments by the police, and over a hundred boys were arrested. That these friendless boys, left very much to their own guidance, should yield to such temptations is not strange. But for the instruction and advice received at the lodging-house more would doubtless go astray and be ruined. We do not wonder that lodging-houses and similar institutions do not save all, but that with their present means they save and help so many. How cheap is virtue; how costly is crime. For one a little money and care discreetly bestowed at the outset; for the other untold suffering, and losses, and expenses for courts and jails, and a ruined man at the end.

Once a fortnight a company of boys start for the West under the auspices of the society, and of these young emigrants an excellent report is often brought back.[2] Doubtless, many street-boys, through the instrumentality of the newsboys' home and the society that maintains it, will grow up intelligent and useful citizens instead of outcasts and criminals.

Let me add that gifts of cast-off boys' clothing of any kind are always acceptable and useful. Perhaps some of the boys who, I hope, will read this article, may have an old cap or other garments which they would like to bestow on some one of these poor boys in the lodging-house, who, without parents, is sturdily fighting the battle of life on his own account.

The success of this establishment should be encouragement to the charitable everywhere to engage in the same great Christian enterprise. Just think what it is to pluck a boy out of the perils and pitfalls of a great city, and save him from a career of vice and crime to one of usefulness and honesty, and you will not hesitate to engage in the great work of practical benevolence.

---

1   See *Ragged Dick*, Chapter 1, p. 55, note 1 and p. 58, note 3.
2   Between 1853 and 1929, under the auspices of the Children's Aid Society, over 150,000 New York children were adopted by families outside the city, transferred to their new homes by so-called "orphan trains." Alger dramatized the experience in his juvenile novel *Julius; or, The Street Boy Out West* (1874).

2. From *Christian Union* (10 May 1883): 368

... I have always held that it is injudicious to write down to the supposed comprehension of children, or to keep them in leading strings too long. An author who shows respect for their intelligence will stand in higher favor with them, and will seldom find that he has overestimated it. When a young boy I applied to a lady for the loan of one of Fredrika Bremer's novels.[1] She was perfectly willing to lend it, and did so, but expressed a doubt as to whether it were not too "old" for me. I silently resented the imputation, feeling my intelligence underrated.

Some children mature mentally much earlier than others. I have known boys of fourteen who could appreciate the Waverley novels,[2] while others would not care for them at eighteen. A thoughtful parent or teacher will not confine a boy or girl to books prepared for children longer than is necessary. The taste for reading ought to be progressive. A young man ought not to be satisfied with the same class of books which he enjoyed as a boy. It will be a sign that he has stood still intellectually. The realm of books opens more widely as we advance in age, and we find ourselves at maturity embarrassed by the wealth of wisdom, wit, and imagination that invites our enjoyment.

The great works which are our most precious legacy from the past should not be abridged or simplified to bring them down to the comprehension of childhood. It is better for the young to wait till their minds are mature enough to enjoy them in their original form.

I do not approve the arbitrary repression of a boy's natural taste. Those who are most ambitious to serve as literary advisers to the young are often most incompetent. Had Sir Walter Scott, instead of being allowed to browse at will in the library where he gathered the store of story and legend of which in after years he made such profitable use, been committed to the tutelage of some such narrow-minded guide, his loss and that of the world would have been incalculable. Books read from the sense of duty seldom benefit. I remember so reading a voluminous history during a college vacation, when I thirsted for something entirely different, and was entitled to it after months of hard study. Instead of being refreshed I was mentally wearied, and gained no advantage from the tiresome chronicle. Children doubtless stand in need of advice, but it should come from one who understands them, since there can be no uniform rule applying to all varieties of taste and temperament.

---

1 Fredrika Bremer (1801–65) was a prominent Swedish writer and feminist.
2 See *Risen from the Ranks*, Chapter IV, p. 207, note 1.

3. "Are My Boys Real?" *Ladies' Home Journal* 7 (November 1890): 29

The idea is suggested that young people will be interested to learn whether the boy characters in my books are taken from real life. I answer in general terms that I have always preferred to introduce real boys into my stories, and have done so in many instances where it has been possible for me to find a character suited to a plot.

The first street boy with whom I became acquainted was Johnny Nolan, a young boot-black, who made daily calls at the office of one of my friends whose office, in 1867, was on Spruce street, on the site now occupied by the "Tribune" building.[1] My conversations with him gave me my first knowledge of New York street-boys and their mode of life. My interest was excited, and led me a few months later to undertake the story of "Ragged Dick," in which Johnny figures. I have described him as he was—a good-natured but lazy boy, without enterprise or ambition. I gave Johnny a copy of the book when it appeared, and he was quite proud of figuring in print. The original of "Micky Maguire" was Paddy Shea, a tough character, who lived not far from the City Hall, and generally passed the summer at "the island." "Ragged Dick" was a real name, but I never knew the boy who bore it.

I met the hero of "Rough and Ready" at the Newsboys' Lodge, in the upper part of the old "Sun" building. "Ben, the Luggage Boy" I met at the same place, and the story of that name substantially accords with his. The boys who made for themselves a home beneath one of the piers were known to Superintendent O'Connor, and he arranged for me an interview with one of them. I had conversations with many street boys while writing "Ragged Dick" and "Tattered Tom" series, and derived from many of them sketches of character and incident.

When I was preparing to write "The District Telegraph Boy," I sent for a boy who had served in that capacity for nearly two years, and used some of the incidents he supplied to me. "Phil the Fiddler" was a real Italian boy. I obtained the picture which appears in the book from a Broadway photographer, to whom he sat for it. Mr. Casali, then editor of an Italian semi-weekly paper in New York,[2] furnished me with many of the incidents.

Some of the characters in "The Young Circus Rider" are still living, in particular Charlie Davis, who left home at an early age and accom-

---

1 See *Ragged Dick*, Chapter II, p. 59, note 1.
2 Giovanni Francesco Secchi de Casali (1818–85), editor of the weekly New York Italian-language newspaper the *L'Eco d'Italia*.

panied a circus to Australia. In "Frank's Campaign," the boys forming the military company commanded by Frank Frost were all real boys, and all, with one exception, are living to-day. The colored boy, little Pomp, in the same story, was intended as a male counterpart to Mrs. Stowe's "Topsy."[1]

I have, by request, given to many of my characters the real names of young friends and acquaintances without necessarily making them portraits. Some of my books and serial stories were suggested in part by incidents in the lives of young persons whom I knew. I am now writing for a juvenile publication a story called "The Erie Train Boy." Fred, the hero, served in that capacity last summer, securing the position through me.

I am often indebted for characters and incidents to paragraphs in the daily press. Whenever I find one that seems available, I follow the example of Charles Reade,[2] and cut it out for future reference. I have probably written seventy-five juvenile books and serials, and I have no hesitation in saying that it would have been quite impossible for me to write half the number if I had not drawn in large part my characters and material from real life. The story of "Joe's Luck," located in California, was written in San Francisco. Years afterwards the name of the book was given to a mine in Southern Africa, of which a picture appeared in the "London Illustrated News." In like manner I went to Chicago in October 1887, to obtain material for a story just published in book-form called "Luke Walton; or, The Chicago Newsboy."

I have, of course, introduced a large number of adult characters in my various stories. Many of these are special studies from life. I hold that a novelist, or writer of fiction, is best situated in a large city, where he has an opportunity to study life in many phases, and come in contact with a large variety of types of character. The experience of prominent American and foreign novelists, notably of Charles Dickens,[3] will bear me out in this statement.

---

1   A young slave girl depicted for comic purpose in *Uncle Tom's Cabin* (1851–52), a best-selling anti-slavery novel by Harriet Beecher Stowe (1811–96).

2   Charles Reade (1814–85) was one of the most popular British novelists of the nineteenth century.

3   Alger was an avid reader of the British novelist Charles Dickens (1812–70). See also Gary Scharnhorst, "Dickens and Horatio Alger, Jr.," *Dickens Quarterly* 2 (June 1985): 50–53.

4. From "The Novel—Its Scope and Place in Literature," *New York Railroad Men* 9 (March 1896): 141–43

... The novel with a purpose ... is perhaps the latest development in the history of the novel. It was not until a recent period that it was discovered how effective a helper the novelist might become to social reform and a broad humanity. Foremost in the list of novels with a mission comes *Uncle Tom's Cabin*. Mrs. Stowe, when she wrote this wonderful novel, probably had a very inadequate idea of the importance of the book and its far reaching effects. That it precipitated the civil war and so led ultimately to the abolition of slavery can hardly admit of a doubt. It has not been given to any other writer to achieve with a single book such wonderful effects. Speeches and editorials by the hundreds had appeared on the same subject, but all the efforts of all the anti-slavery orators sink into insignificance compared with the work of this plain and unassuming woman. Orators appealed to the intellect, she to the heart. She portrayed the cruelties and the infamy of the system of slavery in a way that set the people aflame with indignation. The greatest advance that has been made in the cause of humanity in this age was the work of a woman and a novelist. If *Uncle Tom's Cabin* had been the only novel ever written it would have gained for itself a high place in literature, not as an artistic production, but as a factor in the world's progress.

5. "Writing Stories for Boys," *Writer* 9 (March 1896): 36–37

When I began to write for publication it was far from my expectation that I should devote my life to writing stories for boys. I was ambitious, rather, to write for adults, and for a few years I contributed to such periodicals as *Harper's Magazine*, *Harper's Weekly*, *Putnam's Magazine*, and a variety of literary weeklies. I achieved fair success, but I could see that I had so many competitors that it would take a long time to acquire a reputation. One day I selected a plot for a two-column sketch for the Harpers. It was during the [civil] war. Thinking the matter over, it occurred to me that it would be a good plot for a juvenile book. I sat down at once and wrote to A.K. Loring of Boston,[1] at that time a publisher in only a small way, detailing the plot and asking if he would encourage me to write a juvenile book. He answered: "Go ahead, and if I don't publish it, some other publisher will." In three months I put in his hands the manuscript of "Frank's

---

1   Aaron K. Loring (1836–1911) owned the Boston publishing company that issued most of Alger's juvenile books between 1864 and 1880.

Campaign." This story was well received, but it was not till I removed to New York and wrote "Ragged Dick" that I scored a decided success.

I don't intend to weary the reader with a detailed account of my books and the circumstances under which they were written. It is enough to say that I soon found reason to believe that I was much more likely to achieve success as a writer for boys than as a writer for adults. I therefore confined myself to juvenile writing, and am at present the author of more than sixty boys' stories, besides a considerable number of serials, which may eventually appear in book form.

As may be supposed, I have some idea in regard to the qualifications that are needed in an author who would succeed in this line of work, and will set them down briefly, at the request of the editor of the *Writer*.

A writer for boys should have an abundant sympathy with them. He should be able to enter into their plans, hopes, and aspirations. He should learn to look upon life as they do. Such books as "Sandford and Merton"[1] would no longer achieve success. Boys object to be written down to. Even the Rollo books,[2] popular as they were in their time, do not suit the boys of to-day. A boy's heart opens to the man or writer who understands him. There are teachers and writers who delight to lecture the young. They are provided with a little hoard of maxims preaching down a schoolboy's heart, if I may adapt a well-known line of Tennyson's.[3] Those parents who understand and sympathize with their boys have the strongest hold upon them. I call to mind one writer for boys (he wrote but a single book) whose hero talked like a preacher and was a perfect prig. He seemed to have none of the imperfections of boyhood, and none of the qualities that make boys attractive. Boys soon learn whether a writer understands and sympathizes with them. I have sometimes wondered whether there ever was a boy like Jonas in the Rollo books. If so, I think that while probably an instructive, he must have been a very unpleasant companion for a young boy like Rollo.

A writer for boys should remember his responsibility and exert a wholesome influence on his young readers. Honesty, industry, frugality, and a worthy ambition he can preach through the medium of a story much more effectively than a lecturer or a preacher. I have tried

---

1   *The History of Sandford and Merton* (1789) by Thomas Day (1748–89) was a popular children's book through the mid-nineteenth century.

2   The fourteen Rollo books for juvenile readers by Jacob Abbott (1803–79) were published between 1834 and 1842.

3   Alger adapts the phrase "preaching down a daughter's heart" from "Locksley Hall" (1842) by Alfred, Lord Tennyson (1809–92).

to make my heroes manly boys, bright, cheerful, hopeful, and plucky. Goody-goody boys never win life's prizes. Strong and yet gentle, ready to defend those that are weak, willing to work for their families if called upon to do so, ready to ease the burden that may have fallen upon a widowed mother, or dependent brothers and sisters, such boys are sure to succeed, and deserve success.

It should not be forgotten that boys like adventure. There is no objection to healthy excitement. Sensational stories, such as are found in the dime and half-dime libraries, do much harm, and are very objectionable. Many a boy has been tempted to crime by them. Such stories as "The Boy Highwayman," "The Boy Pirate,"[1] and books of that class, do incalculable mischief. Better that a boy's life should be humdrum than filled with such dangerous excitement.

Some writers have the art of blending instruction with an interesting story. One of the best known—perhaps the best known of juvenile writers—excels in this department.[2] Carrying his boy heroes to foreign lands, he manages to impart a large amount of information respecting them without detracting from the interest of the story. I have never attempted this, because it requires a special gift which I do not possess.

One thing more, and the last I shall mention—a story should be interesting. A young reader will not tolerate dullness. If there are dull passages which he is tempted to skip, he is likely to throw the book aside. The interest should never flag. If a writer finds his own interest in the story he is writing failing, he may be sure that the same effect will be produced on the mind of the reader. It seems to me that no writer should undertake to write for boys who does not feel that he has been called to that particular work. If he finds himself able to entertain and influence boys, he should realize that upon him rests a great responsibility. In the formation period of youth he is able to exert a powerful and salutary influence. The influence of no writer for adults can compare with his. If, as the years pass, he is permitted to see that he has helped even a few of his boy readers to grow into a worthy and noble manhood, he can ask no better reward.

---

1 Alger refers to a pair of blood-and-thunder British novels for boys: *Black Wolf; or, The Boy Highwayman* (1864) and Irving Lyons's *The Boy Pirate; or, Life on the Ocean* (1865).

2 Probably John T. Trowbridge (1827–1916). See "Advice from Horatio Alger, Jr.," *Writer* 6 (January 1892): 16: "My present taste inclines me to prefer the juvenile books of J. T. Trowbridge."

Appendix B: Historical Documents on Children and the Success Myth

1. From Benjamin Franklin, "The Way to Wealth" (1758), in *The Works of Benjamin Franklin*, ed. Jared Sparks (Boston: Gray & Co., 1836), II, 92–103

[In a *tour de force* of the moral maxims he had published in *Poor Richard's Almanac* over the previous quarter-century, Benjamin Franklin (1706–90) composed a type of secular sermon that circulated widely for the next century and became, in effect, an early success manual.]

... I stopped my horse lately where a great number of people were collected at a vendue[1] of merchant goods. The hour of sale not being come, they were conversing on the badness of the times, and one of the company called to a plain clean old man, with white locks, "Pray, Father Abraham, what think you of the times? Won't these heavy taxes quite ruin the country? How shall we be ever able to pay them? What would you advise us to?" Father Abraham stood up, and replied, "If you'd have my advice, I'll give it you in short, for *a word to the wise is enough*, and *many words won't fill a bushel*, as Poor Richard says." They joined in desiring him to speak his mind, and gathering round him, he proceeded as follows: "Friends, says he, and neighbors, the taxes are indeed very heavy, and if those laid on by the government were the only ones we had to pay, we might more easily discharge them; but we have many others, and much more grievous to some of us. We are taxed twice as much by our idleness, three times as much by our pride, and four times as much by our folly, and from these taxes the commissioners cannot ease or deliver us by allowing an abatement. However let us hearken to good advice, and something may be done for us; *God helps them that help themselves*, as Poor Richard says, in his almanac of 1733. "It would be thought a hard government that should tax its people one tenth part of their time, to be employed in its service. But idleness taxes many of us much more, if we reckon all that is spent in absolute sloth, or doing of nothing, with that which is spent in idle employments or amusements, that amount to nothing. Sloth, by bringing on diseases, absolutely shortens life. *Sloth, like rust, consumes faster than labor wears, while the used key is always bright*, as Poor

---

1 A public auction.

Richard says. But *dost thou love life, then do not squander time, for that's the stuff life is made of*, as Poor Richard says. How much more than is necessary do we spend in sleep! forgetting that *the sleeping fox catches no poultry*, and that *there will be sleeping enough in the grave*, as Poor Richard says. If time be of all things the most precious, *wasting time must be*, as Poor Richard says, *the greatest prodigality*, since, as he elsewhere tells us, *lost time is never found again*, and what we call *time-enough, always proves little enough*: let us then be up and be doing, and doing to the purpose; so by diligence shall we do more with less perplexity. *Sloth makes all things difficult, but industry all easy*, as Poor Richard says; and *he that riseth late, must trot all day, and shall scarce overtake his business at night*. While *laziness travels so slowly, that poverty soon overtakes him*, as we read in Poor Richard, who adds, *drive thy business, let not that drive thee*; and *early to bed, and early to rise, makes a man healthy, wealthy and wise*.

"So what signifies wishing and hoping for better times? We may make these times better if we bestir ourselves. *Industry need not wish*, as Poor Richard says, and *he that lives upon hope will die fasting. There are no gains, without pains*, then *help, hands, for I have no lands*, or if I have, they are smartly taxed. And, as Poor Richard likewise observes, *he that hath a trade hath an estate*, and *he that hath a calling hath an office of profit and honor*; but then the trade must be worked at, and the calling well followed, or neither the estate, nor the office, will enable us to pay our taxes. If we are industrious we shall never starve; for, as Poor Richard says, *at the working man's house hunger looks in, but dares not enter*. Nor will the bailiff nor the constable enter, for *industry pays debts, while despair encreaseth them*, says Poor Richard. What though you have found no treasure, nor has any rich relation left you a legacy, *diligence is the mother of good luck*, as Poor Richard says, and *God gives all things to industry*. Then *plough deep, while sluggards sleep, and you shall have corn to sell and to keep*, says Poor Dick. Work while it is called today, for you know not how much you may be hindered tomorrow, which makes Poor Richard say, *one today is worth two tomorrows*; and farther, *have you somewhat to do tomorrow, do it today*. If you were a servant, would you not be ashamed that a good master should catch you idle? Are you then your own master, *be ashamed to catch yourself idle*, as Poor Dick says. When there is so much to be done for yourself, your family, your country, and your gracious king, be up by peep of day; *let not the sun look down and say, inglorious here he lies*. Handle your tools without mittens; remember that *the cat in gloves catches no mice*, as Poor Richard says. 'Tis true there is much to be done, and perhaps you are weak handed, but stick to it steadily, and you will see great effects, for *constant dropping wears away stones*, and *by diligence and patience the mouse ate in two the cable*; and *little strokes fell great oaks*, as Poor Richard says in his almanac, the year I cannot just now remember.

"Methinks I hear some of you say, must a man afford himself no leisure? I will tell thee, my friend, what Poor Richard says, *employ thy time well if thou meanest to gain leisure*; and, *since thou art not sure of a minute, throw not away an hour*. Leisure is time for doing something useful; this leisure the diligent man will obtain, but the lazy man never; so that, as Poor Richard says, *a life of leisure and a life of laziness are two things*. Do you imagine that sloth will afford you more comfort than labor? No, for as Poor Richard says, *trouble springs from idleness, and grievous toil from needless ease. Many without labor would live by their wits only, but they break for want of stock*. Whereas industry gives comfort, and plenty, and respect: *fly pleasures, and they'll follow you. The diligent spinner has a large shift*, and *now I have a sheep and a cow, everybody bids me good morrow*, all which is well said by Poor Richard.

"But with our industry, we must likewise be steady, settled and careful, and oversee our own affairs with our own eyes, and not trust too much to others; for, as Poor Richard says,

> *I never saw an oft removed tree,*
> *Nor yet an oft removed family,*
> *That throve so well as those that settled be.*

"And again, three removes is as bad as a fire, and again, keep the shop, and thy shop will keep thee; and again, if you would have your business done, go; if not, send. And again,

> *He that by the plough would thrive,*
> *Himself must either hold or drive.*

"And again, the *eye of a master will do more work than both his hands*; and again, *want of care does us more damage than want of knowledge*; and again, *not to oversee workmen is to leave them your purse open*. Trusting too much to others' care is the ruin of many; for, as the almanac says, *in the affairs of this world men are saved not by faith, but by the want of it*; but a man's own care is profitable; for, saith Poor Dick, *learning is to the studious*, and *riches to the careful*, as well as *power to the bold*, and Heaven to the virtuous. And farther, *if you would have a faithful servant, and one that you like, serve yourself*. And again, he adviseth to circumspection and care, even in the smallest matters, because sometimes *a little neglect may breed great mischief*; adding, *for want of a nail the shoe was lost; for want of a shoe the horse was lost, and for want of a horse the rider was lost*, being overtaken and slain by the enemy, all for want of care about a horse-shoe nail.

"So much for industry, my friends, and attention to one's own business; but to these we must add frugality, if we would make our industry more certainly successful. A man may, if he knows not how to save as he gets, *keep his nose all his life to the grindstone*, and die not worth a groat at last. *A fat kitchen makes a lean will*, as Poor Richard says; and,

> *Many estates are spent in the getting,*
> *Since women for tea forsook spinning and knitting,*
> *And men for punch forsook hewing and splitting.*

If you would be wealthy, says he, in another almanac, *think of saving as well as of getting: the Indies have not made Spain rich, because her outgoes are greater than her incomes.* Away then with your expensive follies, and you will not have so much cause to complain of hard times, heavy taxes, and chargeable families; for, as Poor Dick says,

> *Women and wine, game and deceit,*
> *Make the wealth small, and the wants great.*

And farther, *what maintains one vice, would bring up two children.* You may think perhaps that a little tea, or a little punch now and then, diet a little more costly, clothes a little finer, and a little entertainment now and then, can be no great Matter; but remember what Poor Richard says, *many a little makes a mickle*, and farther, *beware of little expenses; a small leak will sink a great ship*, and again, *who dainties love, shall beggars prove*, and moreover, *fools make Feasts, and wise men eat them.*

"Here you are all got together at this vendue of fineries and knick-nacks. You call them goods, but if you do not take care, they will prove evils to some of you. You expect they will be sold cheap, and perhaps they may for less than they cost; but if you have no occasion for them, they must be dear to you. Remember what Poor Richard says, *buy what thou hast no need of, and ere long thou shalt sell thy necessaries.* And again, *at a great pennyworth pause a while*: he means, that perhaps the cheapness is apparent only, and not real; or the bargain, by straitning thee in thy business, may do thee more harm than good. For in another place he says, *many have been ruined by buying good penny-worths.* Again, Poor Richard says, *'tis foolish to lay our money in a purchase of repentance*; and yet this folly is practised every day at vendues, for want of minding the almanac. *Wise men*, as Poor Dick says, *learn by others' harms, fools scarcely by their own*, but, *felix quem faciunt aliena pericula cautum.*[1] Many a one, for the sake of finery on the back, have

---

1 From the Latin of Horace (65–8 BCE): "Fortunate are they who learn caution from the risks taken by others."

gone with a hungry belly, and half starved their families; *silks and satins, scarlet and velvets*, as Poor Richard says, *put out the kitchen fire*. These are not the necessaries of life; they can scarcely be called the conveniences, and yet only because they look pretty, how many want to have them. The artificial wants of mankind thus become more numerous than the natural; and, as Poor Dick says, *for one poor person, there are an hundred indigent*. By these, and other extravagancies, the genteel are reduced to poverty, and forced to borrow of those whom they formerly despised, but who through industry and frugality have maintained their standing; in which case it appears plainly, that *a ploughman on his legs is higher than a gentleman on his knees*, as Poor Richard says. Perhaps they have had a small estate left them, which they knew not the getting of; they think *'tis day, and will never be night*; that a little to be spent out of so much, is not worth minding; (*a child and a fool*, as Poor Richard says, *imagine twenty shillings and twenty years can never be spent*) but, *always taking out of the meal-tub, and never putting in, soon comes to the bottom*; then, as Poor Dick says, *when the well's dry, they know the worth of water*. But this they might have known before, if they had taken his advice; *if you would know the value of money, go and try to borrow some*, for, *he that goes a borrowing goes a sorrowing*, and indeed so does he that lends to such people, when he goes to get it in again. Poor Dick farther advises, and says,

> Fond pride of dress, is sure a very curse;
> E'er fancy you consult, consult your purse.

And again, *pride is as loud a beggar as want, and a great deal more saucy*. When you have bought one fine thing you must buy ten more, that your appearance may be all of a piece; but Poor Dick says, *'tis easier to suppress the first desire than to satisfy all that follow it*. And 'tis as truly folly for the poor to ape the rich, as for the frog to swell, in order to equal the ox.

> Great estates may venture more,
> But little boats should keep near shore.

'Tis however a folly soon punished; for *pride that dines on vanity sups on contempt*, as Poor Richard says. And in another place, *pride breakfasted with plenty, dined with poverty, and supped with infamy*. And after all, of what use is this pride of appearance, for which so much is risked, so much is suffered? It cannot promote health; or ease pain; it makes no increase of merit in the person, it creates envy, it hastens misfortune.

What is a butterfly? At best
He's but a caterpillar dressed. .
The gaudy fop's his picture just,

as Poor Richard says.

"But what madness must it be to run in debt for these super-fluities! We are offered, by the terms of this vendue, six months' credit; and that perhaps has induced some of us to attend it, because we cannot spare the ready money, and hope now to be fine without it. But, ah, think what you do when you run in debt; *you give to another power over your liberty.* If you cannot pay at the time, you will be ashamed to see your creditor; you will be in fear when you speak to him, you will make poor pitiful sneaking excuses, and by degrees come to lose you veracity, and sink into base downright lying; for, as Poor Richard says, *the second vice is lying, the first is running in debt.* And again to the same purpose, *lying rides upon debt's back.* Whereas a freeborn Englishman ought not to be ashamed or afraid to see or speak to any man living. But poverty often deprives a man of all spirit and virtue: *'tis hard for an empty bag to stand upright,* as Poor Richard truly says. What would you think of that Prince, or that government, who should issue an edict forbidding you to dress like a gentleman or a gentlewoman, on pain of imprisonment or servitude? Would you not say, that you are free, have a right to dress as you please, and that such an edict would be a breach of your privileges, and such a gov-ernment tyrannical? And yet you are about to put yourself under that tyranny when you run in debt for such dress! Your creditor has authority at his pleasure to deprive you of your liberty, by confining you in gaol for life, or to sell you for a servant, if you should not be able to pay him! When you have got your bargain, you may, perhaps, think little of payment; but *creditors,* Poor Richard tells us, *have better memories than debtors,* and in another place says, *creditors are a super-stitious sect, great observers of set days and times.* The day comes round before you are aware, and the demand is made before you are pre-pared to satisfy it. Or if you bear your debt in mind, the term which at first seemed so long, will, as it lessens, appear extremely short. Time will seem to have added wings to his heels as well as shoulders. *Those have a short Lent,* saith Poor Richard, *who owe money to be paid at Easter.* Then since, as he says, *the borrower is a slave to the lender, and the debtor to the creditor,* disdain the chain, preserve your freedom; and maintain your independency: be industrious and free; be frugal and free. At present, perhaps, you may think yourself in thriving cir-cumstances, and that you can bear a little extravagance without injury; but,

For age and want, save while you may;
No morning sun lasts a whole day,

as Poor Richard says. Gain may be temporary and uncertain, but ever while you live, expense is constant and certain; and *'tis easier to build two chimneys than to keep one in fuel*, as Poor Richard says. So *rather go to bed supperless than rise in debt.*

Get what you can, and what you get, hold;
'Tis the stone that will turn all your lead into gold,

as Poor Richard says. And when you have got the philosopher's stone, sure you will no longer complain of bad times, or the difficulty of paying taxes. "This doctrine, my friends, is reason and wisdom; but after all, do not depend too much upon your own industry, and frugality, and prudence, though excellent things, for they may all be blasted without the blessing of heaven; and therefore ask that blessing humbly, and be not uncharitable to those that at present seem to want it, but comfort and help them. Remember Job suffered, and was afterwards prosperous.

"And now to conclude, *experience keeps a dear school, but fools will learn in no other, and scarce in that, for it is true, we may give advice, but we cannot give conduct*, as Poor Richard says: however, remember this, *they that won't be counseled, can't be helped*, as Poor Richard says: and farther, that *if you will not hear reason, she'll surely rap your knuckles.*" Thus the old gentleman ended his harangue. The people heard it, and approved the doctrine, and immediately practiced the contrary, just as if it had been a common sermon....

2. Mark Twain, "The Bootblacks," *Alta California* [San Francisco] (14 July 1867): 1

[During his months as the New York correspondent of the *Alta California* in early 1867, Mark Twain (Samuel Langhorne Clemens, 1835–1910) apparently visited the Newsboys' Lodging House in the *Sun* Building on Fulton Street, here renamed as "the Boot-Black Brigade Chapel."]

Sometimes, down about the City Hall Park, it does seem to me that every little ragamuffin in New York has bought a brush and a foot-box, and gone in the boot-blacking business. "Blackin', sir, blackin'!" "Shine, sir?—nice shine, sir, only five cents!" So they assail a man at every step, and persecute him from the rising of the sun till the going down thereof. If you give one of them a job, half a dozen of them will crowd around and sit on the ground to see it done and criticise it; and to blackguard each other in a slang that no Christian can understand; and make remarks about the sensation of the day; and speak familiarly and disrespectfully of the gentlemen of the City Government, and abuse their stupidity; and drop critiques concerning "the Japs," discuss the leaders in the Herald, the Tribune and Times, and even find fault with Mr. Seward's statesmanship, and the general conduct of the National Government. I notice that they usually speak of great personages as "old" Seward,[1] "old" Johnson,[2] etc. It is because these free-souled young blackguards scorn to be respectful to anything or anybody. After they have got through discussing the new Russian Possessions purchase,[3] they fall to pitching pennies and engaging in other disreputable species of gambling, and combine business with it as before, in the matter of persecuting passers-by.

I saw a sign on a house in an obscure street, yesterday, which read, "Boot-Black Brigade Chapel," and found out that some well meaning enthusiast is in the habit of drumming a lot of these gamins de [kids of] New York together two or three times a week, and preaching to them and praying for them, under the extraordinary impression that he can save their souls. I certainly wish him well, but I bet nothing on his success.

I went in, and found a preacher earnestly exhorting about two hundred of the rattiest lot of little outlaws that any city can produce. Most of the time they listened pretty intently, but critically—always critically, for behold, the bootblack is nothing if not critical. Part of what the preacher said they seemed to receive as square and proper enough, and part they seemed to receive under mild protest—but when he said that Lazarus was brought to life after he had been dead three days, there was a pretty general telegraphing of incredulity from eye to eye about the assemblage, and one boy with a shock head and rags all over to match nudged his neighbor, and said in a coarse whisper, "I don't go that, Bill, do you?—'cause he'd stink, wouldn't he?" And when the preacher told how the five thousand were miraculously fed with twelve loaves and several little fishes, a boy said:

"Say, Jimmy, do you suck that?"

---

1   William H. Seward (1801–72), US secretary of state from 1861 to 1869.
2   Andrew Johnson (1808–75), president of the United States from 1865 to 1869.
3   The Russian Possessions in North America—i.e., Alaska—finalized on 30 March 1867.

"Well, I do'no. It mought a ben, mebbe, if they warn't many of 'em hongry. I see the time, though, when I could a et them twelve loaves myself, I could, less'n they was busters."

And so they criticised all the while, and cast disrepute upon every statement that seemed a little shaky to them, and the longer I staid the less confidence I had in the speculation of trying to get material for salvation out of the bootblack brigade.

I attended the Old Bowery Theatre in the evening, and there, in the pit, I found the whole tribe. I suppose there were three hundred of them present, closely packed together in their rags and dirt, and the way they guyed the actors and criticised the performance was interesting. They applauded all the "ranting" passages furiously, and hurled uncompromising scorn and contempt upon the sentimental ones.

I asked one of them what he thought of the leading man as an actor?

"Oh, he ain't no force. You'd ought to hear Proctor—Oh, geeminy! —why, you can hear Proctor[1] f'm here to Central Park when he lays hisself out in Richard Third."[2]

Up in the fifth tier—the gallery—there was a multitude of negroes, and a sprinkling of bootblacks and women of the town. There was a bar up there, and two of the women came forward and asked us to treat. A bootblack, who had just blacked my boots and perhaps felt a personal interest in my welfare on that account, tipped at me a wink of wonderful complexity and mystery, and I went and asked him to translate it. He said:

"You keep away f'm them women. I've been around here four years, and I know all about 'em. Don't you go no wheres with that curly-headed one, nor 'tother one either—they'd go through you for everything you've got. That's their style. You ask any cop (policeman,)—they'll tell you. Why, that curly girl's rid in the Black Maria (conveyance for prisoners) oftener'n she's rid in the street cars. And don't you touch that liquor in there—don't tell anybody I told you, 'cause they'd highst me out of this, you know—but don't you drink that dern swipes—it's pi'son."

I thanked the philosopher for his advice, and followed it. The bootblacks and newsboys, who did not happen to be present at the play, were all outside in front of the theatre, I think. There were dozens of them—all holding out their hands for checks, when we started home between the acts. We delivered up ours, and a noisy, struggling scramble ensued for their possession. They are a wild, lawless, independent

---

1 Joseph Proctor (1816–97), a popular nineteenth-century American actor.
2 Shakespeare's *The Tragedy of King Richard the Third*, written c. 1592.

lot, those bootblacks and street boys, and would make good desperado stuff to stock a new mining camp with.

3. Mark Twain, "The Late Benjamin Franklin," *Galaxy* 10 (July 1870): 138–40

[Twain was raised on the moral maxims of Franklin. He visited Franklin's grave during his first trip to Philadelphia in 1853, and he delivered his first public speech in 1856 at a printers' banquet in Keokuk, Iowa, to celebrate the sesquicentennial of Franklin's birth. Fourteen years later, however, Twain famously lampooned the influence of Franklin on the American cult of success.]

[Never put off til to-morrow what you can do day after to-morrow just as well.—B.F.]

This party was one of those persons whom they call Philosophers. He was twins, being born simultaneously in two different houses in the city of Boston. These houses remain unto this day, and have signs upon them worded in accordance with the facts. The signs are considered well enough to have, though not necessary, because the inhabitants point out the two birth-places to the stranger anyhow, and sometimes as often as several times in the same day. The subject of this memoir was of a vicious disposition, and early prostituted his talents to the invention of maxims and aphorisms calculated to inflict suffering upon the rising generation of all subsequent ages. His simplest acts, also, were contrived with a view to their being held up for the emulation of boys forever—boys who might otherwise have been happy. It was in this spirit that he became the son of a soap-boiler; and probably for no other reason than that the efforts of all future boys who tried to be anything might be looked upon with suspicion unless they were the sons of soap-boilers. With a malevolence which is without parallel in history, he would work all day and then sit up nights and let on to be studying algebra by the light of a smouldering fire, so that all other boys might have to do that also or else have Benjamin Franklin thrown up to them. Not satisfied with these proceedings, he had a fashion of living wholly on bread and water, and studying astronomy at meal time—a thing which has brought affliction to millions of boys since, whose fathers had read Franklin's pernicious biography.

His maxims were full of animosity toward boys. Nowadays a boy cannot follow out a single natural instinct without tumbling over some of those everlasting aphorisms and hearing from Franklin on the spot. If he buys two cents worth of peanuts, his father says, "Remember what Franklin has said, my son,—'A groat a day's a penny a year'"; and the comfort is all gone out of those peanuts. If he wants to spin his top when he is done work, his father quotes, "Procrastination is the thief of time." If he does a virtuous action, he never gets anything for it, because "Virtue is its own reward." And that boy is hounded to death and robbed of his natural rest, because Franklin said once in one of his inspired flights of malignity—

Early to bed and early to rise
Make a man healthy and wealthy and wise.

As if it were any object to a boy to be healthy and wealthy and wise on such terms. The sorrow that that maxim has cost me through my parents' experimenting on me with it, tongue cannot tell. The legitimate result is my present state of general debility, indigence, and mental aberration. My parents used to have me up before nine o'clock in the morning, sometimes, when I was a boy. If they had let me take my natural rest, where would I have been now? Keeping store, no doubt, and respected by all.

And what an adroit old adventurer the subject of this memoir was! In order to get a chance to fly his kite on Sunday, he used to hang a key on the string and let on to be fishing for lightning. And a guileless public would go home chirping about the "wisdom" and the "genius" of the hoary Sabbath-breaker. If anybody caught him playing "mumble-peg" by himself, after the age of sixty, he would immediately appear to be ciphering out how the grass grew—as if it was any of his business. My grandfather knew him well, and he says Franklin was always fixed— always ready. If a body, during his old age, happened on him unexpectedly when he was catching flies, or making mud pies, or sliding on a cellar-door, he would immediately look wise, and rip out a maxim, and walk off with his nose in the air and his cap turned wrong side before, trying to appear absent-minded and eccentric. He was a hard lot.

He invented a stove that would smoke your head off in four hours by the clock. One can see the almost devilish satisfaction he took in it, by his giving it his name.

He was always proud of telling how he entered Philadelphia, for the first time, with nothing in the world but two shillings in his pocket and four rolls of bread under his arm. But really, when you come to examine it critically, it was nothing. Anybody could have done it.

To the subject of this memoir belongs the honor of recommending the army to go back to bows and arrows in place of bayonets and muskets. He observed, with his customary force, that the bayonet was very well, under some circumstances, but that he doubted whether it could be used with accuracy at long range.

Benjamin Franklin did a great many notable things for his country, and made her young name to be honored in many lands as the mother of such a son. It is not the idea of this memoir to ignore that or cover it up. No; the simple idea of it is to snub those pretentious maxims of his, which he worked up with a great show of originality out of truisms that had become wearisome platitudes as early as the dispersion from Babel; and also to snub his stove, and his military inspirations, his unseemly endeavor to make himself conspicuous when he entered Philadelphia, and his flying his kite and fooling away his time in all sorts of such ways, when he ought have been foraging for soap-fat, or constructing candles. I merely desired to do away with somewhat of the prevalent calamitous idea among heads of families that Franklin *acquired* his great genius by working for nothing, studying by moonlight, and getting up in the night instead of waiting til morning like a Christian, and that this programme, rigidly inflicted, will make a Franklin of every father's fool. It is time these gentlemen were finding out that these execrable eccentricities of instinct and conduct are only the *evidences* of genius, not the *creators* of it. I wish I had been the father of my parents long enough to make them comprehend this truth, and thus prepare them to let their son have an easier time of it. When I was a child I had to boil soap, notwithstanding my father was wealthy, and I had to get up early and study geometry at breakfast, and peddle my own poetry, and do everything just as Franklin did, in the solemn hope that I would be a Franklin someday. And here I am.

4. From Charles Loring Brace, *The Dangerous Classes of New York* (New York: Wynkoop & Hellenbeck, 1872), 97–108

[In 1852 the philanthropist Charles Loring Brace (1826–90) founded the Children's Aid Society, which sponsored lodging houses, schools, clinics, and the so-called "orphan trains" that enabled New York City orphans to immigrate west. Brace reminisced in his autobiography about the charitable work of the Newsboys' Lodging-House, which he established in 1854.]

There seemed to be a very considerable class of lads in New York who bore to the busy, wealthy world about them something of the same relation which Indians bear to the civilized Western settlers. They had no settled home, and lived on the outskirts of society, their hand against every man's pocket, and every man looking on them as natural enemies; their wits sharpened like those of a savage, and their principles often no better. Christianity reared its temples over them, and Civilization was carrying on its great work, while they—a happy race of little heathens and barbarians—plundered, or frolicked, or led their roving life, far beneath. Sometimes they seemed to me, like what the police call them, "street-rats," who gnawed at the foundations of society, and scampered away when light was brought near them. Their life was, of course, a painfully hard one. To sleep in boxes, or under stairways, or in hay-barges on the coldest winter-nights, for a mere child, was hard enough; but often to have no food, to be kicked and cuffed by the older ruffians, and shoved about by the police, standing barefooted and in rags under doorways as the winter-storm raged, and to know that in all the great city there was not a single door open with welcome to the little rover—this was harder.

Yet, with all this, a more light-hearted youngster than the street-boy is not to be found. He is always ready to make fun of his own sufferings, and to "chaff" others. His face is old from exposure and his sharp "struggle for existence"; his clothes flutter in the breeze; and his bare feet peep out from the broken boots. Yet he is merry as a clown, and always ready for the smallest joke, and quick to take "a point" or to return a repartee. His views of life are mainly derived from the more mature opinions of "flash-men," engine-runners, cock-fighters, pugilists, and pickpockets, whom he occasionally is permitted to look upon with admiration at some select pot-house; while his more ideal pictures of the world about him, and, his literary education, come from the low theatres, to which he is passionately attached. His morals are, of course, not of a high order, living, as he does, in a fighting, swearing, stealing, and gambling set. Yet he has his code; he will not get drunk; he pays his debts to other boys, and thinks it dishonorable to sell papers on their beat, and, if they come on his, he administers summary justice by "punching"; he is generous to a fault, and will always divide his last sixpence with a poorer boy. "Life is a strife" with him, and money its reward; and, as bankruptcy means to the street-boy a night on the door-steps without supper, he is sharp and reckless, if he can only earn or get enough to keep him above water. His temptations are, to cheat, steal, and lie. His religion is vague. One boy, who told me he "didn't live nowhere," who had never heard of Christ, said he had heard of God, and the boys thought it "kind o' lucky" to say over something to Him which one of them had learned, when they were sleeping out in boxes.

With all their other vices, it is remarkable how few of these smaller street-boys ever take liquor. And their kindness to one another, when all are in the utmost destitution, is a credit to human nature.

Their money is unfortunately apt to slip away, especially for gambling and petty lotteries, called "policy-tickets." A tradition in the remote past of some boy who drew a hundred dollars in these lotteries still pervades the whole body, and they annually sink a considerable portion of their hard-earned pennies in "policy-tickets."

The choice of these lads of a night's resting-place is sometimes almost as remarkable as was Gavroche's in "Les Misérables."[1] Two little newsboys slept one winter in the iron tube of the bridge at Harlem; two others made their bed in a burned-out safe in Wall Street. Sometimes they ensconced themselves in the cabin of a ferry-boat, and thus spent the night. Old boilers, barges, steps, and, above all, steam-gratings, were their favorite beds.

In those days the writer would frequently see ten or a dozen of them, piled together to keep one another warm, under the stairs of the printing-offices.

In planning the alleviation of these evils, it was necessary to keep in view one object, not to weaken the best quality of this class—their sturdy independence—and, at the same time, their prejudices and habits were not too suddenly to be assailed. They had a peculiar dread of Sunday Schools and religious exhortations—I think partly because of the general creed of their older associates, but more for fear that these exercises were a "pious dodge" for trapping them into the House of Refuge or some place of detention.[2]

The first thing to be aimed at in the plan was, to treat the lads as independent little dealers, and give them nothing without payment, but at the same time to offer them much more for their money than they could get anywhere else. Moral, educational, and religious influences were to come in afterward. Securing them through their interests, we had a permanent hold of them.

Efforts were made by the writer among our influential citizens and in various churches, public meetings were held, articles written, the press interested, and at length sufficient money was pledged to make the experiment. The board of the new Society gave its approval, and a loft was secured in the old "Sun Buildings," and fitted up as a lodging-room, and in March, 1854, the first Lodging-house for street-boys or newsboys in this country was opened.

An excellent superintendent was found in the person of a carpenter, Mr. C. C. Tracy,[3] who showed remarkable ingenuity and tact in the management of these wild lads. These little subjects regarded the first arrangements with some suspicion and much contempt. To find a good bed offered them for six cents, with a bath thrown in, and a

---

1 The gamin or street urchin Gavroche is a character in the historical novel *Les Misérables* (1862) by Victor Hugo (1802–85).

2 Houses of Refuge were early reform schools for detaining and disciplining juvenile delinquents.

3 Charles O'Connor's predecessor as superintendent of the Newsboys' Lodging House; he later served as the emigration agent or manager of the orphan trains to the West sponsored by the Children's Aid Society.

supper for four cents, was a hard fact, which they could rest upon and understand; but the motive was evidently "gaseous." There was "no money in it"—that was clear. The Superintendent was probably "a street preacher," and this was a trap to get them to Sunday Schools, and so prepare them for the House of Refuge. Still, they might have a lark there, and it could be no worse than "bumming," i.e., sleeping out. They laid their plans for a general scrimmage in the school-room—first cutting off the gas, and then a row in the bedroom.

The Superintendent, however, in a bland and benevolent way, nipped their plans in the bud. The gas-pipes were guarded; the rough ring-leaders were politely dismissed to the lower door, where an officer looked after their welfare; and, when the first boots began to fly from a little fellow's bed, he found himself suddenly snaked out by a gentle but muscular hand, and left in the cold to shiver over his folly. The others began to feel that a mysterious authority was getting even with them, and thought it better to nestle in their warm beds.

Little sleeping, however, was there among them that night; but ejaculations sounded out—such as, "I say, Jim, this is rayther better 'an bummin'—eh?" "My eyes! what soft beds these is!" "Tom! it's 'most as good as a steam-gratin', and there ain't no M.P.'s[1] to poke neither!" "I'm glad I ain't a bummer to-night!"

A good wash and a breakfast sent the lodgers forth in the morning, happier and cleaner, if not better, than when they went in. This night's success established its popularity with the newsboys. The "Fulton Lodge" soon became a boys' hotel, and one loft was known among them as the "Astor House."

Quietly and judiciously did Mr. Tracy advance his lines among them.

"Boys," said he, one morning, "there was a gentleman here this morning, who wanted a boy in an office, at three dollars a week."

"My eyes! Let—me—go, sir!" and—"Me,—sir!"

"But he wanted a boy who could write a good hand."

Their countenances fell.

"Well, now, suppose we have a night-school, and learn to write—what do you say, boys?"

"Agreed, sir."

And so arose our evening-school.

The Sunday Meeting, which is now an "institution," was entered upon in a similarly discreet manner. The lads had been impressed by a public funeral, and Mr. Tracy suggested their listening to a little reading from the Bible. They consented, and were a good deal sur-

---

1   Member of the Police.

prised at what they heard. The "Golden Rule"[1] struck them as an altogether impossible kind of precept to obey, especially when one was "stuck and short," and "had to live." The marvels of the Bible—the stories of miracles and the like—always seemed to them natural and proper. That a Being of such a character as Christ should control Nature and disease, was appropriate to their minds. And it was a kind of comfort to these young vagabonds that the Son of God was so often homeless, and that he belonged humanly to the working classes. The petition for "daily bread" (which a celebrated divine has declared "unsuited to modern conditions of civilization") they always rolled out with a peculiar unction. I think that the conception of a Superior Being, who knew just the sort of privations and temptations that followed them, and who felt especially for the poorer classes, who was always near them, and pleased at true manhood in them, did keep afterward a considerable number of them from lying and stealing and cheating and vile pleasures.

Their singing was generally prepared for by taking off their coats and rolling up their sleeves, and was entered into with a gusto.

The voices seemed sometimes to come from a different part of their natures from what we saw with the bodily eyes. There was, now and then, a gentle and minor key, as if a glimpse of something purer and higher passed through these rough lads. A favorite song was, "There's a Rest for the Weary," though more untiring youngsters than these never frisked over the earth; and "There's a Light in the Window for Thee, Brother,"[2] always pleased them, as if they imagined themselves wandering alone through a great city at night, and at length a friendly light shone in the window for them.

Their especial vice of money-wasting the Superintendent broke up by opening a Savings-bank, and allowing the boys to vote how long it should be closed. The small daily deposits accumulated to such a degree that the opening gave them a great surprise at the amounts which they possessed, and they began to feel thus the "sense of property," and the desire of accumulation, which economists tell us, is the base of all civilization. A liberal interest was also soon allowed on deposits, which stimulated the good habit. At present, from two hundred to three hundred dollars will often be saved by the lads in a month.

The same device, and constant instruction, broke up gambling, though I think policy-tickets were never fairly undermined among them.

---

1   See Matthew 7:12 and Luke 6:31: "Do unto others as you have them do unto you."

2   Brace quotes verses from two traditional Christian hymns.

The present Superintendent and Matron of the Newsboys' Lodging-house, Mr. and Mrs. O'Connor (at Nos. 49 and 51 Park Place), are unsurpassed in such institutions in their discipline, order, good management, and excellent housekeeping. The floors, over which two hundred or two hundred and fifty street-boys tread daily, are as clean as a man-of-war's deck. The Sunday-evening meetings are as attentive and orderly as a church, the week-evening school quiet and studious. All that mass of wild young humanity is kept in perfect order, and brought under a thousand good influences.

The Superintendent has had a very good preliminary experience for this work in the military service—having been in the British army in the Crimea.[1] The discipline which he maintains is excellent. He is a man, too, of remarkable generosity of feeling, and a good "provider." One always knows that his boys will have enough to eat, and that everything will be managed liberally—and justly. It is truly remarkable during how many years he controlled that great multitude of little vagabonds and "roughs," and yet with scarcely ever even a complaint from any source against him. For such success is needed the utmost kindness, and, at the same time, the strictest justice. His wife has been almost like a mother to the boys.

In the course of a year the population of a town passes through the Lodging-house—in 1869 and '70, *eight thousand eight hundred and thirty-five* different boys. Many are put in good homes; some find places for themselves; others drift away—no one knows whither. They are an army of orphans—regiments of children who have not a home or friend—a multitude of little street-rovers who have no place where to lay their heads. They are being educated in the streets rapidly to be thieves and burglars and criminals. The Lodging-house is at once school, church, intelligence-office, and hotel for them. Here they are shaped to be honest and industrious citizens; here taught economy, good order, cleanliness, and morality; here Religion brings its powerful influences to bear upon them; and they are sent forth to begin courses of honest livelihood.

The Lodging-houses repay their expenses to the public ten times over each year, in preventing the growth of thieves and criminals. They are agencies of pure humanity and almost unmingled good. Their only possible reproach could be, that some of their wild subjects are soon beyond their reach, and have been too deeply tainted with the vices of street-life to be touched even by kindness, education, or religion. The number [*sic*] who are saved, however, are most encouragingly large.

---

1 In the Crimean War (October 1853–March 1856), a military alliance of Great Britain, France, and the Ottoman Empire defeated Russia.

The Newsboys' Lodging-house is by no means, however, an entire burden on the charity of the community. During 1870 the lads themselves paid $3,349 toward its expense.

The following is a brief description of the rooms during the past five years:

The first floor is divided into various compartments—a large dining-room, where one hundred and fifty boys can sit down to a table; a kitchen, laundry, storeroom, servants' room, and rooms for the family of the superintendent. The next story is partitioned into a school-room, gymnasium, and bath and wash rooms, plentifully supplied with hot and cold water. The hot water and the heat of the rooms are supplied by a steam-boiler on the lower story. The two upper stories are filled with neat iron bedsteads, having two beds each, arranged like ships' bunks over each other; of these there are two hundred and sixty. Here are also the water-vats, into which the many barrelsful used daily are pumped by the engine. The rooms are high and dry, and the floors clean.

It is a commentary on the housekeeping and accommodations that for eighteen years no case of contagious disease has ever occurred among these thousands of boys.

The New York Newsboys' Lodging-house has been in existence eighteen years. During these years it has lodged 91,326 different boys, restored 7,278 boys to friends, provided 5,126 with homes, furnished 576,485 lodgings and 469,461 meals. The expense of all this has been $132,888. Of this amount the boys have contributed $32,306.

Appendix C: Contemporary Reviews

[The first editions of *Ragged Dick* and its sequel *Fame and Fortune* were mostly advertised in the metropolitan dailies of New York and Boston, cities with large post–Civil War populations of homeless children. Alger doubtless took a hand in preparing these newspaper ads, particularly the one in the *Boston Transcript* for 8 December 1868.]

1. Advertisements

a. *New York Evening Post* (6 May 1868): 2

BOOK NOTICES.

GOOD NEWS FOR THE BOYS.

RAGGED DICK;

OR, STREET LIFE IN NEW YORK WITH THE BOOTBLACKS,

By Horatio Alger, Jr., is for sale this morning.

It is the best book for boys written.

As a serial in THE SCHOOLMATE it attracted great attention, and now it has been rewritten, revised and added to.

With its characteristic illustrations and pretty binding, it will attract a host of buyers and readers.

Price $1 25, at all the Bookstores.

LORING, Publisher, Boston.

b. *Boston Journal* (6 August 1868): 3

d. *Boston Transcript* (8 December 1868): 3

RAGGED DICK,
FAME AND FORTUNE,

are having an enormous popularity and sale in every great city. Sunday evening, at the News-Boys' Lodging House, after the service the boys rushed up to the author, asking all sorts of questions about the new book. When I showed them the picture of Micky Maguire passing the cigar-stump to Gilbert, there was a chorus of ejaculations: "He's got the cheek!" &c. Among the foremost boys was JOHNNY NOLAN, who wanted to know if I had got his name in the book all right.

If the outside world enjoy this book half as much as the newsboys and bootblacks, thousands of copies will be sold, which will delight

LORING, Publisher.

1t   d 8

---

e. *Boston Transcript* (9 December 1868): 3

RAGGED DICK

is the story of a little, keen, wide-awake, grotesquely-dressed New York Bootblack, whose singing "Shine yer Boots, Sir," arrested the attention of every passer-by on Broadway just below the Astor House. He was "a diamond in the rough"—energetic and successful, squandering his earnings, sleeping in empty boxes or secluded doorways, humorous and possessed of a noble nature, a type of a host of newsboys and bootblacks found in every great city. A few kind words, a generous act from a stranger, roused in him the ambition to rise in the world and be a man. How step by step this was accomplished is told, as only HORATIO ALGER, JR., the author, can do it; and at the end of the book we take leave of "Raged Dick" and open with delight the new volume,

FAME AND FORTUNE,
Or, the Progress of Richard Hunter.

How Richard deported himself in his new position; what drawbacks he experienced from his old associations; how he steadily overcame all these obstacles and rose in due time, with hard labor, to be the junior partner in the large firm of Rockwell & Hunter, Pearl street, New York, is told in the most satisfactory manner.

TWO NOBLER BOOKS ARE NOT WRITTEN. They are rendering a great good, and philanthropic individuals are putting them into the hands of the newsboys and bootblacks in New York and other large cities, and causing them to be read aloud in many of our reformatory schools, as inspiring examples of what energy, ambition and an honest purpose may achieve

No one, young or old, will fail to have the greatest delight in reading them, and their influence on boys however positioned in life, will be most beneficial.

If the outside world enjoy these books half as muc as the newsboys and bootblacks, thousands of copie will be sold, which will delight

LORING, Publisher.

1t   d 9

[The thirteen contemporary notices of *Ragged Dick* and twelve notices of *Risen from the Ranks* listed below are the largest sheaf of reviews of the novels ever compiled and underscore the moral purpose of the stories.]

2. Contemporary Reviews of *Ragged Dick*

a. *Providence Press* (11 May 1868): 1

Mr. Alger has projected a "Ragged Dick" series, and an intensely interesting volume is this first installment. If the succeeding volumes are up to the standard of this, the series will be a perfect success. This is simply charming, and we read every word of it. We were so carried away with Dick and his triumphs,—which were the triumphs of *honesty* and *pluck*,—that we forgot all about our pencil and notes. Mr. Alger is a sweet writer, has a good heart behind his pen and will win the love of the lads and lasses, who will and *must* read "Ragged Dick." Loring has given the story a handsome dress.

b. *Salem Register* (11 May 1868): 2

This is the story which excited so wide-spread an interest as it was passing through the pages of that excellent youth's magazine, The Schoolmate. It is one of the brightest and sprightliest juveniles of the season and has made Ragged Dick a universal favorite. A more enter-taining volume it would be difficult to find. Several of the characters are sketched from life and not a few of the facts made use of were obtained from the Superintendent of the Newsboys' Lodging House in Fulton street, N.Y. We hope that Ragged Dick's career will not induce all our young friends to wish themselves boot-blacks in New York, but they might adopt his good principles and determination to make an honest, intelligent, and respectable man of himself, to very great advantage. The little boot-black is now on the road to fame and fortune, and Mr. Alger intends to complete his Ragged Dick Series in six volumes, which will be highly acceptable, if they are all as good as the first two.

c. "A Lively Boy's Book," *Boston Traveller* (13 May 1868): 1

"Ragged Dick" is the story of a lively boy, and a book for lively boys. It is one of the most wide-awake, comical and at the same time instructive and entertaining books that has been issued for young folks in some time. A.K. Loring is the publisher, and his publications are always good. It is a neatly bound volume of 296 pages, and several

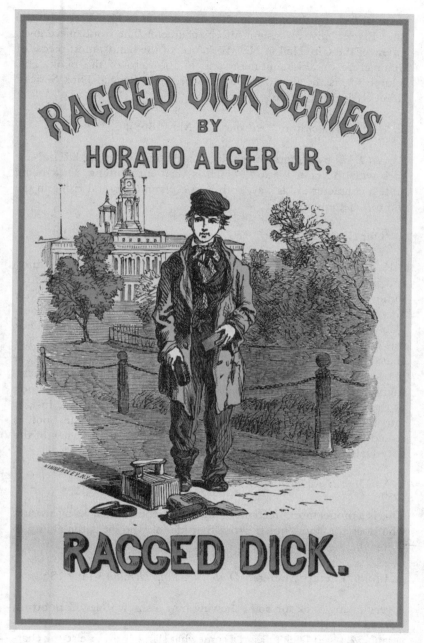

Figure 10. Frontispiece to *Ragged Dick* (1868). Editor's collection.

illustrations, and the sub-title, "Or, Street Life in New York with the Boot-Blacks," give an insight into its character. The frontispiece gives a view of the City Hall in New York, one of the handsomest pieces of architecture on this continent, and of the hero of the book. This volume forms the first of what is to be "The Ragged Dick Series." Horatio Alger, Jr., is the author.

d. "Current Literature," *Advance* (21 May 1868): 6

Ragged Dick, by Horatio Alger, Jr., is a picture of "street life in New York with the boot blacks," which is very entertaining, Dick being quite a character in his way, both in speech and act, and rising in the end to a better condition.

e. "Our Book Table," *Turf, Field, and Farm* (23 May 1868): 329

A.K. Loring of Boston have just issued one of the most entertaining and instructive books that has been published for young folks for some time. It is entitled "Ragged Dick," or "Street Life in New York," and gives the experience and adventures of a New York boot-black in a most lively, wide awake and humorous style. Ragged Dick was emphatically a diamond in the rough, and this and many other characters in the story are sketched from life. The volume is the first of a series intended to illustrate the experiences of the alas too many friendless and vagrant children of New York, and in this first book of the series the Author (Horatio Alger, Jr.) shows a clear insight into their characters and modes of getting a living. The book is issued in an attractive style, and the frontispiece gives a view of the City Hall.

f. *New York Herald* (28 May 1868): 4

This is a model moral account of life among the bootblacks by a writer who does not know much about that life, or who lacks the ability to write what he knows.

g. From "Literary Matters," *Daily Cleveland Herald* (5 June 1868): 1

A very taking book for boys, showing how a shrewd New York boy ... worked his way up from a boot-black's position by honesty and perse-verance. Ragged Dick talks in a somewhat slangy way, or else the char-acter would not be natural, but he is honest and virtuous.

h. From "Books for Boys, by Horatio Alger, Jr.," *Flag of Our Union* (20 June 1868): 392

With a ready and prolific genius, Mr. Alger has contributed some very acceptable books to the juvenile literature of the day. The boys are delighted with him, and his name is the guarantee of a warm welcome to the book in which he appears.... "Ragged Dick; or, Street Life in New York with the Boot-Blacks" is a story to show that those in the very humblest life, by virtuous and proper conduct, may attain success and position. The course of Ragged Dick from his small beginning through his various providences to the pinnacle of his fortune is interesting to those who may have to make like struggles and meet like vicissitudes. The incidents and the principle that underlies them may tend to give strength to hope and furnish new incentive to trial. We felt, while reading his story, that Dick is no fictional character. We have seen him near City Hall, plying his trade, and recognize his features in the picture. We rejoice in his good fortune, and long to congratulate him. Thus his story reacts upon the reader, and quickens his sympathy for the poor and stirring, and thus does a double good.

i. "Ragged Dick," *Christian Register* (27 June 1868): 1

Loring has brought out in his admirable way this excellent story by H. Alger, Jr. Mr. Alger has a clear insight into boy-nature, and knows how to touch their hearts and awaken the aspiration for good in them; he need not desire a nobler sphere than thus to plant good seed in the minds of the future man. He has a keen sense of humor, which gives an irresistible charm to his books. "Ragged Dick" was the most prominent and leading character in that excellent serial, *The Student and Schoolmate*, for 1867.

j. *Putnam's Magazine* 12 (July 1868): 120

"Ragged Dick," by Horatio Alger, Jr., published by A.K. Loring, Boston, is a well-told story of street-life in New York, that will, we should judge, be well received by the boy-readers for whom it is intended.

The hero is a boot-black, who, by sharpness, industry, and honesty, makes his way in the world, and is, perhaps, somewhat more immaculate in character and manners than could naturally have been expected from his origin and training.

We find in this, as in many books for boys, a certain monotony in the inculcation of the principle that honesty is the best policy, a proposition that, as far as mere temporal success is concerned, we believe to be only partially true. However, the book is very much readable, and we should consider it a much more valuable addition to the Sunday-school library than the tales of inebriates, and treatises on the nature of sin, that so often find place there.

k. Rufus Ellis,[1] "Literary Notices," *Monthly Religious Magazine* 40 (July 1868): 84

If you want a spirited and inspiring book for children, get *Ragged Dick*.

l. "Library Table," *Round Table* (11 July 1868): 25

Ragged Dick presents a phase of New York life worthy the attention of philanthropists and those whose love of children makes them desire to keep the little ones from a knowledge of evil, and of those sins from which certain misery ensues. The story of Dick and his adventures is full of interest, and although many of the events are of everyday occurrence, they are none the less true and striking, and the moral lesson they convey is by no means lessened by our familiarity with the subject.

m. "Ragged Dick," *Godey's Lady's Book and Magazine* 77 (August 1868): 178

This story, designed for the perusal of young readers, is the first volume of a series intended to illustrate the life and experiences of the friendless and vagrant children now so numerous in our larger cities. The characters are well and sharply defined, and the story is told in a pleasing style, that will, no doubt, recommend it to the favorable consideration of those for whose amusement and instruction it was written.

3. Contemporary Reviews of *Risen from the Ranks*

a. "Briefer Notices," *Advance* (29 January 1874): 10

"Bound to Rise; or, Harry Walton's Motto," is the second volume of the second series of Horatio Alger's "Luck and Pluck" stories, in

---

1 Rufus Ellis (1819–85) was minister of the First Unitarian Church in Boston and editor of the *Monthly Religious Magazine*.

which the preternaturally wise Harry Walton goes unscathed through various trials and temptations, "rising" with each one as he was "bound" to do. The adventures related in this book are less exciting, and the tone more wholesome than many of the class to which it belongs.

b. "Literary Notices," *St. Louis Republican* (17 October 1874): 5

Risen from the Ranks; or, Harry Walton's Success.... The story is of a boy who rises by pluck more than luck. The author could have made him lucky, but the plucky lesson was better and he taught it.

c. *Gazette* [Alexandria, Virginia] (22 October 1874): 2

This is the seventh book in the Luck and Pluck Series of Horatio Alger, published by Loring, of Boston. This series is spoken of highly, and while the reading is made attractive, it is at the same time very instructive.

d. *Vermont Phœnix* (23 October 1874): 3

Loring, Boston, has just published *Risen from the Ranks*, another of Horatio Alger's books for boys. The hero of this story appeared first in "Bound to Rise," by the same author. In the volume before us he commences as a printer's apprentice and his career is followed step by step as he becomes an editor, a member of Congress, and rises to still higher honors. The side scenes are full of humor, and will interest every reader.

e. "Literary Matters," *Daily Cleveland Herald* (29 October 1874): 4

Horatio Alger ... has brought out another book, which Loring publishes, concerning the further history of Harry Walton, who being in a former book "Bound to Rise" has now "Risen from the Ranks," and graduated from a "printer's devil" to a successful newspaper editor and prominent political leader. We are glad to say that Mr. Alger has dropped the slang talk which made some of his stories rather coarse and objectionable, and this tale is in purpose and execution as commendable as it is fresh and interesting.

f. "Briefer Notices," *Advance* (29 October 1874): 156

"Risen from the Ranks; or, Harry Walton's Success," by Horatio Alger, Jr., is the third of the second series of the "Luck and Pluck" books, with the usual amount of surprising adventures which this author is wont to furnish for his boy readers.

g. From *Daily News* [Galveston, Texas] (30 October 1874): 2

Risen from the Ranks ... is written in that forcible and instructive style peculiar to its author, and is well worth the perusal of the young.

h. From "Literary Notices," *Philadelphia North American and United States Gazette* (2 November 1874): 1

Risen from the Ranks.... Mr. Alger's Luck and Pluck series introduces Harry Walton, a country boy, who, equipped with a good common-school education, is incited by Franklin's life to see to better his own condition. He failed at shoemaking and in the business of showman, but he became a printer's apprentice, and his assiduity and smartness induced the son of a newspaper editor to direct and assist his studies. He studied hard and acquired so much knowledge that he became the reporter [*sic*] of the paper; and still studying, conquered one elevation after another until he was elected to Congress. The progress of the hero is paralleled by the failures of those who started with better prospects and greater advantages. The design of the story, and of the series to which it belongs, is excellent; the method is attractive, and the rewards given to right conduct are well calculated to induce ingenuous youth to propose honorable ends and seek them worthily.

i. From "New Books," *News and Courier* [Charleston, South Carolina] (9 November 1874): 2

Risen from the Ranks ... is one of a series of books written by Mr. Alger exclusively for boys. It treats of an ambitious youth who, fired by reading the life of Franklin, renounces a comparatively good salary as a magician's assistant to become a "devil" in a printing office. Beginning on an infinitesimal salary, he works his way upward into the empyrean occupied by editors and other perfect spirits, and reaps the reward of virtue. It is a simple and unpretending story that any boy might strive to make his own history, and be all the better for imitating.

j. "Recent Publications," *Daily Press* [Portland, Maine] (30 November 1874): 1

"Risen from the Ranks" contains the further history of Harry Walton, who was first introduced to the public in the pages of "Bound to Rise." Those who are interested in learning how far he made good the promise of his boyhood, may here find their curiosity gratified. For the benefit of those who may only read the present volume, a synopsis of Harry's previous life is given in the first chapter. The volume will be joyously welcomed by the young people.

k. From "New Publications," *Arthur's Illustrated Home Magazine* 42 (December 1874): 793

"Risen from the Ranks; or, Harry Walton's Success." ... This is the third volume of the second series of the "Luck and Pluck" books, so deservedly popular among the young folks. It gives a continuation of the history of Harry Walton, who was first introduced to the public in the pages of "Bound to Rise."

l. From "Bound to Rise," *Little Rock Daily Arkansas Gazette* (22 December 1874): 4

The Gazette Library now contains Horatio Alger's new book "Risen from the Ranks; or, Harry Walton's Success." ... Harry Walton, the hero of the story, is a bright country boy with a common school education. "Bound to Rise" was his motto, and by perseverance he rose from the ranks. Harry starts out as a printer's apprentice (printer's devil). In the town where he locates, he makes the acquaintance of a son of one of the editors of an evening journal in Boston, who, though Harry is a poor boy, is proud of him on account of his integrity and ability and good sense. Through the influence of his friend, he became a member of a debating society, where he soon became a leader. At last he became part owner and editor of an influential newspaper, and at last, to crown his history, he was elected to congress. The side scenes in the book are full of humor and will interest everybody. The book is written in an easy, interesting style, alike interesting and instructive.

m. From "Editor's Table," *Ohio Farmer* (2 January 1875): 1

Risen from the Ranks ... is the *seventh* in Loring's popular "Luck and Pluck" series. Harry Walton, the hero, appears first in the previous volume, "Bound to Rise." This was his motto, and every move he makes advances him a step higher, until, from a poor shoemaker's apprentice, he becomes successively reporter for a Boston journal, then its editor, and finally goes to Congress. It is just the book to please and help ambitious boys. Alger's books are all good; and the "Luck and Pluck" series is one of the best that is published.

Appendix D: Early Alger Parodies

[This section reprints two early works in the literary tradition of Alger parodies, which includes later works by F. Scott Fitzgerald, Nathanael West, William Gaddis, John Seelye, and James Thurber. Loomis's "Bernard the Bartender" has never been reprinted until now.]

1. Charles Battell Loomis, "Bernard the Bartender," *Puck* (7 May 1894): 36–37

By the Author of "Horatio Alger."

Chapter I.

Our hero, Bernard, the bartender, was only twenty-eight years of age. He was a very handsome fellow. He had a big, honest black moustache; his hair was neatly oiled, and an air of refinement that you could not place pervaded him.

He was tending bar in a swell saloon on Montague St., Brooklyn, when Alphonse Durand, a flashily dressed youth of scarce twenty five, entered the gilded den.

Alphonse was an evil-looking lad. He had more money that was good for one so young, and he expended it foolishly at matinées and ball games and the like. He had dropped into the saloon to buy a glass of lemonade, for I grieve to state that he had long cultivated a passion for that acid beverage.

"Give me my usual tipple," said he, with a wicked leer on his features. To our hero the concocting of a glass of lemonade was a mere bagatelle, and he soon placed it on the long counter or "bar," with which such places are generally provided.

"When are you going to pay me the half-dollar I won off you at craps?" asked Bernard.

This was a game at which both lads were adepts, and they often whiled away an idle hour at it, although I am pleased to say that Bernard never played it on Sunday. Sunday was the day that he always set apart for fishing off the docks of Cholera Banks.

By way of reply to his question, Alphonse handed Bernard a half-dollar which the practiced eye of the latter immediately discovered to be a poor counterfeit.

"I can't take that piece of money," said Bernard, simply.

"Why not?" asked Alphonse, with an affected air of surprise.

"It's bad," was Bernard's laconic response.

"What's that to me?" sneered Alphonse.

"Alphonse, because you are a jay,[1] shall I be one, too?" replied our honest hero, looking him squarely in the eye. A blind beggar could tell that it is bad, and I would run a great risk trying to pass it."

"A curse on your scruples!" said the wicked Alphonse.

"I may be poor, Alphonse, but, thank heaven, I am discreet! If you can't pay me what you owe me in good money, or at least in a passable counterfeit, I will have you arrested the first time I think of it."

Alphonse's sallow countenance took on a pallid hue. He ground a lemon-pit between his clenched jaws, and, uttering a wicked oath, he left the saloon without paying for his drink. Once outside, he shook his two fists in the direction of the saloon and vowed that he would get even with his too scrupulous friend.

Bernard could ill afford to lose the half-dollar, but the thought that he had been true to himself so consoled him that he forgot to make good the price of the lemonade to his employer.

Chapter II.

"Twenty-seven cents, a two-cent stamp and a bridge ticket, and I have been six months in saving it up. Poor, dear mother! I fear that her delicate fingers will become paralyzed from disuse before I shall have saved up money enough to buy her the Rosewood Grand[2] she so sorely needs. Well, I will enclose this much in the letter I wrote her last night." And the speaker, who was none other than our hero, Bernard, took out an envelope, into which he placed the money and then put it back into his pocket. He was seated on a sofa in front of a second-hand furniture store, in Court Street, Brooklyn. It was his afternoon off, and he was on his way to Carroll Park, there to enjoy a few hours of well-earned pleasure. Feeling somewhat tired, and having no Bromo-Caffeine,[3] he sat down on the sofa before mentioned. We will leave him there for a few minutes and explain the reference to his mother.

That lady had been left at the death of her husband with nothing but her son and a talent for music. After several years' search she had succeeded in getting seven small pupils among the poorer classes for instruction on the piano-forte, but month had succeeded month, and she had not been able to give them a lesson for the lack of an instrument, which she was too poor to buy, and which her pride prevented her from hiring. Lately several of her pupils had hinted that they would

---

1 An innocent or naïve person.
2 A high-priced piano.
3 A patent medicine, an effervescent treatment for headaches and other nervous diseases.

have to seek elsewhere for instruction if she did not hasten and give them their first lesson.

Her son Bernard had studied at some of the best colleges, but had refused to accept a single degree. He was not proud, and was glad to obtain, through the good offices of their pastor, a situation as bartender in the swell saloon in which we first met him. During his off-days he had tried to sell Brooklyn papers in uptown New York, with what success our readers already know. The entire proceeds from their sale he intended to devote to purchasing a piano for the mother he so dearly loved. He lacked about $650 of the required sum.

We will now return to our hero, who, as may possibly be remembered, we left upon the sofa in front of the furniture store.

As he sat there with his head in his hands, a voice at his elbow said, "Ha!" and, looking up, he saw the unpleasant features of Alphonse, whom he had not met since the scene in the saloon.

"Just been evicted?" asked Alphonse, glancing superciliously at the array of cheap furniture with which Bernard was surrounded.

"Sir, this furniture is not mine!" said Bernard, his color rising, although he continued to remain seated, himself.

"That may not be so easy to prove, if I call an officer," said the fellow, in an ugly tone. "And if so, what are you doing with it here at this time of day?" It was high noon and crowds of people were passing. The fellow's voice was loud, and several stopped to see what was the matter.

"What seems to be the trouble?" asked a portly old gentleman of kindly aspect.

"Why, this fellow's a thief. He's making away with this furniture!" replied Alphonse.

"He has an honest eye. My boy, to whom does this furniture belong? You are moving it for someone, are you not?" said the old man, kindly, stepping up to Bernard.

"It belongs to the man who keeps the store, and I am only sitting on the sofa because I am weary," said Bernard, removing his hat in an exceedingly polite way.

"That's a likely story," sneered Alphonse. "What would he be doing with all his furniture out here at this time of day?"

The usual crowd had in the meantime gathered, and the wisdom of his remark seemed to have struck a peculiar chord. "Call a policeman," said one. As often happens in Brooklyn, a blue-coated guardian of the peace was passing, and he was hailed by a score of voices.

"What's the row here?" asked he, sauntering up, and twirling his club.

"This fellow is trying to get away with this furniture," said Alphonse, glibly, pointing to the sofa, the chairs and the dining-room table with which our hero was surrounded.

"It's no such thing," said Bernard, sullenly. "Ask the man inside."

"That seems reasonable," said the benevolent-looking old gentleman, and he stepped up to the door. Appearances were decidedly against the young bartender, for the door was locked, the proprietor having gone to luncheon.

As the terrible predicament in which Alphonse had place him flashed across his mind, he pulled his handkerchief from his inside breast-pocket, in order that he might burst into tears, and the letter to his mother fell to the pavement. He hastily stooped to pick it up; but Alphonse was quicker than he, and in a twinkling he seized and opened it.

He calmly pocketed the enclosure of money, doing it so deftly that no one noticed the act. He then hurriedly read the letter to himself and handed it to the policeman with an air of triumph.

"Read that out loud. It may convince the old gentleman that his young man is not as honest as he pretends to be."

The officer took the letter and read as follows:

"Dearest Mother—
"I hate to think of you, forced week by week to postpose your pupils' lessons for lack of so common a piece of furniture as a piano. It galls your boy, to be unable, at present, by fair means, to bring home even a second-hand piano. I enclose a little money and feel in my bones that before long your house will be furnished as becomes my lady mother.

Your dutiful son,
Bernard."

A shudder of horror crept through the crowd at this seeming instance of our hero's depravity. Bernard saw that so cleverly had Alphonse woven the net of circumstantial evidence around him that he could never hope to prove his innocence. What was to become of his mother when he was at Sing Sing?[1]

The old gentleman whom he had instinctively felt would befriend him, and who looked as if he might have several marriageable daughters, sighed heavily, and, looking at his watch, hailed an approaching car, and was soon borne in the direction of Greenwood.[2]

---

1 A maximum-security prison in Ossining, New York, on the Hudson River thirty miles north of New York City.

2 See Chapter XXVI of *Ragged Dick*, p. 177, note 1.

"You'll refuse to take counterfeit money again, will you?" hissed Alphonse between his teeth.

Bernard was but human, and with a wild cry —————

The rest of this story will be published in book-form, uniformly with "Ragged Tom," "Tattered Dick," "Tough and Steady," etc., etc. etc. See advertisement.

2. Stephen Crane, "A Self-Made Man: An Example of Success That Any One Can Follow," *Cornhill Magazine*, ns 6 (March 1899): 324–29

Tom had a hole in his shoe. It was very round and very uncomfortable, particularly when he went on wet pavements. Rainy days made him feel that he was walking on frozen dollars, although he had only to think for a moment to discover he was not.

He used up almost two packs of playing cards by means of putting four cards at a time inside his shoe as a sort of temporary sole, which usually lasted about half a day. Once he put in four aces for luck. He went downtown that morning and got refused work. He thought it wasn't a very extraordinary performance for a young man of ability, and he was not sorry that night to find his packs were entirely out of aces.

One day, Tom was strolling down Broadway. He was in pursuit of work, although his pace was slow. He had found that he must take the matter coolly. So he puffed tenderly at a cigarette and walked as if he owned stock. He imitated success so successfully that if it wasn't for the constant reminder (king, queen, deuce, and tray[1]) in his shoe, he would have gone into a store and bought something.

He had borrowed five cents that morning of his landlady, for his mouth craved tobacco. Although he owed her much for board, she had unlimited confidence in him, because his stock of self-assurance was very large indeed. And as it increased in a proper ratio with the amount of his bills, his relations with her seemed on a firm basis. So he strolled along and smoked, with his confidence in fortune in nowise impaired by his financial condition.

Of a sudden he perceived an old man seated upon a railing, and smoking a clay pipe.

He stopped to look because he wasn't in a hurry, and because it was an unusual thing on Broadway to see old men seated upon railings and smoking clay pipes.

And to his surprise the old man regarded him very intently in return. He stared, with a wistful expression, into Tom's face, and he clasped his hands in trembling excitement.

---

1   A three card in any suit.

Tom was filled with astonishment at the old man's strange demeanour. He stood, puffing at his cigarette, and tried to understand matters. Failing, he threw his cigarette away, took a fresh one from his pocket, and approached the old man.

"Got a match?" he inquired pleasantly.

The old man, much agitated, nearly fell from the railing as he leaned dangerously forward.

"Sonny, can you read?" he demanded, in a quavering voice.

"Certainly I can," said Tom encouragingly. He waived the affair of the match.

The old man fumbled in his pocket. "You look honest, sonny. I've been lookin' fer an honest feller fur a'most a week. I've set on this railing fur six days," he cried plaintively.

He drew forth a letter and handed it to Tom. "Read it fur me, sonny, read it," he said coaxingly.

Tom took the letter and leaned back against the railings. As he opened it and prepared to read, the old man wriggled like a child at a forbidden feast.

Thundering trucks made frequent interruptions and seven men in a hurry jogged Tom's elbow, but he succeeded in reading what follows:

"Office of Ketchum R. Jones, Attorney-at-Law, Tin Can, Nevada, May 19, 18—.

"RUFUS WILKINS, ESQ.

"DEAR SIR,—

"I have as yet received no acknowledgment of the draft from the sale of the north section lots, which I forwarded to you on June 25. I would request an immediate reply concerning it.

"Since my last [letter] I have sold the three corner lots at five thousand each.

"The city grew so rapidly in that direction that they were surrounded by brick stores almost before you would know it. I have also sold for four thousand dollars the ten acres of outlying sage-bush which you once foolishly tried to give away. Mr. Simpson, of Boston, bought the tract. He is very shrewd, no doubt, but he hasn't been in the West long. Still, I think if he holds it for about a thousand years he may come out all right.

"I worked him with the projected-horse-car-line gag. Inform me of the address of your New York attorneys and I will send on the papers. Pray do not neglect to write me concerning the draft sent on June 25.

"In conclusion I might say that if you have any eastern friends who are after good western investments, inform them of the glorious future of Tin Can. We now have three railroads, a bank, an electric-light plant, a projected-horse-car line, and an art society. Also, a saw manufactory, a patent car-wheel mill, and a Methodist church. Tin Can is marching forward to take her proud stand as the metropolis of the West. The rose-hued future holds no glories to which Tin Can does not—" Tom stopped abruptly. "I guess the important part of the letter came first," he said.

"Yes," cried the old man, "I've heard enough. It is just as I thought. George has robbed his dad."

The old man's frail body quivered with grief. Two tears trickled slowly down the furrows of his face.

"Come, come, now," said Tom, patting him tenderly on the back. "Brace up, old feller. What you want to do is to get a lawyer and go put the screws on George."

"Is it really?" asked the old man eagerly.

"Certainly it is," said Tom.

"All right," cried the old man, with enthusiasm; "tell me where to get one." He slid down from the railing and prepared to start off.

Tom reflected. "Well," he said finally, "I might do for one myself."

"What!" shouted the old man in a voice of admiration, "are you a lawyer as well as a reader?"

"Well," said Tom again, "I might appear to advantage as one. All you need is a big front," he added slowly. He was a profane young man.

The old man seized him by the arm. "Come on, then," he cried, "and we'll go put the screws on George."

Tom permitted himself to be dragged by the weak arms of his companion around a corner and along a side-street. As they proceeded, he was internally bracing himself for a struggle, and putting large bales of self-assurance around where they would be likely to obstruct the advance of discovery and defeat.

By the time they reached a brown stone house, hidden away in a street of shops and warehouses, his mental balance was so admirable that he seemed to be in possession of enough information and brains to ruin half the city, and he was no more concerned about the king, queen, deuce and tray than if they had been discards that didn't fit his draw. Too, he infused so much confidence and courage into his companion that the old man went along the street breathing war, like a decrepit hound on the scent of new blood.

He ambled up the steps of the brown stone house as if he were charging earthworks. He unlocked the door, and they passed along a dark hall-way. In a rear room they found a man seated at table engaged with a very late breakfast. He had a diamond in his shirt front, and a bit of egg on his cuff.

"George," said the old man in a fierce voice that came from his aged throat with a sound like the crackle of burning twigs, "here's my lawyer, Mr.—er—ah—Smith, and we want to know what you did with the draft that was sent on June 25th."

The old man delivered the words as if each one was a musket shot.

George's coffee spilled softly upon the table-cover, and his fingers worked convulsively upon a slice of bread. He turned a white, astonished face toward the old man and the intrepid Thomas.

The latter, straight and tall, with a highly legal air, stood at the old man's side. His glowing eyes were fixed upon the face of the man at the table. They seemed like two little detective cameras taking pictures of the other man's thoughts.

"Father, what d-do you mean?" faltered George, totally unable to withstand the two cameras and the highly legal air.

"What do I mean?" said the old man with a feeble roar, as from an ancient lion; "I mean that draft—that's what I mean. Give it up, or we'll—we'll—" he paused to gain courage by a glance at the formidable figure at his side, "we'll put the screws on you."

"Well, I was—I was only borrowin' it for 'bout a month," said George.

"Ah," said Tom.

George started, glared at Tom, and then began to shiver like an animal with a broken back.

There were a few moments of silence. The old man was fumbling about in his mind for more imprecations. George was wilting and turning limp before the glittering orbs of the valiant attorney. The latter, content with the exalted advantage he had gained by the use of the expression, "Ah," spoke no more, but continued to stare.

"Well," said George finally, in a weak voice, "I s'pose I can give you a check for it, though I was only borrowin' it for 'bout a month. I don't think you have treated me fairly, father, with your lawyers, and your threats, and all that. But I'll give you the check."

The old man turned to his attorney. "Well?" he asked. Tom looked at the son and held an impressive debate with himself. "I think we may accept the check," he said coldly, after a time.

George arose and tottered across the room. He drew a check that made the attorney's heart come privately into his mouth. As he and his client passed triumphantly out, he turned a last highly legal glare upon George that reduced that individual to a mere paste.

On the sidewalk the old man went into a spasm of delight and called his attorney all the admiring and endearing names there were to be had.

"Lord, how you settled him!" he cried ecstatically. They walked slowly back toward Broadway. "The scoundrel," murmured the old man. "I'll never see 'im again. I'll desert 'im. I'll find a nice quiet boarding-place, and—"

"That's all right," said Tom. "I know one. I'll take you right up," which he did.

He came near being happy ever after. The old man lived at advanced rates in the front room at Tom's boarding-house. And the latter basked in the proprietress's smiles, which had a commercial value and were a great improvement on many we see.

The old man, with his quantities of sage-bush, thought Thomas owned all the virtues mentioned in high-class literature, and his opinion, too, was of commercial value. Also, he knew a man who knew another man who received an impetus which made him engage Thomas on terms that were highly satisfactory.

Then it was that the latter learned he had not succeeded sooner because he did not know a man who knew another man.

So it came to pass that Tom grew to be Thomas G. Somebody. He achieved that position in life from which he could hold out for good wines when he went to poor restaurants. His name became entangled with the name of Wilkins in the ownership of vast and valuable tracts of sage-bush in Tin Can, Nevada.

At the present day he is so great that he lunches frugally at high prices. His fame has spread through the land as a man who carved his way to fortune with no help but his undaunted pluck, his tireless energy, and his sterling integrity.

Newspapers apply to him now, and he writes long signed articles to struggling young men, in which he gives the best possible advice as to how to become wealthy. In these articles he, in a burst of glorification, cites the king, queen, deuce, and tray, the four aces, and all that. He alludes tenderly to the nickel he borrowed and spent for cigarettes as the foundation of his fortune.

"To succeed in life," he writes, "the youth of America have only to see an old man seated upon a railing and smoking a clay pipe. Then go up and ask him for a match."

Select Bibliography

Biography

Scharnhorst, Gary, with Jack Bales. *The Lost Life of Horatio Alger, Jr.* Bloomington: Indiana UP, 1985.

Bibliographies

Bennett, Bob. *A Collector's Guide to the Published Works of Horatio Alger, Jr.* Newark, NJ: MAD Book, 1999.

Scharnhorst, Gary, and Jack Bales. *Horatio Alger, Jr.: A Secondary Bibliography of Contemporary Comment and Criticism*. Metuchen, NJ: Scarecrow P, 1981.

Criticism

Beauchamp, Gorman. "*Ragged Dick* and the Fate of Respectability." *Michigan Quarterly Review* 31 (Summer 1992): 324–45.

Bode, Carl. "Introduction" to *Ragged Dick and Struggling Upward*. New York: Signet, 1990. ix–xxi.

Cawelti, John G. *Apostles of the Self-Made Man: Changing Concepts of Success in America*. Chicago: U of Chicago P, 1965.

——. "Portrait of the Newsboy as a Young Man: Some Remarks on the Alger Stories." *Wisconsin Magazine of History* 45 (Winter 1961–62): 79–83.

Coad, Bruce E. "The Alger Hero." *Heroes of Popular Culture*. Ed. Ray B. Browne et al. Bowling Green, OH: Bowling Green U Popular P, 1972. 42–51.

Fink, Rychard. "Horatio Alger as a Social Philosopher." *Ragged Dick and Mark the Match Boy*. New York: Collier, 1962. 5–31.

Fluet, Lisa. "The Unsocial 'Purfessional': Revisiting Horatio Alger's *Ragged Dick*." *Worcester Review* 30 (2009): 109–26.

Garrison, Dee. "Cultural Custodians of the Gilded Age: The Public Librarian and Horatio Alger." *Journal of Library History* 6 (October 1971): 327–36.

Hendler, Glenn. "Pandering in the Public Sphere: Masculinity and the Market in Horatio Alger." *American Quarterly* 48 (September 1996): 415–38.

Hoeller, Hildegard. "Freaks and the American Dream: Horatio Alger, P.T. Barnum, and the Art of Humbug." *Studies in American Fiction* 34 (Autumn 2006): 189–214.

Kanar, Hanley. "Horatio Alger and *Frank's Campaign*: White Supremacy in a Northern Intellectual's Juvenile Novel." *Children's Literature Association Quarterly* 17 (Spring 1992): 36–40.

Marrs, Clinton W. "Paideia in America: Ragged Dick, George Babbitt, and the Problem of a Modern Classical Education." *Arion: A Journal of Humanities and the Classics* 15 (Fall 2007): 39–55.

Miner, Madonne M. "Horatio Alger's *Ragged Dick*: Projection, Denial and Double-Dealing." *American Imago* 47 (Fall–Winter 1990): 233–48.

Moon, Michael. "'The Gentle Boy from the Dangerous Classes': Pederasty, Domesticity, and Capitalism in Horatio Alger." *Representations* 19 (Summer 1987): 87–110.

Nackenoff, Carol. *The Fictional Republic: Horatio Alger and American Political Discourse*. New York: Oxford UP, 1994.

——. "Of Factories and Failures: Exploring the Invisible Factory Gates of Horatio Alger, Jr." *Journal of Popular Culture* 25 (Spring 1992): 63–80.

Nader, Jennifer M. "From Serial to Novel: Horatio Alger's Revisions in *Ragged Dick*." *American Literary Realism* 50 (Fall 2017). Forthcoming.

Packer-Kinlaw, Donna. "The Rise and Fall of the American Dream: From *The Autobiography of Benjamin Franklin* to *Death of a Salesman*." *The American Dream*. Ed. Keith Newlin. Ipswich, MA: Salem, 2013. 3–17.

Pauly, Thomas H. "*Ragged Dick* and *Little Women*: Idealized Homes and Unwanted Marriages." *Journal of Popular Culture* 9 (1975): 583–92.

Photinos, Christine. "The Figure of the Tramp in Gilded Age Success Narratives." *Journal of Popular Culture* 40 (December 2007): 994–1018.

Pickering, Sam. "A Boy's Own War." *New England Quarterly* 48 (September 1975): 362–77.

Scharnhorst, Gary. "Benjamin Franklin's Legacy to the Gilded Age: Manners, Money, and Horatio Alger." *Civilizing America: Manners and Civility in American Literature and Culture*. Ed. Dietmar Schloss (Heidelberg: Universitätverlag, 2009). 242–51.

——. "Had Their Mothers Only Known: Horatio Alger, Jr., Rewrites Cooper, Melville, and Twain." *Journal of Popular Culture* 15 (Winter 1981): 175–82.

——. *Horatio Alger, Jr.* Boston: Twayne, 1980.

Shaheen, Aaron. "Endless Frontiers and Emancipation from History: Horatio Alger's Reconstruction of Place and Time in *Ragged Dick*." *Children's Literature* 33 (2005): 20–40.

Shuffelton, Frank. "Bound to Rise—But Not Too Far." *Illinois Quarterly* 39 (Fall 1976): 51–64.

Trachtenberg, Alan. "Introduction" to *Ragged Dick*. New York: Signet, 1990. v–xx.

Weiher, Carol. "Horatio Alger's Fiction: American Fairy Tales for All Ages." *CEA Critic* 40.2 (1978): 23–27.

Young, Arthur P. "Banish the Books: Horatio Alger, Jr., the Censors, the Libraries, and the Readers, 1870–1910." *Children's Library Association Quarterly* 38 (Winter 2013): 420–34.

Zuckerman, Michael. "The Nursery Tales of Horatio Alger, Jr." *American Quarterly* 24 (May 1972): 191–209.

Historical Background

Decker, Jeffrey Louis. *Made in America: Self-Styled Success from Horatio Alger to Oprah Winfrey*. Minneapolis: U of Minnesota P, 1997.

Huber, Richard M. *The American Idea of Success*. New York: McGraw-Hill, 1971.

Köseman, Zennure. *From the Way to Wealth to the Gospel of Wealth: The Transformation in the Concept of Success from Benjamin Franklin to Theodore Dreiser*. Bethesda, MD: Academica P, 2013.

Kruse, Horst H. *From Rags to Riches: Erfolgsmythos und Erfolgsrezepte in der Amerikanische Gesellschaft*. Munich: Goldmann, 1982.

Lynn, Kenneth S. *The Dream of Success: A Study of the Modern American Imagination*. Boston: Little, Brown, 1955.

Rischin, Moses. *The American Gospel of Success: Individualism and Beyond*. Chicago: Quadrangle, 1965.

Weiss, Richard. *The American Myth of Success: From Horatio Alger to Norman Vincent Peale*. New York: Basic Books, 1969.

Wohl, R. Richard. "The 'Country Boy' Myth and Its Place in American Urban Culture: The Nineteenth-Century Contribution." *Perspectives in American History* 3 (1969): 77–156.

——. "The 'Rags to Riches Story': An Episode of Secular Idealism." *Class, Status, and Power: A Reader in Social Stratification*. Ed. Reinhard Bendix and Seymour Martin Lipset. Glencoe, IL: Free P, 1953. 388–94.

Wyllie, Irvin G. *The Self-Made Man in America: The Myth of Rags to Riches*. New York: Free P, 1964.

From the Publisher

A name never says it all, but the word "Broadview" expresses a good deal of the philosophy behind our company. We are open to a broad range of academic approaches and political viewpoints. We pay attention to the broad impact book publishing and book printing has in the wider world; we began using recycled stock more than a decade ago, and for some years now we have used 100% recycled paper for most titles. Our publishing program is internationally oriented and broad-ranging. Our individual titles often appeal to a broad readership too; many are of interest as much to general readers as to academics and students.

Founded in 1985, Broadview remains a fully independent company owned by its shareholders—not an imprint or subsidiary of a larger multinational.

For the most accurate information on our books (including information on pricing, editions, and formats) please visit our website at www.broadviewpress.com. Our print books and ebooks are also available for sale on our site.

On the Broadview website we also offer several goods that are not books—among them the Broadview coffee mug, the Broadview beer stein (inscribed with a line from Geoffrey Chaucer's *Canterbury Tales*), the Broadview fridge magnets (your choice of philosophical or literary), and a range of T-shirts (made from combinations of hemp, bamboo, and/or high-quality pima cotton, with no child labor, sweatshop labor, or environmental degradation involved in their manufacture).

All these goods are available through the "merchandise" section of the Broadview website. When you buy Broadview goods you can support other goods too.

broadview press
www.broadviewpress.com

MIX
Paper from
responsible sources
FSC® C103567

The interior of this book is printed on 30% recycled paper.

PERMANENT

BIO GAS®
ENERGY

30%